SECOND EDITION

# TEACHER SUPERVISION & EVALUATION

## Theory Into Practice

## THE WILEY BICENTENNIAL—KNOWLEDGE FOR GENERATIONS

$\mathcal{E}$ach generation has its unique needs and aspirations. When Charles Wiley first opened his small printing shop in lower Manhattan in 1807, it was a generation of boundless potential searching for an identity. And we were there, helping to define a new American literary tradition. Over half a century later, in the midst of the Second Industrial Revolution, it was a generation focused on building the future. Once again, we were there, supplying the critical scientific, technical, and engineering knowledge that helped frame the world. Throughout the 20th century, and into the new millennium, nations began to reach out beyond their own borders and a new international community was born. Wiley was there, expanding its operations around the world to enable a global exchange of ideas, opinions, and know-how.

For 200 years, Wiley has been an integral part of each generation's journey, enabling the flow of information and understanding necessary to meet their needs and fulfill their aspirations. Today, bold new technologies are changing the way we live and learn. Wiley will be there, providing the must-have knowledge you need to imagine new worlds, new possibilities, and new opportunities.

Generations come and go, but you can always count on Wiley to provide the knowledge you need, when and where you need it!

**WILLIAM J. PESCE**
PRESIDENT AND CHIEF EXECUTIVE OFFICER

**PETER BOOTH WILEY**
CHAIRMAN OF THE BOARD

SECOND EDITION

# TEACHER SUPERVISION & EVALUATION
## Theory Into Practice

**JAMES F. NOLAN, JR.**
*Pennsylvania State University*

**LINDA A. HOOVER**
*Shippensburg University*

John Wiley & Sons, Inc.

| | |
|---|---|
| VICE PRESIDENT AND PUBLISHER | Jay O'Callaghan |
| ACQUISITION EDITOR | Robert Johnston |
| SENIOR PRODUCTION EDITOR | Valerie A. Vargas |
| MARKETING MANAGER | Emily Streutker |
| CREATIVE DIRECTOR | Harry Nolan |
| SENIOR DESIGN ASSISTANT | Hope Miller |
| EDITORIAL ASSISTANT | Eileen McKeever |
| MEDIA EDITOR | Lynn Pearlman |
| COVER PHOTO | (Woman in Meeting) Ryanstock/Taxi/Getty Images; (Books) Corbis Digital Stock |

This book was set in 10/12 Times Roman by Thomson Digital

This book is printed on acid free paper.

To order books or for customer service please, call 1-800-CALL WILEY (225-5945).

ISBN-13  978-0-470-08405-2

10 9 8 7 6 5 4 3 2 1

# *DEDICATION*

*We dedicate this edition of our book to Zack Topper (1975–2006). He was not a teacher by profession, but he taught us by example how to live passionately and how to die courageously. Though he lived far too short a time, his playful zest for life, the gusto with which he embraced adventure, family, and friends, and his indomitable spirit in the face of a debilitating disease touched the hearts of so many. In his words, "It is not the end, but a new beginning."*

# CONTENTS

## CHAPTER 3    *PEER COACHING*    58

## PART III

# *DIFFERENTIATED SUPERVISION STRATEGIES*

## CHAPTER 4    *SELF-DIRECTED TEACHER GROWTH*    80

## PART IV

## *TEACHER EVALUATION*

### CHAPTER 7   *STANDARDS FOR EFFECTIVE TEACHING AND TEACHER EVALUATION*   164

### CHAPTER 8   *PROCEDURES FOR EVIDENCE-BASED TEACHER EVALUATION*   183

## PART VI

## *SUPERVISION AND EVALUATION: TRANSFORMING THE SYSTEM*

**CHAPTER 12**   *DEVELOPING YOUR OWN SYSTEM OF TEACHER SUPERVISION AND EVALUATION*   **268**

# PREFACE TO THE SECOND EDITION

The phrase "teacher supervision and evaluation" provokes a variety of emotional responses on the part of teachers. For some, it gives rise to pleasant, even invigorating memories of well-designed and well-supported learning opportunities that resulted in a renewed sense of professionalism and improved teaching and learning. For others, the memories are of hostile, unfair, negative judgments made by administrators who appeared to have at best a superficial understanding of the teacher's work. For the majority of teachers, it often calls to mind emotionally neutral, yearly rituals that included a brief compliment or an innocuous suggestion for improvement but had no lasting impact. Friends who are educators ask why we, the authors, would want to write a book about teacher supervision and evaluation. The answer is that we are passionate about the subject. Our work in schools over the last two decades has enabled us to see the powerful growth opportunities created by well-designed systems of teacher supervision and evaluation. Our dream in writing this book is that every educator experience that power. So we begin.

In crafting this second edition of our book, we have used feedback from a variety of sources including students and faculty members who have used this book at a variety of institutions, official reviews of this book solicited by our publisher, John Wiley & Sons, and feedback from students who have used the book with us in our supervision and professional development courses. As a result of this feedback, we have made several significant changes in this book including

    **a.** Separating the chapter on evidence-based teacher evaluation into two separate chapters, one focusing on principles of evaluation and standards for evaluating teaching and the other focusing on evaluation procedures.

    **b.** Including an expanded definition of professional learning communities and their role in supervision and evaluation processes.

    **c.** Providing case studies of self-directed teacher growth, action research, and critical friends groups in the respective chapters in which the supervision strategy is discussed.

    **d.** Including a discussion of lesson study as a form of collegial development groups in Chapter 6.

    **e.** Weighing in on the advantages and disadvantages of classroom walk-throughs as part of a district's supervision and evaluation plan.

We hope that these changes will retain the thoroughness and substance of the first edition while making this book more user-friendly. The remainder of the preface provides a brief overview of each chapter as well as suggestions for how to use this book more effectively.

# CHAPTER OVERVIEWS

This book is divided into six major parts. Part I, consists of a single chapter that articulates the foundations of a teacher supervision and evaluation system. Part II (Chapters 2 and 3) focuses on classroom supervision and coaching. Part III (Chapters 4–6) presents differentiated supervision and professional development strategies for promoting teacher growth. Part IV (Chapters 7 and 8) focuses on principles, standards, and procedures for effective teacher evaluation. Part V (Chapters 9–11) addresses the supervision and evaluation of preservice, novice, and marginal teachers. Finally, Part VI (Chapter 12) provides guidance in developing your own high-quality system of teacher supervision and evaluation. The chapters are briefly described below.

Chapter 1, *Understanding the components of a comprehensive teacher supervision and evaluation system* has three main topics. First, it looks at the historical roots of teacher supervision and evaluation and explains some of the current confusion regarding the relationship between the two. Second, it explains and justifies the conception of teacher supervision and evaluation as separate but complementary functions. We contend that a school system must perform both functions well for teachers and students to be able to achieve high standards of performance and that the failure to separate the two functions results in a system in which neither is performed very well. The chapter concludes with a set of specific criteria that can be used by the stakeholders in a school or school district to assess the overall quality of its teacher supervision and evaluation system.

Part II of this book focuses on supervision options that use classroom-based observation and conferencing as the primary vehicles for enhancing teacher performance. Chapter 2, *Key concepts and skills in classroom supervision,* discusses concepts and skills that are essential in implementing classroom-based teacher supervision. The chapter focuses on seven such essential concepts and skills: trust building and engendering positive communication, uncovering espoused platforms and platforms in use, encouraging continuous reflection and inquiry into teaching, systematic data collection, interpreting and making use of data, conferencing, and, finally, fostering a professional learning community. Taken together, these seven concepts and skills provide the foundation for a differentiated system of teacher supervision.

Chapter 3, *Peer coaching,* focuses on explaining peer coaching, its rationale, the phases of the peer-coaching cycle, and the administrator's role in the coaching process. It provides concrete examples and suggestions to ensure optimal success in implementing a peer-coaching program. This chapter also discusses in detail the potential of peer coaching for fostering higher-level teacher development. It also connects peer coaching to notions of professional learning communities. The literature on adult learning has identified specific conditions for fostering adult development and growth. These conditions are all present in well-designed peer-coaching programs.

The concepts discussed in Chapter 3 build upon the ideas introduced about classroom observation in Chapter 2. Observation-based classroom supervision and peer coaching share the same basic goals and procedures. When a teacher and a supervisor carry out the process, we label it as supervision; when two or more teachers carry out the process, we label it as peer coaching.

Part III of this book focuses on those supervisory options for promoting professional growth that do not rely on classroom observation as their primary mechanism. These strategies tend to be very much teacher directed with consultation and collaboration from administrators. Chapter 4, *Self-directed teacher growth,* features the differentiated supervision strategy known as individualized teacher development or self-directed teacher growth.

Although self-directed growth may refer to the process of a teacher working alone to meet established goals, it may also refer to teachers working together to do so. In either case, the responsibility for deciding on the goals to pursue and the strategies for achieving them lies primarily with the teachers. The chapter provides the rationale for including self-directed growth as a component of the teacher supervision system and as an opportunity for job-embedded learning. In addition, it gives a detailed explanation of each of the components of the process—goal setting, action planning, providing resources and support for teachers, evaluating action plan achievement, facilitating networking, establishing system-wide record keeping and accountability, and the important role that the administrator plays in the process. Examples and vignettes of self-directed growth plans and their impact are also provided in the chapter.

Chapter 5, *Action research,* focuses on teacher research, carried out either individually or collectively. Although teacher research has not been a common supervision strategy, we believe that it has great potential as a tool for professional development. The chapter presents the history of action research and the potential benefits for individual teachers and the school culture. Detailed explanations of the action research process help you understand how to go about carrying out and supporting teacher research. Suggestions for administering the action research process as a component of the teacher supervision and evaluation system are also provided.

Chapter 6, *Collegial development groups,* discusses the establishment of three types of collegial development groups: study groups, critical friends groups, and lesson study groups. Collegial development groups are formed by teachers as a mechanism for sharing perspectives and practices and for deepening their understanding of particular educational phenomena. As we see it, such groups have the potential to be a catalyst for transforming school cultures. The chapter suggests how to structure the work of study groups and provides an example of the work of a study group composed of middle school teachers. The chapter also provides examples of the types of activities that critical friends groups engage in when examining student work and/or teacher thinking and practice. The third strategy for collegial development groups focuses on the phenomenon of lesson study in which groups of teachers work together to plan, deliver, and reflect on particular lessons or units of instruction. The chapter concludes with guidelines for incorporating collegial development groups into the teacher supervision system as a whole.

Part IV of this book focuses on principles, procedures and standards for effective teacher evaluation and consists of two chapters focused on teacher evaluation. Chapter 7, *Standards for effective teacher evaluation,* shifts the focus from promoting teacher growth to developing an evidence-based process to promote accountability. The chapter focuses on the design of a high-quality teacher evaluation process by suggesting eight principles that should provide a foundation for thinking about the evaluation system. The chapter also addresses some of the substantive criteria that might be used to assess teacher quality. Examples of five different sets of criteria for teacher evaluation are provided. Four sets of criteria come from others, whereas the authors developed the fifth themselves.

Chapter 8, *Procedures for evidence-based teacher evaluation,* addresses the procedural aspects of the evaluation process including the roles that teachers and administrators and other stakeholders play, potential data sources, creating the evaluation portfolio, and making the summative evaluation decision. In keeping with our platform of beliefs, this chapter lays out a much more substantive role for the teacher in the process of evaluation while maintaining administrator judgment as the final arbiter of teacher performance.

Part V of this book focuses on the application of supervision and evaluation to the specific cases of preservice, novice, and marginal teachers. Each chapter in this part explains why the specific group in question should be considered a special case in supervision and evaluation and then outlines specific suggestions for adapting supervision and evaluation to meet the needs of that special group.

Chapter 9, *Supervision and evaluation of the preservice teacher,* focuses on the roles of both the university supervisor and cooperating teacher in the supervision and evaluation of the preservice teacher. The complexity of the student teaching experience is discussed in terms of the student teacher's developmental journey from college student to beginning professional. In consort with this developmental journey to beginning professional, the student teacher's concerns shift from concerns about self to concerns about students and their learning. Four supervisory activities that are especially powerful in working with preservice teachers frame the discussion of supervision during student teaching, preobservation conferences, postobservation conferences, structured videotape analyses of teaching, and the creation of electronic growth portfolios to encourage reflection. These same procedures, though explained in detail in Chapter 9, are also very useful in working with novice and marginal teachers. The evaluation of student teaching performance, a high-stakes evaluation process, serves an important gate keeping function for the profession. The chapter suggests a variety of evaluation procedures for carrying out this task effectively as well as advice about dealing with failure in student teaching.

Chapter 10, *Supervision and evaluation of the novice teacher,* gives special attention to the needs of new teachers and the development of induction programs that meet those needs. New teachers require a strong induction program guided by an excellent mentor who has received specialized training designed to help him or her carry out the mentoring task effectively. The mentor and novice work together to develop a first-year portfolio, a supervisory activity that engenders reflection and prepares the novice to create evaluation portfolios in subsequent years.

The evaluation of novice teachers is of crucial importance. In most states tenure requires the completion of 3 years of successful teaching. School districts and supervisors therefore have a golden opportunity to make the process of evaluating new teachers very rigorous, ensuring that only good or excellent teachers are granted tenure. The chapter provides a 3-year plan for socializing the novice teacher into the district's teacher evaluation system and for collecting a variety of types of data that enable the administrative team to make an accurate decision concerning whether to grant tenure or not.

Chapter 11, *Supervision and evaluation of the marginal teacher,* focuses on the paradoxical world of working intensively to help the marginal teacher improve while simultaneously collecting the documentation necessary to dismiss the teacher if remediation proves fruitless. In contrast to the separation of evaluation and supervision that occurs for other veteran teachers, the questionable competence of the marginal teacher requires the intertwining of evaluation and supervision. Evaluation becomes the guiding force in setting improvement targets within a specified time frame. Supervision activities to assist the teacher in meeting improvement targets include directive preobservation and postobservation conferences as well as the development of an intensive assistance plan implemented with the help of a support team. Evaluation of the marginal teacher is carried out by an administrative team and is carefully designed to ensure that the teacher's due process rights are protected. The chapter ends with a discussion of options for dealing with incompetent teachers including induced exit and dismissal.

Part VI of our book again consists of a single chapter. Chapter 12, *Developing your own system of teacher supervision and evaluation,* focuses on strategies for combining all of the supervision and evaluation processes into a coherent, high-quality system of teacher supervision and evaluation, thereby enabling you to understand how to operationalize the principles of teacher supervision and evaluation encountered throughout the book. We distinguish between situations where it is appropriate to import ideas from others and situations where reinventing the wheel is important, even if time consuming. A set of guidelines for involving various stakeholders in the process of developing, maintaining, and evaluating the system is presented. This chapter also provides a concrete example of a high-quality system of teacher supervision and evaluation that is currently in operation in public schools. We intend this final chapter to serve as an action plan that can guide the development and implementation of a high-quality teacher supervision and evaluation system in most school districts. Developing the systems design that is outlined in Chapter 12 is a critical skill for those educational leaders who want to promote of a coherent school vision as advocated by Standard 1 of the ELCC Standards for School Leaders (see Appendix B).

## SUGGESTIONS FOR USING THIS BOOK

Throughout the chapters in the book, you will find six types of teaching and learning tools: (1) guiding questions for prereading journaling and reflection; (2) skill and concept development exercises; (3) case studies, vignettes, and examples; (4) end-of-chapter discussion questions; (5) theory-into-practice applications; and (6) suggestions for further reading.

### Guiding Questions for Prereading, Journaling, and Reflection

A set of questions follows each chapter overview. The questions are intended to help you bring your own thoughts, ideas, and experiences to the reading of the chapter. As prior knowledge is a key factor in determining what one takes from reading any text, readers may find it useful to jot down their responses to these questions and then, if possible, to engage others in discussions before continuing with the remainder of the chapter.

### Skill and Concept Development Exercises

Educators must have the opportunity to develop the knowledge and skills necessary to put theory into practice. In relevant places in the text we provide exercises that aim at developing a deeper understanding of concepts or at development of specific skills. Concept development exercises engage the reader in activities that make abstract ideas more concrete. Skill development exercises ask the reader to practice doing supervision and evaluation activities. The exercises come primarily from our own supervision classes. They represent the types of activities that our own students are asked to engage in. One of the most powerful ways to use these concept and skill development exercises is to work as a pair or to form a triad. Each member of the partner pair or triad then carries out the activity. Afterward the partners can compare notes. For those exercises where it is appropriate, partners can give each other feedback on their level of skill development.

Three exercises in this book are somewhat different from the others. Exercises 1.1, 3.1, and 7.1 are designed as introductory activities. They bring to the surface beliefs and attitudes concerning issues discussed in the respective chapters. The most appropriate use of these exercises would be to complete them in class the week before that particular chapter is assigned for reading. This approach will allow you to examine your own ideas before encountering the authors' take on the issues.

### Case Studies, Examples, and Vignettes

The book provides concrete examples of the concepts and principles that are introduced. Readers will find multiple examples of data collection tools, conference strategies, goal-setting formats, action research projects, collegial development group protocols, supervision and evaluation forms and timelines, and so on. Where appropriate, case studies and vignettes (That is, extended examples that illustrate supervision and evaluation processes and procedures) are also provided.

## Discussion Questions

Each chapter ends with open-ended questions that are intended to promote additional thinking about the ideas presented in the chapter. We have found that using questions like these in our classes has led to some powerful insights on the part of our students. Discussion questions could also serve as the impetus for electronic student chats.

## Theory-Into-Practice Applications

Theory-into-practice applications differ from skill development exercises in that they help the reader find concrete ways to relate abstract concepts or principles to a personal, practical context. The applications are more extensive than skill development exercises. They involve more thought and discussion and require more time to complete. We have found them to be particularly useful as homework assignments. In some cases they make good topics for electronic chats and in-class discussions. We suggest that readers use both face-to-face and electronic discussions to think through and talk through these activities.

## Suggestions for Further Reading and Research

At the end of each chapter, suggestions for additional reading, including both print materials and web sites are made. Our intention is to encourage deeper engagement with content that we have begun to explore but have not fully developed because to do so would take us beyond the scope of the chapter or book. These suggestions for further reading also provide the reader with more insight into the type of literature that has influenced our thinking about supervision and evaluation.

This book can be used by individuals and by school districts for different purposes. Individuals can use this book to improve their personal understanding of the processes of teacher supervision and evaluation. They can also use it to enhance their skills in these domains by practicing the techniques and procedures described. School districts or stakeholder groups within school districts can use the ideas offered in the book as an opportunity to assess their current system of teacher supervision and evaluation. A comparison of an existing system to the principles, guidelines, and criteria for high-quality supervision and evaluation systems that are offered in the book should clearly identify the strengths and weaknesses of their current system. The suggestions provided in Chapter 12 can then be used as an action planning tool for improving the effectiveness of the current system. It is our hope that, taken seriously, these suggestions can lead to the improvement of systems of teacher supervision and evaluation and to the betterment of the supervisors who work in those systems.

## Acknowledgements

Deirdre Bauer, Paul Daniels, David Hoover, Janet E. Alleman (Michigan State University), Dennis Buss (Rider University), Margaret R. Dolan (University of Missouri), Lynn H. Doyle (Old Dominion University), Ann Hassenpfulg (University of Akron), Helen M. Hazi (West Virginia University), Beverly B. Kasper (Loyola University of Chicago), Megan Tschannen-Moran (The College of William and Mary), Robert C. Morris (State University of West Georgia), George Perreault (University of Nevada), Eva Weisz (DePauw University).

# CHAPTER 1

# *UNDERSTANDING THE COMPONENTS OF A COMPREHENSIVE TEACHER SUPERVISION AND EVALUATION SYSTEM*

**T**HIS CHAPTER helps you to build a clear understanding of what a high-quality teacher supervision and evaluation system looks like. To build that understanding, having some idea of the history of instructional supervision and its close connection to teacher evaluation important. The first section in the chapter focuses on that history. We do not, by any means, try to present a complete history of teacher supervision and evaluation. Instead, we focus on the historical basis for our contemporary confusion about teacher supervision and its relationship to teacher evaluation.

The second section of the chapter builds the case for conceptualizing supervision and evaluation as two separate, complementary, and essential functions of schools as organizations.

The final section of the chapter provides a set of criteria that can be used to assess the quality of any system of teacher supervision and evaluation, including the system in which you presently function. The criteria have been derived from the scholarly literature on teacher supervision and evaluation, but they have also been tested in practice in several school districts.

## GUIDING QUESTIONS FOR PREREADING REFLECTION AND JOURNALING

- As you see it, how do the following terms differ: teacher supervision, teacher evaluation, and teacher observation?
- Given your past experience, what are the most important purposes of teacher evaluation?
- What is the purpose of teacher supervision? Do all teachers need supervision? Why or why not?
- If you were asked to identify an excellent teacher supervision and evaluation system, what characteristics would you look for?

**EXERCISE 1.1   Attitudes and Beliefs About Supervision and Evaluation**

**Introduction**   This three-part exercise is intended to help you to articulate some of your underlying beliefs and attitudes about teacher supervision and evaluation and to share your perspectives with colleagues. The purpose of the activity is not to find the correct answer but rather to explore the underlying issues. Completing the activity now should help you to interact more fully with the concepts presented in the remainder of the chapter.

**Part 1** Respond to the following nine statements concerning supervision and evaluation with one of the five following responses: SA-strongly agree, A-agree, N-neutral, D-disagree, SD–strongly disagree. Circle your response.

1. The same individual can carry out the roles of supervisor and evaluator effectively.
   SA—A—N—D—SD
2. Supervision is best accomplished through a one-to-one relationship between teacher and supervisor.
   SA—A—N—D—SD
3. In order to evaluate teaching effectiveness appropriately, the evaluator must posses content knowledge in the subject being observed.
   SA—A—N—D—SD
4. The same procedures can be used effectively for both supervision and evaluation.
   SA—A—N—D—SD
5. Teachers must be observed at least once a year in order to evaluate their performance effectively.
   SA—A—N—D—SD
6. All teachers need to participate in both supervision and evaluation each year.
   SA—A—N—D—SD
7. The most valid source of data concerning teacher performance is classroom observation data gathered by a trained observer.
   SA—A—N—D—SD
8. Teachers in a single school building are a group who share similar needs for professional development.
   SA—A—N—D—SD
9. In order to evaluate teaching performance effectively, the evaluator must have experience teaching at the grade level being observed.
   SA—A—N—D—SD

**Part 2** Find two or three partners and discuss your responses to the various items. Try to reach consensus on as many items as you can. Identify those items that were the easiest and the most difficult to reach consensus on.

**Part 3** Compare your group responses with those of other groups. Discuss which items caused the greatest difficulty for all of the groups. What do those items have in common? What does that say about teacher supervision and evaluation?

We express our appreciation to the Pennsylvania ASCD Supervision Committee for allowing us to adapt this exercise for use in this text.

# TEACHER SUPERVISION AND EVALUATION: HISTORICAL ROOTS

Many current systems of teacher supervision and evaluation lack precise descriptions of the relationship between teacher supervision and evaluation. As a result, both teachers and administrators are not clear regarding purposes of either function (McGreal, 1983). The struggle to understand the relationship between supervision and evaluation is not new. The problem has its roots in the history of school supervision. Over time, competing educational philosophies and movements defined the role of the supervisor in often contradictory ways. The pendulum has swung back and forth throughout the decades from inspector to helper to evaluator to counselor. By understanding this history, you will be in a better position to confront the complex issues surrounding the relationship of teacher supervision and evaluation.

Instructional supervision finds its historical roots in the inspectorial function of the school committees of the early eighteenth century. Inspectors were often ministers, selectmen, schoolmasters, and other distinguished citizens. In fact, as Glanz notes, supervision as a function performed by specifically trained professionals did not exist until after the Civil War. Lay methods of supervision stressed strict control and close inspection of school facilities (Glanz, 1998, p. 47). This inspectorial model continued to flourish even after the role of the professionally trained school superintendent had been established in the early nineteenth century (Pajak, 2000). Supervisors were concerned with the tasks of overseeing the curriculum, improving the efficiency of the methods of instruction used by teachers, and evaluating teacher performance and student achievement (Bolin, 1987). "Teachers, who were mostly female and disenfranchised, were seen as a bedraggled troop, incompetent and backward in outlook" (Bolin & Panaritis, 1992, p. 33).

Balliet, writing in 1894, suggested that the only way to reform schools was to secure a competent superintendent and allow him to reform the incompetent teachers who could be reformed and to bury the rest who were dead (as cited in Glanz, 1998). Glanz explains how getting rid of teachers was linked to school quality, in the minds of some educational reformers. 'The mission of eliminating incompetent teachers, as the central thrust of supervision during this time, does not contradict the essential purpose of supervision that was to achieve quality schooling. In fact, supervisors maintained that the best way to achieve quality schooling was to remove "deficient" teachers. The methods employed by the supervisors were inspectorial and rather impressionistic, but nonetheless served to achieve the stated objective' (Glanz, 1998).

In the early twentieth century, Frederick Taylor's efficiency movement had a powerful influence on how administrators saw their tasks (Bolin, 1987; Glanz, 1998). Taylor and his associates conducted time and motion studies with the aim of making the physical movements of laborers in industry more efficient, thus conserving their energy and increasing productivity. This efficiency orientation, as applied to education by Franklin Bobbit and others, was one of the major forces that drove the processes of school supervision in the early portion of the twentieth century.

Social efficiency philosophies, combined with the increasing bureaucratization of school systems and the emergence of a class of middle level school managers who carried out the task of supervision, led to the vigorous development of rating scales designed to rate teacher effectiveness. The underlying assumptions were that scientists could study those teachers who seemed to be most effective and efficient and develop descriptors of their behaviors. These descriptions could be transformed into scales to rate the efficiency and effectiveness of other teachers. Skilled supervisors could then use the ratings and the descriptions on the rating scales to make teachers more efficient. Edward Elliot and Clifton Boyce were two of the pioneers in development of teacher efficiency rating instruments, whose categories ranged from physical to moral to social efficiency. (Glanz, 1998).

The number of teacher rating scales grew tremendously throughout the first quarter of the twentieth century, resulting in a wide variety of teacher rating instruments, albeit very little agreement as to what constituted effective teaching. Despite rather vigorous opposition from those who saw rating scales as anti–democratic and anti-intellectual, the teacher rating scales were widely used. The role of the supervisor was plainly teacher evaluation. Criticisms of rating scales and of the emphasis on evaluation increased as the Progressives became more prominent, and, eventually, the social efficiency and inspectorial models of teacher supervision came under heavy attack. Supervisors, who had legitimized their positions by devising better evaluation methods for rating teachers, suddenly found themselves in a very vulnerable position and began to embrace helping teachers to grow as an important function (Glanz, 1998).

The alternative conceptions of supervision were grounded in democratic principles of autonomy and freedom. The Progressive era, with its philosophy of inquiry, democratic processes, and scientific investigation, led to a supervisory process that was seen as helpful, improvement oriented, and collaborative. "Drawing directly on the work of Dewey and other progressives, Barr and Burton's 1926 text on supervision devoted an entire chapter to encouraging reflective thought among teachers and administrators through experimentation in classrooms and schools" (Pajak, 2000, p. 3).

Progressive supervision, while downplaying teacher evaluation, emphasized collaboration, group processes, inquiry, and experimentation. In marked contrast to the social efficiency model, teachers were seen as part of the solution rather than as the problem. Barr, Brueckner, and Burton (1938) announced in *Supervision* that they were deliberately setting out to replace the old concept of the supervisor as inspector with responsible leadership that would rely on scientific reason and experimentation for enlightenment and direction. Democratic supervision, according to this view, recognized the worth of each individual and emphasized flexibility in organization, free participation by all, and pursuit of the common good (Pajak, 2000, p. 3).

These principles of democratic supervision, however, were not employed universally. Democratic supervision processes coexisted with bureaucratic, controlling methods for rating and weeding out incompetent teachers. The Progressive's democratic challenge to the role of supervisor as autocrat and rater of teacher efficiency marked the beginning of an ongoing conflict between the dual role of supervisor as teacher evaluator and as helpful colleague.

The remainder of the twentieth century saw a constant tug-of-war between the evaluative and helping functions of the supervisor. Until the mid-1950s, the helping or collegial function was emphasized. Collaborative problem solving, group supervision, and curriculum development were seen as the primary tools used by supervisors to facilitate the development of those with whom they worked. Supervisors were cognizant of the task of developing people and considered human relations an important component of their work (Pajak, 2000). However, following the launching of Sputnik in 1957, the rush to improve student learning especially in mathematics and science led to an increasing emphasis on the role of the supervisor as the instrument of school change. Collaboration and cooperation were seen as less important than getting innovations into practice. In some cases, the desire to see innovations put into practice led school districts to develop teacher evaluation systems that monitored implementation and punished those who resisted with lower evaluation ratings. In others, the vehicle for promoting innovation was seen as developing collegial, helpful relationships with teachers. These relationships could then be used to nudge ideas into practice.

From the late 1960s, the field of supervision has been marked by a disconnect between the theoretical literature and the realities of practice. Much of the theoretical literature on teacher supervision has focused on the tradition of clinical supervision as developed by Cogan (1973) and Goldhammer (1969). Their model emphasizes the supervisor as colleague who develops a trusting relationship with the teacher and provides intellectual service designed to improve the teacher's practice and student learning. Both Cogan and Goldhammer eschew the role of supervisor as evaluator, believing it to be basically incompatible with the supervisory helping function. In the world of practice, however, most of those employed as supervisor find themselves saddled with the tasks of both teacher evaluation and teacher improvement. Various factors, including inadequate supervisory knowledge and skills, role overload that leads to a lack of time for supervision, and issues related to contractual agreements restricting supervisory activities, cause most supervisors to focus their efforts on teacher evaluation and do relatively little in the area of teacher help and improvement. As a consequence, clinical supervision never achieved popularity in the schools.

In the late 1970s, Madeline Hunter, an educational psychologist, developed a model of supervision that made sense to many practitioners (see Hunter, 1984). Although her model also became known as "clinical supervision," it bore little resemblance to Cogan and Goldhammer's conceptions. Hunter's model was much more authoritarian, much more supervisor directed, and entirely compatible with teacher evaluation. Despite many admonitions by its developer, Hunter's model of clinical supervision was turned into a teacher-rating checklist in district after district. Its use spread like wildfire, prompting scholars in supervision to ask, is there life after Madeline Hunter? (Garman & Hazi, 1986). For the most part, Hunter's model of clinical "supervision" was really a process of teacher evaluation. Labeling this process of teacher evaluation as clinical supervision further exacerbated the confusion between teacher supervision and evaluation in the minds of many educators.

The late 1980s and the 1990s saw the development of alternative models of teacher supervision that were intended to counteract the impact of Hunter's model on the world of supervisory practice. Developmental supervision (Glickman, Gordon, & Ross-Gordon, 1998) and reflective supervision (Garman, 1990) were philosophically similar to Cogan and Goldhammer's model in espousing collaborative efforts to improve teaching and insisting that evaluation and supervision be viewed as separate activities. These developmental and reflective approaches dominate the current landscape of supervisory practice in the field of preservice teacher education. Though they enjoy growing popularity in in-service teacher supervision, they are still not widely used in that domain. The long-standing tradition of teacher evaluation as an important function of supervisors prevents many school systems from embracing these collegial supervisory models. Such districts often embrace collegiality in rhetoric, but continue to practice inspectorial evaluation as the predominant mode of interaction between teachers and supervisors.

It short, the continuing failure to resolve the dilemma between teacher supervision and evaluation has created major difficulties in the practice of instructional supervision since the 1920s. As a result, we find a scholarly literature that advocates collegial improvement and practitioners who find themselves unable to accept the collegial role due to the hierarchical superiority that is implied and, indeed, necessitated by the role of teacher evaluator. Jeffrey Glanz, one of the few scholars in the field of supervision who has focused his work on supervision history, concurs with our assessment of this unresolved conflict.

> *The evaluative function of supervision is historically rooted in bureaucratic, inspection-type supervision. Maintaining an effective and efficient school organization as well as a sound instructional program mandates that teachers are assessed for competency. In other words, the evaluative aspect of the supervisory function emanates from organizational requirements to measure and assess teaching effectiveness. The origins of the helping or improvement function of supervision can be dated back to early democratic practices in colonial America and later in the twentieth century. In other words helping teachers to improve instruction and promote pupil achievement grew out of the democratic theory of supervision. Supervisors or people concerned with supervision have faced a basic role conflict; namely, the unresolved dilemma between the necessity to evaluate (a bureaucratic function) and the desire to genuinely assist teachers in the instructional process (a professional goal) (Glanz, 1998).*

Now that we have examined this long-standing dilemma in the role of school supervisor, we will turn our attention to resolving the dilemma by explicating the separate but complementary functions of teacher supervision and teacher evaluation.

## TEACHER SUPERVISION AND EVALUATION: SEPARATE, ESSENTIAL, COMPLEMENTARY FUNCTIONS

As noted above, the question of whether teacher supervision and teacher evaluation are compatible roles for the same individual has plagued both practice and scholarship for many decades. Individuals who have developed models of teacher supervision are divided on the issue. Some (e.g., Hunter and Acheson and Gall) see no inherent conflict between the two roles; others (e.g., Cogan, Glickman, Smyth) believe that the roles should be separated by process and time, if not by person; still others (e.g., Blumberg) suggest that the two are best separated but can be carried out simultaneously, if necessary (Pajak, 2000).

The world of practice is at least as confused as the world of scholarship. Some school districts define teacher supervision and evaluation as the same function both in policy and in practice. Many districts make a distinction between teacher supervision and evaluation in policy but end up practicing what McGreal (1983) called "common law evaluation," that is, using the exact same procedures for both functions, with the result that teachers end up perceiving the entire process as evaluative. Many of these districts attempt to soften the threat of evaluation by couching evaluation in a language of growth and improvement, but this euphemistic strategy often ends up creating mass confusion and excessive entanglements between supervision and evaluation (Hazi, 1994). Finally, some districts, growing in number over the last decade, have managed to separate the two functions both in policy and in practice.

The world of supervision has also suffered from a failure to develop commonly accepted definitions for important concepts. As commonly accepted definitions for supervision and evaluation do not exist, it is particularly important that we make clear the definitions we are using.

As we define it, teacher evaluation is an organizational function designed to make comprehensive judgments concerning teacher performance and competence for the purposes of personnel decisions such as tenure and continuing employment. Though improvements in the teacher's performance may result from the process and may be a desired outcome, the process as a whole is aimed primarily at making a summative judgment about the quality of the teacher's performance in carrying out both instructional duties and other responsibilities. This is a state-mandated function carried out only by those who are properly certificated by the state. Typically, the superintendent of schools is officially responsible for teacher evaluation and chooses to delegate this responsibility to individuals within the school district who are properly certificated, administrators and supervisors.

As we define it, teacher supervision is an organizational function concerned with promoting teacher growth, leading to improvement in teaching performance and greater student learning. Supervision is not concerned with making global judgments concerning the teacher's competence and performance. It is a function that can be carried out by multiple individuals who find themselves in multiple roles within the school system, teachers, administrators, supervisors, and so on. Teacher supervision is a broad label that encompasses many different activities designed to enhance teacher growth. Classroom coaching designed to examine and improve specific aspects of teaching performance is a supervisory process whether carried out by two teaching colleagues or by a teacher and someone

**FIGURE 1.1**   Dimensions on which Supervision and Evaluation Differ

1.  Their basic purpose
2.  The rationale for their existence
3.  Their scope
4.  The nature of the relationship between the teacher and the administrator
5.  The focus for data collection procedures
6.  The role of expertise
7.  The teacher's perspective on the entire process

designated as a supervisor. In the former case, we refer to it as peer coaching or colleague consultation. In the latter case, we refer to it as classroom supervision. Also included under the broad label of teacher supervision are activities such as self-directed teacher development, action research, and collegial development groups, as they are organizational functions aimed at promoting teacher growth.

Notice the use of the term function to refer to both teacher supervision and evaluation. We use function as opposed to role. Our reason is that, while teacher evaluation responsibilities are confined to those in certain organizational roles, supervision is not the sole purview of those who occupy a role known as supervisor. As we make explicit in our platform of beliefs, every professional within the system has the capability and responsibility of contributing to the function of supervision.

One of the most fundamental planks in our platform of beliefs is that teacher supervision and evaluation are two essential functions, each separate from the other, but complementary. Although many school districts attempt to combine the two functions into a single activity, we believe that this approach is doomed to failure because the two functions are fundamentally different. Teacher supervision and evaluation differ on at least seven dimensions (Figure 1.1).

Though the two functions must be carried out separately from each other, they are key complementary functions of schools as organizations. The two functions complement each other in that teacher evaluation ensures that all teachers function at a satisfactory level of performance, whereas teacher supervision provides opportunities for teachers to grow far beyond minimally acceptable levels of performance.

We now turn our attention to explaining the fundamental differences between evaluation and supervision in terms of the seven dimensions.

## Basic Purpose

The purpose of teacher evaluation is to make judgments concerning the overall quality of the teacher's performance and the teacher's competence in carrying out assigned duties as well as to provide a picture of the quality of teaching performance across the professional staff. The process results in some form of summative rating, numerical (e.g., 78/80) or qualitative (e.g., outstanding, satisfactory, or unsatisfactory). Developing either a numerical or qualitative rating demands that the evaluator have in mind some explicit or, at the very least, implicit model or standard of desired performance against which the performance of the teacher can be compared. Absent some such explicit standard of performance and evaluation data, it is impossible to make and justify a numerical or qualitative rating. In short, the basic purpose of teacher evaluation is to ascertain whether or not all teachers meet at least a minimum standard of competent performance as judged by an evaluator with appropriate expertise. Even though teachers may improve (in a small number of cases) as a result of going through the evaluation process, the primary objective in the mind of the evaluator is to ascertain the quality of the teacher's performance.

Evaluation provides assurance that every teacher in the system will be performing at some minimal level of competence. Though there are huge differences across school districts in the quality of performance that is considered to demonstrate a minimal level of competence, there is some threshold level of minimal competence in every school district's evaluation system. The threshold is clear and explicit in some districts, and it is much more implicit in others. Teachers who are not tenured or whose performance is marginal or worse can be forced to improve by being threatened with an unsatisfactory rating. However, as long as tenured teachers are performing at or above that minimum level of competence, evaluators do not have the power to force them to grow. Although the evaluator often suggests areas for improvement, the satisfactory, tenured teacher is free to accept or reject those suggestions. Administrators, school board members, and politicians who would opt to put all of their resources for teacher improvement into teacher evaluation fail to understand the limited power of teacher evaluation for forcing people to grow. Others, who really understand the limits of evaluation, see the need for teacher supervision as a vehicle for promoting (not forcing) growth.

The purpose of supervision is to promote individual teacher growth beyond the teacher's current level of performance. It is not important in supervision to make a global pronouncement of teacher proficiency. The task is to start where the teacher is, wherever that might be, and reach beyond that level. This involves making sense of the complex world of the classroom and helping the teacher to become aware of his or her behavior and its consequences for learners.

As opposed to being driven by some externally adopted model of teacher performance, the supervisory process is driven by the teacher's and school's platforms of beliefs about teaching and learning. The teacher is motivated to grow by a desire to find ways to better achieve his or her own goals for students. Supervision attempts to capitalize on our knowledge of adults as learners. Adults, in contrast to most children, are likely to change their behavior when they see that there may be a better way to accomplish goals that are important to them as opposed to improving because someone else says that they need to (Knowles, 1990). Teacher ownership over the growth process is an important motivating variable.

## Rationale

The rationale for the function of teacher evaluation derives from the legitimate right of the state to protect children from harm through incompetent, immoral, or unprofessional teacher behavior. This right is operationalized through a process of inspection delegated to the local school district by the state. Districts that abandon teacher evaluation or fail to take it seriously do not live up to their moral commitment to ensure that no child is harmed by the instruction that he or she receives. Consequently, teacher evaluation is a legalistic and bureaucratic process that must be carefully articulated to ensure that the rights of the state and its children are protected and to ensure that the teacher's rights to due process are not violated. Teacher tenure laws further delineate the teacher's due process rights and shift the burden of proof in a dismissal hearing. School districts must pay close attention to these legal issues and also to the implications of collective bargaining agreements in designing teacher evaluation processes.

The rationale for supervision, on the contrary, derives from the complex nature of the teaching environment itself. Classrooms environments are marked by simultaneity and multidimensionality, requiring teachers to make hundreds of nontrivial decisions on a daily basis (Doyle, 2001). The task of promoting cognitive, affective, and psychomotor growth for 25 or more students simultaneously is amazingly complex. No other professional works with so many clients at the same time.

For example, suppose that doctors had to see 25 patients at the same time. Some doctors appear to schedule multiple patients for the same time slot, but most see only one at a time. Imagine what medicine would be like if the doctor had a limited amount of time, say one half hour, to diagnose and treat 25 patients. One might assume that the doctor would take a sampling of symptoms and then prescribe some general treatment that would address the symptoms of as many people as possible. So that if everyone else in your patient group has a sore throat, you would get penicillin too, even though it probably would not heal your broken wrist.

We might also imagine what it would be like for a trial lawyer to try several cases simultaneously in adjoining courtrooms. We realize that lawyers often work on multiple cases at the same time, but they try only one at a time. If the daily work of lawyers involved multiple cases being tried simultaneously, he or she might examine a witness in one courtroom and then rush to an adjacent courtroom to cross-examine a witness whose direct testimony the lawyer had not heard.

These examples of doctors and lawyers may sound ludicrous, but we use them to make an important point about teachers' daily lives. Teachers' work is very much like that of a doctor who has to treat 25 patients simultaneously or a lawyer who tries multiple cases at the same time. If you doubt that, think about a teacher who has 25 diverse students with a variety of strengths, needs, and interests and has a limited amount of time and instructional resources with which to meet their varying needs. Does the hypothetical doctor's work seem any more complex? Consider also the teacher who is moving around the room monitoring five groups of students who are working on a cooperative learning activity. She hears group A answer questions one and two, and then she moves to group B to listen to their discussion of questions three and four without any inkling of what they said about the first two questions. This example strikes us as being very similar to the lawyer who must cross-examine a witness whose direct testimony has not been heard. Teaching one single individual how to complete a complex task, e.g., knitting a sweater, can seem tremendously overwhelming. How much more complex is the world of the classroom where teachers attempt to reach two-dozen students or more?

Given complexity of their work environment, teachers benefit tremendously from having a skilled colleague who can act as another set of eyes and ears to capture classroom events and then talk with the teacher to help to make sense of what is happening in the classroom and what impact it is having on individual learners. Supervision is not intended as a legalistic or bureaucratic process; it is a professional, community building activity that recognizes that teachers are motivated by internal drives such as a desire to improve their own professional competence and a desire to maximize student learning.

## Scope

By its very nature teacher evaluation must be very broad in scope. Teacher evaluation examines not only the teacher's classroom teaching performance but also the teacher's contribution to the school as an organization, including meeting contractual obligations, interacting with professional colleagues, communicating with parents, continuing his or her own professional development, and making a contribution to the total life of the school. In fact, many teachers who are dismissed through the teacher evaluation process are dismissed not for poor classroom performance but rather for issues and behaviors that are connected to minimal contractual obligations and extra-classroom behavior.

Even in terms of classroom teaching, the evaluation task is broad. Effective teacher evaluation demands that the teacher be observed teaching the entire spectrum of classes that the teacher teaches. For elementary teachers, this means observing language arts, math, science, social studies, and so on. There are very few elementary teachers who are equally capable in teaching all of these content areas. In order to state that the process has resulted in a comprehensive evaluation of even the teacher's classroom teaching, all of these various subjects must be observed.

For secondary teachers, this means observing the entire spectrum of courses and students that the teacher is assigned. Many secondary teachers teach more than one subject (e.g., algebra and geometry or general science and chemistry), and almost all secondary teachers teach a variety of different types of students with different strengths and needs. Few secondary teachers are equally good in teaching all subjects and all students. If the system is designed to obtain a comprehensive picture of the teacher's classroom teaching performance, all of these various contexts must be observed. Additionally, effective evaluation depends on seeing the teacher over time rather than only once or twice. Many of us can put our best foot forward for a limited time. However, as someone observes our work more frequently, a much clearer picture of our typical behavior emerges. Unless the evaluator takes the time to develop a comprehensive view of teacher performance, both inside and outside the classroom, it is not possible to make or defend a global judgment of teacher's effectiveness such as that demanded by most state teacher evaluation systems.

Teacher supervision, on the contrary, can narrow its focus considerably. As improvement in performance rather than a global judgment of competence is the goal, the supervision process can be focused on one class or one type of teaching situation over time. In fact, case studies in clinical supervision indicate that a specified focus in the same environment over time is a critical dimension of supervision that improves teacher performance (Nolan, Hawkes, & Francis, 1993). The best way for most of us to improve is to focus our attention on one or two factors at a time. If we try to focus globally and say we will improve without being specific about exactly what we will improve, nothing ever changes. Thus, if supervision is to be effective in helping teachers grow, it must have a narrow rather than a broad focus.

### EXERCISE 1.2   Developing an Evaluative Observation Schedule

**Introduction**   The purpose of this exercise is to enable you to understand the complex task of attempting to match the scope of teacher evaluation activities to the complex role of the classroom teacher at the various levels of basic education. It should help to make the previous ideas more concrete.

**The Teachers**
- Cathy is a first-grade teacher in Parkview Elementary School. She teaches a group of 25 first graders. Four of her students have Individualized Education Plan (IEPs) and three additional students receive specialized services of some sort. Cathy teaches all required subjects—math, language arts and reading, science, social studies, technology competencies, and so on.
- Howard is a sixth-grade teacher in Parkview Middle School. Howard has a homeroom of 28 students. He instructs these homeroom students in language arts and social studies. For math, he teaches the top group of sixth graders, who are studying prealgebra and will take algebra in seventh grade. For science, he teaches the lowest group of sixth graders in his building.
- Kathy is a social studies teacher at Parkview High School. She teaches five periods per day in traditional 45-min periods. She has two advanced classes of 10th grade world cultures (30 per class) and two average classes for 11th grade U.S. history (27 per class). In addition, she teaches one section of rather unmotivated seniors (20 students) in a course called Problems of Democracy.

**The Task**   You and a partner have been assigned the task of developing an observation schedule for each teacher's yearly evaluation. Using the knowledge about their class schedules, identify the minimum number of observations that would be required to gain an accurate picture of each teacher's classroom teaching performance over the course of an entire school year.

## Nature of the Relationship

The evaluator's role is to make a professional judgment concerning the teacher's overall performance and competence. As stated earlier, one of the evaluator's major responsibilities is to protect the interest of the state and its children. For that reason, only properly certificated personnel can fill the role of teacher evaluator. Although the evaluator may know and like the teacher in question, it is imperative that he or she maintain a certain degree of distance in order to make a fair assessment of the teacher's performance. It is also imperative that the roles remain distinct. The evaluator is always the evaluator; the evaluatee is always the evaluatee. The roles can never be merged or blended. It seems that the most appropriate stance for the evaluator would be what Garman (1982) calls a "neutral observer," and the highest level of collaboration one could hope for would be "working-acceptance involvement." Working acceptance implies that both parties know the rules and their respective roles and agree to live by them. The degree of collaboration is limited to that type of understanding. The evaluator cannot be "on the teacher's side" because in some cases this might imply not being on the children's side.

Establishing an atmosphere of trust in this relationship is also extremely difficult the evaluator has all the power and the teacher has all the vulnerability. Additionally, the teacher has no choice about whether to participate in the process or not; it is a state-mandated activity. As Blumberg and Jonas (1987) pointed out, it is very unlikely in this type of relationship that the teacher will grant the evaluator access to his or her deepest hopes, fears, and beliefs about the teaching and learning process. Some highly skilled principals are able to establish collegial relationships with teachers even when they are engaged in evaluation. These highly skilled individuals build such good relationships in spite of the system, not because of it.

In supervision, on the contrary, distance is a barrier and rigid adherence to organizational roles hinders rather than facilitates the process. In the process of supervision, both partners agree to work together as colleagues. Sometimes the teacher takes the lead in the process, and sometimes the supervisor takes the lead. By watching the process of supervision develop over time, we come to realize that leadership is shared and roles are blended and exchanged freely. When the process unfolds as it should, it is possible to reach what Garman (1982) described as organic reciprocity, in which goals, leadership, expertise, respect, and trust are shared mutually among the participants.

In contrast to the neutral stance demanded of the evaluator, the supervisor should be on the teacher's side in helping the teacher to accomplish mutually set goals and objectives. In contrast to evaluation, where the evaluator is all-powerful and the teacher is an all-vulnerable, forced participant, supervision is a voluntary relationship with mutual vulnerability and shared power. The fact that the teacher is allowed to select specific areas of teaching on which to focus the supervision process empowers the teacher and also makes the supervisor accountable for collecting the type of data that the teacher requests. Shared responsibility, trust, and mutual vulnerability are three important characteristics of collegial relationships (Nolan, Hawkes, & Francis, 1993).

## The Focus for Data Collection

The process of teacher evaluation is standardized and criteria driven, that is, the process is driven by established criteria that are used to judge the teacher's performance and competence. Because the evaluator's task is to make a global judgment, the evaluation data must take a more global focus, encompassing the teaching–learning environment in its entirety rather than just one or several selected aspects of the teacher's behavior. Failure to maintain this global focus over time risks capturing an incomplete picture of the teacher's behavior, resulting in an unfair evaluation. Moreover, the outcome of the evaluation process is a summative judgment that is communicated by a written narrative that loc remarkably similar for all teachers.

Finally, and perhaps most importantly, the standards that drive classroom observation for purposes of teacher evaluation must be the same for all teachers. In keeping with due process rights and contractual agreements, all teachers in the same job category must be evaluated using the same criteria. Issues of fairness across teachers as well as issues of validity and reliability take precedence over individual teacher needs in the arena of teacher evaluation. If the criteria are different for some teachers, charges of arbitrary and capricious behavior will surely be hurled at the evaluators in any type of dismissal hearing.

Data collection for purposes of teacher supervision, by contrast, should be differentiated, individualized, and teacher driven (Nolan & Francis, 1992). The focus on data collection in supervision is typically very narrow, converging on some teacher-selected aspect(s) of teacher and/or student behavior. In addition, this narrow focus is typically captured during several lessons over time in an attempt to document improved teacher or student performance and to capture what Garman (1990) called the "unfolding lesson." The supervisor's role is not to make and communicate judgments but rather to collect observational and inferential data that can be used to enable the teacher to make better judgments about his or her own teaching performance and its impact on learners. The supervisor may help the teacher in making these judgments but does not make the judgments for the teacher. As a result, one of the outcomes of the supervision process should be the development of a teacher who is more self-directed and a better decision maker.

We believe that if the supervisory process does not improve teacher's decision making and self-direction, then the entire process is not very useful at all. We make this claim based on the reality of teacher supervision. Let us take the case of a typical high school teacher, just to make the math easier. The typical high school teacher teaches five classes per day for 180 days, a total of 900 classes per year. In even the most exemplary teacher supervision system, it is very unlikely that the teacher will be observed nine times during the course of the school year, but, for the sake of argument, let us assume that the teacher is observed nine times. This means that observers have seen 1% of the teacher's classes. Ninety-nine percent of the time the teacher will be on his or her own with students. If the supervisor does all the problem solving, all the directing, and all the decision making, and does not enable the teacher to develop those skills, the teacher will be unable to improve the teaching in 99% of his or her classes. So, as you can see, improved teacher decision making and problem solving is a sine qua non of good supervision.

## The Role of Expertise

Only those who are properly certified by the state are allowed to carry out the process of teacher evaluation certification implies that special knowledge and skills are required for this role. Throughout the process, the evaluator maintains the role of expert. The evaluations responsibility is to make a fair assessment of the teacher's performance and competence using the district standards and the evidence collected during the process. The teacher may be asked for his or her opinion (we will argue in Chapters 7 and 8 that self-evaluation should be an important aspect of teacher evaluation); however, if this opinion conflicts with that of the evaluator, it is the evaluator's opinion that must prevail. Therefore, expertise for making judgments concerning teacher performance and competence resides solely in the evaluator(s).

Further evidence for one-sided expertise is provided by the fact that teachers are often presented with a written text that describes and judges their performance before there has been an opportunity for the teacher and evaluator to discuss what has been observed. This places a heavy burden on the evaluator, who must possess both pedagogical and content expertise in order to make a fair, informed, comprehensive assessment of teacher performance and competence. If the evaluator does not possess content expertise, it is imperative that other properly certificated experts in the content area be brought into the process.

We believe that an accurate judgement of poor teacher is possible without any knowledge of the content being taught. For example, classroom management may be so poor that the vast majority of students are completely off-task most of the time. However, we believe to making a defensible judgment that someone is a good teacher is not possible without some understanding of the content being taught. An obvious example is a fifth-year foreign language class in which the evaluator does not speak the language. If the majority or all of the class is conducted in the target language, the evaluator has no basis whatever for assessing the teacher's performance. Content expertise is an essential aspect of assessing good teaching performance. The importance of content expertise is very clear in the negative attitudes, expressed or implied, of secondary teachers toward evaluators who do not have expertise in the content areas they teach.

By contrast, teacher supervision relies on shared expertise. The supervisor brings expertise in supervision (data collecting, inquiry, and conferencing), pedagogy, and perhaps content whereas the teacher contributes expertise in pedagogy, content, and perhaps supervision as well as intimate knowledge of his or her students and the history of that particular classroom context. If any of these areas of expertise are missing or untapped, it is extremely difficult to make sense of the teaching–learning environment. Because each of the partners recognizes the expertise of the other and its importance, leadership and power are shared. When disagreements about the meaning of classroom events occur, they are resolved through dialog and further hypothesis testing, data collection, and interpretation. Neither partner seeks nor accepts the role of resident expert because neither partner is responsible for making a summative judgment about the quality of teaching.

## Teacher Perspective

Teachers see the process of teacher evaluation as a situation in which they are supposed to put their best foot forward for the benefit of the evaluator. It is a "hit me with your best shot" type of approach. The evaluator plays the role of drama critic whereas the teacher is playwright, actor, producer, and director. Because of the negative consequences that can result from poor performance during an observation for evaluation purposes, teachers take few risks. They do not put on plays that are likely to fold. They are much more likely to put on old favorites that have received rave reviews. Showcase lessons that are repeated in whole or in part, year after year, are not unheard of in the realm of teacher evaluation.

One of the authors, a former German teacher, was evaluated by a principal who loved to see lots of classroom interaction. The typical pattern of teaching on nonobservation days, all 178 of them, was to begin the class with a 5-min oral warm-up in which students were questioned about everyday events, their families, the weather, school activities, and so on. On the one or two days of unannounced observation by the principal, the oral warm-up continued for about 20–25 min, 50% or more of the class time, because the principal could see lots of student interaction. Though the author is not proud of having behaved in this way, the example does illustrate the "best foot forward" attitude toward teacher evaluation that most teachers possess. Employing the procedures that we suggest in Chapter 8 for increasing the teacher's responsibility for data collection can diminish this best foot forward attitude to some degree, but it can never be eliminated completely.

Supervision, on the contrary, should be an opportunity for risk taking and experimentation. Often supervision is used to enable teachers to try out new behaviors and techniques in a safe, supportive environment. As there is no fear of a negative judgment about competence, the teacher can allow the supervisor to see lessons that are not perfect. In fact, the teacher may ask the supervisor to observe purposely a lesson with which the teacher is struggling in hopes that the supervisor can be helpful in improving it.

Joyce and Showers (2002) have demonstrated the importance of supportive, nonevaluative coaching in helping teachers transfer new teaching models to the classroom. They suggest that without classroom coaching as a follow-up to training activities only 15–20% of the teachers are able to transfer the use of complex teaching techniques to the classroom. With appropriate coaching and supervision, up to 90% of teachers are typically capable of making the transfer. As supervision is aimed at growth over time, experimentation and risk taking are tremendously important characteristics.

## Summary

Both teacher evaluation and teacher supervision are essential functions. As Sergiovanni and Starratt (2006) suggest, evaluation establishes an individual teacher's right to enjoy continuing membership in a given school community whereas supervision helps that teacher to exercise his or her responsibility to promote continuing growth in that particular community and in the profession of teaching as a whole. Though both functions are important, evaluation and supervision differ significantly from each other in terms of their basic purpose, the rationale for their existence, the nature of the relationship between the participants, the scope of the process, the observation procedures employed, the role of expertise, and the teacher's perspective on the process. Figure 1.2 summarizes these fundamental differences.

These differences are fundamental, not trivial, and they demand that the two functions be separated. Although we firmly believe that the two processes must be separated, we also assert that the same individual can carry out both functions effectively as long as the processes are different. If the procedures for supervision and evaluation are not noticeably different, teachers will always see any individual who carries out both roles as an evaluation. The system's failure to separate teacher evaluation from teacher supervision means that most schools do a very poor job of both processes in most schools.

Though supervision and evaluation are separate functions, they can be used together as powerful, complementary components of a school district teacher supervision and evaluation system. The evaluation component of the system allows all stakeholders to be assured that the performance of all professionals is at least at a minimal level of competence. It also provides a mechanism for deciding whether new teachers should be granted

**FIGURE 1.2**  Fundamental Differences Between Teacher Supervision and Evaluation

| Dimension | Evaluation | Supervision |
|-----------|-----------|-------------|
| Purpose | Minimal competence | Growth |
| Relationship | Protect children | Complexity of teaching |
| Rationale | Hierarchical | Collegial |
| Scope | Comprehensive | Focused |
| Data focus | Standardized | Individualized |
| Expertise | Evaluator as expert | Shared expertise |
| Perspective | Best foot forward | Risk taking |

tenure and for remediating the performance of or eventually dismissing teachers who fail to perform at satisfactory levels. The supervisory component of the system allows teachers to grow in ways that are personally meaningful and compatible with their career stages, learning styles, and general life circumstances. A well-designed supervision component of a teacher evaluation and supervision system helps to establish the norm that teachers are expected to grow continually and that the status quo is not an option. But what does a well-designed system of teacher supervision and evaluation look like? The following section describes the criteria that can be used to assess the quality in this domain.

## CRITERIA FOR HIGH-QUALITY SUPERVISION AND EVALUATION SYSTEMS

The criteria that follow are based on the scholarly literature (e.g., Danielson & McGreal, 2000; Peterson, 2000) and have also been tested, in practice, through the statewide awards process for exemplary practices in teacher supervision and evaluation established by the Pennsylvania Association for Supervision and Curriculum Development.

1. *The processes for judging competence (evaluation) are clearly differentiated from processes for promoting growth (supervision).* Having built the rationale for this separation of supervision and evaluatic, we turn our attention now to the question of how the two functions can be separated in practice. There are two basic ways to separate evaluation from supervision: by people or by time and procedures.

The most obvious way to separate the two is by using different people to carry out the two different functions. In this model, administrators carry out the process of teacher evaluation, whereas teachers and/or other specialists such as content supervisors carry out the process of supervision. The two processes remain completely separate. What happens in the supervision process is confidential, with all data and notes being kept by the two participants. In many districts that use this type of arrangement, supervision becomes peer coaching carried out by teachers who have been given the opportunity through staff development to develop the knowledge and skills necessary to engage in effective coaching. This method of separating evaluation from supervision makes an unmistakably clear distinction between the two functions.

Despite its clarity of separation, this model has some drawbacks. The approach requires a significant increase in the resources directed toward teacher supervision and evaluation. Either supervisory personnel must be employed to engage in supervision, or teachers must be provided with staff development and some release time to carry out the process of peer coaching. In addition, many administrators really would like to be involved in helping teachers grow and would find it very difficult to carry out a role that allows them to engage only in making summative judgments about the quality of teacher performance. Those districts that do not have enough resources or do not prefer this type of structure can consider the second alternative.

This alternative is to develop a system of teacher supervision and evaluation that separates the functions by time and procedures. In this model, the same administrator can be engaged in carrying out both functions. However, the functions are carried out at different times with different procedures. When this model is used, teachers are typically placed on differing supervision and evaluation tracks. Figure 1.3 depicts this differentiated model of supervision and evaluation in which the same administrators can be involved in both functions.

Nontenured teachers and teachers who are new to the district are often placed in a probationary track until they successfully complete the typical 3-year period required for

**FIGURE 1.3** A Differentiated System of Teacher Supervision and Evaluation

|  | **Probationary track** | **Cyclical evaluation and supervision** | **Intensive assistance** |
|---|---|---|---|
| Participants | Novice teachers and teachers new to the district | Veteran teachers whose performance is satisfactory or better | Veteran teachers whose performance is marginal |
| Evaluation process | Each year until probationary period is over (usually 3 years) | Formal evaluation every 3 years | Each year until performance is satisfactory or teacher is dismissed |
| Goal of evaluation | Make accurate judgment concerning granting tenure | Assess quality of performance and identify areas for growth | Return to a satisfactory level of performance |
| Supervision process | Each year. Primarily classroom observation but may include other supervisory modes as well. Focused on growth but related to evaluation | Two nonevaluative years of 3-year cycle. Mode chosen by teacher from classroom supervision, peer coaching, self-directed growth, action research, and collegial development groups | Each year. Administrated directed but augmented by help from intensive assistance team. Tied closely to evaluation process |
| Goal of supervision | Maximize growth in support of evaluation | Enhance growth toward excellence | Remediate identified deficiencies |

earning tenure. Once the probationary period has passed and tenure has been granted, teachers are typically in an evaluative mode once every 3 years and in a supervisory mode the other 2 years. During the evaluative year of the cycle, the teacher participates in the standardized evaluation process. Activities during the supervisory years vary. Teachers may engage in self-directed staff development, goal setting and supervision with the principal, peer coaching, action research, or collegial development groups. Typically, teachers in this track are asked in the spring to select their supervisory option for the following school year.

If the principal engages in supervision with the teacher during the supervision years of the cycle, the procedures used differ substantially from the evaluation procedures used during the evaluation year. For example, observations for the purposes of evaluation are both announced and unannounced, driven by the teacher evaluation criteria and used to communicate observer judgments concerning the effectiveness of the teacher's performance. By contrast, observations for the purpose of supervision are preceded by a preconference in which the teacher selects a focus. Observations are used to collect data that enable the teacher to make collaborative judgments with the supervisor about how to improve his or her teaching.

During the supervisory years of the cycle, the teacher is not formally observed for the purposes of evaluation although the administrator visits the classroom periodically to keep in touch with what is happening. The teacher (who has already passed through the probationary period) is presumed to be teaching at a satisfactory or better level. State-mandated yearly evaluation ratings for these veteran teachers can be marked legitimately as satisfactory on the basis of three pieces of evidence: the teacher's past performance, the teacher's participation in supervision, and the administrator's informal observations unless some evidence to the contrary surfaces. If such evidence does surface, the teacher is immediately moved into an intensive assistance mode where a thorough evaluation of his or her performance is conducted.

A final component of this differentiated system of teacher supervision and evaluation is an intensive assistance mode for teachers whose performance is considered marginal or worse. Typically, the administrator is given the authority to place teachers into the intensive assistance category as a result of a poor evaluation during the evaluation year of the cycle. If the teacher believes that this placement is unfair or inappropriate, he or she is usually given the opportunity to appeal this placement to the superintendent. If the administrator's recommendation is upheld, then a process of intensive remediation begins.

Typically, a team of administrators and teachers is assembled with the purpose of helping the teacher to improve. The goal of the process is not teacher dismissal. Rather, it is to return the teacher's performance to a level of satisfactory or beyond and to allow the teacher to return to the cyclical system of teacher supervision and evaluation. If improvement does not occur, the administrative team must decide whether to give the teacher an unsatisfactory rating or to continue the intensive assistance process. This decision is a difficult one and will be addressed in greater detail in Chapter 11. You will note that even in this differentiated model depicted in Figure 1.3 the only clear separation between supervision and evaluation occurs for veteran teachers who are performing well. For both novice and marginal teachers, supervision and evaluation are still connected to each other. We believe that this is appropriate. Until teachers have demonstrated the capacity to perform well over time, ongoing evaluation is important. Once that ability has been demonstrated, periodic formal evaluation is sufficient.

In both of these models for separating supervision from evaluation, a strong commitment is made to both teacher evaluation and teacher supervision. Teachers are required to complete a rigorous period of intense evaluation before they are granted full membership in the community and before a district commitment to their long-term growth is made. Once this probationary period has passed, the district makes a long-term commitment to provide the resources necessary to carry out both teacher evaluation and teacher supervision separately and effectively.

2. *Supervision and evaluation are high district priorities.* Developing a high-quality teacher supervision and evaluation system is a very demanding activity. Human and fiscal resources must be devoted to the processes of developing, implementing, maintaining, and evaluating the system. Administrators alone cannot develop a high-quality system of evaluation and supervision. A variety of stakeholders including teachers, school board members, parents, and community members should be involved in the process. School board members play an essential role in the process because the outcomes of the development process will be new policies for district implementation as well as requirements for more resources committed to teacher supervision and evaluation. The presence of parents and community members in the committee can help to legitimize the process in the eyes of the community at large.

Teacher ownership of the system is critical in order to achieve the desired outcomes of improved teaching and learning. When teachers do not buy into the system, they can find subtle ways of undermining the goals that the system is attempting to achieve. They go through the motions necessary to comply with the letter of the law, but they also make sure to follow the path of least resistance. They choose to participate in those aspects of the system that will require the least amount of effort on their part and also result in the lowest possible level of improvement. Although some teachers may make these choices because they are uninterested in improvement, others do so because they resent being treated as children who cannot be trusted to play a role in developing systems that are intended to promote their own growth.

In our work with school districts engaged in the process of developing or revising their systems of evaluation and supervision, we have been deeply impressed by two aspects of teacher involvement in the process. First, teachers who participate in development committees are often even more dedicated than administrators and school board members to raising the level of teacher performance across the district. Second, we are impressed by the number of teachers who choose supervisory modes of growth that require much, much more work on the part of the teacher than the once-a-year visit by the principal for evaluation. They choose more work simply because they believe that it will result in improvement for them and increased learning for their students.

Development of the system is an essential indicator that supervision and evaluation are high district priorities. A second powerful indicator of the importance of the two functions is the attention given by the district to the implementation of the system and its ongoing evaluation and maintenance. Implementing the system will require staff development for all the players in the system, both administrators and teachers. Staff development must be provided concerning the mechanics of the system and participation in it as well as the standards and criteria for teacher evaluation. It is also likely to be needed for particular components of the system, for example, peer coaching and action research.

After the initial training and staff development have been provided and the system is put into operation, a committee of stakeholders should meet on a regular basis to monitor the implementation of the system and troubleshoot problems. Our experience tells us that it is very common to have different administrators implement the system in different ways, even after they have all received the same training. If implementation is not monitored, serious problems can arise in the system as a result of perceived unequal and unfair implementations. Awareness of such problems in the early stages of implementation can avoid serious problems later on.

After the system has been implemented successfully, periodic evaluation of the system and its impact is crucial. No system is perfect. There are always minor adjustments that can be made to improve quality. We suggest that a committee of stakeholders solicit feedback from participants at least every 3 years in order to evaluate the efficacy of the system and to refine and improve it. This ongoing evaluation function results in improvements in the system and also models the process of continuous improvement for which everyone in the system should be striving. The degree to which any school district takes seriously the processes of development, implementation, and ongoing maintenance of its teacher supervision and evaluation system is a very strong indicator of the district's commitment to these processes. Chapter 12 contains much more explicit information about the development, implementation, and evaluation processes.

3. *The district provides opportunities for differentiated supervision.* One of the hallmarks of excellent teaching is the ability of the teacher to meet the varying needs of the students with whom he or she is working. As noted in our platform of beliefs, teachers, like students, differ from each other in many respects. Nevertheless, the vast majority of teacher supervision and evaluation systems in the United States do not account for individual differences beyond the first 3 years of teaching. Typically, teachers who have not yet earned tenure are seen as different from tenured teachers and treated differently in terms of both supervision and evaluation. Once tenure has been earned, however, most systems of teacher evaluation and supervision treat everyone the same. A single model of supervision for teachers does not make any more sense than a single model of instruction for children.

The deeper tragedy of this failure to meet individual teacher's needs is the fact that many models of supervision and evaluation are designed with the case of the marginal teacher in mind. The entire system consists of regulations and practices that are designed to force marginal teachers to improve. As a result the systems are administrator-centered, very directive, and sometimes punitive in nature. Although such heavy-handed systems may be necessary for some marginal teachers, they are exactly the opposite of what the vast majority of teachers require. Designing such a system is analogous to designing a system of instruction that meets the needs of the least cooperative, most unmotivated child in the school and then teaching all students by that method.

High-quality systems of teacher supervision and evaluation provide a variety of options for teacher growth including but not limited to classroom supervision, peer coaching, collegial development groups, self-directed professional development, and action research. Chapters 2 to 6 provide detailed information concerning the development, implementation, and evaluation of many of these options for differentiated supervision and growth.

4. *The process for evaluation makes clear the criteria by which performance is judged.* As suggested earlier in this chapter, every system of teacher evaluation is based on some implicit or explicit conception of what satisfactory teaching performance looks like. One of the indicators that differentiates high-quality systems of teacher evaluation from low-quality systems is the presence of a clear and explicit set of standards for describing successful teacher performance. When all of the participants in the evaluation process have a deep understanding of the criteria for successful teaching, it is much more likely that teaching performance across the district will match or exceed the minimal level of competence. When either administrators or teachers are unclear or confused about the standards for satisfactory performance, each individual is free to develop his or her own interpretation. One result of this muddled situation is a tremendous variance in the quality of teaching performance across schools.

The lack of specificity and clarity concerning standards and criteria for satisfactory performance is responsible in many cases for the horrible situation in which a teacher whose performance has been judged to be satisfactory for 20 or more years is suddenly found to be marginal or unsatisfactory. This situation often occurs when a new administrator or evaluator steps on to the scene. This new evaluator sees the act of teaching very differently from the former evaluator. As a result, the same teaching performance is rated as satisfactory or even better in May and as unsatisfactory in October. Obviously, this situation is unfair for both the teacher and the new administrator.

As we suggest in Chapter 7, there are many sources of help to which a district can turn in developing the standards and criteria for satisfactory teaching performance. There are state-approved formats that can be used, although some of these are quite broad and not particularly helpful in focusing on the instructional act per se. Other sophisticated and highly developed systems that can be used to assess the teaching act are available. We present 5 sets of standards in Chapter 7. We suggest that each school district develop its own set of criteria and standards for teaching after examining preexisting standards from external experts. The authors have been involved in the development of teacher supervision and evaluation systems in many districts and have been quite amazed at the commonalities one finds when teachers and administrators are asked to respond to the question of what good teaching looks like.

The development of the standards and criteria does not complete the task of making the standards and criteria clear. Staff development must be provided for all participants so that each individual has the opportunity to understand the standards and criteria and has a chance to ask questions that will clarify any unclear or confusing areas. In addition, evaluators must participate in both initial and ongoing staff development aimed at helping all evaluators interpret the criteria in the same way and apply them uniformly. Unlike teacher supervision, which is optimized by a differentiated, individualized approach, teacher evaluation demands consistency and uniformity across evaluators. Specific training should be provided so that all evaluators attain a high degree of reliability in assessing teacher performance. After this initial training has been held and the system is operationalized, periodic sessions should be held in which evaluator reliability is reestablished. This will help to prevent what researchers call "observer drift." Observer drift is a phenomenon in which researchers who are trained initially to achieve a very high degree of reliability gradually drift into their own individualized interpretation once they go out observing on their own.

5. *The organizational climate is conducive to effective supervision and evaluation.* Teacher supervision and evaluation do not occur in a vacuum. They take place within both school and district organizational contexts. There is no doubt that climate varies considerably across and even within the same school districts. The climate in small elementary schools is often very different from the climate that one finds in large high schools that must rely on bureaucracy and standardization to some degree, simply because of their size. The most well intentioned and carefully crafted system of teacher supervision and evaluation will sputter and die in an organizational climate marked by distrust, animosity, and cynicism. Because teacher evaluation, as we noted earlier, requires only working acceptance on the part of the teacher and does not imply a collaborative relationship between the teacher and the evaluator, the impact of a negative climate on the evaluation function is rather limited. Teacher supervision, on the contrary, with its emphasis on trust, collaboration, and teacher direction, is extremely dependent on the climate of the school and district in general.

The importance of school climate for successful supervision implies that districts should concern themselves with the readiness of the district as a whole for developing sophisticated systems of teacher supervision and evaluation. When the climate is already fairly open and trusting, the district can forge ahead with establishing a stakeholder group to develop the system. When the climate is cynical or negative, it would be wise to begin very slowly. The district might find particular buildings or even departments in which the climate is more positive and begin to pilot supervisory processes with selected volunteers. Over time, the number of volunteers and the number of school sites can be gradually increased as the successes of the pilot programs are made known to broader constituencies through staff development activities.

It should be obvious that developing a high-quality system of teacher supervision and evaluation in a negative climate requires vision, patience, persistence, and consistency in district leadership over time. When district leadership changes frequently or when stakeholders become too impatient, there is often a push toward accelerated system development and implementation. The result is usually a system that has no chance of being successful in promoting growth and an increase in the climate of hostility and negativism. We should also point out that the very process of developing, implementing, and evaluating a system of teacher supervision and evaluation can improve the climate of the district as a whole if carried out in accordance with principles such as those outlined in Chapter 12.

6. *The entire system of supervision and evaluation is aimed at enhancing student learning.* As important as teacher supervision and evaluation are, they are not ends in themselves. Both are aimed at enhancing the quality of student learning. This improvement in student learning should be the primary purpose of any system of teacher supervision and evaluation as we assert in our platform of beliefs. One of the questions that we are asked most frequently when we conduct workshops for school board members is whether our notions about teacher supervision and evaluation will improve student test scores. We always answer the question honestly by saying that we have no evidence that student test scores will improve. We also explain that the causal chain from a system of supervision and evaluation to improved test scores on the part of an individual student is a very long chain of events with the opportunity for interference from a very large number of intervening variables (teacher effort, student motivation, test–curriculum match, etc.). Attributing improved test performance to supervision and evaluation is a difficult measurement task.

**FIGURE 1.4**  Criteria for High-Quality Systems of Teacher Evaluation and Supervision

1. The processes for judging competence (evaluation) are clearly differentiated from processes for promoting growth (supervision).
2. Supervision and evaluation are high district priorities.
3. The district provides opportunities for differentiated supervision.
4. The process for evaluation makes clear the criteria by which performance is judged.
5. The organizational climate is conducive for effective supervision and evaluation.
6. The entire system of supervision and evaluation is aimed at enhancing student learning.

However, in our work with schools, we have seen many instances of improvement in student learning and performance that we could document and attribute to the process of teacher supervision. One of the authors was involved in a peer-coaching project as part of a district differentiated supervision system in which two peer coaches were able to provide clear documentation of improvement in student writing as a direct result of the peer-coaching process. The other author was involved in a peer-coaching project in another district where increases in student learning resulted from the efforts of a calculus teacher and a physics teacher who joined forces to create an interdisciplinary advanced placement course for their students. In interviewing teachers about teacher supervision, we have heard several well-documented stories of changes in student behavior and learning that resulted from differentiated supervision opportunities. None of these cases involved standardized test scores; they did involve significant student learning.

The unfortunate aspect of these stories of improved student learning, however, was that none had been documented or recorded beyond the level of the individual teacher. We believe it is very important that district-wide procedures be developed for reporting and recording changes in student learning that occur as a result of differentiated supervision and evaluation. Enhanced learning can be captured through the data collection procedures that are used to evaluate the efficacy of the system. They can also be captured as part of the routine record keeping that is used for each of the various supervisory options as suggested in Chapters 2–6.

There are several important reasons for developing procedures to document and record enhanced student learning. Such efforts testify to the effectiveness of the system as a whole in meeting its basic purpose, and they also provide opportunities for teachers and administrators to recognize and celebrate their impact on individual students. Finally, such efforts provide parents, community members, and school board members with concrete evidence of the positive impact of the human and fiscal resources devoted to teacher super-vision and evaluation. Unfortunately, we have seen a couple of cases in which a few new school board members or a new superintendent were able to undermine and dismantle a high-quality system of teacher supervision and evaluation simply because the district administrators had not collected any concrete information concerning the impact of the system on students. We believe that if these two districts had collected such data (similar to the vignettes, cases, and examples in Chapters 4–7), the systems would have survived.

Figure 1.4 restates the six criteria for high-quality teacher supervision and evaluation systems that have been discussed above.

## CHAPTER SUMMARY

From the beginning of the twentieth century, school supervisors have been handicapped by an ongoing tension between the roles of supervisor and evalua-tor. Although most supervisors would like to work with teachers in helpful and supportive ways, they have also been saddled with the duties of teacher evaluation. As most schools have not been able to develop systems of teacher supervision and evaluation that reconcile these two important functions, the vast majority of supervisors have become de facto teacher evaluators who do little or no supervision.

We assert that teacher supervision and evaluation are two critically important but separate functions for improving the quality of education. In this chapter, we build a case for the separation of teacher supervision from evaluation based on seven dimensions in which the two functions differ. Supervision and evaluation differ in terms of their basic purposes, the rationales for their existence, the scope of the two processes, the relationship established with the teacher, the observation procedures, the nature of expertise, and the teacher's perspective on the process.

We then used this understanding to describe how the two separate functions can be related to each other in complementary ways in a well-designed system of teacher supervision and evaluation. This differentiated system employs three supervision and evaluation tracks: a probationary track for novice teachers, a cyclical process of evaluation and supervision for veteran teachers, and an intensive assistance mode for marginal teachers.

The final section of the chapter delineated six criteria by which the quality of any system of teacher supervision and evaluation may be assessed. A well-designed system separates evaluation from supervision, promotes differentiated growth opportunities, makes evaluation criteria clear, is a high district priority, aims at enhancing student learning, and exists within and contributes to a collaborative organizational climate.

## DISCUSSION QUESTIONS

**1.** Look back at Exercise 1.1. Have any of your beliefs and attitudes about supervision and evaluation changed as a result of what you have read in the chapter? If so, what caused them to change? If your attitudes and beliefs differ from the authors, what arguments would you use to convince the authors that their beliefs are wrong?

**2.** Think about the last time you were evaluated by an administrator. What was the relationship between you and the administrator like during the evaluation process? Was your relationship different when you are/ were not being evaluated? If so, how was the relationship different?

**3.** Thinking solely of performance evaluations that you have received, describe the degree to which they

were helpful in improving your performance. What made them helpful or not helpful? How could they have been made more helpful?

**4.** Describe the process of supervision that was used the last time you were supervised as a professional. What elements of the process made it feel like supervision as opposed to evaluation? What elements made it feel like evaluation and not supervision? What improvement in your performance, if any, resulted from the process? Why did improvement occur or not occur?

**5.** Consider the six criteria suggested for evaluating the quality of a teacher supervision and evaluation system. Do you agree with each? Why or why not? Would you modify any? Eliminate any? Add any? Why?

## THEORY-INTO-PRACTICE APPLICATIONS

**1.** Obtain a copy of the written plan for teacher supervision and evaluation in the school where you are currently working or in which you have worked most recently. Apply the six criteria for high-quality teacher supervision and evaluation systems to that plan. Identify strengths and weaknesses of the plan. How could the weaknesses be improved? Also, identify those criteria on which judgments were readily possible based on the plan alone and those criteria that would require more intense study of actual processes before a judgment is possible.

**2.** Obtain a copy of the teacher observation instrument that is used for teacher evaluation in a local school district. What does the instrument tell you, as an observer, about how the district sees teaching competence? Relate it to your own views about good teaching. What changes would you make? Why? Now separate those qualities on the instrument that are directly observable from those that are not. What data sources would be needed to ascertain the presence of those qualities that are not directly observable?

**3.** Design a survey that could be used to obtain feedback from the teachers in a local school district concerning the quality of the district's teacher supervision and evaluation system. Now, adapt the survey for principals; for central office administrators; for board members. Administer the survey and compare the results across groups.

**4.** Interview three teachers and three administrators (try to get elementary, middle, and high school teachers and administrators) concerning what they would perceive as high-quality teacher supervision and evaluation. Compare the perceptions of the teachers and administrators. What are the differences? What are the similarities?

# REFERENCES

BARR, A., BURTON, W., & BRUECKNER, L. (1938). Supervision: Democratic leadership for the improvement of learning (2nd ed.) New York: Appleton-Hartley.

BLUMBERG, A., & JONAS, S. (1987). Permitting access: The teacher's control over supervision. *Educational Leadership 44*(8), 58–63.

BOLIN, F. (1987). On defining supervision. *Journal of Curriculum and Supervision 2*(4), 368–380.

BOLIN, F., & PANARITIS, P. (1992). Searching for a common purpose: A perspective on the history of supervision. In C. Glickman (Ed.), *Supervision in transition* (pp. 30–43). Alexandria, VA: Association for Supervision and Curriculum Development.

COGAN, M. (1973). *Clinical supervision*. Boston: Houghton Mifflin.

DANIELSON, C., & MCGREAL, T. (2000). *Teacher evaluation to enhance professional practice*. Alexandria, VA: Association for Supervision and Curriculum Development.

DOYLE, W. (2001). Classroom organization and management. In M. Wittrock (Ed.) *Handbook of research on teaching* (4th ed.) (pp. 392–431). New York: Macmillan.

GARMAN, N. (1982). The clinical approach to supervision. In T.J. Sergiovanni (Ed.), *Supervision of teaching* (pp. 35–52). Alexandria, VA: Association for Supervision and Curriculum Development.

GARMAN, N. (1990). Theories embedded in the events of clinical supervision: A hermeneutic approach. *Journal of Curriculum and Supervision 5*, 201–213.

GARMAN, N., & HAZI, H. (1986). Teachers ask: Is there life after Madeline Hunter? *Phi Delta Kappan 69*(9), 669–672.

GLANZ, J. (1998). Histories, antecedents, and legacies of school supervision. In G. Firth & E. Pajak (Eds.), *Handbook of research on school supervision*. New York: Macmillan Library Reference. (p. 39–79)

GLICKMAN, C., GORDON, S., & ROSS-GORDON, J. (1998). *Developmental supervision* (4th ed.), Boston: Allyn and Bacon.

GOLDHAMMER, R. (1969). *Clinical supervision: Special techniques for the supervision of teachers*. New York: Holt, Rinehart and Winston.

HAZI, H. (1994). The teacher evaluation-supervision dilemma: A case of entanglements and irreconcilable differences. *Journal of Curriculum and Supervision 9*, 195–216.

HUNTER, M. (1984). Knowing, teaching and supervising. In P. Hosford (Ed.), *Using what we know about teaching*. Alexandria, VA: Association for Supervision and Curriculum Development. (p. 169–192)

JOYCE, B., & SHOWERS, B. (2002). *Student achievement through staff development* (3rd ed.), Alexandria, VA: Association for Supervision and Curriculum Development.

KNOWLES, M. (1990). *The adult learner: A neglected species* (4th ed.), Houston, TX: Gulf Publication Co.

MCGREAL, T. (1983). *Successful teacher evaluation*. Alexandria, VA: Association for Supervision and Curriculum Development.

NOLAN, J., & FRANCIS, P. (1992). Changing perspectives in curriculum and instruction. In C. Glickman (Ed.), *Supervision in transition* (pp. 44–60). Alexandria, VA: Association for Supervision and Curriculum Development.

NOLAN, J., HAWKES, B., & FRANCIS, P. (1993). Case studies: Windows onto clinical supervision. *Educational Leadership 51*(2) 52–56.

PAJAK, E. (2000). *Approaches to clinical supervision: Alternatives for improving instruction* (2nd ed.), Norwood, MA: Christopher Gordon Publishers.

PETERSON, K. (2000). *Teacher evaluation: A comprehensive guide to new directions and practices*. Thousand Oaks, CA: Corwin Press.

SERGIOVANNI, T. J., & STARRATT, R. J. (2006). *Supervision: A redefinition (8th ed.)*, Boston: McGraw Hill.

# SUGGESTIONS FOR FURTHER READING AND RESEARCH

FIRTH, E., & PAJAK, E. (Eds.). (1998). *Handbook of research on school supervision*. New York: Macmillan Publishing.

NOLAN, J., PALKO, L., BUREAU, E., CLAPPER, J., GOODNACK, J., GOODWIN, S., HEALEY, P., HOOVER, L., MEISTER, D. (1995). *Teacher Supervision and evaluation: A process for school district self-assessment and improvement*. Lancaster, PA.: Pennsylvania Association for Supervision and Curriculum Development.

# CHAPTER 2

# KEY CONCEPTS AND SKILLS IN CLASSROOM SUPERVISION

$\mathbf{I}$N **CHAPTER** 1, we defined teacher supervision as an organizational function concerned with promoting teacher growth, thus leading to improvement in teacher performance and greater student learning. "Teacher supervision" is a broad label. It encompasses a variety of activities that can be carried out by multiple individuals, both in class and out. In **Part II**, we focus on observation of teaching as an in-classroom supervisory activity. The present chapter deals with classroom supervision involving a teacher and an individual designated as a certificated supervisor. In Chapter 3, we describe peer coaching as a differentiated form of supervision, a process of observation carried out by teaching colleagues.

The foundation for the processes of classroom observation that we espouse stems primarily from the pioneering work of Morris Cogan (1973) and Robert Goldhammer (1969) at Harvard University. Although their original models of clinical supervision have evolved in myriad ways over the past 40 years, their underlying philosophy and clinical cycle remain essential to supervisors observing in today's classrooms.

Cogan and Goldhammer advocate a collegial, rather than a hierarchical approach to supervision designed to enhance student learning. Continuous reflection and inquiry into one's teaching are at the center of a multistage cycle that includes establishing readiness, a preconference, the teaching observation, analysis of the data, a postobservation conference, and an overall evaluation of the process.

Throughout the cycle, supervisors are encouraged to develop genuine and supportive relationships with teachers. They develop those relationships by recognizing and building upon the teachers' existing strengths, individual styles, and unique teaching contexts, rather than by focusing on shortcomings. The supervisor's task is to start wherever the teacher might be in terms of classroom practice and to facilitate the teacher's growth beyond that point through data-driven decision making. The underlying assumption is that most teachers are professionally competent and seek to make instructional choices that will have a positive impact on student learning (Pajak, 2000). They are appreciative of a supervisor's efforts to collaborate with them to collect, interpret, and discover the meaning of data because, in doing so, they can consciously make informed decisions about their practice.

To truly affect the teaching–learning process, a supervisor must understand and practice seven salient skills of classroom-based supervision. With a firm foundation in these skills, a supervisor should be well equipped to promote individual teacher growth beyond current levels of performance. Chapter 2 captures what we believe is the essence of that complex and differentiated process. The seven essential skills of classroom-based supervision are

- Build trust and positive communication
- Uncover espoused platforms and platforms in use
- Encourage continuous reflection and inquiry into teaching
- Collect systematic data
- Interpret and use the data
- Conference
- Foster a professional learning community

The chapter explains these skills in depth and provides practice in using them.

## GUIDING QUESTIONS FOR PREREADING REFLECTION AND JOURNALING

- Think about the characteristics of the supervisors whom you most vividly recall being helpful to your professional growth. Using your course journal, create a list of the attributes or skills that those individuals have in common.
- When was the last time you articulated the philosophy that guides your teaching? Take a few moments to reflect and list some key points that serve as the foundation of your belief system.
- What types of data have your supervisors collected during classroom observations in the past? What do you remember about their observation summaries? What have you found most helpful in improving your practice? Least helpful?
- Describe the characteristics of an "ideal" school climate, one in which you would feel valued as a stakeholder who possesses a shared voice and genuine ownership in striving toward maximum student achievement.

## BUILDING TRUST AND POSITIVE COMMUNICATION

One of our favorite anecdotes concerning typical classroom observation was related by Art Blumberg (1996). He recalled a course that he had once taught on communication networks in organizational life. Because many of his students were teachers, they chose schools as organizations for analysis:

*It was in that setting that I learned about the warning systems—communications structures—that teachers used while they were in their classroom to tell each other that the principal or other type of supervisor was prowling around the school. The systems involved such activities as this: the teacher who first discovered that the supervisor was on "grand rounds" might give a particularly colored pencil to a youngster to take to the teacher next door. It was a prearranged signal. The pencil would be passed from room to room and soon the whole school was aware of what was going on. ... The thing which struck me most was not the method used, which was actually pretty efficient, but that a method for warning the faculty about a possible supervisory visit was used. How odd it was, or so I thought. Large numbers of teachers seemed to feel it was necessary to warn each other when the person who was supposed to help them was in the process of trying to do just that. (p. 3)*

As we discussed in chapter 1, when schools fail to separate supervision from evaluation, neither function is performed very well. One of the resulting problems is that teachers respond to observation as Blumberg describes—with mistrust and apprehension.

Recognizing that trust is a cornerstone in the foundation for effective in-class supervision, Blumberg focused much of his research on trust building and positive communication or interpersonal relationships in supervisory practice. As he makes clear, teachers cannot refuse their supervisors entry to their classrooms, but they can and do control access to themselves and their belief systems. Thus, any substantive changes that may occur in the classroom environment or instructional delivery are also controlled (Blumberg & Jonas, 1987). Because long-term change in a teacher's instructional behaviors or practice seldom occurs without a corresponding change in the assumptions and attitudes that underlie and shape those behaviors and that practice, one of the questions that supervisors struggle with is how to "open the door" to teachers' belief systems and thought processes. Unless the door is opened metaphorically as well as literally, time together is more likely to be spent "going through the motions" or in meaningless ritual to which a teacher gives lip service than in improving teaching. Thus, the first stage of the in-class supervision model is to establish readiness by building trust and positive communication.

In our workshops on supervision, we frequently ask the educators with whom we work to identify the traits of an "ideal" supervisory partner—someone in whom they could place their trust and confidence. Invariably, teachers draw the same conclusions about trusted interpersonal relationships. They describe the ideal supervisory partner as one who

- maintains a spirit of confidentiality, making the teacher feel safe in sharing;
- is nonjudgemental and open minded, supporting the teacher in trying new ideas in a nonthreatening manner;
- is confident and possesses a strong knowledge base in content, pedagogy, and supervisory skills, earning the teacher's respect as a professional;
- practices good communication skills, including active listening, sensitivity, and tact;
- sets a good example by modeling a positive attitude, enthusiasm for teaching, and self-reflection in personal practice; and
- maintains a sense of humor.

Blumberg's research exploring administrator–teacher supervisory relationships (1987) highlights two crucial factors in promoting trust. The first is a collaborative approach to problem solving—the sense of "our being in this together." Rather than adopting an "us versus them" mentality, the supervisor and teacher both recognize that they share a basic goal, namely, that the results of their working together have a positive impact on students' learning. They realize that to achieve that goal, they must freely exchange ideas and share responsibility in the supervisory process. They need not agree, but they must respect one another's right to hold differing viewpoints. The second factor, closely related to the first, is the supervisor's ability to communicate a genuine belief that teachers possess the expertise to participate meaningfully in supervision. Supervisors may have knowledge beyond the teacher in many competency areas, but they must recognize that, as professional educators, teachers contribute specialized knowledge and skills. No one knows the abilities and needs of a particular group of students, the classroom dynamics, or the history of a class better than the individual who works in that classroom on a daily basis. Supervisors must openly demonstrate shared ownership in the process through a genuine commitment to and acknowledgement of the competent teachers with whom they work.

Positive communication is also essential to establishing readiness. Clear communication begins with a shared understanding of the observation process, including its goals, the varied processes that can be used to attain those goals, and the roles that all stakeholders can play.

A shared understanding of this kind does not develop immediately. It must be nurtured through a carefully planned sequence of activities. For example, at the beginning of the supervision cycle, the supervisor should take time to explain the entire process to the teacher. This includes the goals and the stages of the process and the roles that the teacher and supervisor are expected to play. Supervisors may meet individually with each teacher or in a group format.

Ideally, communication starts at the district level. The central office administration should facilitate a common conception of what it means to be supervised and what it means to be evaluated. Principals must consistently reinforce the philosophy in both words and actions as they review and model the procedures of supervision at the building level. If teachers understand and believe that observations for supervision are separate from those for evaluation—that they are a means of working in collaboration with another individual to promote professional growth and students' learning—teachers are far less likely to resort to Blumberg's example of a warning device.

On an individual level, positive communication involves the supervisor's taking a genuine interest in the teacher's work, remaining nonjudgmental, and employing active listening (discussed in the section on conferencing later in this chapter). Positive communication builds gradually over time as supervisors and the teachers with whom they work come to know one another beyond a superficial level. Supervisors must "walk the talk" of a collaborative approach to supervision. Without a foundation of trust and mutual respect, teachers will seldom "open their doors" to seek help from administrators when challenging dilemmas arise in the classroom, to work collaboratively with administrators to solve problems, or to continue to "set the bar" at higher levels for themselves and for their students.

## UNCOVERING ESPOUSED PLATFORMS AND PLATFORMS IN USE

Another useful means of establishing readiness is tapping into a teacher's (oftentimes implicit) belief system. Every educator, no matter what role he or she plays, operates from a set of values and convictions about the fundamental purposes of education and how those purposes should be translated into the teaching and learning process. This is called the teacher's espoused platform, and because a teacher's philosophy about teaching and learning so powerfully influences that teacher's classroom behaviors, the impact of the supervisory process will be far greater if the espoused platform can be made explicit and open to examination. Teachers are far more likely to change their behaviors when they come to a self-realization of the underlying reasons for doing so.

We, the authors, are no different. We possess a deeply held set of beliefs about teacher supervision and evaluation that drives our thinking and our practice. (As authors, we have written our espoused platform about supervision and evaluation—see Box). A teacher's espoused platform includes key aspects such as the teacher's views on the goals of education and the curriculum, expectations for the students as a class and as individuals, preferred pedagogy, preferred school climate, and theories about what factors most impact student learning. The platform stems from personal history, formal education, and actual classroom experience (Sergiovanni & Starratt, 2006).

When a supervisor accesses and understands a teacher's espoused platform, that supervisor is able to view and appreciate what occurs in the classroom from the teacher's perspective, making it far more likely that the two professionals can work effectively together.

# Nolan and Hoover's Espoused Platform on Teacher Supervision and Evaluation

*The most basic purpose of both supervision and evaluation is to enhance the educational experiences and learning of all students.* It is possible to become so involved in the procedural or conceptual processes of supervision and evaluation that the original intent of the activity becomes lost. Whether they are collecting data in classrooms, watching videotapes, collaborating on self-directed growth projects, reviewing portfolios, or designing individualized professional development plans, supervisors must continually return to one fundamental question, "What impact will this have on students?" The needs of students must be paramount.

*All educators should be treated ethically, fairly, and respectfully as they engage in the work of educating children.* When teachers are treated respectfully and sensitively, the likelihood that the school climate for students will be sensitive and caring increases greatly. In their interactions with one another, educators must model the behaviors that they expect to see exhibited by teachers as they work with their students. Information about each individual should be treated confidentially. The diversity that each individual brings to the profession should be appreciated and honored. All actions must attempt to keep each individual's long-term best interests at heart. When the values of caring, ethical treatment, and respect undergird individual behavior, building a positive organizational climate and creating a system of teacher supervision and evaluation that enhances professional growth and increases individual and organizational accountability are far more likely.

*Educational leaders must foster an organizational climate that is conducive to developing relationships among educators marked by trust, mutual respect, and the willingness to work collaboratively to solve problems.* Teacher supervision and evaluation do not occur in a vacuum. The most well-intentioned procedures and most highly sophisticated activities will not result in effective supervision and evaluation if the organizational context is inhospitable. When educators do not trust one another, do not respect one another, or do not have the skills to work together effectively, supervision and evaluation are likely to be reduced to mechanical processes carried out in ritualistic fashion. In such an organizational climate educators generally seek to get through the encounter as quickly, as painlessly, and as thoughtlessly as possible. In contrast, when a climate of trust, collaboration, and mutual respect exists, educators can successfully work together to solve complex problems, with mutual growth and enhanced student learning as the result.

*Teaching is a complex, problem-solving activity, and supervision and evaluation require sophisticated knowledge and skills.* Attempting to meet the needs of individual students is a tremendously complex process. Competing goals to which the teacher might attend are always present. A teacher may do an excellent job by one standard (e.g., promoting student success on advanced placement history exams) while failing miserably by some other standard (e.g., meeting the adolescent need for social development). It is also possible, indeed probable, for a teacher to succeed spectacularly with some types of learners while failing just as spectacularly with others. The multitude of decisions that teachers make on a daily basis demands that they engage in ongoing reflection and problem solving. Teaching is by nature recursive, multifaceted, and nonlinear. Therefore, supervision and evaluation procedures must be able to capture the complexity of the teaching and learning process. They cannot be reduced to a checklist containing a series of behaviors or steps that all teachers must follow. The act of teaching is always contextualized. Judgments about its effectiveness must also be contextualized.

*Supervision and evaluation are separate but complementary functions that should provide the cornerstones of a comprehensive system of professional growth and accountability.* Many school systems emphasize accountability at the expense of professional growth. The result is a system that can deal somewhat effectively with poor or marginal teacher performance, but that remains ineffectual at fostering growth when a teacher's performance is good or excellent. Other school systems focus on professional growth and de-emphasize accountability. Such systems provide many opportunities for teachers to grow professionally, but appear impotent when it comes to remediating marginal teacher performance or weeding out incompetent teachers. An effective teacher supervision and evaluation system must be capable of eliminating poor performance as well as nurturing excellent performance.

*Staff development is an integral component of an effective teacher supervision and evaluation system, not a separate activity.* Too often teacher supervision and evaluation are viewed as functions that are separate from staff development. This separation potentially results in a system that is unable to provide ongoing support to help teachers meet the needs that are identified through supervision and evaluation activities. While staff development may emphasize out-of-classroom training, does it follow through assistance needed for implementation? Separating supervision from staff development also results in reduced opportunities for job-embedded learning. We envision a supervision system that employs both out-of-school training activities and a variety of job-embedded learning experiences as key components of differentiated supervisory options for professional growth. High quality staff development includes supervisory activities such as classroom observation, peer coaching, self-directed growth, action research and collegial development groups.

*Teachers are unique individuals who learn and grow in a variety of different ways, and systems of teacher supervision and evaluation must provide differentiated growth opportunities.* Although teachers as a group share many characteristics, each teacher is a unique individual. Teachers differ in terms of preferred learning styles, levels of motivation, cognitive abilities and characteristics, and personal lives. A one-size-fits-all approach to teacher supervision and evaluation makes no more sense than a one-size-fits-all approach to teaching children and adolescents. Yet, remarkably, many school districts that advocate differentiated instruction for children take a one-size-fits-all approach to supervision and evaluation. We endorse a system of teacher supervision that allows the teacher and supervisor to work collaboratively to identify and meet the needs of the teacher. The supervision and evaluation system should include a variety of different processes to maximize teacher growth, from the marginal to the exceptionally able, at all stages of career development, from novices to those close to retirement.

*Teacher supervision is a function to which all professional educators can contribute.* Many educators see supervision as a role reserved for those individuals who have some type of administrative credential. We do not. We see supervision as an organizational function that is designed to promote professional growth for everyone within the system. All educators, therefore, have two roles to play. First, they are the primary movers in their own professional growth. Second, they help to foster the growth of other educators by participating in processes such as peer coaching, collegial development groups, collaborative self-directed professional growth, action research, and curriculum development. Teachers are professionals. By participating in these activities, they fulfill their responsibility to the profession itself. It is incumbent upon school districts to recognize these two important roles that teachers play in supervision and to develop comprehensive systems of supervision and evaluation that include these growth-oriented processes.

*All educators must have a deep understanding of the system of teacher supervision and evaluation as well as the skills necessary to carry out their roles within the system.* If the system of teacher supervision and evaluation is to work as designed, then everyone must understand the basic goals of the system as well as the various processes that are employed to achieve those goals. When this level of understanding is shared throughout the organizational hierarchy, the likelihood that leadership will be truly diffused throughout the system increases. Also, the possibility for collaboration is enhanced. When only certain individuals within the system understand the system thoroughly, then they alone must play the leadership roles. Concentration of leadership in the hands of a few limits the potential of the school to function as a learning organization and limits the possibilities for collaborative problem solving. In addition to understanding the goals and procedures of each component of the system, all educators must have the skills necessary to carry out their particular roles. Among the many skills that any individual is likely to need are question asking, data collecting, active listening, short- and long-term goal setting, interpersonal communicating, collaborating, and problem solving. An important implication of this belief is that all educators need ongoing professional development in order to enhance these crucial skills.

In the previous section on trust building, we explored "opening the door" to teachers' belief systems and thought processes. Supervisors can encourage teachers to articulate their belief systems by conducting a series of conversations about practice with those teachers. The platform can be a potential source of dialog and reflection for all pre- and postconferencing.

In addition to an espoused platform, a teacher possesses a "platform in use"—that is, actual teaching behaviors and interactions with students as revealed by the data. By articulating the espoused platform and comparing it to the platform in use, the supervisor and teacher can discover the extent to which the two are congruent. That exercise can be extremely useful if a teacher espouses one philosophy and discovers through the supervision process that the platform in use differs significantly. The stage is then set for cognitive dissonance: recognition on the part of the teacher of the inconsistency between personal beliefs and performance.

For example, a middle-level English teacher may espouse a student-centered classroom in which students are actively engaged in higher level thinking and discussion about the literature they are reading. However, the data may reveal that the percentage of teacher talk far outweighs student contributions to the discussion. Recorded teacher questions and student responses may show little in the way of the desired critical thinking. In this case, the teacher faces an in-depth comparison between the ideal and the real—cognitive dissonance between articulated beliefs and recorded behavior. Hopefully, to resolve the disparity, the teacher will consciously set such future goals as asking more divergent questions, allowing more wait time for student responses, and refraining from unnecessary explication that may discourage student-to-student interaction. On the contrary, a teacher's recognition that the espoused platform matches the platform in use can be a powerful form of affirmation and reinforcement of effective practice.

Platform clarification can also provide other benefits for the teacher and supervisor. Without consciously articulating and probing into the assumptions underlying their philosophies, teachers have little hope of a sustained change in perspective or teaching practice. Moreover, a supervisor may encourage a teacher to compare a personal platform with the school's platform and its goal statements concerning best practice. Exploring discrepancies between the two serves as a good starting point for reflection and conversation leading toward a common purpose and a shared commitment to improve instructional competence and professional practice. For example, if a teacher espouses a more traditional platform of passive learning but the district's mission values the active engagement of students in exploration of content, then a platform conference provides an opportunity to address the disparity openly.

A teacher's espoused platform can be uncovered individually through writing prompts, in small-group sessions facilitated by a discussion leader, or in pairs as teacher and supervisor work one to one at the beginning of a supervisory cycle (Sergiovanni & Starratt, 2006). Exercise 2.1 provides some sample questions that can be used as a starting point to interview a teacher concerning his or her espoused platform.

## EXERCISE 2.1   Conducting an Espoused Platform Conference

**Directions**   Find a partner. Take turns using the following set of questions in an interview format. What did you discover about one another's belief systems?

1. Think back and share some of the most important reasons why you entered the teaching profession. Have your feelings changed in any way? Explain.

2. Five years after your students have left your classroom, what would you like them to be saying about you? About your teaching? About their learning in your classroom?

3. Why should students learn the content that you teach? How does that content relate to the world outside the classroom?

4. How do you handle the constant tension between covering the content and exploring topics in depth to promote deeper understanding?

5. What indicators tell you that you have taught a successful lesson? How do you know when your students have learned what you hoped to convey?

6. If I were a new student moving into your classroom, what would you say if I asked, "What will you expect from me?"

7. If I were a parent of a new student, how would you respond if I asked you to describe the classroom climate or learning environment?

8. Think about the colleagues whom you most respect. Which of their strengths would you most like to integrate into your own teaching style?

9. What questions do you have about your instructional practices?

10. What questions do you have about your students' learning?

# ENCOURAGING CONTINUOUS REFLECTION AND INQUIRY INTO TEACHING

After establishing readiness by promoting trust, facilitating shared communication, understanding the supervision process, and uncovering a teacher's espoused platform, the supervisor and teacher are ready to focus on the ongoing skills of reflection and inquiry that serve as the center of the observation cycle. In our supervisory belief platform, we stated that teaching is a complex, multifaceted, problem-solving activity. Few supervisors who embrace that belief would argue against the importance of reflection upon teaching and of inquiry or problem posing about practice as continuous components of an educator's professional responsibility. However, coming to a shared understanding of exactly what it means to be a "reflective practitioner" has proved far more challenging. We suggest a return to Dewey's (1933) original notion, crafted more than 70 years ago, of teacher reflection as "problematic" and "purposeful," driven by the need to intellectually confront and generate questions, and subsequently to search for answers or a repertoire of solutions to classroom-based problems.

Inquiry into what we typically do is central to reflective teaching because it forces us to question our teaching beliefs and behaviors in light of student learning. As teachers constructively frame and reframe essential classroom questions (e.g., Do I really believe that "all students can learn"? If so, how do I convey my high expectations for their success and implement differentiated instruction to meet their needs?), they in essence study their own practice. Schon (1988) explains that honest and deliberate problem-posing of that type "opens a person to confusion, to not knowing" and therefore to a search for alternatives to the all-too-common tendency to accept the status quo (p. 23).

Reflection and inquiry into teaching are of little value, however, unless the increased consciousness raising has an impact on day-to-day practice through accompanying action. The blend of deliberation on practice and resulting action is called praxis (Freire, 1970).

Four simple, self-examining questions can lead an educator from thought to action—praxis (Smyth, 1989):

**1.** *(Describe)* What do I do?
Describing might be accomplished through artifacts such as a teacher's reflective journal, data collected during an observation, videotapes of teaching, examining student work, and so on.

**2.** *(Inform)* What does it mean?
Finding meaning might involve comparing one's beliefs to one's actual teaching actions and behaviors or identifying patterns in the data and analyzing the implications of those patterns for students' learning.

**3.** *(Confront)* How did I come to be like this?

**4.** *(Reconstruct)* How might I do things differently? (pp. 5–6)

Moreover, there are various categories of teacher reflection (Clift, Veal, Holland, Johnson, & McCarthy, 1995):

- *Technical analysis of one's own actions*: Action is analyzed in light of best practice and research on effective teaching (e.g., Do I have a good anticipatory set to introduce my lesson and effective closure to review my lesson outcome?).

- *Personal analysis of one's own development as an educator*: Analysis of development focuses on interpersonal relationships with students, colleagues, administrators, and parents (e.g., How effective am I as a teacher leader? Do I model what I believe? Am I really supporting my colleagues in improving their instruction?).

- *Critical analysis of the implicit and explicit values embedded in educational practice*: Values analysis develops insight into why certain norms and routines exist and how they affect children (e.g., How do I really feel about the middle school policy of homogeneous grouping for reading, language arts, and math? Is it better for students to be heterogeneously grouped for all subjects? What are the advantages and disadvantages of homogeneous grouping for learning-disabled children?).

- *Communal analysis*: Communal analysis moves reflection from oneself as an individual to oneself as a member of a community (e.g., I have been really interested in the possibility of multi-age, flexible grouping. Perhaps we can form a collegial development group to research and investigate the feasibility of a pilot project in our elementary school.). (p. 25)

In addition, teachers might also focus on practical wonderings that relate directly to their daily responsibilities. Questions for exploration might be "How do I balance student interest with the prescribed curriculum for the district, especially when I find myself unmotivated by some of the topics I teach?" or "How much time do I spend merely introducing certain topics as opposed to exploring them in depth so that my students grasp the essential concepts?"

Reflective questioning should be a part of every conference before or after observation. Figure 2.1 includes a sampling of questions that a supervisor might use during a conference to spark an experienced teacher's reflection and inquiry. These questions might also be used to spark conversations in small groups during grade-level, departmental, or building-level faculty meetings.

Note that control for reflection and inquiry lies internally with the teacher. The powerful combination of purposeful inquiry or of generating knowledge about one's teaching through question posing and the actions that a teacher then takes based upon investigation and experimentation leads to the teacher's becoming a self-directed professional who contributes to his or her own growth.

**FIGURE 2.1**  Reflective Questions to Guide an Experienced Teacher's Inquiry Into Practice

1. In what areas of my teaching do I tend to cling to the known and predictable?
2. Can I provide concrete examples of how I individualize my instruction to accommodate my students' unique differences and varied learning styles?
3. To what extent do I apply "quick fixes" or seek temporary compliance to classroom management problems rather than explore the underlying reasons behind my students' behavior?
4. Do my students view themselves as part of a community of learners within my classroom? How do I know?
5. In what ways have I worked to overcome professional isolation within my grade level, subject area, or school to extend the idea of a learning community beyond my classroom?
6. In what ways do I model the importance of lifelong learning for my students?
7. To what extent have I demonstrated a cynical belief that "this too shall pass" when introduced to an educational initiative through district staff development?
8. How do I build in the time and opportunity to keep myself up to date on what the research in my field suggests about best practices to promote student learning?
9. How do I gather data or concrete evidence on the impact that a new initiative or practice has on my students' learning?

Adapted from Brown, J. L., & Moffett, C. A. (1999). *The hero's journey: How educators can transform schools and improve learning.* Alexandria, VA: Association for Supervision and Curriculum Development.

Ultimately, however, we as authors are mindful that the reflective process must always return to a consistent focus on the most central of questions: What impact are various aspects of my teaching practice having on my students' learning? How can I better meet the needs of my students? As Barth (1990) declares, the greatest benefit of teacher reflection lies in its potential effect on students:

> *Probably nothing within a school has more impact on students in terms of skill development, self-confidence, or classroom behavior than the personal and professional growth of teachers. The crux of teachers' professional growth, I feel, is the development of a capacity to observe and analyze the consequences for students of different teaching behaviors and materials, and to learn to make continuous modifications of teaching. (p. 49)*

In summary, the supervisor's role is to serve as a guide who facilitates a teacher's continuous self-improvement through an informed "reshaping" of underlying assumptions and overt actions. As Garman (1986) notes, continuous reflection and inquiry into teaching leads to self-understanding, which is truly the "heart of clinical supervision" (p. 17).

## COLLECTING SYSTEMATIC DATA

In this section and the two that follow, we explore ways in which supervisors systematically encourage continuous reflection and inquiry into teaching through data collection, data interpretation, and conferencing. During a teaching observation, the supervisor or coach collects nonjudgmental, descriptive information. Although teachers may possess a general sense of what occurred during a lesson, the complexity and rapid pace of classroom interactions mean that teachers are frequently unaware of some of their own teaching behaviors or their students' actions and reactions. Analyzing objective data in collaboration with a supervisor or coach helps teachers to become more thoughtful about their actions rather than functioning on "automatic pilot."

Because teachers work alone in the classroom most of the time, the supervisor's responsibility lies in assisting them to become self-directing. One of the greatest disservices to a teacher is the untrained supervisor's tendency to sit in the back of the room and record personal judgments about what is occurring during a lesson. Providing summative judgments that require little or no reflection on the part of the teacher defeats the goal of teacher self-direction. Additionally, recorded judgments can automatically cause a teacher to become defensive. They thus destroy any trust that was established during the readiness phase of the cycle.

Note the difference between judgments, inferences, and observations. Judgments are statements that give the observer's opinion about the quality or effectiveness of what was observed ("There was a good deal of off-task behavior during the lesson"). Inferences are statements that guess what another person is thinking or feeling based on observable behavior ("I noticed that Ted was bored. He kept looking out the window"). Observations are statements that describe events that can be seen or heard ("Robert raised his hand three times during the lesson").

In the first instance, a supervisor's judgment can automatically cause teachers to rationalize that the supervisor is biased or "out to get me." Moreover, it robs teachers of the opportunity to form their own judgments. Teachers have far more difficulty denying or refusing to reflect on the concrete data provided by observations. They are forced to look beyond perceived reality and view themselves in light of data-driven reality. Exercise 2.2 provides practice in distinguishing among observations, inferences, and judgments.

**EXERCISE 2.2   Observations, Inferences, or Judgments**

**Directions**   The statements that follow are taken from actual written comments found in administrative observation narratives. Use them to practice distinguishing a supervisor's recorded observation **(O)** from an inference **(I)** and from a judgment **(J)**. If you mark a statement as a judgment, try to revise it so that it reflects objective data. Compare your answers with a partner.

1. My first impression as I walked into the classroom was the excessive noise level coming from the students.

2. You paused at least 3 seconds after each question asked before responding or calling on another student.

3. The students were very confused by your directions as their questions indicated.

4. Thirty percent of the students responded at least once to your questions.

5. You dominated the discussion.

6. Each direction that the teacher gave orally was also written on the whiteboard.

7. Kevin was indifferent to all of your requests that he pay attention to the demonstration.

8. Karen left her seat six times to sharpen her pencil during the seatwork assignment.

9. Only five students participated by answering questions about the homework assignment.

10. You gave positive reinforcement to the six students who volunteered; however, other than nodding your head, you gave no verbal reinforcement to the six nonvolunteer students whom you called upon.

## Data Collection Devices

Once they are able to clearly distinguish between observations based upon data, inferences, and personal judgments, supervisors are ready to explore specific methods of collecting data during teacher observations. Acheson and Gall (2003) describe three types of data collection techniques: wide-lens techniques, selective verbatim, and visual diagramming instruments such as SCORE (seating chart observational recording). Each technique has its strengths and limitations. Together they provide a strong starting point for data-driven supervision and a useful initial "toolbox" for the practicing supervisor or coach.

***Wide-Lens (Global) Techniques***   A wide-lens data collection technique records a holistic or global picture of the overall lesson, providing a "panoramic view" of instructional phenomena. If neither the teacher nor the supervisor knows exactly where to begin to focus in the observation process, wide-lens data oftentimes provide a good starting point. After analyzing the data collected, the teacher might be better able to identify specific questions or concerns about the implementation of a lesson or its impact on student learning.

The strength of wide-lens techniques lies in their comprehensiveness; however, they put the supervisor in control. In gathering such open-ended data, the supervisor chooses what to record and what *not* to record.

The most common techniques for observational wide-lens data collection are script taping, anecdotal notes (often accompanied by a timeline), and videotape analyses. (Although analyzing a videotape of one's teaching can be educative regardless of the level of experience, we find videotape analysis to be particularly helpful in guiding reflection for preservice teachers. We examine this wide-lens technique more closely in Chapter 9, on supervising the preservice teacher.)

**Figure 2.2** Sample Excerpt of Script Taping

| | | |
|---|---|---|
| **T** | Teacher | October 8, 2002 |
| **S** | Student | 8:53 a.m. |
| **Ss** | Students | AM Kinder |
| **C** | Choral response from group | |

Sharing time

| | |
|---|---|
| T | Time to stop tlking & come to circle |
| Ss | Much chatter |
| T | Claps pttern |
| Ss | Clp in resps |
| T | Sgnls: Look@ me |
| Ss | All look to T |
| T | Jeremy, this not time to tlk |
| T | Gd mrnng! |
| C | Gd mrnng! |
| T | We'll go round crcl. Tell eye color & share |
| Ss | Eye clr & shrg (1 by 1) |
| T respses | Be little loudr. Snds like fun! |
| | Wait til yr trn |
| | Em, scoot arnd. Face ths way |
| | Do u like tht? (Gameboy) |
| T | Taps S head to stp talkg |
| | Wow. Did it work? |
| 9 a.m. | |
| T | Who's alphbt ledr tody? |
| T | Stay sttng |
| T | Trevor (smles) |
| T | Use your magc lettr fingr to wrte nam in air |
| S | T-r-e-v-o-r (wrts in air/says out ld) |
| T | How many r's in yr nm? |
| S | 2 |

Special thanks to principal Deirdre Bauer from Radio Park Elementary School for sharing her script taping expertise.

Script taping became popular in conjunction with Madeline Hunter's seven "essential elements of instruction" movement in the 1980s (1983). The technique yields a detailed written record and timeline of the verbal (as close to word-for-word as possible) interactions that occur within the context of a specific lesson. The words of the teacher and of the students alike are recorded.

Capturing the data requires that the supervisor practice a system of abbreviations or shorthand. Supervisors trained and experienced in script taping can record the intricate and multidimensional aspects of lessons. It is important to note that although some observers can become quite adept at script taping, devising their own system of shorthand, others find the process cumbersome. Figure 2.2 shows an excerpt of a principal's "shorthand" in script taping a portion of a kindergarten teacher's morning meeting.

Anecdotal notes are a scaled down version of scripting. Resembling an anthropologist's field notes in a qualitative study, anecdotal notes include nonevaluative, summary descriptions of what occurs in the classroom. Although anecdotal notes are broad in focus, the lens can be modified or narrowed to view teacher behaviors, instructional strategies or activities that occur throughout the lesson, whole-class teacher–student interactions, or perhaps the actions of a small group or just one student. Figure 2.3 shows an example of anecdotal notes charting a teacher's behaviors during a lesson. The notes have been word processed and are in their final form.

It is again important to note that in script taping or anecdotal notes, control of what is recorded rests with the supervisor. In other words, although the supervisor records actual descriptive data, a judgment is first made about which actions or behaviors are significant enough to record and which are to be ignored. How that judgment is exercised may interfere with the goal of giving the teacher control over the type of data being collected.

***Selective Verbatim*** Wide-lens techniques offer a panoramic view of the classroom; selective verbatim on the contrary affords a narrow focus or telephoto view of classroom communication. Selective verbatim as a data-recording device provides teachers with the

**FIGURE 2.3** Anecdotal Notes on Teacher Behaviors

| | |
|---|---|
| Teacher: | Jennifer Monn |
| Class observed: | 9th- and 10th-grade Survey Science 1 |
| Date: | February 18, 2006 |
| Time: | 10:05 –10:50 a.m. |
| Enrollment: | 25 |

10:05    Miss Monn begins class by assisting her students in organizing their science notebooks. Using an overhead transparency, she reviews the class notes, list of completed study guides, data from in-class experiments, and science log entries that students should have as a record of their learning as part of the current unit. She informs anyone who was absent or missing information to check the four corresponding folders located on the table at the back of the room or to check with the assigned study buddy.

10:15    Miss Monn then orally introduces a research project. The class will be spending the next 2 days in the library using Web-based and print sources to complete their choice of one of the following assignments: (a) investigating the causes and treatment of one of a list of bone disorders; (b) comparing and contrasting the bone structure of another mammal with the human skeleton (this project includes the creation of some form of visual); or (c) exploring a career that might be related to the study of bones.

10:20    Miss Monn provides each of the students with a guide sheet and rubric explaining the criteria for success in this research project. Among the descriptors is information for sharing an 8 minute presentation about their findings with the rest of the class at the completion of the project.

10:28    Miss Monn accepts questions from the students and clarifies any concerns that they have.

10:34    Miss Monn has selected a collection of books from the school and community libraries for the students to peruse to help them in deciding which research project they would most be interested in completing. Students are given the time and opportunity to begin reading to decide on the topic they will explore in the library tomorrow. Students work individually and in pairs. Miss Monn circulates, answering questions.

10:45    Miss Monn reminds the students that she will be collecting their notebooks next week. She instructs them to report directly to the library at the start of class tomorrow. As they enter, they are to turn in their choice of assignment on a 3 x 5 index card (with their name!) that she distributes at the conclusion of class. She distributes cards before students leave.

opportunity to improve their instruction and impact on student learning by a careful analy-sis of communication patterns with students or among students (Acheson & Gall, 2003).

Selective verbatim is a targeted, word-for-word record of anything stated during the observation that pertains to a particular question or concern that the supervisor and teacher may wish to address. Among the specific data on which the supervisor and teacher might focus are teacher questions, teacher feedback after student responses, teacher directions, teacher transitional statements between various activities in a lesson, and teacher manage-ment or discipline statements. If the observation is designed to zoom in solely on evidence of student learning (or lack thereof), data can be collected on student questions, student responses to teacher questions, or student-to-student interactions. Depending upon a supervisor's skill and comfort level, that supervisor may choose to audiotape the lesson to supplement written notes.

Some supervisors object to the selective verbatim method because they fear that if the supervisor and teacher have predetermined its use, then the teacher will be consciously focus-ing on that aspect of the verbal exchange while the observer records. Although that fear may be well founded, a compensating advantage is that the verbal aspect is brought to the fore-front of the teachers' thinking and will most likely remain there long after the observation.

Because we as authors believe that behavior cannot truly be changed unless brought to a conscious level, we see selective verbatim as a technique that can be a powerful first step in creating change. Figure 2.4 provides a sample of the management and discipline

**FIGURE 2.4**   Selective Verbatim of a First-Year Teacher's Management and Discipline Statements

| | |
|---|---|
| Teacher: | Jeffrey Potter |
| Class observed: | First-grade reading class |
| Date: | March 12, 2006 |
| Time: | 9:45 –10:45 a.m. |
| Enrollment: | 25 |

**9:45 a.m. Begin**
First graders, eyes on me while I give directions.
I said eyes on me.
I'm not going to begin until you are in your seats and quiet!
Shhhhhhhhhh!
Thank you, Polar Bears, for being ready to learn. Your group may come to the reading carpet.
I'm waiting for the rest of you.
Excuse me —
If you continue to waste my time, I will make sure I take time from your a.m. recess.
Okay, Leopards, up front.
You know I expect you to sit pretzel-style with your hands in your lap. Do it now!
We're wasting too much time. The rest of you come forward.
Keep your hands to yourself!
Jeremy, move over so you are sitting next to me if you cannot behave.
Don't tell me you weren't doing anything. Move over here right this minute.
First graders, please quiet down. We have a lot of work to do this morning.
I cannot hear Carol's question with all this noise.
Shhhhhhhhhh!
Jeremy, do you want to stay in during recess?

**10:00 a.m. Teacher begins reading from Big Book**

statements of Mr. Potter, a first-year teacher who is experiencing classroom management problems. The data reveal that he spends more than 15 min. of class time trying to regain control and the students' attention in the transition from individual seats to the carpeted area at the front of the classroom. Hopefully, seeing those concrete data will lead him to reflect on the wasted learning time and to ask for assistance in problem-solving solutions.

**SCORE Instruments**   SCORE (Seating Chart Observational REcording) instruments can provide detailed information on individual students (such as the types of verbal interactions or student engagement) or on the class as a whole (e.g., "traffic patterns" if movement is a concern). Unlike script taping, anecdotal notes, or selective verbatim, SCORE instruments provide a more visual representation of the data. The technique is extremely versatile because the supervisor and teacher can be flexible in devising a coding system to gather data that address a question or concern the teacher might have. The SCORE chart is easily adapted for any room arrangement. Moreover, a large amount of data can be condensed on a single page.

Two important consideration in using SCORE are keeping the coding system from becoming too cumbersome for the supervisor to use and remembering to analyze the recorded behaviors contextually in relation to the lesson.

Figure 2.5 provides a concrete illustration of how a supervisor might use four major codes (the recommended average) on a SCORE instrument to collect data concerning student engagement. Note that after the data are collected, the teacher and the supervisor collaborate to relate recorded student behavior to the overall context of the lesson. In the present scenario, assume that a third-grade communications arts teacher, Miss Alexander, introduces a new spelling pattern (e.g., _ail versus __ale; sail/sale) and list of words to her class each week on Monday through direct instruction. On Tuesday through Friday, her 16 third graders practice using the skills in four centers. Groups of four are assigned as a team to a different spelling center each day.

Center 1 involves a word puzzle using the spelling words. Center 2 features a newspaper cut-and-paste activity in which the students look for like spelling patterns in other words in print (e.g., mail/male). Center 3 is essentially a writer's workshop where students listen to directions on tape and then use their spelling list in context. Finally, Center 4 includes a self-selected reading station where students look for examples of the identified pattern as they read from their choice of predetermined trade books.

Miss Alexander wonders whether the four groups function effectively as teams. She also questions whether the students are working efficiently and staying on task during the half hour assigned as center time.

She and her supervisor collaborate to come up with a system of codes to describe student actions during the lesson. Are they *actively* involved in the lesson (**A/C, A/P, A/R, A/W, A/L:** cutting, pasting, reading, writing, listening), obviously *off-task* (**O:** head down, staring out the window, writing a note), *socializing* (**S:** chatting with one another about topics other than spelling), or have they *left their seats* (**L**) for some reason? Miss Alexander and the supervisor also agree to a student-by-student sweep to record data on the whole group once every 5 min. Because Miss Alexander expresses an interest in how her movement in the room (**T**) affects student engagement, the supervisor agrees to record her location at the start of each sweep.

The first sweep might begin with Miss Alexander's location in the room, followed by the supervisor's immediately turning attention to Dave in Center 1 at the upper left-hand corner of the room. After recording a code to reflect Dave's behavior at the moment of the first scan, the supervisor moves to observe and record data for the next student. That pattern repeats at 5-min. intervals.

**FIGURE 2.5**   SCORE Instrument for Collecting Data on Student Engagement During Learning Center Time

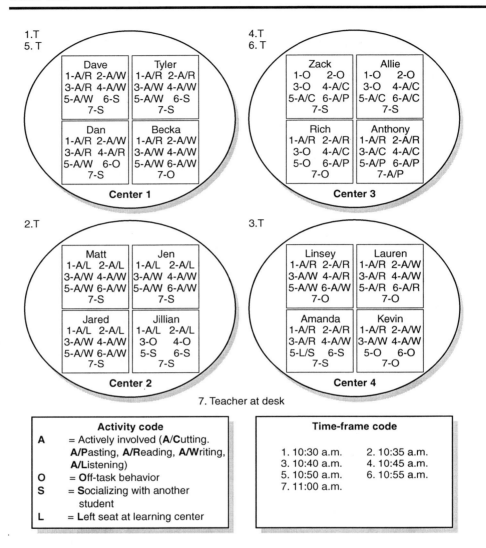

Following the observation, the teacher and supervisor have a wealth of data to inform practice. The data will both reinforce what Miss Alexander does well and point out potential questions to address. For example, among 112 recorded behaviors, students were actively involved in the centers 78 times, for total engagement of 70%.

Miss Alexander is pleased, but she would like to improve the percentage of academic learning time. She notes that Dan, Becka, Zack, Allie, Rich, Jillian, Lindsey, Lauren, and Kevin were off task on one or more occasions (19 off-task behaviors) and that students were socializing about unrelated topics 15 times. However, a closer look shows her that, except for Zack, Allie, Rich, and Jillian, the remainder of the off-task behavior occurred near the conclusion of center time. Miss Alexander also discovers that the students in Centers 1, 2, and 4 are functioning well together. She decides that she needs to separate Zack and Allie. Additionally, she makes a mental note to keep a closer watch on Jillian, and perhaps to move her away from Amanda, who left her seat to join Jillian at Center 2 near the end of class.

When analyzing her part in the classroom interactions, Miss Alexander determines that her presence at each center affects student engagement positively. She cannot be at each center simultaneously, but she can reflect on her ability to monitor the entire group while simultaneously assisting at an individual center. She and the supervisor collaboratively reach the conclusion that she might want to monitor Centers 1 and 2 from the middle of the quads rather than from the perimeter of the classroom. Miss Alexander wonders if 30 min. is too long to engage in independent center time. Moreover, she explores with the supervisor the possibility that returning to her desk 5 min. before the conclusion of center time might influence students to shut down and quit early. (The data reveal that only one of the students was actively engaged during the final sweep.)

In reviewing Figure 2.5, notice a limitation in using a SCORE instrument: It sometimes requires the supervisor to infer what individuals are thinking based on their overt behavior. For example, a student who is doodling could appear to be off-task when in reality that student is able to both doodle and actively listen to the center group's discussion. Thus, SCORE instruments are typically categorized as producing high-inference data.

SCORE instruments also work well in collecting information on the verbal flow in a classroom discussion. "Verbal flow" refers to the teacher's verbal actions and reactions to students or to student interactions during classroom discussion. SCORE data collection can reveal how a teacher encourages or inhibits participation, either by individual students (where patterns may reflect biases related to ability level, ethnicity, gender, or room location) or by the group as a whole. The coding system might include such descriptors as

**V**   Student *volunteers* to answer a question.

**C**   Student is a nonvolunteer whom the teacher *calls upon.*

**I**   Student *initiates* a comment or question related to the lesson.

**X**   Student initiates a comment *unrelated* to the lesson.

Other codes that a supervisor uses would depend on the question or concern that the teacher is addressing. Such codes might be

**E**   Teacher *elaborates* on a student response.

**PR**  Teacher asks a follow-up *probing question* following a student response.

**+**   Teacher offers *positive* reinforcement to a student following a response.

**–**   Teacher issues *criticism* or a discipline statement.

Unlike selective verbatim, which emphasizes the *content* (substance) of the interactions, a SCORE chart accentuates the frequency and kind of communication between the teacher and the students, or among students. Exercise 2.3 provides practice in using a verbal flow chart.

A SCORE chart (with arrows) is a useful tool to focus on teacher or student movement throughout the classroom. For example, Figure 2.6 shows the data collected at the request of a first-grade teacher who feels that she never has enough time to devote to individual children during center activities. Her students are engaged in independent work at four centers in reading, writing, math, and music/art activities around a weekly theme. The teacher always feels rushed as she tries to circulate and formatively assess her students' progress. SCORE movement data collection can help her to determine why she experiences that problem and how she can better pace her movement.

**FIGURE 2.6** SCORE Instrument for Charting Teacher Movement Among Learning Centers

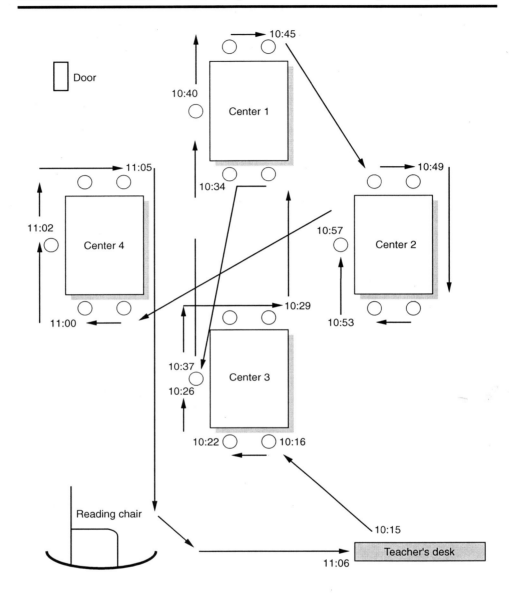

The data reveal that she becomes so involved with the first children she works with (beginning at Center 3, closest to her desk) that she devotes less time and attention to those at Centers 2 and 4.

A limitation of a SCORE movement chart is that keeping the arrows organized over a long period of time can be difficult.

***Other Ways of Collecting Data*** The preceding examples of data collection devices represent only a few of the tools available to supervisors. Data collection methods range from simple frequency counts of selected categories—such as the number of cognitive questions asked from each level of Bloom's taxonomy—to formal, more complex instruments originally developed for use in educational research—such as Flanders Interaction Analysis System (Acheson & Gall, 2003).

In our work in schools, we have discovered that during data collection the device itself is less important than the ability of the supervisor and the teacher, during the preconference, to match the teacher's questions or concerns with the most appropriate observation instrument. In some instances, making the match may entail modifying a data collection technique to better meet the teacher's described need. For example, in using a SCORE instrument for student engagement (as in Figure 2.5), the supervisor and the teacher might create unique activity codes to match a specific classroom context or lesson. (See Chapter 3 on peer coaching for further examples of matching data collection methods to a teacher's specific question or concern.) In other cases, adapting the most appropriate data collection technique may require experimentation, with slight modifications being made to the instrument or coding process over time. Exercise 2.5 provides practice in matching data collection instruments to a teacher's question or concern.

Increasingly, supervisors and teachers are turning to analysis of teacher and student artifacts as a powerful source of information to supplement data collected during an observation. Relevant artifacts provide a varied, extended source of data that augments the data actually captured by the supervisor to make the act of teaching tangible. According to Danielson and McGreal (2000)

> It has been well documented that the majority of students in preK–12 classrooms spend as much, if not more, time interacting with the "stuff" of teaching than they do being directly instructed by the teacher. As student involvement with technology becomes more prevalent in classrooms and as the emphasis on engaged learning continues to escalate, the need for artifact collection or document analysis will be even more obvious. (p. 89)

A supervisor and teacher can collaboratively review any combination of written lesson plans, teacher-created curriculum materials and assessments, corrected student homework, and performance-based student projects. For example, to enhance the anecdotal notes collected on Miss Monn's lesson in Figure 2.3, the supervisor and teacher might shift the focus to student learning by reviewing a sampling of the students' science notebooks and corrected research projects. Additionally, the supervisor working with Mr. Potter in Figure 2.4 might request that he share his classroom management plan, including a list of classroom expectations and consequences for inappropriate behavior. *Chapters 8 and 10 explain more about the use of artifacts captured in a portfolio to complement observational data collection.*

**_Summary of Data Collection Strategies_**    Figure 2.7 summarizes the data collection strategies discussed here, their potential uses, their strengths and limitations.

## INTERPRETING AND MAKING USE OF THE DATA

Once raw data have been described or collected, the next step is to summarize the data and make sense of it. The process of data interpretation entails reconstructing the observed lesson, searching for salient patterns or behaviors repeated over time, seeking to understand why the data look as they do, and projecting what the findings reveal about the teacher's instructional practice in terms of consequences for student learning. The supervisor and the teacher should not only examine and search for meaning in patterns that may be problematic, but also celebrate positive teaching practices that should be affirmed and strengthened. In other words, analysis involves reinforcing, modifying, or extinguishing the repetitive

**FIGURE 2.7** Data Collection Strategies and Their Potential Uses, Strengths, and Limitations

| Data type | Potential uses | Strengths | Limitations |
|---|---|---|---|
| **Wide-lens/global** | | | |
| *Script taping or anecdotal notes* | Panoramic view as a starting point of the process | Observer has freedom and choice; comprehensive in nature | Observer, not teacher, controls decisions about what to record |
| **Selective verbatim** | | | |
| *Selective verbatim* | Versatile: can record questions, feedback, directions, transitions, or discipline statements; can also record students' questions and comments | Easy to understand conceptually; emphasizes content of interactions; records observations, not inferences or judgments; teacher input; can see a pattern quickly | Hard to capture fast-paced lessons accurately (use tape recording for backup); data relate more to whole class than to individual students |
| **SCORE** | | | |
| *Time on task* | Charts use of instructional time and actual student engagement | Provides detailed information on each individual student; pictures activity over time; can be easily adapted to teacher needs | Contains inferential data; quality of data depends on observer's skill; observer must sit in position to see students' faces |
| *Teacher–student or student–student verbal flow* | Charts questioning or participation in terms of gender, ethnicity, ability level, or location in room | Provides detailed information on each individual student, objective picture of classroom interaction patterns; captures large amount of data on one page | Gives quantity, not content, of interactions; can be complicated to record |
| *Movement charting* | Captures either teacher or student movement throughout a lesson | Shows teacher proximity to students; gives clear picture of student out-of-seat time | Difficult to chart over a long time period |
| **Teaching artifacts** | | | |
| *Lesson and unit plans, handouts, assessments, student work* | Augments data collection by the observer | Provides a rich and varied context for data captured by the observer | Usefulness depends on appropriateness of artifact selection; document analysis can be time consuming |

teaching behavior patterns that constitute each teacher's individual professional performance (Goldhammer, 1969).

Although it is important for both the teacher and the supervisor to examine and interpret the data independently before conferencing, one of the most important decisions that a supervisor must make is who will lead data interpretation and initiate the issues to be addressed in the postobservation conference. That decision should be based on the teacher's developmental level. Glickman, Gordon, and Ross-Gordon (2004) base their four supervisory approaches to data interpretation and conferencing on a continuum. More specifically, the choice of approach depends on the teacher's knowledge base, instructional skills, intrinsic motivation, and capacity for introspection and reflection on practice:

- *Nondirective*:  At this end of the continuum, the teacher has control of data interpretation and analysis and takes the lead in suggesting a course of action based on that data. The supervisor acts as a sounding board, listening, clarifying, and encouraging without judgement: "I see what you mean. You're right; I agree that the data reveal that the girls in the back of the room are frequently off task. Their body language seems to indicate lack of interest in the lesson." The nondirective approach is most often used in peer coaching or with professionally responsible, self-directed, highly reflective teachers.

- *Collaborative*:  A true partnership (two-way interaction between the teacher and the supervisor) characterizes this approach. The participants share equal responsibility for data interpretation and analysis during the postobservation conference and for initiating any future course of action: "Now that we have identified the problem by examining the data, let's work together to brainstorm a list of ways we might tackle this concern." The two educators present their ideas, jointly problem solve, and jointly create a plan for future teaching. Although the supervisor might possess expertise on observational techniques and data analysis, the teacher's expertise lies in knowing the curriculum and the unique needs of the students. Supervisors and teachers who can successfully use a collaborative approach exemplify the spirit of supervision, as we have outlined it in this chapter.

- *Directive informational*:  The supervisor takes a more dominant role by providing the lead in data analysis and the parameters for possible action. As the teacher is not yet able to interpret data accurately and lay out a course of action based on the data, the teacher selects from among the supervisor's suggestions. The teacher has choice in decision making, but selects from a repertoire of ideas that the supervisor provides. This style is best matched to situations in which the teacher feels inexperienced, confused, or at a loss as to how to proceed in problem solving and in which the supervisor clearly possesses expert knowledge that the teacher lacks. Notably, the supervisory goal is not just to solve the problem, but to leave the teacher in a better position to independently solve similar problems in the future. Thus, it is critical that the supervisor model personal thinking concerning the dilemma and brainstorm possible solutions: "According to the data, you spent more time dealing with noninstructional issues and organizing for activities than you spent in teaching. To avoid confusion and loss of instructional time during transitions, you could try prearranging the triads rather than asking the children to choose their own groups, or you might have them draw names to form triads. It might also be useful to specifically state your expectation that, as they form their groups, they remember to take their rulers and pencils with them. Have you thought about reinforcing your oral directions with a poster of key points or an outline on the whiteboard?" University supervisors of preservice teachers or mentors working with novice teachers might use the directive informational approach (see Chapters 9 and 10).

- *Directive control*: At the opposite end of the continuum from the nondirective approach, directive control occurs when the supervisor dictates to the teacher what is to be accomplished by modeling data analysis and mandating the future course of action. Because of the teacher's chronically borderline performance or inability to follow through with appropriate action, the supervisor is obliged to assume maximum responsibility in determining a plan of action for improvement. In other words, the supervisor directs the teacher in understanding that certain standards must be attained within a stated time period to ensure that students will not be adversely affected: "The next time I come in to observe, I expect to see a written plan indicating lesson objectives that relate to the curriculum and content standards for this grade level. I want you to be sure that you approach the lesson knowing exactly what you want students to understand and be able to do." The supervisor also concretely articulates the consequences of inaction (e.g., an unsatisfactory rating). No choices are available in the postobservation conference because the supervisor has had to assume responsibility. The supervisors tells the teacher what to do because the teacher is not capable of making decisions in the students' best interest. (For further explanation, see Chapter 11 on the marginal teacher.)

Because of varying developmental level among teachers, a supervisor will probably use each of the approaches over time. However, the long-term goal must always be to reduce dependency on the supervisor by helping teachers acquire the ability to analyze their own teaching. Given the opportunity to analyze data, to frame problems, and to search for solutions in collaboration with a supervisor or colleague, teachers will be far more likely to internalize self-inquiry and reflectiveness.

Another important decision that a supervisor must make is which data should be the focus of the postobservation conference. That decision is particularly important when the directive informational or directive control approaches are being used. When planning for a more directive follow-up conference, an effective supervisor thinks in terms of salience and selectivity (Goldhammer, Anderson, & Krawjewski, 1993). "Salience" means focusing on issues that have the greatest demonstrable impact on students' learning. For example, a salient issue would be a first-year teacher's spending more class time on management and discipline statements than on actual instruction (recall Figure 2.4).

A supervisor might use these three questions to determine the salience of a behavior or a pattern of behaviors:

1. Do the data reveal a demonstrable effect on the students (e.g., after a teacher ridicules a student's incorrect answer, the amount of student volunteering declines dramatically)?

2. Does learning theory predict that the behavior is likely to affect students (e.g., teachers who use little proximity or movement during class are likely to have more off-task student behavior)?

3. Is the behavior likely to affect the teacher's ability to achieve his or her espoused platform (e.g., recall our earlier example of the English teacher who espouses a student-centered classroom in which students are actively engaged in discussion about the literature they are reading, when the data reveal that the percentage of teacher talk far outweighs student contributions)?

The supervisor has responsibility to focus attention on the data that matter most in terms of student learning. In the case of Mr. Potter (Figure 2.4), those data concern the loss of valuable class time.

Selectivity comes into play because no one likes to be overwhelmed. In observing a teacher who is uncertain, inexperienced, or marginal, a supervisor might uncover myriad patterns to address. Mindful of selectivity, the supervisor must be especially careful not to overload the teacher, either intellectually or emotionally. Exercise 2.3 provides an opportunity to practice salience and selectivity in data analysis and to prepare to conference from collaborative and directive control supervisory approaches alike.

### EXERCISE 2.3  Analyzing Collected Data

1. Imagine that you have just completed an observation of a second-year English teacher. Her class consists of 24 juniors enrolled in American literature. Because she is unsatisfied with the general tone or climate, she has requested that you track the types of teacher and student verbal statements that occur during a classroom discussion. She makes it clear that she is most interested in her interactions with individual students, rather than with the class as a whole. Although you and the teacher plan to engage in collaborative data analysis, in preparation for the postconference, you decide to look over the data and take some preliminary notes. Work with a partner to review the data in Figure 2.8, and list several open-ended questions that you might ask the teacher during the meeting to guide her in inquiry and self-reflection.

2. Using the observational data in Figure 2.8, assume that you are a supervisor working with a teacher who is in danger of an unsatisfactory rating. Take a *directive informational* approach in this case. Role play with a partner who assumes the role of the teacher in the postobservation conference. Be prepared to share your scenario with the group. Be ready to discuss how the concepts of salience and selectivity entered into your thinking.

3. As a class, discuss the differences in the two supervisory approaches.

# CONFERENCING

Included among the stages of a supervision cycle are a preobservation conference, which takes place between a supervisor and a teacher before the actual classroom observation; a postobservation conference; and a cycle evaluation. In this section, we explore each of these stages.

## The Preobservation Conference

Earlier in this chapter, we discussed creating readiness through a series of conversations that establish trust, communicate a consensual understanding of supervision goals and processes, and uncover a teacher's espoused platform. The next step in setting the stage for an effective classroom observation is to conduct a preobservation conference. A preconference can help the supervisor to avoid forming presuppositions about a teacher's thoughts or behaviors. A well-executed preconference has three phases: fluency, rehearsal, and contract (Goldhammer, 1969). If a supervisor invests the time and energy to meet face to face with the teacher before a classroom observation, then including these three components will maximize the results.

The first element, fluency, refers to the supervisor's developing a thorough understanding of the teacher's intended lesson (becoming "fluent" in the lesson almost as if it were a language). Recall how many times you, as a teacher, have had a supervisor come into your classroom "cold"—with no knowledge of what has happened previously, of what

**FIGURE 2.8** Observational Data from a Literature Class for Use in Exercise 2.3

**Teacher verbal statement codes**

**E** Elaboration by teacher following student answer

**PR** Probing follow-up question asked of student

**VB** Teacher's verbatim repetition of student's answer

**+** Some type of positive reinforcement acknowledging correct answer

**−** Criticism or discipline statement directed toward student

**Student verbal statement codes**

**V** Volunteers to answer a question

**C** Called upon by teacher; nonvolunteer, hand not raised to participate

**I** Initiates a question or comment independent of teacher

**Front of the room**

| F | M | M | M | M | M |
|---|---|---|---|---|---|
| −I− | V+<br>C+ | V+<br>V+<br>I PR+ | V+ | V PR PR+<br>C PR+ | I+<br>C+<br>C |

| F | F | F | F | M | |
|---|---|---|---|---|---|
| − | C− | V | V | V+<br>V+PR | Absent |

| F | F | M | M | M | F |
|---|---|---|---|---|---|
| | | C PR+<br>V+ | V+<br>V+<br>C+ | C+ | − |

| F | M | F | M | F | F |
|---|---|---|---|---|---|
| C | − | − | | | |

*Note*: F indicates female student; M indicates a male student.

your objectives for student learning might be, or of the reasoning behind the learning strategies that you selected to meet those objectives.

Fluency offers an opportunity for a teacher to walk the supervisor through that teacher's oftentimes unspoken planning processes. Fluency creates a shared understanding and joint exploration of how the lesson fits into the total scheme of the teacher's curricular and instructional decision making. The teacher articulates the goals for student learning, the instructional strategies and activities in which students will participate to achieve those goals, and the methods for formatively assessing whether the desired student learning actually took place. A supervisor can be far more effective when approaching an observation from the teacher's frame of reference.

The second element, rehearsal, occurs when the supervisor engages the teacher in actually practicing or role playing selected aspects of the lesson. The teacher "mentally rehearses" or "walks the supervisor through" the upcoming lesson. That informal preview offers an opportunity for anticipating problems, clarifying elements of the plan that may be vague, and identifying and addressing the teacher's concerns about the lesson before it begins. For example, if a teacher will be giving directions for a student project that is being implemented for the first time, walking through the procedure step by step with the supervisor may help the teacher ensure that the directions are clear and easy to follow. Rehearsal during the preconference is particularly useful in the supervision of preservice teachers (see Chapter 9).

The final element of the preconference is a contract negotiated between the supervisor and the teacher. The contract clarifies and summarizes the expectations of both parties regarding the intended focus for data collection and the data collection technique that should provide the most useful information.

Supervisors must be mindful to employ active listening strategies when conferencing. Active listening strategies are behaviors that convey to the teacher the supervisor's sincere intent to hear and understand what the teacher is saying. The underlying mindset is critical. In the absence of the appropriate mindset, active listening strategies are meaningless at best, manipulative at worst.

Active listening begins simply. It starts with positive nonverbal feedback, such as a welcoming posture, receptive eye contact, and affirming head nods. It involves meeting with the teacher in a comfortable setting and sitting next to the teacher, rather than formally (and authoritatively) behind a desk.

Supervisors who engage in active listening focus on asking open-ended questions. They then attentively receive the teacher's responses before sharing their own impressions and perceptions. Five recommended active listening moves are structuring, probing, feeling checks, summarizing, and wait time or silence.

Structuring moves are used to uncover a teacher's thought processes, needs, or concerns. They can also be used to transition from one part of the conference to another:

- "Let us begin with an overview of the lesson I will be observing. Can you tell me about the content you will be covering and your goals for student learning?"
- "Now that I understand what you want students to know and to be able to do, can you walk me through the steps of the lesson? How will you begin?"
- We have discussed the lesson and your concern about pacing because of the complex material that you are introducing to your students. Let us decide on the type of technique that would be most useful to gather data."

A supervisor uses probing moves to elicit further information from the teacher and to seek extension, clarification, or justification. In probing, the supervisor requests additional information:

- "Now that you have described your objectives for student learning, can you explain how your lesson fits into the curriculum, what you have taught previously, and what will follow?"
- "That sounds like a motivating activity with which to open the lesson. How will it allow you to tap into your students' prior knowledge?"
- "What do you mean when you say this unit will be particularly problematic for your students? Can you provide some examples of student questions or behaviors that you expect will cue us to their possible confusion?"

Feeling checks acknowledge or confirm the teacher's emotions by paraphrasing. Such statements provide an excellent opportunity for a supervisor to show support, respect, and empathy for a teacher's feelings and concerns:

- "You seem really frustrated by your past experiences in teaching this unit. You seem to think that although students can distinguish among the defining characteristics of simple machines, they cannot apply those attributes to examples you had not covered in class."

- "You seem really surprised by the patterns in the data. Were they not what you were expecting?"

Summarizing moves are used to confirm shared understanding and to demonstrate that the supervisor has captured the teacher's ideas accurately.

- "I hear you emphasizing two key issues for data collection. First, you want me to record students' responses to your questions so that we can analyze their thinking and can search for the reasons underlying their confusion. Second, you want me to review a sample of homework assignments to look for additional clues as to why they cannot apply the concepts."

- "So, I will be in tomorrow at 2 p.m. to record students' questions while you provide concrete examples and check their understanding of the material."

Finally, wait time allows the teacher and supervisor the opportunity to process and think deeply about what has been stated before moving on.

Exercise 2.4 reinforces an understanding of active listening moves.

### EXERCISE 2.4   Active Listening Moves for Conferencing

| 1. | Structuring moves | Uncover a teacher's thought processes, needs, or concerns |
| | | Relate one part of the conference to another |
| | | Expand the boundaries of a topic to new ideas or directions |
| 2. | Probing moves | Elicit further information from the teacher |
| | | Seek extension, clarification, or justification |
| 3. | Feeling checks | Acknowledge or confirm the teacher's emotions |
| 4. | Summarizing moves | Confirm shared understanding |
| | | Demonstrate that the supervisor captured the teacher's ideas accurately |
| 5. | Silence | Allow the teacher and supervisor time to think and process what has been said |

**Directions**   Read each of the following supervisory statements. For each, decide which of the four types of active listening moves is used. Explain your decision.

1. How do you perceive that the students responded to your demonstration?

2. Can you tell me a little more about why you chose that particular instructional strategy to convey the learning objective?

3. Walk me through the anticipatory set of this lesson, including how you intend to connect today's material with students' prior knowledge.

4. In other words, you plan to frequently ask questions to formatively check students' understanding of the material?

5. You are wondering if it is your fault that your students have seemed unmotivated during this unit.

6. Can you tell me a little bit more about the homework assignment?

7. How does your use of pair problem solving relate to your goals for classroom climate?

8. You seem very pleased with the number of individual students who initiated questions during the discussion.

9. What might be some ways that we can collect data that would be most useful during this activity?

10. Because this is the first time you will be using so many different learning centers, you would like me to focus on the students' transitioning from one center to another with as little confusion and time off task as possible.

Adapted from Goldsberry, L. F., & Nolan, J. F. (1983). *Active listening skills for reflective conferences.* Unpublished manuscript. The Pennsylvania State University, University Park.

## The Postobservation Conference

After careful data analysis and strategy planning, the postobservation conference follows naturally. The supervisor or coach and the teacher exchange views by discussing their interpretations of the data. They compare the aims and learner outcomes for the lesson as articulated in the espoused platform or preobservation conference with the actual classroom actions and behaviors and the resulting impact on students. The hallmarks of a successful postobservation conference include inquiry and decision making based on data interpretation and analysis, a teacher's reflectiveness about the data and willingness to generate and experiment with alternative approaches, and an emphasis on identifying and reinforcing teacher strengths. The supervisor's role is to encourage teachers to construct knowledge about their practice in powerful and productive ways.

Whenever appropriate and possible, the supervisor assumes a nondirective or collaborative approach to accomplish the goals of the postobservation conference. Acheson and Gall (2003) refer to supervisor as a "catalyst" in the follow-up discussions. They caution against the temptation to dominate with a "conclusions first" conference. If the supervisor

### EXERCISE 2.5  Choosing a Data Collection Method During the Preconference

**Directions**  Work with a partner. One of you assumes the role of the teacher; the other takes the role of the supervisor. You are at the contract stage of the preconference. Using the information and examples provided in this chapter on collecting systematic data, plus your own professional knowledge and experience, decide on the data collection instrument that you will use or modify to match each of the following teacher questions or concerns:

1. Mrs. Brown is at her wits' end. She worked hard over the summer to create motivating, educational learning centers for most of her third-grade language arts units. Yet now she finds herself unable to keep up with the constant questions, complaints, and failure to follow directions. She has four different centers in operation. She hopes that you can gather data to reveal why her students are having so much difficulty during independent activities.

2. Mr. Atkins is a second-year, seventh-grade math teacher. Three boys in his seventh period are disrupting the entire group and making the end of his day miserable. He has been reflecting about what he can do to alter the classroom climate in this challenging section. He has explained that he has three ideas. First, he is going to change the pace of classroom activities more frequently and incorporate more hands-on learning. Second, he is going to be mindful of his physical proximity in relation to the three troublemakers. Finally, he is going to look for ways to offer positive encouragement to all of the students when they *are* on task. He would like you to observe and offer feedback on how effective his new strategies are.

3. Mrs. Jackson is not satisfied with the discussion in her high school social studies classes. She tries to get the students involved in relating current events to the lessons from the past that they have been studying, but she finds herself doing most of the talking. Her goal is to increase student-initiated responses and student-to-student interaction. Your observation will be the starting point. By collecting and analyzing data, she hopes that the two of you can plan a strategy for increased student participation.

lays out personal perceptions and analysis concerning what the teacher did and might do differently, the teacher has no choice but to *react*. The spirit of trust is violated.

It also stands to reason that expecting a teacher to change behavior without personal reflection and inquiry into the assumptions influencing that behavior or without coming to conclusions supported by data will have little impact or lasting effect upon practice. If teachers understand and appreciate the "why?" of what they might do differently to have a positive impact on student learning, they will be far more willing to effect lasting change. They will also become better able to self-supervise.

Additionally, collaboratively recognizing and affirming a job well done (as supported by data) will serve to strengthen the teaching behaviors that have a positive impact on students' learning. (*See Chapters 9 and 11 for further information on taking a directive approach to postobservation conferences.*)

### Cycle Evaluation

Most postobservation conferences conclude with the teacher and the supervisor both candidly reviewing the cycle and agreeing on future goals for the next round of classroom observation. (An exception to this joint process occurs when the supervisor is using a directive approach. The supervisor will then engage in the cycle evaluation independently because the teacher may be not be ready for, or capable of, this final step.)

If conducted with candor and honesty, the cycle evaluation fosters a continuing spirit of trust and a sense of ongoing support and collaboration. The supervisor and the teacher should both feel that the supervision cycle was of value to the teacher, leaving that professional better able to problem solve alone in a similar teaching situation in the future. Moreover, the supervisor and the teacher should both reflect on what was learned. Seldom do we as authors come away from a supervision cycle without feeling that we have been in some way enriched by the experience. Goldhammer et al. (1993) refer to this final stage in the supervision cycle as its "superego" or conscience, and they suggest the following questions for reflection on the process:

- How skillfully did we conduct the preconference? Was a good plan developed for the observation?
- Did our data collection procedures make sense and match the questions or concerns expressed by the teacher?
- Did the teacher leave the supervision process with a greater understanding of professional strengths, as well as a valid perception of how those strengths can be increased?
- As a supervisor, what did I learn by sharing in the teacher's classroom? What did I learn about my own supervisory behavior? How might I do a better job in the future?

## FOSTERING A PROFESSIONAL LEARNING COMMUNITY

We began this chapter with a focus on a supervisor's skill in building trust and communication and in encouraging a cycle of continuous reflection and inquiry. Now we have come full circle and return to the idea of trust and positive communication, but more holistically and pervasively as it pertains to the school as a professional learning community.

Barth (2002) describes a school's culture as a "complex pattern of norms, attitudes, beliefs, behaviors, values, ceremonies, traditions, and myths that are deeply ingrained in the very core of the organization" (p. 7). All too often, the bureaucratic and hierarchical nature of schools as organizations conflicts with a culture of collaboration and inquiry (Lieberman & Miller, 2004). In our platform of beliefs about supervision and evaluation, we join the voices of those who advocate "reculturing" schools to create a climate that supports teacher as learner in a supportive professional learning community. In such a community, learning occurs by doing and as an inherent part of a teacher's practice. Learning is social, collective, and experiential rather than individual, isolated, and mandated from top down (Lieberman & Miller, 2004). Teachers engage with their colleagues to assess their students' learning, collect and interpret data, and then use that data to drive their decisions about revising curriculum or adapting instruction to enhance achievement.

DuFour, Eaker, and DuFour (2005) suggest that educators in a professional learning community work together to plan lessons and clarify questions such as

1. What is it we all want students to learn?
2. How will we know when each student has mastered the essential learning?
3. How will we respond when a student experiences difficulty in learning?
4. How will we deepen the learning for students who have already mastered the essential knowledge and skills? (p. 15)

In order for such a culture to flourish, teachers must feel respected and be empowered to collaborate with administrators and one another in a spirit of "trust, candor, openness, risk taking, and commitment to continuous improvement" (Hargreaves, 1997, p. 2). In essence, teachers have always been leaders of students. The question we might ponder is how to capitalize on their leadership characteristics and extend them beyond the walls of their own classrooms toward the good of the greater community within the building or district.

The ability to promote the development of a strong organizational culture that promotes the success of all students is an important capability required of all school leaders according to the National Policy Board for Educational Administration's *Educational Leadership Constituent Council: Standards for Advanced Programs in Educational Leadership* (see Appendix A). Creating a schoolwide climate that values community, collaboration, and continuous growth is a process of evolution, not revolution. It requires active participation by supervisors who consciously and consistently serve as role models. Through their words—even more crucially—through their *actions*, they genuinely recognize and openly show appreciation for the work of teachers. They convey a belief that the vast majority of teachers have a voice and shared ownership in supervision. These educational leaders recognize and celebrate the contributions of those surrounding them. They commit the necessary human and fiscal resources for teacher supervision in terms of time, opportunity, and variety of roles. (In Chapters 3–6, we will examine such roles in the form of peer coaching, self-directed teacher growth, action research possibilities, and collegial development groups.) Most important, they themselves engage in ongoing reflection and professional growth, modeling their own commitment to improve teacher and student learning. In essence, fostering such a schoolwide climate may be the most important element in readiness building for supervision.

In such an environment, goal setting by teachers aligns with the goals of the district and focuses upon student learning. Teachers openly discuss their teaching with one another and willingly share what they know about best practices and ways to maximize student learning. They collaborate in pairs or in teams on curricular and instructional issues, and they coach one another as they visit classrooms other than their own. They collect data on their instruction and on students' learning, and they candidly reflect about the meaning of those data as a basis for teacher decision making. In such a schoolwide climate, teacher risk taking is embraced as a learning opportunity. The norm of high expectations and continuous assessment starts with the individual and extends throughout the school as an organization.

We vividly recall serving as part of a statewide audit team assessing the supervision and evaluation plan of a district nominated for an exemplary practices award. One of the teachers being interviewed remarked, "in our district, maintaining the status quo is not an option!"

In summary, faculty and administration that think in terms of "we" characterize a professional learning community. Teachers move beyond a focus on their own classrooms to a schoolwide commitment and sense of ownership in improving student learning. They view themselves as participants connected to the whole—members of an "organic unit" with collective potential that was unimaginable when they worked in isolation (Garman, 1982, p. 42). Everyone feels a responsibility for nurturing excellence.

## CLASSROOM-BASED SUPERVISION AND COACHING AS A CYCLICAL PROCESS

Supervision and coaching are marked by frequent and ongoing teacher–supervisor cycles over time. Figure 2.9 provides a visual summary of the multistage supervision cycle explained in this chapter. The cycle includes establishing readiness through trust building and positive communication to build interpersonal relationships and some type of individual or small-group session designed to uncover espoused platforms. After readiness building, supervisors engage in a preobservation conference; an observation during which they collect nonjudgmental, descriptive data; a period for data interpretation; a postobservation conference in which teacher and supervisor or coach share ideas and reach conclusions about the data; and a follow-up discussion to carefully and honestly appraised the effectiveness of the cycle (Goldsberry, 1998).

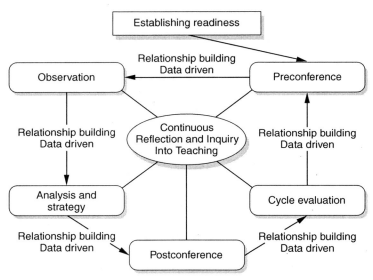

**FIGURE 2.9**   The Supervision Cycle

Garman (1982) points outs out that, just as good teaching surpasses a "technical competence" or "cookbook approach" of step-by-step procedures, supervision is also far more than just a set of prescribed, linear steps. The cycle of supervision is "a metaphor as well as a method ... suggest[ing] dynamic forms of collaboration in educational alliances" (p. 52). We therefore urge supervisors to embrace the larger concepts of professional practice inherent in the model by (a) striving to build and strengthen collaborative relationships among educators; (b) encouraging teachers to continuously and consciously reflect upon and inquire into their practice; and (c) engaging in data-driven decision making to improve students' learning.

# CHAPTER SUMMARY

In-classroom supervision refers to a process of observation and conferencing that promotes individual teacher growth beyond current levels of performance; fosters reflective, self-directed professionalism; and ultimately has a positive impact on students' learning. In this chapter we identified, described, and provided concrete examples of the seven essential skills that a supervisor must understand and practice.

First, the supervisor must focus on creating readiness through building trust and communication with teachers. Readiness includes a mutual understanding of the knowledge, goals, processes, and roles of supervision. Another part of creating readiness is uncovering the teacher's belief system or espoused platform. Productive and meaningful collaboration is enhanced when supervisors understand the teacher's frame of reference.

The supervisor then encourages teachers to engage in continuous introspection and inquiry into teaching so that the teachers are empowered to become self-supervisory. To encourage teacher deliberation on practice, supervisors use various means to collect systematic, nonjudgmental data during classroom observations. Those means include wide-lens, selective verbatim, and SCORE instruments. The observational data is oftentimes augmented by analysis of artifacts such as the teacher's written plans or samples of student work.

Before data collection begins, face-to-face preconferencing ensures that the supervisor has a context for the lesson and taps into the teacher's questions and concerns, so that the data generated match the teacher's stated needs. Following the observation, the supervisor engages in data analysis and strategizing prior to the postobservation conferences. The approach can range from nondirective through collaborative to directive supervisory control, depending on the developmental level of the teacher. During the postobservation conference, the supervisor and the teacher discuss patterns found in the data in terms of their impact on student learning. Based on their discoveries, the supervisor and the teacher affirm existing practices or explore a plan for generating alternative approaches.

The cycle concludes with an examination of the goals that were set in the preconference and a search for ways to be more effective during subsequent observation cycles. Supervision done well helps to foster a schoolwide learning community characterized by genuine collaboration, ongoing reflection and inquiry, and continuous growth.

# DISCUSSION QUESTIONS

**1.** Focus for a moment on Figure 3.9. As a group, discuss what this model for the supervision cycle implies about teacher observation. How does its inherent "platform" match with your beliefs about becoming an effective supervisor? Talk about how your beliefs have been affected by what you have read in this chapter.

**2.** From among the seven essential skills of classroom-based supervision, discuss the skill that you feel will be among your strengths as a supervisor. Why? Which skill do you believe will be a personal goal in your future supervisory work with teachers?

**3.** As you look back, do you perceive your own classroom observations to have been at the more perfunctory and ritualistic end of the continuum, or were they a vehicle for encouraging you to be inwardly reflective and inquiry-oriented? In the context of this chapter, explore the reasons underlying your response.

**4.** During an observation in your classroom, have any of your supervisors employed the data collection devices described in this chapter? Which ones? From a teacher's perspective, what do you see as the advantages and disadvantages of those techniques for collecting and analyzing data? From a supervisor's perspective?

**5.** Have any of your supervisors used data collection methods that you found particularly helpful but that were not discussed in this chapter? Share an example of an alternative method with the rest of the group. Explain why you found it particularly helpful to your teaching situation.

**6.** Discuss some concrete steps that you as a new principal might take to transition from a more hierarchical school climate to one of shared leadership and teacher ownership.

## THEORY-INTO-PRACTICE APPLICATIONS

**1.** In Exercise 3.1, you and a partner used the questions provided to articulate and share your espoused platforms. Join with another pair to form a quad. Now move beyond sharing to *comparing* your platforms. Explore the similarities and discrepancies across your philosophies. What conclusions about individual teacher platforms and their effect on supervision might you draw from this activity?

**2.** Try to articulate your school district's formal mission and goal statements. Now secure a copy of the actual strategic plan. Briefly summarize what the written documentation acknowledges as important to the teaching–learning process. How does your individual platform compare to the school's platform? Could you accurately explain the district's written mission statement, or did it surprise you?

**3.** Have one member of the class share his or her district's supervision plan. Does it have elements in common with the supervision cycle as illustrated in Figure 3.9? Role-play the part of a member of the district's supervision committee. What recommendations for changes might you ask the committee to consider?

**4.** Select two volunteers to teach separate 10-minute mini-lessons. Divide the remainder of the class into two groups. During the first lesson, one group role-plays the students, and the other group acts as supervisors using the script taping technique to collect data. During the second lesson, the two groups switch roles. This time, the supervisor group uses anecdotal notes to collect data. Afterwards, have the role-

playing supervisors compare data and share their reactions to the process. Did the volunteer teachers and students feel that the data accurately portrayed classroom occurrences? Create a list of strengths and concerns regarding the use of each of these wide-lens techniques.

**5.** Work in triads. One person assumes the role of supervisor; one, the role of teacher; and the third, the role of process observer recording notes on what can be seen and heard. The supervisor arranges to visit and observe in the teacher's classroom. Before the site visit, practice a cycle beginning with a preconference in class. The supervisor guides the teacher through the steps of fluency, rehearsal, and contract. Be cognizant of using all four active listening moves, including structuring, probing, feeling checks, and summarizing.

**6.** In your triad conduct an actual classroom observation and a postobservation conference, collecting the mutually agreed-on data and analyzing that data. Write a reaction paper summarizing your reflections on the process of data collection and analysis from the point of view of supervisor, teacher, or observer. Be sure to include a discussion of *why* you decided upon the particular data collection instrument and *how* you reacted to using it. Include a copy of the data collected and a summary of the interpretations.

**7.** Staying in the same triad, complete the cycle by conducting a follow-up evaluation of the supervisory experience. What do you perceive as the strengths and limitations of using our in-class supervision model?

## REFERENCES

ACHESON, K. A., & GALL, M. D. (2003). *Techniques in the clinical supervision of teachers: Preservice and inservice applications* (5th ed.). Hoboken, NJ: Wiley.

BARTH, R. S. (1990). *Improving schools from within.* San Francisco, CA: Jossey-Bass.

BARTH, R. S. (2002). The culture builder, *Educational Leadership, 59*(8), 6–11.

BLUMBERG, A. (1996). You know where you're going when you get there: Reflections on a quarter century of teaching supervision. *Wingspan: The Pedamorphosis Communiqué, 11*(2), 2–6.

BLUMBERG, A., & JONAS, R. S. (1987). The teacher's control over supervision. *Educational Leadership, 44*(8), 58–62.

BROWN, J. L., & MOFFETT, C. A. (1999). *The hero's journey: How educators can transform schools and improve learning.* Alexandria, VA: ASCD.

CLIFT, R. T., VEALL, M. L., HOLLAND, P., JOHNSON, M., & MCCARTHY, J. (1995). *Collaborative leadership and shared decision making.* New York: Teachers College Press.

COGAN, M. L. (1973). *Clinical supervision.* Boston, MA: Houghton Mifflin.

DANIELSON, C., & McGREAL, T. L. (2000). *Teacher evaluation to enhance professional practice.* Alexandria and Princeton: ASCD and ETS.

DEWEY, J. (1933). *How we think: A restatement of the relation of reflective thinking to the educative process.* Chicago, IL: Heath.

DUFOUR, R., EAKER, R., & DUFOUR, R. (2005). Recurring themes of professional learning communities and the assumptions they challenge (pp. 7–30). In R. DuFour, R. Eaker, & R. DuFour (Eds.), *On common ground: The power of professional learning communities.* Bloomington, IN: National Educational Service.

FREIRE, P. (1970). *Pedagogy of the oppressed.* New York: Continuum.

GARMAN, N. B. (1982). The clinical approach to supervision. In T. J. Sergiovanni (Ed.), *Supervision of teaching* (pp. 35–52). Alexandria, VA: ASCD.

GARMAN, N. B. (1986). Reflection, the heart of clinical supervision: A modern rationale for professional practice. *Journal of Curriculum and Supervision, 2*(1), 1–14.

GLICKMAN, C. D., GORDON, S. P., & ROSS-GORDON, J. M. (2004). *Supervision and instructional leadership: A developmental approach* (6th ed.). Boston, MA: ALLYN & BACON.

GOLDHAMMER, R. (1969). *Clinical supervision: Special methods for the supervision of teachers.* New York: Holt, Rinehart, & Winston.

GOLDHAMMER, R., ANDERSON, R. H., & KRAWJEWSKI, R. J. (1993), *Clinical supervision: Special methods for the supervision of teachers* (3rd ed.). Fort Worth, TX: Harcourt, Brace, & Jovanovich.

GOLDSBERRY, L. F. (1998). Teacher involvement in supervision. In G. R. Firth & E. F. Pajak (Eds.). *Handbook of research on school supervision* (pp. 428–462). New York: Simon and Schuster Macmillan.

GOLDSBERRY, L. F., & Nolan, J. F. (1983). *Active listening skills for reflective conferences.* Unpublished manuscript. The Pennsylvania State University, University Park.

HARGREAVES, A. (1997). Rethinking educational change: Going deeper and wider in the quest for success. In A. Hargreaves (Ed.), *Rethinking educational change with heart and mind* (pp. 1–26). Alexandria, VA: ASCD.

HUNTER, M. (1983). Script taping: An essential supervisory tool. *Educational Leadership, 41*(3), 43.

LIEBERMAN, A., & MILLER, A. (2004). *Teacher leadership.* San Francisco, CA: Jossey-Bass.

National Policy Board for Educational Administration, (2002). *Educational Leadership Constituent Council: Standards for advanced programs in educational leadership.* Retrieved from http://www.npbea.org/ELCC/ELCCStandards%20 5-02.pdf.

PAJAK, E. (2000). *Approaches to clinical supervision: Alternatives for improving instruction* (2nd ed.). Norwood, MA: Christopher Gordon.

SCHON, D. A. (1988). Coaching reflective teaching. In P. P. Grimmet, & G. L. Erickson (Eds.), *Reflection in teacher education.* New York: Teachers College Press.

SERGIOVANNI, T. J., & STARRATT, R. J. (2006). *Supervision: A redefinition* (8th ed.). Boston, MA: McGraw Hill.

SMYTH, W. J. (1989). Developing and sustaining critical reflection in teacher education. *Journal of Teacher Education, 40*(2), 2–9.

# SUGGESTIONS FOR FURTHER READING AND RESEARCH

BLASÉ, J., & BLASÉ, J. (2001). *Empowering teachers: What successful principals do* (2nd ed.). Thousand Oaks, CA: Corwin Press.

DUFOUR, R. (2004). What is a "professional learning community?" *Educational Leadership, 61*(8), 6–11.

LAMBERT, L. (2003). *Leadership capacity for lasting school improvement.* Alexandria, VA: ASCD.

National Staff Development Council. *Learning communities.* http://www.nsdc.org.

SCHON, D. A. (1987). *Educational the reflective practitioner: Toward a new design for teaching and learning in the professions.* San Francisco, CA: Jossey-Bass.

SERGIOVANNI, T. J. (2000). *Creating culture, community, and personal meaning in our schools.* San Francisco, CA: Jossey-Bass.

SPARKS, D. (2005). *Leading for results: Transforming teaching, learning, and relationships in schools.* Thousand Oaks, CA: Corwin Press.

WALD, P. J., & CASTLEBERRY, M. S. (Eds.). (2000). *Educators as learners: Creating a professional learning community in your school.* Alexandria, VA: ASCD.

ZEICHNER, K. M., & LISTON, D. P. (1996). *Reflective teaching: An Introduction.* Mahwah, NJ: Erlbaum.

# CHAPTER 3

# PEER COACHING

▌N CHAPTER 2, we explored the seven skills that provide the foundation for in-classroom supervision and coaching. We believe that each teacher is responsible for contributing to his or her professional growth and for playing an important role in supervision as an organizational function. In the present chapter, we explain the peer-coaching process—an option in which competent professionals engage in classroom supervision of one another without the presence of an administrator. Moreover, we provide a research-based rationale for empowering teachers as peer coaches.

Peer coaching fosters conditions that support adult learning, takes into account the impact that teacher career stages have on effective supervisory practice, and frees time for administrators to conduct effective classroom observations that focus effort on the teachers who truly need the assistance. We explore peer coaching in action by reviewing the cycle and offering concrete examples of teachers engaged in the process. In addition, we explain the administrator's function as a viable part of a peer-coaching program—in a different, yet meaningful, supervisory relationship. Finally, drawing on our close work with school districts representing a wide range of demographics, we present practical suggestions for optimum success in implementing and sustaining a peer-coaching program.

## GUIDING QUESTIONS FOR PREREADING REFLECTION AND JOURNALING

- Have you ever been personally involved in peer coaching? What were your impressions of the process? What impact did peer coaching have on you as a teacher?

- What steps could you as a future supervisor take to contribute to a supportive climate for teacher observation in one another's classrooms?

- As a member of a committee looking into implementing a peer-coaching program, what would be your recommendations regarding the issues of teacher trust and confidentiality?

- What barriers in addition to those related to climate, trust, and confidentiality might prevent teachers from participating in a peer-coaching program?

## ASSUMPTIONS ABOUT PEER COACHING

The first two exercises in this chapter, Exercises 3.1 and 3.2, are designed to activate thinking about peer coaching and share perceptions in group discussion. In these exercises, there are no right or wrong answers.

**EXERCISE 3.1    An Individual Decision Model Grid for Peer Coaching**

***Directions***    Imagine that you are serving on a team implementing a peer-coaching program in your school district. To uncover each committee member's underlying assumptions concerning peer coaching, you are asked to read each of 12 numbered statements and then to write its corresponding number in one of the squares on the grid provided below. For each statement, decide if you strongly agree, agree, disagree, or strongly disagree. You must prioritize, because you may write *only one number per square.*

| Strongly agree | Agree | Disagree | Strongly disagree |
|---|---|---|---|
|  |  |  |  |
|  |  |  |  |
|  |  |  |  |

1. Peer coaching should only be implemented in schools with a positive, supportive climate.
2. Peer coaching makes sense because teachers have varied expertise and professional development needs.
3. Peer coaching reduces feelings of teacher isolation.
4. Participating in a peer-coaching program should be mandatory.
5. Many teachers are reluctant to participate in peer coaching because they fear being "judged" by their colleagues.
6. Peer-coaching partners should have the same grade level or content expertise.
7. Training in classroom observation and conferencing is a necessary prerequisite for peer coaching.
8. Peer coaching can be used in place of annual observation by the principal.
9. Data collected during peer coaching may be used as part of a teacher's evaluation.
10. Release time should be provided for peer coaching.
11. The most successful peer coaching is linked to district professional development initiatives.
12. Administrators have little involvement with teachers in the years the teachers are engaged in peer coaching.

Special thanks to the Supervision Committee of Pennsylvania's Association of Supervision and Curriculum Development for sharing this exercise.

**EXERCISE 3.2    Reaching Group Consensus on Peer Coaching**

***Directions***    Now that everyone has individually completed Exercise 3.1, form groups of three. Assign the roles Artist, Discussion Leader, and Consensus Builder. The Artist receives a large sheet of chart paper and a marker with which to recreate the decision model grid. The Discussion Leader reads the 12 statements one at a time. The group members share their responses to each statement and the thinking that led to the placement that they assigned it on their individual grids. The Consensus Builder attempts to bring the group to a collaborative decision on where the Artist should place each statement number on the team grid. On completion of the team grid, the Artist in each group posts the large grid. The class as a whole can then compare the team grids and discuss the various viewpoints about peer coaching.

# WHAT IS PEER COACHING?

*Lauren Laslow is a high school English teacher with 17 years of experience. She is still enthusiastic and loves coming to work every day. Lauren is well respected by her colleagues and her students alike. However, she is troubled by what she perceives as a lack of opportunity for continuous growth. She is at a point where she feels as if she could easily fall into the trap of complacency. Lauren completed her master's degree 10 years ago. Now she faithfully stays abreast of best practice by reading journals and attending the required professional development workshops to keep her certificate current; however, she is not sure whether she is effectively implementing the ideas she reads about. Moreover, she leaves seminars motivated to revise a unit or to implement a new instructional practice, but she then feels isolated in her efforts, finding little in the way of support or feedback. Lauren respects her principal, but he always appears overwhelmed by the demands of the job. Because the principal knows that Lauren is an exemplary teacher, he often puts off his observation of her classroom. Last year, to her disappointment, he did not turn up until she was administering the final examination! That observation report certainly offered nothing to help her grow as a professional. The traditional supervision and evaluation system seems like a joke to many of her colleagues. They view it as a once-a-year "performance." Lauren senses that there must be another way, but she is not sure what it might be.*

Competent teachers such as Lauren would most certainly benefit from the opportunity to engage in peer coaching. Coaching—also called "colleague consultation," "peer observation," or "peer supervision"—is a voluntary, confidential process in which competent professionals, with adequate training, observe and conference with one another, sharing their expertise and experience. They provide one another with feedback, support, and opportunities to reflect upon practice.

Peer coaching is a form of supervision designed to assist teachers in refining present skills, learning innovative instructional strategies, and analyzing and seeking solutions for classroom-related problems. Coaching has the potential to enhance student learning by differentiating teachers' learning according to their unique needs and interests. In peer coaching, the teacher who is being observed directs the process. The coaching partner (or partners) visits the classroom to collect data and, later, to engage in meaningful dialog about the findings. Never evaluative, when done well peer coaching energizes teachers to inquire into practice, to take risks in a nonthreatening environment, and to subsequently reflect on the results in terms of their students' learning.

Garmston (1987) discusses technical and collegial coaching as two different models. Technical coaching is most often used as a follow-up to district in-service workshops. Joyce and Showers (2002) describe its major purpose as the transfer of training—particularly innovations in curriculum or instruction—to classroom practice. They found that teachers who engage in peer coaching as part of ongoing follow-up to district staff development initiatives practice the new methods more consistently, develop greater skill in using the methods, and add the new learning most appropriately to their repertoire of instructional strategies. For example, following a summer workshop on Dimensions of Learning as a research-based teaching framework, a pair of coaches may observe one another as they integrate aspects of the five dimensions into specific lessons.

The effectiveness of technical coaching is diminished when the observer uses some sort of mandated, training-related checklist of necessary skills to record the presence or absence of prescribed teaching behaviors (e.g., The teacher greeted students at the door as they came into class. Observed or not observed?). In that case, the teacher has little ownership of, or input into, the kind of data to be collected, and the opportunity for inquiry and reflection into practice is severely limited. During the 1980s, many school districts used a standardized checklist for technical coaching following workshops in Hunter's essential elements of instruction. As a result, technical coaching seemed more in line with evaluation than supervision.

Collegial coaching occurs when the teachers who are being observed establish the focus of the observation in response to questions or concerns that they have about their existing teaching practice or their students' learning. They identify a self-selected area for inquiry and analysis, ask their partner to collect data based on the selected foci, analyze those data, and deliberate on the results.

Teachers' individual questions or concerns are not necessarily connected to a professional development workshop or a districtwide model of teaching. Thus, collegial coaching helps teachers to become more self-directed and reflective, independent of schoolwide initiatives. For example, a math teacher may wonder if she is helping her students engage in self-regulated thinking. Although she is concerned that her students arrive at the correct answers to word problems, she is even more interested in the reasoning processes behind their answers, particularly when they are experiencing difficulty. She might ask her coach to collect data about the kinds of questions that she asks to encourage her students to become aware of their own thinking, or she might choose to explore the kinds of questions that her students pose as they engage in problem solving. If the data reveal that students are not thinking at the higher levels she aspires toward, she can brainstorm ways in which to restructure her questioning or to reinforce her approach to teaching problem-solving strategies.

It is important to note that peer coaching can extend beyond the actual classroom observation. For example, the teacher may ask the coach to supplement the observation by helping to analyze a random sampling of students' mathematical thinking logs as additional data about their reasoning abilities.

In building a comprehensive system of teacher supervision and evaluation, we embrace the idea of a coaching model that blends technical and collegial coaching, encouraging teachers to grow and learn not only as individuals but also as part of a collaborative schoolwide community. Returning to the example of the two teachers who engaged in the district-sponsored summer professional development workshop on Dimensions of Learning, those teachers might still use the five dimensions as the basis for peer coaching. However, rather than using a district-formulated checklist encompassing all five of the dimensions, the teacher being observed would have the freedom to select, from one of the dimensions, an aspect that is of particular interest to her and her students.

For example, after reviewing the research about how teachers unconsciously treat high-achieving and low-achieving students differently, the teacher might wonder about the nonverbal and verbal signals she sends. She then might request that the coach collect descriptive data about her nonverbal behaviors during one visit and use a SCORE (seating chart observational recording) chart to record verbal interactions during a follow-up observation. Afterward she can search the data for biases in her treatment of students at different achievement levels. Although Dimensions of Learning is a district initiative, the teacher has selected one area of personal concern to investigate and has decided how best to collect data relevant to her concern.

## WHY PEER COACHING IS IMPORTANT AS PART OF A COMPREHENSIVE SYSTEM OF TEACHER SUPERVISION AND EVALUATION

During the 1990s, professional development efforts evolved to put teachers at the center of their own learning. Rather than relying on the more traditional 1-day in-service training with minimal follow-up, those responsible for teacher development began to structure ongoing, school-based learning that was embedded in the daily work of teachers (National Staff Development Council, 2000). During the same period, supervision also underwent marked changes. From a process meant to ascertain minimum competence, it changed into a method for encouraging all teachers to strive beyond their current level of performance by increasing their understanding of best practice and its impact on student learning. A role previously undertaken only by administrators, supervision became a more collaborative inquiry in which teachers played an important part (Nolan & Francis, 1992). The integration of those paradigm changes into professional development and supervision theory facilitated the widespread introduction of peer coaching, which provides teachers with an active and viable part in supervision.

Peer coaching makes sense for several important reasons. First, it capitalizes on the research base about conditions that support adult learning. Second, it takes into account the impact of teachers' varying developmental levels on effective supervisory practice. Finally, it extends the role of supervisor to teachers who possess the knowledge and skills to engage in classroom observation, giving busy administrators more time to intensify their efforts in supervising the teachers who truly need their assistance.

## Fostering the Conditions That Support Adults as Learners

Reiman and Thies-Sprinthall (1998) note the importance of the better understanding that behavioral science has reached concerning adult development in general and teacher development in particular. Brookfield's (1986) research, for example, investigated the factors needed to effectively facilitate adult learning. He identified four conditions that apply directly to peer coaching:

- *Mutual respect and trust:*   Adults need to feel that they work in a climate of professional trust and that they are valued as unique individuals.
- *Sense of ownership and self-direction:*   Adults respond well when they are empowered to take responsibility for their own learning and when the learning matches their interests and meets their specific needs.
- *Voluntary participation:*   Adults learn best when they actively engage in learning at their own volition.
- *Collaborative spirit:*   Adults learn best as part of a community whose members share their knowledge rather than working in isolation.

The sections that follow explore the ways that peer coaching supports adults as learners.

***Mutual Respect and a Sense of Ownership and Self-Direction***   In their seminal work *In Search of Excellence: Lessons from America's Best-Run Companies* (1982), Peters and Waterman discuss basic principles that lead to successful management. Among them is "productivity through people," or the creation in all employees of an awareness that their best efforts are essential to the well-being of the organization. That philosophy, simple yet profound, embraces a humanistic approach to motivation that emphasizes treating each individual with respect and dignity as a valued professional.

The importance of nurturing a school climate conducive to mutual respect and productivity through people is recognized in Standard 1 of the National Policy Board for Educational Administration's *Standards for Advanced Programs in Educational Leadership* (Educational Leadership Constituent Council, 2002; see Appendix A).

Standard 1 describes an administrator as an educational leader who engages in activities that provide autonomy, support innovation, delegate responsibility, and develop leadership in others.

Glickman, Gordon, and Ross-Gordon (2004) apply the idea of productivity through people when they consider supervision as a process leading toward increased teacher decision making and autonomy; giving teachers increased responsibility signals that their efforts are recognized as important. The authors base their model on Herzberg's (1987) 30 years of research into human motivation. Herzberg discovered that positive factors called "satisfiers" motivate individuals to work harder. Among the satisfiers are recognition and increased responsibility (e.g., factors leading to mutual respect) and the possibility of professional growth. Furthermore, Glickman et al. relate Herzberg's motivating factors to the top two levels of Maslow's (1968) classic hierarchy of human needs: esteem and self-actualization. Being appreciated and respected by others meets an individual's esteem needs. "Self-actualization" is Maslow's term for self-fulfillment—the realization of one's talents and personal potential. The authors write, "Herzberg's motivation factors ... correspond with Maslow's higher stages. This interaction between motivation and higher level needs defines an area in which the teacher is 'going beyond competence.' The individual knows performance is acceptable and now strives for excellence" (p. 92).

Recall from Chapter 2 that Glickman's developmental supervision is based on locus of control. Good peer coaching is a perfect example of nondirective supervisory control, in which the teacher who is observed maintains ownership and guides the process. The coaching partner, who is collecting data, acts as a sounding board (using active listening moves). For example, when conferencing, the coach uses structuring moves to ensure a deep understanding of the teacher's beliefs and thought processes. The coach asks probing questions to help the teacher clarify points and problem solve based on the data. The coach then summarizes or restates the teacher's conclusions to ensure shared understanding. It is as if coaches were holding up a mirror: Teachers can then view themselves in a different light, with increased self-awareness. A case in point is an eighth-grade communication arts teacher who told one of the authors that a metaphor to describe her peer-coaching partner would be a "*thinking* video recorder who walks and talks and offers another perspective!"

Figure 3.1 provides a sample transcript of what the verbal interaction in a peer coaching approach might sound like when the teacher who is being observed directs the conference.

Peer coaching as a supervision option contributes to a climate of mutual respect between teachers and administrators and among the teachers themselves. The resulting sense of ownership and self-direction encourages career-long teacher development and a climate supportive of professional learning.

***Voluntary Participation and a Collaborative Spirit***    Because adults learn best when they engage in learning of their own volition, the decision to act as a peer coach should be strictly voluntary. In a system of differentiated supervision, competent teachers can choose from among various supervisory options. Moreover, because the coach is there to serve as another set of eyes and ears in the classroom, and because the teacher must feel comfortable with the coach's presence, we advise that teachers select the partners with whom they want to work.

In Chapter 2, we discussed the importance of fostering a schoolwide climate that values collaboration among teachers. In his landmark work *Improving Schools from Within,* Barth (1990) emphasized the need to build a professional community among teachers. He

**FIGURE 3.1** Sample Transcript of Peer Coaching with a Nondirective Approach

| | |
|---|---|
| Coach: | Did you have a chance to look at and analyze the data I collected in your math class yesterday? |
| Teacher: | Yes, Tony. Thanks so much for coming in to observe. I'm really interested in my students' ability to identify and articulate exactly where they become bogged down in solving word problems. Your recording their answers to my questions confirmed some of my hunches about why so many of them are having difficulty with this unit. |
| Coach: | Did you discover a pattern in their responses? |
| Teacher: | As long as I provide only the necessary information in the word problem, most of my students are able to transfer from words to a mathematical equation and solve the problem. But when I introduce extraneous information, they're unable to differentiate between what to use and what to discard before tackling the problem. |
| Coach: | So, the mathematical concepts don't seem to be causing students' frustration. It is transferring the word problem into a mathematical equation, particularly when the word problem presents more information than is necessary. |
| Teacher: | Exactly. |
| Coach: | Now that you have a handle on where students are having difficulty, how might you approach the problem? |
| Teacher: | I think I need to model, model, and model some more. I need to backtrack. Rather than focusing on the mathematics involved, I need a lesson on relevant versus extraneous information and how to tell the difference when faced with word problems that give extraneous information. I was thinking I could... |

makes an extremely incisive distinction between an educational environment of *congeniality* and one of *collegiality*.

Most faculty rooms abound in examples of congeniality, with teachers discussing the victories and losses of their favorite sports teams, their weekend plans, and the local gossip over cups of coffee. Barth realized that congeniality is a good starting point for positive communication and collaboration, but emphasized that healthy, high-achieving schools move beyond congeniality toward collegiality—a spirit of community and collaboration. He offers a characterization of such a milieu based upon the research of Little (as cited in Barth, 1990):

> *Adults in schools talk about practice. These conversations about teaching and learning are frequent, continuous, concrete, and precise. Adults in schools observe each other engaged in the practice of teaching and administration. These observations become the practice to reflect on and talk about. Adults in schools teach each other what they know about teaching, learning, and leading. Craft knowledge is revealed, articulated, and shared. (p. 31)*

To some readers, Barth's description may sound like "pie in the sky"; however, as researchers and staff developers we can attest to myriad examples of such collegiality in schools that have effectively implemented peer coaching. Teachers are in and out of one another's classrooms, sharing ideas and expertise and conducting substantive conversations about their practice.

When coaching relationships are characterized by the highest degree of trust and reciprocity, they frequently extend beyond a nondirective approach toward more collaborative supervisory behavior. In other words, the teacher who is observed invites the coach to participate as more than a sounding board. They take a joint approach to problem solving and planning for acceptable action. The teacher and the coach ask each other hard questions, attempt to understand the other's point of view, and search together for answers. They view themselves as teachers–learners and regard differing opinions and divergent perspectives as a positive means of challenging one another to develop new insights and encouraging one another to engage in in-depth reflection about their work.

That kind of collaboration is essential to adult learning. New learning brings about a sense of intellectual and psychological disequilibrium, as learners compare previously held perspectives to new viewpoints. To truly learn and change, teachers need ongoing and sustained support in dealing with the disequilibrium (Reiman & Thies-Sprinthall, 1998). By building a collaborative spirit, peer coaching contributes to a climate of teacher support.

Another positive outgrowth of such collaboration is that teachers assume more of a leadership role. Showers and Joyce (1996) reported that successful peer-coaching teams who developed skills in collaboration enjoyed the experience so much that they often wanted to continue their collegial partnerships after they accomplished their initial goals. A dynamic peer-coaching team that we worked with provides an excellent example of teacher leadership.

Maxine is a high school science teacher, and Sue is a high school mathematics teacher. Until they collaborated and observed one another, Maxine and Sue had no idea how many connections existed between their separate curricula. After 2 years of observing in one another's classrooms as peer coaches, they applied for a National Science Foundation grant to write the curriculum for an integrated Advanced Placement calculus and physics course that they now team teach. According to Sue,

> *This course is an outgrowth of our collaboration. The motivation to plan for it (and write a successful grant) comes from the input and excitement of working closely with another person. The students see the interrelatedness of our two subjects and watch us learning from one another. (Hoover & Guinn, 1998, p. 22)*

Close collaboration through peer coaching created a synergy between Maxine and Sue. It motivated them to continue to grow as professionals, even though each, on her own, was considered an outstanding teacher. Ultimately, Maxine and Sue extended their teamwork from coaching observations to such self-directed activities as grant writing, curriculum writing, and co-teaching a newly designed course that benefited students. They happily reported that, with the implementation of their combined course, they increased the number of girls enrolled in advanced mathematics and science by 20%.

The collaboration between Maxine and Sue provides the perfect example of the five interacting conditions that form the framework for teacher development: role taking, reflection, balance, continuity, and support/challenge (Reiman & Thies-Sprinthall, 1998). The framework builds on research illustrating that teachers function at varying levels of adult growth in three dimensions:

- *ego development* or *interpersonal growth,* which ranges from self-protecting, to conforming, to self-aware and autonomous (Loevinger, 1976);
- *moral* or *ethical development,* which ranges from self-concerns, to concerns based on the opinions of others or on social norms, to decisions based on a sense of justice and equality (Kohlberg, 1969); and
- *conceptual development* or *problem-solving abilities* as related to human interaction, which ranges from concrete to highly abstract thinking (Hunt, 1971).

Teachers who function at higher levels, no matter in which dimension, are typically more effective at fostering a positive environment for learning. They are more creative, perceptive, and reflective. They display a high tolerance for ambiguity and frustration; they are more willing to take risks after weighing a wide variety of alternatives; and they can more easily differentiate their instruction to meet the needs of their students. Thus, contributing to the conditions that support teacher development is an important goal of the Reiman and Thies-Sprinthall framework.

The first condition, role taking, places teachers in the complex social role of offering assistance to one another. Teachers take that assistance and use it to construct new knowledge and skills to meet the demands of a more stimulating task. Peer coaching puts teachers in such a social role. It capitalizes on the breakdown of barriers between classrooms as trusted colleagues like Maxine and Sue observe one another. Moreover, the learning is clearly a two-way phenomenon: the teachers with whom we have worked report that they often learn as much from observing a colleague as they do from being observed.

Chapter 2 introduced the crucial part that the second and third conditions, guided reflection and balance, play in teacher development. As Reiman and Thies-Sprinthall (1998) note, "Our research has shown time and again that complex new experiences without reflection make no impact on moral and conceptual development" (p. 72). They explain that role taking and reflection together form a cycle of action and reflection, also known as praxis: "The role taking experience contains the seeds of growth. Guided reflection helps the person extract meaning from the experience" (p. 73). The third condition, balance, is the equilibrium or effective interplay between action and reflection. Peer coaching provides teachers with the opportunity and time to collaboratively deliberate on their actions in terms of student learning.

The final two conditions needed for adult growth and development are also inherent in peer coaching. Continuity requires that any lasting change in teacher thinking evolve at a slow pace over time. Coaching as a cyclical process of continuous reflection and inquiry over the course of a school year (see Figure 2.9) provides for such continuity. Finally, simultaneous support/challenge calls for a paradoxical process of nurturing a teacher while simultaneously nudging that teacher to stretch beyond current levels of performance. The nurturing/nudging phenomenon is precisely what occurred in the collaborative coaching relationship shared by Maxine and Sue.

In summary, participation in peer coaching contributes to adult learning by building and affirming the knowledge, experience, skills, and professionalism of teachers. The teachers who are observed are volunteers who select a trusted colleague as a partner and maintain control of the process. They therefore feel a genuine sense of ownership not only in their learning but also in the learning that takes place throughout the school. The autonomy and empowerment contribute to their feeling self-direction, which facilitates adult learning and continuous professional development.

## Taking Into Account the Impact of Teacher Career Stages on Effective Supervisory Practice

Like the students in their classrooms, educators are unique individuals with widely different knowledge, experiences, skills, and needs (Hoover & Guinn, 1998). In their Teacher Career Cycle, Fessler and Christensen (1992) examine the interrelationships among a teacher's personal environment (e.g., family dynamics or crisis situations), organizational environment (e.g., the administration's management style or societal expectations), and career development (see Figure 3.2). They portray a flexible progression from preservice teacher education, through induction of the novice into a new work environment, to differentiated stages in a teacher's career-long journey.

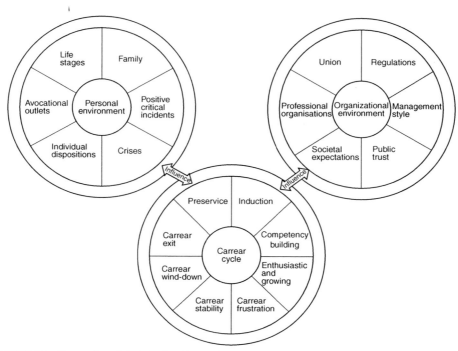

**FIGURE 3.2**   Dynamics of the Teacher Career Cycle (Fessler & Christensen, 1992)

According to Fessler & Christensen and (1992), the eight stages to the teacher career cycle (Figure 3.3) are

**FIGURE 3.3**   The Teacher Career Cycle (Fessler & Christensen, 1992)

- *Preservice:* Period of preparation at the university level for the professional role of a teacher
- *Induction:* First 2 or 3 years of employment, when a teacher is socialized into the system and eventually receives tenure
- *Competency building:* The teacher strives to improve personal repertoire of skills and abilities, and moves beyond self-concerns to enhance personal practice
- *Enthusiastic and growing:* The teacher has attained a high level of competence, but continues to learn as a professional
- *Career frustration:* The teacher feels growing disillusionment with the profession, showing waning job satisfaction and early signs of burnout
- *Stable but stagnant:* Plateau where the teacher is resigned to doing what is expected, but little more
- *Career wind-down:* The teacher plans to leave the profession
- *Career exit:* The teacher leaves the job for an alternative career or retirement

The career cycle, with its various stages, illustrates the need for effective supervisors who match their efforts to the individual needs of the teachers with whom they work. (Indeed, our belief in that need is so strong that in Part V we devote three chapters to special supervisory support systems for preservice, novice, and marginal teachers.) Although we do not view teachers' development as leaner and fixed, we do find peer-coaching a particularly effective supervisory tool for teachers at the "competency-building" and "enthusiastic and growing" stages. Teachers in the competency-building stage are striving to improve their knowledge base, skills, and abilities; they are eagerly seeking new methods, materials, and instructional strategies. Fessler and Christensen (1992) describe competency building as "a time of 'grabbing the handles' of teaching and developing a feeling of comfort in the profession" (p. 88). As they note, peer coaching can be tailored by the teacher-as-learner who is discovering and defining individual growth needs.

Teachers like Lauren, whom we introduced at the beginning of this chapter, can be categorized as enthusiastic and growing. They have attained a high level of competence, yet they are constantly reflecting on ways to enrich their practice. "These individuals are not only experiencing very positive periods in their own professional lives, but also tend to have a very positive influence on school climate and upon other teachers" (Fessler & Christensen, 1992, p. 151). Moreover, as was illustrated by the case of Maxine and Sue, peer coaching builds bridges across classrooms to share teacher expertise and to create a more collaborative working environment. Maxine and Sue are a case in point for Schmoker's (2001) premise that "we want to multiply rather than squander teacher expertise," for, by doing so, we dignify teachers' work and create a "self-perpetuating intellectual legacy" (p. 16). Lauren was searching for such a bridge.

The usefulness of peer coaching is by no means limited to those two career stages. The opportunity to collaborate on a regular basis with colleagues has a positive impact on the professional growth of teachers at all stages. In fact, many teachers have shared with us their thoughts that, although the ritualistic nature of teacher supervision and evaluation as practiced in their district contributed to feelings of career frustration or job stagnancy, participating in peer coaching and working closely with a trusted colleague enlivened their day-to-day teaching and renewed their devotion and sense of professionalism.

The Teacher Career Cycle fits well with Duke and Stiggins' (1986) contention that "we make a crucial mistake if we assume all teachers must travel exactly the same route to precisely the same destination" (p. 14). Differentiated supervision that features peer coaching as one component offers teachers at various developmental stages the opportunity to individualize to meet their specific needs for professional growth.

## Building in More Time for Administrators to Focus on Teachers Who Truly Need Assistance

As you read in Chapter 2 about the skills essential to in-class supervision, you may have wondered how an administrator in the real world could ever have enough time to be an effective supervisor and instructional leader when faced with mounds of bureaucratic paperwork, discipline referrals, and telephone calls from parents. Our answer is simple: The principal cannot do it all! However, a differentiated approach to supervision that incorporates peer coaching (among other options) helps administrators to escape from a one-size-fits-all system in which they can easily become overwhelmed by a seemingly geometric progression of formal classroom visits and follow-up conferencing. The principal focuses time and effort on teachers who most need assistance—for example, nontenured teachers in the induction stage of the career cycle or marginal teachers experiencing career frustration. Meanwhile, competent teachers who volunteer to do so can engage in peer coaching. Instead of visiting every tenured teacher once or twice annually, administrators can concentrate on quality in-class supervision and more frequent cycles with a smaller group of faculty. At the same time, administrators send the message that they respect and dignify teaching as a profession, that they encourage teachers to engage in reflective and collaborative working relationships, and that they recognize teachers as capable of self-directed learning.

## PEER COACHING IN ACTION: THE CYCLE REVISITED

As we outlined in Chapter 2, the in-class supervision cycle incorporates readiness building, a preobservation conference, an observation with some form of objective data collection, interpretation and analysis of the data, a postobservation conference, and a follow-up discussion in which the success of the cycle is carefully and honestly appraised. Peer coaching follows the same pattern, except that the readiness-building phase is increased. Moreover, keeping in mind that in-class supervision is a cyclical process, we recommend that peer-coaching partners commit to a *minimum* of three mutual observation/conferencing cycles annually. That is, to establish continuity of focus over time, the partners observe one another on at least three occasions.

Much of the readiness building for coaching occurs before either teacher enters the other's classroom. It begins with a districtwide committee comprising multiple stakeholders. Those stakeholders include board members, central office administration, principals, teachers from each building, and union leaders who come together to investigate various models of coaching and to make a decision on the policy and procedures that would best match the district's needs and culture (see Chapter 12).

Throughout this book, we emphasize that teachers possess unique and varied needs. So, too, do school districts. A good starting point for the committee is to research (or even to conduct site visits to) other schools with thriving peer-coaching models; however, each educational context has differing requirements for building a successful coaching program.

Following a period of committee research and planning, peer coaching should be introduced at the district level to the faculty as a whole. The introduction should promote a widespread understanding of the goals and processes of coaching. Communication throughout the planning stage makes adoption and acceptance of whatever model the committee chooses far easier in the long run. Additionally, follow-up and support are needed to explain the process at the building level. General question-and-answer sessions at faculty meetings work well, with the principal and teacher/union representatives from the committee present to address concerns.

Teachers must then indicate interest, select a partner with whom to team, and commit to attend training. Voluntary participation and the teacher's personal selection of a trusted colleague are musts. We recommend that districts start small, with a committed pilot group, and build gradually. A general rule of thumb is that faculty are eligible for peer coaching if they

- are tenured,
- have worked in the district for at least 3 years,
- have earned satisfactory ratings during that time, and
- have participated in the requisite supervision training (at minimum, a 2-day workshop).

Supervision training for teachers is a crucial part of readiness building. Professional development in the difference between supervision and evaluation, and in the key skills for observation and conferencing (see Chapter 2), reduces anxiety about the process. Participating in training together also enhances the sense of trust and collegiality that the teachers develop toward one another. The peer-coaching facilitator can address salient issues. These key issues include the importance of confidentiality, teacher ownership and control of the process, the links that peer coaching has to district priorities and professional development, nonjudgmental data collection techniques, active listening skills, conferencing, and the handling of the paper trail. Figure 3.4 provides a suggested outline for a 2-day peer-coaching workshop.

**FIGURE 3.4** Sample Format for 2-Day Peer Coaching Workshop

*Day 1/morning*
- Team-building exercise to tap into teachers' prior knowledge (see Exercises 3.1 and 3.2)
- Presentation on the differences between supervision and evaluation; explanation of the way in which peer coaching fits into a model of differentiated supervision
- Rationale for peer coaching
- Presentation on peer coaching links to district and building initiatives

*Day 1/afternoon*
- Introduction of the knowledge base on the seven essential skills of classroom-based supervision (see Chapter 2 for relevant exercises)
- Building readiness: issues of trust building, ownership and control of the process, confidentiality, and communication
- Building readiness: conducting espoused-platform conferences with a partner (role play; see Exercise 2.1)

*Day 2/morning*
- How to conduct a preconference that promotes inquiry and reflection (role play with emphasis on fluency, rehearsal, and contract; see Exercise 3.3)
- Understanding of and experimentation with a variety of nonjudgmental data collection instruments (suggested resource: Association of Supervision and Curriculum Development's "Improving Instruction Through Observation and Feedback," Tape 2: Observation Techniques)
- Data collection instrument matched to a teacher's question or concern (see Exercise 3.4)

*Day 2/afternoon*
- Data-driven decision making (practice analyzing and interpreting data; see Exercise 2.3)
- How to conduct a postconference and cycle evaluation (role play)
- Review of the elements of the in-class supervision cycle
- District specifics on periodic meetings with principals, logistics of scheduling observations and conferences, paper trail, and accountability issues

To ensure that peer coaching remains separate from evaluation, the teacher who is observed maintains sole possession of all peer-coaching data. The coach neither retains a copy nor shares it with the administration. The results of peer coaching never become a part of a teacher's summative evaluation unless the individual teacher chooses to use such data as part of a professional portfolio demonstrating growth over time (see Chapter 8).

## Sample Peer-Coaching Cycle

After deciding to participate in peer coaching together because of their mutual respect, Marilyn, a fourth-grade teacher, and Linda, a kindergarten teacher, attended a 2-day summer workshop on peer coaching. To begin their first cycle of in-class peer coaching, they met one day after school for a preobservation conference.

Marilyn's concern was related to the district initiative of providing authentic contexts for student writing. Marilyn began by discussing her upcoming lesson, an integrated social studies–communication arts activity in which students would be working in small groups. She explained that the class had been working in pairs to investigate various states in the Southwest. The outcome for Thursday was to begin formulating a business letter. The pairs would be contacting local chambers of commerce to gain additional information about specific states as part of their research. Marilyn would start with about 10 min. of whole-group instruction in which the students would brainstorm the general form and content for a good business letter. Then she intended to separate the students into teams of four to write a first draft. At the conclusion of the lesson, she would pull them all together and use a combination of the ideas and examples

---

**EXERCISE 3.3    The Preobservation Conference**

*Directions*    As discussed in Chapter 2, the preobservation conference is the stage of the cycle before the actual observation. At the conference, the teacher who is being coached gives a general overview of the lesson to be observed (fluency) and reviews the steps in its implementation (rehearsal). The teacher and coach then decide on the data collection instrument that appropriately addresses the teacher's question or concern (contract). It is a violation of trust for the observing teacher to stray from the contract, collecting data or commenting on other aspects of the lesson without an invitation to do so.

Based on that description, work with a partner. One takes the part of the teacher; the other, the coach. To practice conducting a preconference, the coach uses the questions that follow as a guide. Incorporate *fluency, rehearsal,* and *contract* into the conference.

1.  Can you tell me a little bit about the goals and objectives of the lesson I will be observing this afternoon? What do you want your students to learn?
2.  To give me a context, explain how this lesson relates to what you have previously covered and to upcoming lessons.
3.  Now that I have an understanding of what you hope to achieve, can you walk me through what I will actually see? What will be the major segments of the lesson as it unfolds? What instructional approaches and learning activities are you using? Why did you choose them?
4.  Are there any parts of the lesson that you would like to discuss in more detail?
5.  What question or concern about your teaching or your students' learning do you hope to address? How does it relate to district initiatives? How might it affect your students' learning?
6.  What type of data would be most helpful to you? Do you have an idea of an instrument that would provide the most useful information? Let us discuss the approach that would be most practical.

generated in small groups to create a class model of an ideal business letter that each pair could use.

Marilyn's question arose from the fact that this particular class lacked social skills. She found that implementing group work was challenging this year because the children had difficulty cooperating. Prior to this lesson, she and her students had created a class T chart describing what a person would see and hear if the students were working well together. Marilyn's specific concern for the observation was whether her students, divided into six separate quads, were meeting the social skills objectives.

As part of the preobservation contract, Marilyn asked Linda to record the students' behaviors during the student-centered portion of the lesson. For a data collection instrument tailored to specific needs, Marilyn asked Linda to use the class T chart and to add anecdotal notes. Linda agreed to spend about 5 min. observing each quad. As part of the contract, she also agreed to move around the room, sitting on the periphery but positioning herself so that she could see and hear what was transpiring in each group.

After the observation, Linda made a copy of the data for Marilyn to review before their scheduled postobservation conference the next day. That meeting took place before school, over coffee. Marilyn was pleased with the progress her fourth graders had made toward working together cooperatively. By comparing the six T charts (Figure 3.5 shows one of the completed charts), she realized that the two weakest skills were "giving each other eye contact" and "compliments to each other" for good ideas and positive contributions. She decided to discuss both of those concepts the following week during Morning Meeting and to create a mini-lesson in communication arts in which she herself modeled those social skills. One group had neglected to assign roles. Marilyn therefore also made a mental note to remind that group of why it was important to assign each team member a role or specific job. For continuity over time, Linda agreed to come back the following

**FIGURE 3.5** Completed Cooperative Learning Social Skill Observation Form

Group name:     Arizona Proud
Time:           2:10–2:16

Observer places a check mark on the class's T chart beside each social skill noticed and makes anecdotal notes to support the observations.

| **We should see** | **We should hear** |
|---|---|
| _____ Following directions | _X_ Inside voices |
| _X_ Staying on the topic | _X_ Each individual voice |
| _____ Giving each other eye contact | _____ Compliments to each other |
| _X_ Everyone's participation | _X_ No put-downs of people! |
| **Supporting anecdotal notes:** | **Supporting anecdotal notes:** |
| Technically, this group did not follow directions because they did not assign roles as you had instructed. However, at no time did I see any member visibly off task. Although they did not take roles, each student took a turn sharing ideas. I did not observe them looking directly at one another as they spoke. | The students kept their voices low. At no time did I notice them distracting other groups. They kept their discussion focused on composing the draft of the business letter. I heard Kristen, Kate, Karen, and Ryan all offer opinions. Although I definitely heard no put-downs, neither did I hear them acknowledge one another's positive contributions to the group. |

month for another cooperative learning lesson (cycle 2) and to chart the same behaviors to see if the students showed improvement. In the evaluation of the process, both partners felt that the peer-coaching cycle had been effective and that the data gathered had answered Marilyn's question about her students' social skills.

### EXERCISE 3.4    Kathy's Case Study: Practice in Selecting a Data Collection Instrument

*Kathy is a high school art teacher with 8 years of experience. Her schedule consists of studio art classes for 9th and 10th graders. She involves her students in hands-on, performance-based practice using a variety of media and weaves art history into the curriculum. For several years, Kathy has been struggling with a vague notion that her students are not putting forth their best effort. She feels that many of them are capable of producing higher quality work, but that they stop short of doing so.*

*A district initiative in the strategic plan emphasizes students' active role in self-assessment. Kathy wants to explore how involving her students in self-evaluation might be the key to their creating quality student products more often. She has decided to add a component on self-evaluation in her next unit. In the past she has consistently used rubrics for assessing projects, but she has never formally asked students to rate their own projects using the predetermined criteria for success. She has decided to take a risk and experiment with using small-group art criticism circles. In that way, she can have her students formatively assess their own projects, both individually and in a team context before the projects are completed and turned in. She has invited her peer coach to observe the particular lesson using criticism circles.*

*Directions*    Form pairs to assume the roles of Kathy and her peer-coaching partner. Discuss various ways that you might approach collecting data that Kathy needs to assess the effectiveness of the new technique of art criticism. In addition to brainstorming an in-class observational instrument that you think would be effective, plan a means using teacher or student artifacts to collect data that extend beyond the actual classroom observation. Be ready to report your plan of action to the whole group.

## THE PRINCIPAL'S ROLE IN PEER COACHING

When, as consultants, we introduce the idea of peer coaching in workshops for school board members and administrators, we are frequently asked if administrators lose touch with the work of faculty when teachers engage in peer coaching. Our reply is that, on the contrary, we find that the administrator–teacher supervisory relationship remains strong; it simply functions in a different, less traditional way.

Earlier in the chapter, we discussed the principal's role in readiness building. First, the principal communicates with teachers to develop a shared understanding of the goals and procedures involved in peer coaching. Second, many principals join their teachers as part of a team during the requisite training. In doing so, they not only show their support for peer-coaching, but also model educator as learner in a professional community. Third, in lieu of the annual observation, the principal meets with each teacher involved in peer coaching in an individual, face-to-face conference at the beginning of the school year. At that conference, the principal discusses the teacher's goals, deals with any questions about the scheduling of supervisory cycles, and offers support in the form of suggested resources or class coverage. For example, in Kathy's case, having discovered that her goal is student self-assessment through art criticism, the principal might inform her of a future workshop dealing with that topic. The conference is an excellent opportunity for principals to offer tangible assistance and to communicate the expectation that peer coaching is a valued part of the school's culture of collaboration.

At midyear, the principal can support the faculty by facilitating a meeting for all teachers engaged in coaching. The meeting can be structured as a collaborative sharing session, with the principal on hand to facilitate. If additional help is needed, the principal can offer to serve as a process observer to give feedback to coaching partners who may feel the need for further clarification and assistance. Moreover, just because a teacher is engaged in peer coaching certainly does not preclude a supervisor from maintaining visibility by engaging in informal, 5–10-minute drop-in visitations to the teachers' classrooms (Glatthorn, 1997).

At the conclusion of the academic year, the administrator should schedule a final conference with each peer-coaching pair. That conference should reflect on movement toward the teachers' goals, should discuss insights gained through the experience, and should show recognition of their effort to positively contribute to their own self-directed professional growth. We also recommend that the principal maintain some written system of accountability for teachers engaged in the coaching process. See Figure 3.6 for an example of a record-keeping form that each teacher can complete and submit at the end of the year without violating the spirit of confidentiality.

**FIGURE 3.6**   Peer Coaching End-of-the-Year Report

Name: _____

Building: _____

Coaching partner: _____

Central focus/peer-coaching question/concern: _____

Connection to building or district goals: _____

Dates of observations and conferences

Cycle 1: _____

Cycle 2: _____

Cycle 3: _____

(Optional)

Cycle 4: _____

Insights I gained from engaging in peer coaching (both from being observed and from observing another teacher): _____

_____

_____

Implications for student learning or impact my participation in coaching had upon my students: _____

_____

_____

Other comments or suggestions: _____

_____

_____

# IMPLEMENTING AND SUSTAINING A SUCCESSFUL PEER-COACHING PROGRAM

Among the pitfalls or obstacles that a school district might face when implementing or sustaining a peer-coaching program are (a) a top-down decision-making process that fails to include teachers; (b) failure to engage in readiness building, particularly in terms of teacher training; and (c) lack of administrative support in terms of human and fiscal resources. Based on our years of working closely with school districts that have thriving peer-coaching programs, we offer a number of guidelines.

First, capitalize on input from multiple stakeholders and give those stakeholders a shared voice in decision making. As mentioned earlier in the chapter, we recommend beginning with a districtwide committee who come together to investigate various models of coaching and to make a decision on the policy and procedures that best match the district's needs. Sustaining a strong public relations effort districtwide and in each building is important. Periodically revisit the program to assess its strengths and weaknesses and to ensure that it is matching the specific needs of the teachers. Continuous communication and evaluation are essential.

Second, teacher readiness for peer coaching is a fundamental consideration. The district must make a commitment to provide and support opportunities for teacher professional development in peer coaching. Teachers need to be clear on the distinction between supervision and evaluation. They also need to acquire a formal background in planning and executing a supervision cycle. Moreover, questions and challenges inevitably arise along the way. We therefore recommend that districts offer mandatory training for anyone wishing to become involved in peer coaching, and that they also invest in follow-up sharing sessions. All peer coaches must clearly understand that a nondirective or collaborative approach can be used but not a directive approach, because colleagues do not have the authority to direct each other about what to do. Peer-coaching programs that are implemented without the requisite training often indicate an "on-paper policy" that has little administrative commitment or support and that causes a general sense of confusion among teachers regarding exactly what they should be doing.

As in all new initiatives, administrators that work as part of a collaborative team with their teachers convey common purpose and develop a shared knowledge base and understanding of the process. Such teamwork also helps to facilitate operational and internal consistency across buildings and among administrators. We suggest establishing an in-house professional library of books, videotapes, and Web-based resources (see "Suggestions for Further Reading and Research" at the end of this chapter) that provide teachers with extra assistance or skill practice.

Finally, if teachers are to visit one another's classrooms and to collaborate, then district leadership must make an effort to provide release time and support for those activities. In some districts, peer-coaching programs are doomed to failure because teachers find the logistics (scheduling observations and conferences without administrative assistance) too overwhelming. They thus opt not to participate. A district must be creative in offering opportunities for observations. Creative solutions may include occasional class coverage by an administrator or planning to provide an all-day building substitute who can "float" from classroom to classroom to relieve peer coaches during the periods when they are serving in the role of observer. In some districts, principals also make an effort to schedule peer coaches with common planning time. Figure 3.7 contains suggestions for implementing peer coaching.

**FIGURE 3.7**   Practical Guidelines for Implementing and Sustaining a Peer-Coaching Program

1. Involve and regularly communicate with all stakeholders, including board members, central office personnel, building administrators, teachers, and union representatives. Peer coaching cannot be a top-down mandate.

2. Research successful peer-coaching programs. If feasible, conduct site visits to talk to administrators and teachers about their perspectives. However, be sure to shape your program to meet the specific needs of your school district.

3. Make sure that no teacher engages in peer coaching without the requisite training. Trust building, collaboration, confidentiality, communication skills, observational techniques, conferencing, and data-driven decision making should be the cornerstones of this training.

4. Show visible administrative support by having principals work as part of a team with their teachers during training, by scheduling individual meetings with coaches at the beginning and the end of the year, and by facilitating at least one sharing session during the year for those involved in the process.

5. Clearly communicate and seek a shared understanding that a distinction exists between supervision for individual growth and evaluation for accountability. Peer coaching is designed to promote a teacher's professional growth and thereby to have an impact on student learning. It never serves an evaluative function.

6. Make a district commitment to building in the time for observations and conferencing to take place.

7. Routinely assess the program's effectiveness, and refine the procedures if necessary.

# CHAPTER SUMMARY

Peer coaching is part of a differentiated model of supervision. It extends the role of classroom observer to the teacher. It is a voluntary, confidential process through which competent professionals who are adequately trained share their expertise, learn to incorporate new instructional strategies or methodologies into their repertoire, and search for answers to classroom-related questions or concerns in a nonthreatening environment. Peer coaching gives control to the teacher who is being observed. It is based on the belief that teachers collaborating with trusted colleagues can increase their understanding of, and reflection on, best practice. Teacher learning leads in turn to enhanced student learning.

Observation of teachers by teachers makes sense because it fosters the conditions that support adult learning: mutual respect, a sense of ownership and self-direction, voluntary participation, and a collaborative spirit. It also takes into account the impact of teacher career stages on effective supervisory practice and builds in more time for administrators to focus their efforts on the teachers who truly need their assistance.

Peer coaching follows the same in-class cyclical process described in Chapter 2. That process includes readiness building, a preobserva-tion conference, the observation, data collection and analysis, a postobservation conference, and evaluation of the process. Readiness building begins with a districtwide committee composed of multiple stakeholders who research and subsequently develop a peer-coaching program tailored to meet the needs of the district. It also encompasses the professional development required to provide teachers with the knowledge and skills essential to effective observation.

Although building principals may not be engaged in formal classroom observation, they play an important role in collaborating with teachers in the process. Typically, administrators conduct individual, face-to-face conferences with the involved teachers at both the beginning and the end of the school year. The role of the administrator also includes scheduling sharing sessions for teachers midway through the year, arranging logistics so that observations can be scheduled, providing resources, and maintaining a written record for accountability. Additionally, principals can serve as process observers to offer feedback to the coaching partners if necessary.

Guidelines for implementing a peer-coaching program include (a) regularly communicating with all stakeholders in the process; (b) ensuring teacher readiness by providing professional development on the function of peer coaching and on the skills of in-class supervision and (c) showing visible administrative support through commitment of time and resources for observation and conferencing.

## DISCUSSION QUESTIONS

**1.** Return to the grid that you completed concerning your views on peer coaching (Exercise 3.1). Have your initial perceptions changed since reading this chapter? If so, in what ways?

**2.** As you contemplate your years in education, can you personally identify with the eight-step Teacher Career Model? Can you think of colleagues who match each of the stages? What are your views on peer coaching as a tool to meet the needs of teachers at the various stages?

**3.** In your opinion, how does the role that the principal plays as facilitator of the peer-coaching process compare to more traditional role of principal as observer? What are the pros and cons of this less traditional role?

**4.** Given the climate in your school district, what do you think might pose the greatest obstacle in introducing a peer-coaching program there? What steps might you take to overcome that challenge?

## THEORY-INTO-PRACTICE APPLICATIONS

**1.** As a class, gather as many peer-coaching plans as you can—from your home district, from contacts in other districts, or from an Internet search. Divide into groups. In each group, distribute one or two of the plans. Use the information in this chapter to assess the strengths and weaknesses of each peer-coaching program. Report your findings to the whole group. Create a class list of the characteristics that all the peer-coaching models have in common.

**2.** If possible, interview a teacher who has participated as a peer coach or an administrator who has facilitated a peer-coaching program. Ask about the benefits derived and the concerns encountered. Moreover, ask at least one question about the perceived

impact of peer coaching on student learning. After the interview, summarize your impressions about the effectiveness of the peer-coaching model.

**3.** Report back to the class on the results of your interview. As a group, search for patterns across interviews. How do those patterns compare to the information presented in this chapter?

**4.** Using the supervision cycle presented in Chapter 2, pair up with another member of the class or a willing colleague in your district to conduct a full cycle of in-class supervision. Taking the role of the peer coach, write a reflection paper on the experience. Include the data that you collected.

## CASE STUDY: PEER COACHING

This case focuses on peer coaching as described in Chapter 3. You will encounter a description of a peer-coaching initiative in a private, preschool setting. The director of the Montessori program learned about peer coaching and brought it back to the staff. After reading about the peer-coaching process, you will have the opportunity to reflect on questions about the case.

Michelle, the principal of a private Montessori school, was introduced to the concept of peer coaching while taking a summer course on supervision. At

the time, she and her faculty had been discussing alternatives to the supervision and evaluation process already in place. Michelle decided to take the idea back to her teachers. She was particularly intrigued by the research that indicated the peer-coaching model increased teacher efficacy, collegiality, and craftsmanship.

When the school year began, Michelle was enthusiastic about presenting coaching to her teachers as a possible alternative to principal observation. She introduced the concept during the first faculty meeting. Because one of the teachers had taken the course with her, Michelle asked her to invite another colleague to join her to model the cycle during weekly faculty meetings.

The initial step that they presented to the rest of the group was "establishing readiness." Sally, the "trained" teacher, took the role of the teacher who was to be observed, whereas her partner Jan was assigned as "coach." At the first faculty meeting, Michelle and Sally explained that before school began they had used a series of informal meetings and follow-up correspondence by e-mail to explain the goals of coaching, the procedures for nondirective supervision, and the process of systematic data collection and analysis to Jan. Michelle gave the rest of the group a brief overview.

Sally and Jan conducted their first preconference in front of the entire early childhood staff at a subsequent faculty meeting. Sally explained that she wanted to be sure that she was asking questions that challenged her students to really tap into their innate sense of curiosity and wonder. She asked Jan to observe her during a hands-on science lesson and to script all of the questions that she asked so that she could examine them. Michelle then demonstrated to the teachers selective verbatim as a method of data collection.

In the postconference, which was also shared in front of the entire group of their colleagues, Sally agreed to have the questions that Jan scripted displayed upon the Smart Board. She thanked Jan for observing and collecting the data. Sally then used a "think-aloud" protocol to demonstrate searching for patterns and using those patterns to draw conclusions about their meaning in relation to student learning.

Upon reviewing the two teachers' journals after the entire peer-coaching cycle was conducted, Michelle discovered that Jan's journal revealed that, as a coach, taking a nondirective approach made her feel underappreciated and undervalued in

her role. She was proud of how well she scripted Sally's questions as a novice coach. However, the idea of allowing the data that she collected to "speak for itself," without the opportunity for her to add her opinion and commentary, made her feel as if she had wasted valuable time away from her students. She did not understand why the same results could not have been reached through the use of a camcorder recording. She indicated that she would not choose peer coaching again.

Sally, however, displayed a vastly different attitude in her journal. She commented that she respected the safety of the coaching process, in that it allowed her to feel as if she could truly be herself and admit her concerns to a trusted colleague. She wrote: "It definitely made me openly reflect upon and actually 'inspect' the types of questions that I ask and to challenge myself to do better." She was looking forward to inviting Jan in to observe another science lesson in the near future.

### Questions for Discussion

1. Obviously, Sally and Jan had vastly different perceptions of peer coaching. Were you surprised by their disparate reactions? Please explain.

2. Turn to Brookfield's four conditions that support adult learning in Chapter 3. Examine those four conditions as they relate to Sally's experience. To Jan's.

3. According to the research that Michelle read in her graduate course, engaging in peer coaching leads to increased teacher efficacy, collegiality, and craftsmanship. Did you find this true in this case?

4. If you were Michelle, what might you have done differently in presenting the peer-coaching model to the faculty as a whole?

# REFERENCES

BARTH, R. S. (1990). *Improving schools from within.* San Francisco, CA: Jossey-Bass.

BROOKFIELD, S. D. (1986). *Understanding and facilitating adult learning.* San Francisco, CA: Jossey-Bass.

DUKE, D. L., & STIGGINS, R. J. (1986). *Teacher evaluation: Five keys to growth.* Washington, DC: National Education Association.

FESSLER, R., & CHRISTENSEN, J. C. (1992). *The teacher career cycle: Understanding and guiding the professional development of teachers.* Boston, MA: Allyn & Bacon.

GARMSTON, R. J. (1987). How administrators support peer coaching. *Educational Leadership, 44*(5), 18–26.

GLATTHORN, A. A. (1997). *Differentiated supervision* (2nd ed.). Alexandria, VA: Association for Supervision and Curriculum Development.

GLICKMAN, C. D., GORDON, S. P., & ROSS-GORDON, J. M. (2004). *SuperVision and instructional leadership: A developmental approach* (6th ed.). Boston, MA: Allyn & Bacon.

HERZBERG, F. (1987). One more time: How do you motivate employees? *Harvard Business Review, 65*(5), 109–120.

HOOVER, L. A., & GUINN, F. C. (1998). Differentiated supervision and evaluation: Reflections on the Gettysburg model. *Pennsylvania Educational Leadership, 18*(1), 17–24.

HUNT, D. E. (1971). *Matching models in education.* Toronto: Institute for Studies in Education.

JOYCE, B., & SHOWERS, B. (2002). *Student achievement through staff development* (3rd ed). Alexandria, VA: Association For Supervision and Curriculum (Development.

KOHLBERG, L. (1969). Stage and sequence: The cognitive–developmental approach to socialization. In D. Goslin (Ed.), *Handbook of socialization theory and research.* New York: Rand McNally.

LOEVINGER, J. (1976). *Ego development.* San Francisco, CA: Jossey–Bass.

MASLOW, A. (1968). *Toward a psychology of being.* New York: D. Van Nostrand.

National Policy Board for Educational Administration (2002). *Educational Leadership Constituent Council: Standards for advanced programs in educational leadership.* Available: http:// www.npbea.org/ELCC/ELCC-Standards%20_5—02.pdf.

National Staff Development Council. (2000). Revisioning professional development. *Journal of Staff Development, 21*(3), 1–19.

NOLAN, J. F., & FRANCIS, P. (1992). Changing perspectives in curriculum and instruction. In C. D. Glickman (Ed.), *Supervision in transition: 1992 ASCD yearbook.* Alexandria, VA: Association for Supervision and Curriculum Development.

PETERS, T. J., & WATERMAN, R. H. (1982). *In search of excellence: Lessons from America's best-run companies.* New York: Warner Books.

REIMAN, A. J., & THIES-SPRINTHALL, L. (1998). *Mentoring and supervision for teacher development.* New York: Longman.

SCHMOKER, M. (2001). *The results fieldbook: Practical strategies from dramatically improved schools.* Alexandria, VA: Association for Supervision and Curriculum Development.

SHOWERS, B., & JOYCE, B. (1996). The evolution of peer coaching. *Educational Leadership, 53*(6), 12–16.

# SUGGESTIONS FOR FURTHER READING AND RESEARCH

ACKERMAN, R., & MACKENZIE, S. V. (2006). Uncovering teacher leadership. *Educational Leadership, 63*(8), 66–70.

AMAU, L., KAHRS, J., & KRUSKAMP, B. (2004). Peer coaching: Veteran high school teachers take the lead on learning. *NASSP Bulletin, 88*(639)26–42.

Association for Supervision and Curriculum Development. (2002). Videotape. *Improving instruction through observation and feedback.* Alexandria, VA: Association for Supervision and Curriculum Development.

BECKER, J. M. TeachersNetwork: TeachNet: Peer coaching for improvement of teaching and learning. Retrieved from website:http://www.teachnet.org/ntpi/research/growth/becker.htm.

COSTA, A. L., & GARMSTON, R. J. (2002). *Cognitive coaching: A foundation for renaissance schools* (2nd ed.). Norwood, MA: Christopher Gordon.

COSTA, A. L., & KALLICK, B. (1993). Through the lens of a critical friend. *Educational Leadership, 51*(2), 49–51.

ROBBINS, P. (1991). *How to plan and implement a peer coaching program.* Alexandria, VA: Association for Supervision and Curriculum Development.

ROONEY, J. (1993). Teacher evaluation: No more "super" vision. *Educational Leadership, 51*(2), 43–44.

Southwest Educational Development Laboratory. (1997). Professional learning communities. What are they and why are they important. *Issues About Change, 6*(1), 1–8. referred from http://www.sedl.org/change/ issues/ issues61.html.

Video Journal of Education. (1993). Videotape. *The collaborative workplace and peer coaching.* Salt Lake City, UT: Video Journal of Education.

WALEN, E., & DEROSE, M. (1993). The power of peer appraisals. *Educational Leadership, 51*(2), 45–48.

# CHAPTER 4

# SELF-DIRECTED TEACHER GROWTH

**P**ART II of this book focused on in-classroom supervision through a cycle that included readiness-building, observation, conferencing, and assessment of the process. Observation represents one approach to working with teachers to improve instruction. Part III deals with three options that rely on supervisory activities other than observation: self-directed teacher growth, action research, and collegial development groups. We explore these activities as school-based differentiated strategies designed to promote teachers' professional development so as to improve teaching and enhance student learning. These three approaches are designed for supervising tenured, experienced educators who have consistently demonstrated teaching competence over time. These approaches offer school systems specific strategies that can be used to provide authentic growth opportunities for those teachers who perform at high levels and who are often underserved by traditional supervision systems.

The specific focus of the present chapter is self-directed teacher growth. In the self-directed mode, teachers as individuals, pairs, or teams develop and submit a plan to increase knowledge, skills, or teaching performance (or any combination) or to focus on students' performance. A self-directed plan delineates a specific area of teaching or learning that the teacher wants to explore in depth. The plan includes goals, strategies for accomplishing the stated goals, the proposed value of the project in terms of students' learning, a timeline, required resources and support, documentation of progress through data collection, and some form of reflective self-assessment.

We discuss self-directed teacher growth as an integral part of job-embedded learning. Moreover, we illustrate the vital role of the principal in facilitating self-directed teacher growth as a professional development option. Finally, we provide real-world examples from school districts that incorporate self-directed teacher growth as part of their supervision plan.

## GUIDING QUESTIONS FOR PREREADING REFLECTION AND JOURNALING

- Take a moment to consider and jot down what motivates adults in general, and you in particular, to learn.
- Create a list of the professional development experiences that have had the greatest impact on your teaching and your students' learning. Based on your list,

how would you fuel a teacher's desire to engage in continuous professional growth?

- In your opinion, what are the advantages of involving teachers in self-directed teacher growth projects as part of a districtwide supervision plan? The limitations?
- If you were writing your own self-directed professional growth plan, what kind of information do you think would be important to include to help you accomplish your goal?
- As a teacher, what role would you like your principal to play in supporting your self-directed growth plan?

# WHAT IS SELF-DIRECTED TEACHER GROWTH?

Based on the belief that adults are more intrinsically motivated to learn when they have ownership in the process, Knowles (1990) defined self-directed learning as individuals' taking the initiative to identify, explore, and design experiences to meet their needs and enrich their learning. In contrast to the option of having a principal or colleague come into the classroom to observe, the self-directed option affords teachers the opportunity to work independently, in pairs, or in small groups to set meaningful goals, to devise a concrete action plan for meeting those goals, and to reflectively assess progress. Observation of teaching may occur as one means of data collection in an individualized growth plan, but the self-directed mode goes far beyond in-class supervision. As with peer coaching, we recommend that the self-directed option be elected by teachers who are tenured, who have worked in the district for at least 3 years, who have consistently demonstrated teaching competence over time, and who have participated in some form of training in goal setting.

Although some researchers might contend that self-directed growth is professional development, separate from the field of teacher supervision, we maintain that any organizational function designed to promote learning and to improve individual teaching performance is directly associated with supervision. This view is in fact becoming generally accepted. Gordon and Nicely (1998) report "increasing value on staff development as a supervisory task," noting that professional development is one of Wiles and Bondi's "six skill areas of supervision," one of Olivia's "three domains of supervision," and one of Glickman, Gordon, and Ross-Gordon's "five tasks of supervision" (p. 803).

In Chapter 1, we shared our belief that, to promote teacher learning and to provide teachers with ongoing support, a high-quality system of teacher supervision and evaluation must be closely integrated with professional development initiatives. As Barth (2001) notes, "The self-renewal of educators and the self-renewal of our schools go hand in hand" (p. 28).

More recently, the National Policy Board for Educational Administration (2002) developed the ELCC Standards for Advanced Programs in Educational Leadership. Standard 2 advocates for educational leaders who can design and implement comprehensive, context-appropriate professional growth plans for teachers (see Appendix A). To have a positive impact upon student learning, quality supervision and evaluation systems must be supported by complementary professional development efforts.

## Self-Directed Teacher Growth as Job-Embedded Learning

In the decade that preceded the writing of this book, a paradigm shift occurred in professional development. The orientation changed from one of transmitting knowledge and skills to teachers to one in which teachers construct their own knowledge through authentic opportunities to learn from and with colleagues (Lieberman, 1995). Instead of conducting teacher training away from the classroom, with teachers as passive recipients who sit and receive knowledge provided by consultants on designated in-service days, staff developers have been emphasizing multiple forms of experiential learning called "job-embedded learning."

Job-embedded learning is professional development that is ongoing, meaningful, relevant, and closely integrated with supervision (Sparks & Hirsh, 2000). It is in keeping with Sergiovanni and Starratt's (2006) view of professional authority, the belief that administrators must consider the experience and expertise of teachers: "Professional authority is not external but is exercised within the teaching context and from within the teacher" (p. 32). In other words, professional authority assumes that through daily practice, the individual teacher creates knowledge that can improve instruction.

Rather than looking outside the school for expertise or scheduling professional workshops on specially designated days, administrators encourage teachers engaged in job-embedded learning to build expertise continuously within their own environment. Learning occurs by doing, and it occurs as teachers perform their daily routines and then purposefully reflect on their actions in terms of their students' learning (Sparks & Hirsh, 2000; Wood & McQuarrie, 1999). The assumption is that learning is most powerful when linked to the individual needs and developmental levels of teachers and to real-life challenges. Job-embedded learning "pervades the classroom and the school" as teachers "continually draw understanding about their performance from student performance" (National Partnership for Excellence and Accountability in Teaching, 2000, p. 2). It is teacher-as-on-the-job-active-learner, engaged in gathering and analyzing data on student learning and subsequently using those data to inform instruction.

Self-directed teacher growth is an ideal form of job-embedded learning because it intrinsically motivates competent professionals through ownership in and a personal commitment to long-term individual growth. Teachers have "the power to make independent judgments, to exercise personal discretion, initiative and creativity through their work—what Schon described as defining the heart of professional action" (Hargreaves, 1994, p. 178). Sandra, a middle school teacher whom we interviewed, confirmed that point: "When our district moved to a differentiated supervision plan, the self-directed option gave me a voice and a choice and dared me to venture beyond my comfort zone."

More and more districts are encouraging teachers to develop individualized self-directed growth plans. In lieu of the more traditional, one-size-fits-all models of supervision and professional development, teachers are engaging in a variety of activities that support job-embedded learning based on a foundation of competence rather than one of deficiency. For example, Ohio incorporates Individual Professional Development Plans (IPDPs) as part of the state's licensure requirements. Moreover, various school districts in Florida, Kansas, and Texas, recipients of the U.S. Department of Education's Model Professional Development Awards, have long required individual learning plans as "crucial cogs in a system of staff development that links individual learning with schoolwide learning and district goals" (Richardson, 2002, p. 2).

# THE INITIAL STEP: GOAL SETTING

Teachers choosing the self-directed growth option must first identify growth goals for increasing their knowledge or skills in ways that will have an impact on students' learning (Glatthorn, 1997). However, Duke (1990) discovered that many teachers experience difficulty when asked to set specific, meaningful, and challenging goals, especially if they have not been invited to do so in the past. Therefore, when implementing the self-directed growth option as a form of supervision, administrators will find it useful to build readiness by offering a districtwide workshop on how to set appropriate goals.

Written goals must be clear, concrete, realistic, and measurable. Moreover, effective goals should be data driven. Holloway (2003) notes that many school districts have begun to pay more attention to student performance data as they collaborate with teachers in designing professional development to improve classroom practice. For example, after reviewing the results of a statewide achievement test in mathematics or after looking closely at student writing samples over the course of the school year, teachers are more likely to relate their professional growth goals directly to their students' learning.

Another important consideration in goal setting is to ensure that individual teachers are moving in the same direction as the school's vision and mission. We recommend that self-directed growth goals be connected to the standards of professional practice identified by the district, to the district's strategic planning goals, or to the grade-level, departmental, or building goals. Making such a connection empowers teachers to meet their learning needs and, at the same time, to move in the direction of the district's priorities. Ideally, then, the self-directed option blends individual improvement goals with organizational development. Zmuda, Kuklis, and Kline (2004) refer to the power of "collective autonomy" that serves the entire professional learning community as the "school as a system becomes a united body in its determination to achieve the desired results but still fosters open inquiry and individual creativity" (p. 61).

The importance of that blending of goals is underscored by Covey's (1996) description of the three fundamental roles of leadership: pathfinding, aligning, and empowering. After defining pathfinding as communication of the organization's vision and value system, or its overall sense of purpose, Covey explains aligning and empowering as follows:

*People have enormous talent, ingenuity, intelligence, and creativity. Most of it lies dormant. When you have true alignment toward a common vision, a common mission, you begin to co-mission with those people. Individual purpose and mission are commingled with the mission of the organization. When these purposes overlap, great synergy is created. A fire is ignited within people that unleashes their latent talent. . . . this is what we mean by empowerment. (p. 153)*

Danielson and McGreal (2000) suggest three categories for goal setting that we find helpful in organizing teacher self-directed growth goals in conjunction with a district's vision and mission statements. The first category is "improvement goals," which are designed to refine or "fine tune" current teaching practice. The second category, "renewal goals," relates to acquiring and demonstrating new knowledge and skills. Finally, "restructuring goals" refer to redesigning curriculum, instruction, or assessment. Restructuring goals are typically achieved through collaborative effort, and they lead to a new way of doing things—such as developing a nongraded primary program.

For each category of goals, we provide an example of a focused teacher goal that is data driven and that correlates to a specific district priority:

- *Refining current teaching practice—improvement goals*
  *District priority:* To engage students as actively as possible in the learning process.

  *Teacher goal:* Through data collected as part of my peer-coaching experience, I realize that my middle school students are more passive learners than I would like them to be. Accordingly, I plan to review each major unit that I teach to incorporate additional student-centered instructional activities and performance-based assessment wherever appropriate. I want my students to be more involved in constructive, hands-on learning.

- *Acquiring new knowledge or skills—renewal goals*
  *District priority:* To appropriately integrate the use of technology into the curriculum at all grade levels.

*Teacher goal:* I plan to familiarize myself with Blackboard, a Web-based software, and then to integrate that technology into writing in my high school English courses. I reviewed the number of opportunities that my students had to respond to one another's writing this past school year. Although I had hoped to incorporate more peer review, I noted that I implemented such assignments only twice each marking period. (I always feel such time constraints!) Therefore, my goal is to use a discussion board format to have students submit and respond online to one another's reactions to literature. Students will have the opportunity to extend their discussions and learning beyond the walls of my classroom; at the same time, they will be increasing their comfort with technology. Additionally, my more introverted students will have the chance to voice their thoughts and ideas.

- *Redesigning curriculum, instruction, or assessment—restructuring goals*
  *District priority:* To provide support structures in reading and mathematics based on student need as indicated by scores on district or state assessments.

  *Teacher goal:* Now that our third-grade curriculum is aligned with the mathematics standards, my partner and I would like to spend the next year collecting data on how many of our students need extra assistance in meeting the benchmarks that we have designed to assess their progress toward meeting the standards. In conjunction with the data collection, we plan to design and implement a program of differentiated learning opportunities to support the students that need extra help and practice.

Notice that, in every instance, the teacher's professional development goal relates to meeting the needs of students. See Figure 4.1 for a guide to reflective goal setting that teachers might use as a model when they engage in individualized goal setting for a self-directed action plan. Use Exercise 4.1 to practice individualized goal setting for yourself.

---

**EXERCISE 4.1   Engaging in Personal Goal Setting**

**Directions**   Imagine that you work in a district that has introduced self-directed professional development as a supervisory option. Using Figure 4.1 as a guide, develop one or more relevant and meaningful professional growth goals for yourself for the upcoming school year.

---

**FIGURE 4.1**   Teacher's Reflective Goal-Setting Worksheet

1. What curricular, instructional, or assessment area am I most interested in exploring?
2. What do I perceive as my existing strengths and needs in that goal area, especially as it relates to my students' learning?
3. What evidence (data) do I have to support my thinking in question 2?

*Based on questions 1–3, my initial goal statement is*

---

4. Is my goal clear, concrete, realistic, and measurable as stated?
5. How will achieving that goal have a positive impact on my students' learning?
6. In what way does my professional goal correlate to a district standard for professional practice, to a district priority, or to a building initiative?

*Based on questions 4–6, my revised goal statement (if appropriate) is*

---

# THE SECOND STEP: FORMULATING AND IMPLEMENTING AN ACTION PLAN

Brookfield (1986) suggests that facilitating self-directed learning "is best accomplished through a learning contract method in which objectives, relevant resources, specific activities, and evaluative procedures are outlined" (p. 71). Developing a relevant goal (as in Exercise 4.1) is just the first step in the process.

Teachers choosing the self-directed option submit a written proposal or action plan to the principal for approval. The action plan provides a rationale for pursuing the stated goal, including the potential impact on students. Moreover, it outlines concrete steps and a timeline for achieving the goal or goals. At minimum, the action plan includes the method of teacher learning, the required resources, and the roles that others, including colleagues and principal, will play in the process. Additionally, teachers devise some format to monitor and document their progress along the way, providing evidence of whether they have met their goals. Documentation of results might include statistical measures or performance-based artifacts such as a professional portfolio, reflective logs kept throughout the year, videotapes of teaching, unit plans, software, or samples of completed student work. Figure 4.2 presents a sample format that teachers might use in preparing an action plan at the beginning of the school year. Figure 4.3 shows an authentic example of a teacher's completed individual action plan. The plan, which is coordinated with the district's professional development plan, was provided by

**FIGURE 4.2**  Sample Format of an Individual Action Plan for a Teacher's Self-Directed Growth Option

Name: _____

Building: _____

Date: _____

1. Individual professional development goal: _____
2. Rationale for selection of this goal: _____
3. Expected impact on student learning: _____
4. Correlation to grade level, building, or district priorities: _____

*Note: Items 1–4 taken from the Goal-Setting Worksheet*

5. Outline of an action plan. Includes the concrete steps that I can take to achieve my goal and a proposed timeline.

_____

_____

6. Roles that others will take to support me in accomplishing my goals (e.g., networking with colleagues, supervisory support).

_____

_____

7. Method of assessing/measuring attainment of goal, including documentation.

_____

_____

8. Resources required and statement of need (include conference registration, materials, cost of a substitute, etc.).

_____

_____

**FIGURE 4.3** Sample Individual Action Plan for a Teacher's Self-Directed Growth Option

---

Name: Lyne C. Aurand
Building: Lincoln Elementary School
Gettysburg Area School District
Date: October 1, 2006

1. Individual professional development goals
   A. I will develop a 2-year multi-age fourth- and fifth-grade curriculum establishing a year A and B sequential presentation of curricular units.
   B. I will continue my work on the LEAP project with an emphasis on building business partnerships to establish annual funding for LEAP.

2. Rationale
   This is my first year teaching in a multi-age, fourth- and fifth-grade classroom setting. Because I will be putting a new curriculum into practice, that is where I feel the need to concentrate my efforts. Additionally, LEAP, an after-school program for at-risk students, needs outside funding to continue.

3. Expected impact on student learning
   A. Students will benefit from the creation of a developmentally appropriate, multi-age fourth- and fifth-grade curriculum aligned with state standards. The multi-age setting will facilitate greater flexibility in grouping and instruction to meet students' needs.
   B. At-risk students at Lincoln Elementary will be provided with enrichment opportunities, as well as tutoring in reading and math, in a safe and nurturing after-school program.

4. Correlation to building or district priorities
   A. Develop and maintain a written curriculum designed to help students achieve local and state standards. Indicator 1—Curriculum*
   B. Develop and maintain a safe and secure teaching and learning environment for staff and students to concentrate on achieving local and state standards. Indicator 4—Climate*
   C. Develop and maintain knowledge and skills associated with special education programs and students. Indicator 5—Support Services*
      *These goals are taken from the district's Act 48 Continuing Professional Development Plan.

5. Steps in the action plan
   A. Attend multi-age workshops (to be jointly identified and scheduled with principal).
   B. Write and submit the multi-age curriculum in four parts at the conclusion of each marking period in November, January, March, and June.
   C. As a member of the LEAP committee, I will continue to search for and meet with community businesses (Chamber of Commerce) to form partnerships for annual funding to support the after-school tutoring program. I will schedule one meeting per month.

6. Role of others
   I will work with colleague Donna Kluck to develop multi-age units of instruction because she, too, will be teaching a new 4–5 curriculum. We will collaborate with other teachers in the district who have previously developed and who are currently teaching multi-age curriculum.

7. Method of assessment, including documentation
   A. A completed draft of the full year's multi-age curriculum.
   B. A record of funding received from individual businesses.

8. Resources required
   A. Release time and funding to attend multi-age workshops. This will include the cost of a substitute for the days that I am out of the district.
   B. Release time to meet with business leaders as necessary.

**FIGURE 4.4**   Sample Format of a Final Report for a Teacher's Self-Directed Growth Option

Name: _____

Building: _____

Date: _____

1. Professional development goal:
   _____
   _____

2. Summary of steps followed in working toward stated goal:
   _____
   _____

3. Assessment of final outcome; impact of self-directed project on you as a professional and on your students' learning (please include collected documentation):
   _____
   _____

4. Ideas for future goal development:
   _____
   _____
   _____

Lyne Aurand of Gettysburg Area School District. As a teacher experienced in self-directed growth, Lynn lists a new goal as well as ongoing work on a goal from a previous action plan.

After the action plan is approved, the teacher begins implementation. Typically, teachers submit a brief midyear progress report that reviews the steps completed to that point and that proposes adaptations to the design or timeline if necessary. Finally, at the conclusion of the year, the teacher shares the outcome with the administrator and submits a final written report, including attached documentation as illustrated in Figure 4.4.

## THE PRINCIPAL AS FACILITATOR OF THE SELF-DIRECTED GROWTH OPTION

Although responsibility for carrying out the steps of the plan lies with the teacher, the principal provides leadership and a supportive context for self-directed growth by taking an active interest in the teacher's plan, by offering guidance and help in terms of allocated resources and assistance, and by recognizing individual teacher efforts. The principal's responsibility begins with a survey of the staff to see who might be interested in pursuing the self-directed option. Many teachers have told us that, until their principal personally encouraged them, they had not considered developing an individualized plan.

Typically, teachers select self-directed growth in the spring. That timing allows them to attend professional development on goal setting over the summer and to begin drafting an action plan. Early in the school year, the principal holds a face-to-face meeting with each teacher who has submitted a written action plan. The meeting confirms whether the proposal meets predetermined criteria. (Usually the criteria are established by the district's supervision committee.) In keeping with our earlier discussion, we suggest that criteria include (a) the clarity, specificity, and feasibility of the plan; (b) instructional benefit to the students; and (c) value of the self-directed project in relation to school or district initiatives. The initial meeting also ensures that the principal and teacher have a shared understanding of the teacher's plan and of the desired outcomes. The principal might also clarify the assistance that the teacher requires, including training, resources, and networking opportunities.

The principal now has three courses of action. The first is to accept the action plan as written. Another option is to discuss possible revisions. For example, the principal might help the teacher clarify the goal or might suggest modifications to enhance the action plan. The teacher would then edit and resubmit the plan. Third, the principal may, on rare occasions, decide to reject the action plan as inappropriate according to the stated criteria.

Figure 4.5 presents a sample format that an administrator might use to formally assess teacher action plans.

After approving the proposal, the principal serves as mentor and resource facilitator (depending to some extent on the individual district). For example, some districts offer small incentive grants to fund teachers' efforts; others channel professional readings or notifications of workshops to teachers according to their particular goals. Publication of a list of names with the foci of their self-directed projects gives teachers the option to network, to collaborate with others, and to seek advice from those with similar interests across the district.

In addition to mentoring as needed throughout the year, the principal typically meets briefly with teachers when they submit their midyear and final reports. At the midyear meeting, the principal reviews the teacher's progress, provides positive reinforcement, and discusses any stumbling blocks encountered and ways of dealing with those challenges. At the final meeting, the principal and teacher meet to discuss results and look to the future. They can consider continuation of the action plan or other growth opportunities.

**FIGURE 4.5**  Administrative Assessment of a Teacher's Action Plan

Teacher's name: _____

Date of submission:  _____

1. Is the plan submitted in the appropriate format?
2. Is the goal specific, measurable, and data driven?
3. Will the goal have an impact on student learning?
4. Is the goal integrated with building-level or district priorities or performance standards?
5. Are the steps of the plan explicitly outlined?
6. Is the plan realistic and manageable?
7. Are there appropriate methods for documenting/assessing the steps toward achieving the goals in the action plan?
8. In what ways can I provide supervisory support/resources to the teacher?

Comments:

_____

_____

_____

Accepted for implementation _____

Accepted after revision _____

Not accepted for implementation _____

Principal signature: _____

Teacher signature: _____

Although individual teachers often have records of the impact that their self-directed growth plans have on their students, seldom do districts take the extra step to formalize individual data collection procedures as evidence of the impact of teacher growth on student learning. We strongly recommend that administrators work as a team to gather and provide to their faculty, board members, parents, and community the systemwide evidence that investment of human and fiscal resources in self-directed teacher growth is worthwhile.

Evidence can be collected and disseminated in several ways. First, it is feasible to organize the final reports created by teachers into a database or body of evidence that illustrates the impact of self-directed growth on teachers and students alike. The data entered might include the type of project, a brief description of the project, and the reported impact on teacher and student learning. Figure 4.6 shows a sample database of that type. It documents teacher vignettes that are presented later in this chapter. Keeping a database of this kind gives the administration a clear picture of whether the district reporting forms reflect growth in terms of student learning.

Second, in the spirit of a professional learning community, we suggest that principals collaborate districtwide to develop a formal mechanism (e.g., faculty meetings, in-service opportunities, day conferences, or a web site) for sharing self-directed growth "products" or experiences. The use of a public format not only evidences and celebrates teacher excellence, but also provides a forum in which all teachers can benefit from the learnings of their colleagues. A public format also serves to reinforce connections between individual teacher growth and districtwide goals for curriculum and professional development. Videotaping a sharing session is an easy way to capture and document teacher growth for stakeholders outside the school. Positive stories about self-directed growth plans and the resulting impact on student learning can also be publicized through school or district newsletters or community newspapers.

In Chapter 1, we explored the scheduling of supervision and evaluation for tenured teachers in 3-year cycles: 2 years of supervision followed by 1 year of formal teacher evaluation. The self-directed growth option clearly falls within the principal's role as supervisor. The procedure is not part of a method for formally evaluating teachers. If meeting a self-directed growth goal were to be linked to a teacher's formal evaluation, then the purpose of nurturing growth would most likely be undermined. The stakes involved in receiving a positive evaluation are high, and teachers might be less inclined to take risks to stretch themselves beyond their current level of competence. They would likely be more

**FIGURE 4.6**  *Sample Database*

| Project title | Name | Description | Teacher growth | Student growth |
|---|---|---|---|---|
| Differentiated instruction | Stollar, Lori | Incorporating diff. instruct'n | Becoming a trainer | Future plans to conduct action research on the impact of DI |
| Hello, Mrs. Willman… | Willman, Ann | Summer voicemail reading | Manuscript published | No remedial reading student lost ground |
| Reflective journaling | Blanchette, Sue Hendrixson, Fran | Peer mentoring/ teaming | Implementing new strategies | Informal teacher observation |
| LIFT | Brunner, Rhonda | Preschool literacy intervention | Wrote successful grant | 77% of students now at grade level |

**FIGURE 4.7** Checklist for a Principal Who Is Facilitating the Self-Directed Teacher Growth Option

---

☐ Survey staff to determine who might be interested in choosing the self-directed growth supervisory option.

☐ Conduct a faculty meeting or workshop on teacher goal setting.

☐ Use the Assessment Worksheet to evaluate each completed action plan.

☐ Meet face to face with each teacher who selected the self-directed growth option to discuss the relevance of the goals, the specific steps of the action plan, the method of documentation, the necessary support, and the ultimate value in terms of student learning.

☐ To facilitate collaboration, networking, and resource sharing across the district, publish a list of teachers engaged in self-directed growth options and their topics.

☐ Hold a midyear conference with each teacher to review progress toward goals, to offer positive reinforcement, and to discuss any unexpected challenges encountered.

☐ Engage in an end-of-year conference to review and celebrate the teacher's accomplishments, and if necessary, to decide upon an extension for a second year.

☐ Plan a mechanism for sharing individual teacher projects with the rest of the faculty, either in the building or across the district.

☐ Create a database for documenting project results in terms of teacher growth and enhanced student learning.

---

inclined to select safe, easily attainable goals. Moreover, teachers sometimes discover that their action plans are too ambitious to complete in one school year (see Lori's vignette later in the chapter). Revising and extending the plan for a second year may therefore become necessary. Rather than focusing on whether a teacher's goal was met, we recommend that a supervisor judge accountability through documentation that the action plan was implemented with integrity. Accountability lies in accurate record keeping and in sharing what was learned collaboratively with colleagues. Figures 4.7 and 4.8 provide a principal's checklist for facilitating a teacher's action plan and a principal's record of accountability.

# OPTIONS TO PROMOTE SELF-DIRECTED GROWTH

The possibilities for individual self-directed professional growth projects are endless, but we think that focusing on several options is helpful as a starting point. In this section, we explain and provide examples of four types of job-embedded learning choices:

- projects related to curriculum, instruction, or assessment;
- reflective journals;
- grant writing applicable to the classroom; and
- participation in a "training of trainers" model.

We also encourage school districts to explore other alternatives for self-directed growth that complement their vision, mission, and strategic goals. Two other types of job-embedded learning—action research and collegial development groups—are discussed separately in Chapters 5 and 6.

**FIGURE 4.8** Sample Format of a Principal's Record of Facilitating a Teacher's Self-Directed Growth Option

Date of initial meeting: _____

Teacher's goal: _____

Budget/resource needs: _____

Principal's notes: _____

_____

_____

_____

_____

Date of midyear conference: _____

Progress toward goal: _____

Challenges faced: _____

Additional resources: _____

Principal's notes: _____

_____

_____

_____

_____

Date of final conference: _____

Summary of accomplishments: _____

_____

_____

_____

Professional employee's signature: _____

Principal's signature: _____

Date: _____

## Projects Related to Curriculum, Instruction, or Assessment

Growth plans that focus on projects related to curriculum, instruction, or assessment could entail creating new units or redesigning existing units. For example, such projects can examine the core curriculum or essential questions that drive instruction and assessment, or they can match standards to curricular content. Other action plans might involve acquiring new knowledge and skills through in-depth research and subsequent implementation of innovative teaching strategies, learning activities, or technology. Every modification to curriculum, instruction, or assessment is viewed in terms of meeting the learning needs of students (Loucks-Horsley, Hewson, Love, & Stiles, 1998). The two vignettes that follow provide real-life examples of teachers engaged in projects related to curriculum, instruction, or assessment.

### Vignette 1

*Type of job-embedded learning:* Projects in curriculum, instruction, or assessment

*Teacher goal:* Acquiring new knowledge or renewing skills; learning what constitutes differentiated instruction and working toward providing differentiated opportunities for my heterogeneously grouped students

*Impact on students:* Better use of class time and materials to respond to the needs of a variety of students' ability levels and interests

*District priority:* Initiatives leading to instructional improvement

Lori Stollar is a 10th-grade world history teacher and chair of the social studies department in Dover Area School District, a rural district with 3500 students and 240 professional staff. She had been teaching for 17 years when the district adopted a differentiated supervision plan with a self-directed growth option.

The building principal invited several teachers to consider an individualized plan. Lori looked at the challenge as a real learning opportunity. She noted, "Under the traditional system, I was observed once a year. It was like a snapshot—1 day in time. I want to be consciously aware of my teaching the other 179 days as well. I welcomed the opportunity to focus on a topic that would be relevant and meaningful to my classroom."

Lori's goal was to familiarize herself with additional ways of incorporating differentiated instruction and then to refine her practice to do so. Her classes included students with a wide range of abilities, from honors-level students to students with learning disabilities, and she was searching for ways to more effectively meet their diverse needs, skills, and interests.

Much of the year involved a process of self-study as Lori immersed herself in reading and researching about differentiated classrooms. She simultaneously kept a reflective journal to promote and document her learning. She recorded notes on her reading, her thoughts in response, new ideas and insights, and questions along the way. She found, however, that the more she delved into the topic—studying the "what" and the "why"—the more questions she uncovered about the "how to." For example, in a differentiated classroom, teachers offer students the opportunity to explore essential understandings at various degrees of difficulty by modifying content, process, and products for individual students. In a journal entry Lori wondered, "How can I provide enrichment and motivate my students who need a more appropriate level of challenge that matches their abilities?"

Lori noted that her principal was invaluable as a "sounding board," but she described the first-year process as one of merely "planting the seeds." In other words, she realized that much more remained to be done before she felt capable of implementing in her classroom the ideas that she had read about. She realized that she needed to extend that first year of awareness and information gathering into a second year devoted to the task of actual classroom implementation.

With the support of her principal, Lori began the second year by attending a 3-day professional development workshop sponsored by the Association for Supervision and Curriculum Development. Then, using what she learned through her reading and workshop participation, she focused on flexibility in varying content, process, and product to maximize student learning. For example, in a lesson on the social impact of the Industrial Revolution, students read a passage from Dickens' *Hard Times*. Lori decided to differentiate content to challenge her above grade-level students by providing them with more detailed and complex excerpts from the novel. She differentiated process for the inclusion students by meeting with them in small groups and taking a more directed reading approach. Finally, she differentiated products by having them write response papers choosing from a variety of genres, including expository writing, poetry, or first person journaling.

At the midyear conference during the second year of the plan, the assistant superintendent encouraged Lori to share her growth plan with the other teachers by becoming a "trainer" for differentiated instruction the following year. Lori was offered the services of a consultant to assist her as she refined her units, so that she could increase her knowledge, skills, and confidence. Her attendance at a national conference where she could participate in sessions devoted to differentiated instruction would also be arranged. Lori, in turn, would assume the role of a teacher leader or in-house trainer, assisting her colleagues by sharing her experiences and offering help in incorporating differentiated instruction. Her 2 years devoted to differentiated instruction caused her to be continuously aware of individual differences and to search for ways to modify what she does in the classroom to provide enrichment and remediation opportunities for all students.

### Vignette 2

*Type of job-embedded learning:* Projects in curriculum, instruction, or assessment

*Teacher goal:* Redesigning curriculum or assessment/restructuring; providing summer enrichment opportunities to motivate at-risk readers to continue to read over the summer

*Impact on students:* Maintenance of students' reading skills during vacation to prevent regression or "summer slippage"

*District priority:* Enhancement of educational opportunities for students of all ability levels

When reading specialist Ann Willman moved into her newly renovated classroom in Rose Tree Media Elementary School, she was delighted to have a voice-mail system. As summer approached, it struck her as a waste to have the new communication system lie dormant for almost 3 months. Thus, she came up with the idea for her growth goal: to create a developmentally appropriate, motivating summer reading program for at-risk students in first through fourth grades via voice-mail contact with her students. She even gave her action plan project a name: "Hello, Mrs. Willman, It's Me!" One of Rose Tree Media's self-directed options is to implement some form of "best practice" and write about it for publication. Although teachers are required to submit a manuscript for publication, it need not be accepted for completion of the goal. Ann decided to take advantage of the opportunity.

To keep the children focused on reading throughout the summer, Ann wanted to secure three at-level reading books per child and to use the district's Homework Hotline to have the children respond to comprehension questions about their reading. The first year, she wrote a mini-grant for district professional development money and received $300 to purchase the books. The children were invited to practice reading their books and then to call Ann's voice mail to read to her "personally." Ann called into her voice mail at school regularly, kept a log recording each child's progress, and responded by sending out postcards commenting on their reading. The children loved receiving personal mail, and Ann hoped that her notes home would give them the incentive to stay faithful to the assignment. Additionally, all students who completed their three books were invited to join her for an end-of-the summer celebration—a free movie at the local theater with Mrs. Willman.

Ann logged 96 student voice-mail calls the first year of the project. Upon return to the classroom in the fall, Ann tested the students using an informal reading inventory. Although she was not expecting gains, she was delighted that more than 95% of the remedial reading students lost no ground over the summer; they scored at or above their previous spring's reading levels.

Documentation included the log that recorded each student's read aloud, the results of the reading inventory given before the school year ended in June and again in September, and a survey sent home to parents asking for feedback. As a result of the suggestions received from parents, Ann had the children practice using voice mail at school during the second year of the action plan. That way, they were familiar with the format and could focus solely on their reading. She also abandoned the Homework Hotline idea as too cumbersome. Instead, she created individualized learning packets stressing comprehension and vocabulary skills.

Ann described the encouragement that she received from her supervisor as "awesome." "Hello, Mrs. Willman, It's Me!" which her supervisor helped her edit, appeared in *The Reading Teacher,* a journal of the International Reading Association (April 1999). Ann notes, "The self-directed project made me realize I could do something that I didn't think was possible: write for publication about one of my ideas. I have a renewed confidence in my abilities."

In fact, the Summer Voice Mail Reading program has become an annual event. The local educational foundation and Parent–Teacher Group are so supportive of Ann's efforts that they have assumed the cost of the books and the end-of-summer celebration. Moreover, reading teachers from around the country who read about her idea have contacted her about implementing similar summer programs.

## Reflective Journals

Teachers in classrooms around the country ask students to keep journals to summarize what they have learned and to make sense of it. The practice of writing to learn is no less powerful for teachers. A reflective journal includes a record of key events, oftentimes revolving around a specific topic, such as the use of literature circles to discuss trade books in language arts class. In addition to that chronicle of events, it incorporates reflective analyses of experiences, including thought processes, questions, and professional growth that occur related to the topic. Killion (1999) offers the following guidelines for journaling:

1. Describe your teaching actions.
2. Analyze student response to, or the consequences of, those actions.
3. Form conclusions based upon research and best practice to confirm or disprove your thinking. What are you discovering about your teaching?
4. Reflect on how the experience will affect future decisions and teaching actions.

The vignette that follows provides an example of how two elementary teachers used an interactive reflective journal that they shared as part of a collaborative self-directed project.

### Vignette 3

*Type of job-embedded learning:* Reflective journals

*Teacher goal:* Acquiring new knowledge or renewing skills; teaming through writing to share teaching expertise and instructional innovations related to inclusion, the use of literature circles, and the use of multiple intelligence theory

*Impact on students:* Meeting the diverse needs of students by mentoring one another in effectively implementing the three strategies

*District priority:* Developing forums that nurture critical thinking and problem solving

Fran Blanchette and Sue Hendrixson, third- and fourth-grade teachers, respectively, are among the 367 professional staff of Rose Tree Media School District. When the district first offered the self-directed growth option to experienced teachers as part of a differentiated supervision model, their principal encouraged Fran and Sue to try it. They decided that they wanted to collaborate by journaling in a dialog format. They shared a love of writing and considered journals to be a helpful way to reflect outside of face-to-face meetings.

As Fran commented when we interviewed them, "Emotionally, the journal was an outlet for the heart and mind of teaching, while, practically, it allowed us to give and get back instructional ideas."

Sue provided many reasons for the success of their self-directed growth project. First, professional respect and good rapport already characterized their relationship. Both of them felt that comfort level of that kind is a must. Second, they possessed complementary teaching strengths; each could benefit from the other.

Fran was piloting a first-time inclusion project for social studies and science instruction. She was interested in adapting lessons and assessments for her inclusion students. Sue, who had a degree and experience in teaching special education, could provide support and guidance. The district had provided training in adaptation techniques, but Sue would be available daily for practical advice on curriculum considerations and individual needs. Sue could also mentor Fran in the use of literature circles, which she was using in language arts.

Many of Fran's third graders would eventually be in Sue's fourth-grade class. The two of them, therefore, decided that Fran's introduction of circle roles at the conclusion of third-grade year would help to provide a smooth transition to Sue's implementation of fourth-grade literature circles. In a relationship built on a synergistic exchange, Fran, who was a 15-year veteran, could provide advice and serve as a sounding board for Sue, as Sue incorporated multiple intelligence (MI) opportunities into center time.

Fran and Sue's journals documented not only their results, but also their progress toward their stated goals. For example, in one of her first journal entries while experimenting with MI, Sue wrote, "I need to learn to be more comfortable taking chances and getting away from the textbook work to incorporate more activities like this. The children loved the results [of the visual–spatial activity] once the watercolor hit the paper!"

Later, Fran replied, "Sue, your idea to make visuals for students to manipulate when learning equivalent fractions was very clever. May I use it also? Can you see a difference in 'staying power' or how long the children hold onto the concepts with MI? It becomes so much more a part of them, I think."

More exchanges followed, like this one, after Fran visited Sue's classroom to observe Sue's use of literature circles:

> *Fran: It was helpful and positive to come into your room for the literature circles. I appreciate the opportunity. I was so impressed by the children's work. All seemed so actively involved, clear about their role and assignments, and positive and encouraging to one another. From the discussions I heard, it was certainly apparent that they were reporting, inferring, and evaluating. I have several questions: How did you organize? How often do the roles change? How do you monitor their work?*
>
> *Sue: In answer to your question, I organized by reading the book Literature Circles by Harvey Daniels, and then talking over the concepts with Karen [a fifth-grade teacher with extensive experience in reading and language arts]. I think this form of reading is really great for my class. It provides an opportunity for the students to use their pro-social skills with their classmates and a chance to make decisions for themselves. The roles change daily. I float from group to group and join in as a participant. I also have daily journal checks to monitor their entries. Thanks for your support! [She includes several sample ideas and a few pages copied from the book on assigning roles.]*
>
> *Fran: Thanks for your ideas and especially the handout. I have taken a page from your journal and decided to use the index card idea to help the students organize. It is making such a difference. I appreciate the details on literature circles. I admire how creative you are! Sometimes you write about an idea and it just clicks for me and I can make an adaptation to my instruction. Do you mind? Or is this what this [journaling] is all about?*

Neither Fran nor Sue viewed keeping a journal as an overload: "We established a rhythm for writing and responding. Good teachers would reflect anyway, and we love the idea of sharing. It was infused in what we did, not an add-on."

An added benefit was that the two of them shared their journal writing with their students; the passing of the journal back and forth became an eagerly anticipated ritual. For their students, Fran and Sue were modeling collaboration and teamwork, writing as a way of learning, and the importance of lifelong learning.

Notice that, in contrast to the situation in peer coaching, where the observer refrains from communicating judgments to the teacher being observed, Fran and Sue conveyed opinions to one other. Because of their long-term, trusting relationship, they welcomed the feedback, recognizing that they were under no obligation to act on it.

At the conclusion of the first project year, both teachers shared the project with the other teachers on their grade-level teams. Their collaboration had been so successful in terms of teacher learning that their principal suggested they continue for a second year.

Fran explained, "The reflective journaling was individualized for our needs, and thus very rewarding. The administration sent an important message of professional trust in us as teachers. Our principal's confidence in us made us want to soar!"

## Grant Writing and Implementation Applicable to the Classroom

A variety of "teacher friendly" grants are available to individual educators or school districts through businesses, foundations, and state funding. The monies provide resources and materials to supplement district funding and can be a source of significant support for self-directed growth options. For example, the Mathematics Education Trust of the National Council of Teachers of Mathematics supports the improvement of classroom practice and instruction, and increasing teachers, mathematical knowledge by awarding annual grants. In Chapter 3, we shared the story of Maxine and Sue, two high school teachers who first collaborated as peer-coaching partners. An outgrowth of observing in one another's classrooms was that they selected the self-directed growth option and applied for a National Science Foundation grant to write the curriculum for an integrated Advanced Placement calculus and physics course that they now team teach. Another example follows in Vignette 4.

### Vignette 4

*Type of job-embedded learning:* Grant writing and implementation

*Teacher goal:* Redesigning curriculum or assessment/restructuring; designing a 6-week summer intervention program with continued support throughout the school year for prekindergarten students identified as at risk for reading

*Impact on students:* Literacy enrichment opportunities and other supportive measures, such as parent education, are extended to students who might otherwise fall behind and also to their families

*District priority:* As a proactive measure, to "even the playing field" so that every child entering kindergarten has the opportunity to succeed

Elementary reading specialist Rhonda Brunner, a teacher with 9 years of experience, was concerned about the children in her rural school district who entered school already at a disadvantage because of limited language experiences. Research and her years of teaching both suggested that children who begin school far behind their peers in language experience seemed unable ever to "catch up." She knew that the state offered Read-to-Succeed grant money annually. As a leader on the West Perry School District's communication arts committee, she was interested in applying for funding to assist at-risk readers entering kindergarten. In collaboration with the assistant superintendent, she wrote a successful grant that gave birth to LIFT (Literacy Intervention by Families and Teachers).

LIFT, a 6-week summer intervention program that Rhonda designed and coordinated, provides intensive language and literacy experiences for children entering kindergarten who are identified as most at risk for nonachievement in reading, writing, speaking, and listening. Identified students and their parents are invited to attend a 6-week summer literacy program held at the elementary schools. The summer sessions run 2 days per week, and the grant provides funding for transportation to those who need it. The program includes an engaging environment that immerses the children in early literacy activities. Instruction is individualized to meet each child's needs as related to letter identification, phonemic awareness, and exposure to print materials.

Once school begins, the kindergarten teachers, in collaboration with the reading specialist and the speech-and-language clinician, continue the intervention by providing assessment-driven extended learning opportunities. Parent involvement is an integral part of LIFT; parents must consent to participate in the summer enrichment program one evening per week with their children. Parents must also attend evening parent education programs facilitated by Rhonda throughout the school year. The children receive ongoing formative assessments.

Three cohorts of children have participated in LIFT and have completed periodic standardized reading assessments. According to the data, 58 of 75 students (77%) are now performing at or above grade level in reading.

## Training of Trainers Model

In the "training of trainers" model of job-embedded learning, a teacher volunteers to become a "resident expert" in an area of curriculum, instruction, assessment, or technology that is of high interest to that teacher. After first building skills and knowledge in the specific area (often as a self-directed growth project), teachers present in-house workshops or seminars to their colleagues and offer follow-up support when needed (Loucks-Horsley et al., 1998).

Lori Stollar's 2-year self-directed growth project on differentiated instruction, described in Vignette 1, led her to become a trainer of other teachers in the district. She facilitated a group of 18 high school teachers on differentiating instruction. Similarly, with the fiscal support provided by her Read-to-Succeed grant, Rhonda, the reading specialist in Vignette 4, was able to spend a year as the district's literacy specialist, coaching classroom teachers as they implemented a new communication arts program. She modeled lessons on guided reading, shared reading, and interactive writing based on the needs and requests of teachers.

## Summary

As evidenced by the examples and teacher vignettes in this section on self-directed growth, numerous options exist for formulating an action plan. Practitioners new to the process of designing their own professional growth experiences may wish to choose from one of the examples of job-embedded learning provided in this chapter: projects related to curriculum, instruction, or assessment; reflective journals; grant writing applicable to the classroom; and becoming a resident expert or trainer.

# SUCCESSFULLY IMPLEMENTING THE SELF-DIRECTED GROWTH OPTION

We have offered a strong rationale for incorporating self-directed teacher growth plans as a powerful tool for structuring individualized learning experiences for teachers. Here, we summarize our recommendations to administrative teams piloting this form of differentiated supervision:

1. Offer training to teachers on how to use available data from in-class observations, teacher or student artifacts, examination of student work, and standardized assessments to set specific, meaningful, and challenging goals that clearly relate to students' learning. The goals may be categorized as "improvement goals" to refine current teaching practice, "renewal goals" to acquire new knowledge or skills, or "restructuring goals" to redesign curriculum, instruction, or assessment.

2. Use the self-directed growth option as a means of blending individual improvement goals with organizational development. The integration of supervision with professional development efforts strengthens a schoolwide vision and mission, helping to ensure that all stakeholders move toward common goals.

3. Provide a comprehensive and consistent structure that can serve as a road map in formulating an action plan to meet stated goals. Include strategies for accomplishing the goals, a timeline, required resources, documentation of progress, and some form of concluding self-assessment.

4. Take an active leadership role in collaborating with teachers involved in self-directed projects. Offer guidance, fiscal and emotional support, networking opportunities with colleagues or outside resource people, and recognition of teachers' efforts. After approving the teacher's action plan, keep in mind that, although teachers are "self-directed," they continue to look to their administrators for advice, expertise, and encouragement. Be sure to meet with them periodically.

5. Formally gather evidence that illustrates the impact of self-directed growth on teachers and on students across the district. Share examples of teacher learning with faculty, board members, parents, and community members. Celebrate teacher innovation and excellence as part of a professional culture of continuous growth.

---

**EXERCISE 4.2  Jigsaw Activity on Job-Embedded Learning Vignettes**

---

*Step 1*   Form "home groups" of four. Count off from 1 to 4 within each group. Each team member becomes an expert on the correspondingly numbered vignette. Read and take notes on your assigned vignette. List what you perceive to be the strengths of the project, making connections between the key concepts in the chapter on self-directed professional growth options and the teacher's individualized action plan. After outlining the strengths, consider any suggestions that you might have to enhance the teacher's action plan.

*Step 2*   Join with the two or three other experts assigned to the same vignette as you. Share your list of strengths and personal reactions to this actual example of teacher experience with a self-directed growth plan. Try to reach several points of consensus regarding strengths as related to key concepts.

*Step 3*   Return to your home group. Lead a discussion about your assigned vignette. Continue in a round-robin fashion until all vignettes are covered in detail.

*Step 4*   For further discussion, make a summarizing list of the common characteristics that you discovered across vignettes.

---

# CHAPTER SUMMARY

Self-directed teacher growth is a supervisory option in which experienced, competent teachers are given the opportunity to work alone, in pairs, or in small groups to design job-embedded learning experiences to further their professional growth and to have a positive impact on their students' learning. Teachers begin by identifying a focus area of curriculum, instruction, or assessment that they are interested in exploring. They devise a goal statement that is clear, specific, and measurable, and that in some way correlates with building or district goals. The goal statement should be data driven and should relate to refining current practice (improvement goals), acquiring new knowledge or skills (renewal goals), or redesigning curriculum, instruction, or assessment (restructuring goals). The action plan submitted to the principal includes concrete steps to be taken, the roles to be played by others, resources needed, and a proposed timeline. For accountability, teachers document their progress along the way and prepare a year-end report.

Administrators play a key role in facilitating teachers' self-directed plans. Initially, they review the action plan to ensure that it matches the predetermined criteria, and they accept or reject it on that basis. They meet face to face with each teacher who has selected the self-directed option. This meeting establishes a shared understanding of the teacher's goals, steps for implementation, timeline, resource needs, method of documentation, and evaluation procedures. Principals then connect with the teachers periodically throughout the year to provide support, to share relevant resources, to review progress, and to assist with unexpected challenges. Principals also arrange some form of sharing mechanism to celebrate accomplishments and to extend individual teacher learning throughout the building or district. Evidence of impact on student learning as a result of self-directed projects should be collected and disseminated to faculty, board members, parents, and the community.

Supervision that occurs through structured, experiential opportunities for teachers to collaborate and grow in an authentic context as part of their daily routines is known as job-embedded learning. The types of job-embedded professional growth options discussed in this chapter are projects in curriculum, instruction, or assessment; reflective journals; grant writing and implementation; and a training-of-trainers model. The vignettes that exemplify these types of job-embedded learning illustrate the power of the self-directed option, when offered in a supportive supervisory climate, to motivate competent professionals to become risk takers who set meaningful goals and achieve unexpected levels of professional growth.

# DISCUSSION QUESTIONS

**1.** Having read this chapter, what do you perceive as the advantages of giving teachers the option to create and implement a self-directed growth plan?

**2.** Return to the limitations of self-directed teacher growth that you noted at the beginning of this chapter. Have you opinions changed, or do you still perceive them as reality? Explain.

**3.** Discuss the role of the principal in facilitating self-directed teacher growth. What problems might principals encounter in this role? Explain.

**4.** Discuss the advantages and disadvantages of providing teachers with job-embedded learning opportunities in addition to structured, formal in-service days set aside for professional development.

**5.** Discuss a project that you personally might implement based on the four types of job-embedded learning discussed in the chapter.

# THEORY-INTO-PRACTICE APPLICATIONS

**1.** Using Figure 4.2 and the personal goal-setting worksheet that you completed in Exercise 4.1 as guides, create an action plan that you might complete during the course of the school year.

**2.** Pair up with another member of the class. Exchange the action plans that you completed above. Now take the role of the building principal. Use the Administrator Assessment form in Figure 4.5 to review your partner's action plan and make suggestions for revisions or improvement. Work individually. Afterward, hold a conference in which the principal provides feedback and the teacher responds to the feedback.

**3.** If possible, search in surrounding school districts for teachers who are engaged in some form of self-directed individualized growth plan. Interview those teachers to discover their perceptions of the rewards that they gain and challenges that they face while participating in that supervisory option.

# CASE STUDY: SELF-DIRECTED TEACHER GROWTH

Middletown Area School District's Differentiated Supervision and Evaluation Plan incorporates a 3-year cycle for tenured teachers who have been rated as satisfactory. The principal, on a rotating basis, observes one-third of the experienced faculty. The teacher and administrator collaborate to decide whether they will engage in traditional administrative monitoring (one unannounced observation and postconference) or a more clinical cycle. The cycle includes a preobservation conference to establish a teacher-initiated focus for data collection, followed by the observation, data analysis, and a postobservation conference. In the 2 years following the observation year, teachers are required to choose from a number of differentiated supervision options. These options include peer coaching and self-directed professional development. During the 2 years in an alternative mode, the teachers keep a portfolio of artifacts from their professional growth years, which they, in turn, share with their principal when they return to the third year of the cycle.

Ken and Kevin, two enthusiastic eighth-grade social studies teachers, have enjoyed the opportunities provided to them and, more important, to their students, through the self-directed growth option. Ken, with 5 years' experience, entered teaching as a nontraditional student pursuing a second career. Kevin has worked in the district for 10 years. Both of them look at differentiated supervision as a meaningful approach to their own professional development, tailor-made to fit their needs. Middletown, the location of their school district, is a community steeped in history. They share the philosophy that studying history at the local level offers the perfect venue for middle school students' awareness and appreciation of and ownership in their historical roots.

Ken and Kevin have collaborated on more than one occasion, and each time their collegiality leads to more sophisticated self-directed growth projects that tie into the state and national history standards. One of their early foci was revising their units of planned instruction to promote more active learning. As Kevin explains, "History isn't teaching facts and events.

We want the students to take the role of actual historians; it's a historiographical perspective. Our kids visit museums, state archives, and historical societies to explore primary source documents. They've discovered several 'Negro cemeteries' [burial sites for veterans of the Civil War] in their own backyards."

The pair began applying for grants at the district level to fund their innovative ideas, successfully attaining a "One for the Kids" mini-grant. In 2003–2004, with a new sense of confidence, they set their sights higher. Their self-directed project was directly related to facilitating their students' participation in National History Day by applying for a technology grant to the Teaching American History Project. They were elated to receive an $8000 award to equip their students with state-of-the-art hardware and software to create multimedia presentations.

Did they collect data to support the impact of their professional growth upon their students? Ken reported that in 2002–2003, only eight of their students went on to compete at the district level. This year, 51 students advanced to district. Moreover, one team, whose project explored the Union Canal, which originates in Middletown, made it to state level. Their students found meaning and relevance in the curriculum as it came alive during their investigative work. They were encouraged to focus on theme-based issues and to develop lifelong skills, such as cooperation, commitment, self-direction, critical thinking, and citizenship.

Ken and Kevin are already looking forward to their next collaborative project. This time they plan to research and create a local history textbook with the help of their students.

## Questions for Discussion

1. After reading and reflecting on Chapter 4, what are your thoughts about requiring teachers to engage in a differentiated supervision option during 2 years of a 3-year cycle?

2. Do you perceive a direct correlation between Kevin and Ken's professional development project and student learning?

3. Relate the two teachers' supervisory experience with the concept of job-embedded learning.

4. Using the research base, what suggestions might you offer Kevin and Ken to maximize their self-directed growth project?

5. If you were Kevin and Ken's principal, how would you encourage them to proceed when you met with them to review their artifacts during the administrative monitoring (third year) of the cycle?

# REFERENCES

BARTH, R. S. (2001). *Learning by heart.* New York: Wiley: Jossey-Bass.

BROOKFIELD, S. D. (1986). *Understanding and facilitating adult learning.* San Francisco, CA: Jossey-Bass.

COVEY, S. R. (1996). Three roles of the leader in the new paradigm. In F. Hesselbein, M. Goldsmith, & R. Beckhard (Eds.), *The leader of the future: New visions, strategies, and practices for the next era* (pp. 149–160). San Francisco, CA: Jossey-Bass.

DANIELSON, C., & MCGREAL, T. L. (2000). *Teacher evaluation to enhance professional practice.* Alexandria, VA & Princeton, NJ: Association for Supervision and Curriculum Development & Educational Teaching Services.

DUKE, D. (1990). Setting goals for professional development. *Educational Leadership, 47*(8), 71–75.

GLATTHORN, A. A. (1997). *Differentiated supervision* (2nd ed.). Alexandria, VA: Association for Supervision and Curriculum Development.

GORDON, S. P., & NICELY, R. F. (1998). Supervision and staff development. In G. R. Firth & E. F. Pajak (Eds.), *Handbook of research on school supervision* (pp. 801–841). New York: Simon Schuster Macmillan.

HARGREAVES, A. (1994). *Changing teachers, changing times: Teachers' work and culture in the postmodern age.* New York: Teachers College Press.

HOLLOWAY, J. H. (2003). Research link: Linking professional development to student learning. *Educational Leadership, 61*(3), 85–87.

KILLION, J. (1999). Journaling. *Journal of Staff Development, 20*(3), 36–37.

KNOWLES, M. S. (1990). *The adult learner: A neglected species.* Houston, TX: Golf Publication.

LIEBERMAN, A. (1995). Practices that support teacher development: Transforming conceptions of professional learning. *Phi Delta Kappan, 76*(8), 591–596.

LOUCKS-HORSLEY, S., HEWSON, P. H., LOVE, N., & STILES, K. E. (1998). *Designing professional development for teachers of science and mathematics.* Thousand Oaks, CA: Corwin.

National Partnership for Excellence and Accountability in Teaching. (2000). *Revisioning professional development.* Oxford, OH: National Staff Development Council.

National Policy Board for Educational Administration. (2002). *ELCC standards for advanced programs in educational leadership.* Retrieved from http://www.npbea.org/ELCC/index.html.

RICHARDSON, J. (2002, February/March). Reach for the stars: Individual learning plans allow teachers to take charge of their own learning. *Tool for Schools.* Oxford, OH: National Staff Development Council.

SERGIOVANNI, T. J., & STARRATT, R. J. (2006). *Supervision: A redefinition* (8th ed.). Boston, MA: McGraw-Hill.

SPARKS, D., & HIRSH, S. (2000). A national plan for improving, professional development. Retrieved from: http://www.nsdc.org/library/authors/NSDCPlan.cfm.

SPECK, M., & KNIPE, C. (2001). *Why can't we get it right? Professional development in our schools.* Thousand Oaks, CA: Corwin.

WILLMAN, A. (1999). Hello, Mrs. Willman, it's me! *The Reading Teacher. 52*(7), 788–789.

WOOD, F. H., & MCQUARRIE, F. (1999). On-the-job learning. *Journal of Staff Development, 20*(3), 10–13.

ZMUDA, A., KUKLIS, R., & KLINE, E. (2004). *Transforming schools: Creating a culture of continuous improvement.* Alexandria, VA: Association for Supervision and Curriculum Development.

# SUGGESTIONS FOR FURTHER READING AND RESEARCH

GUSKEY, T. R., & HUBERMAN, M. (Eds.). (1995) *Professional development in education: New paradigms and practices.* New York: Teachers College Press.

SCHLECHTY, P. C. (2001). *Shaking up the schoolhouse: How to support and sustain educational innovation.* San Francisco, CA: Jossey-Bass.

SCHMOKER, M. (1999). *Results: The key to continuous school improvement* (2nd ed.), Alexandria, VA: Association for Supervision and Curriculum Development.

SPARKS, D. (2002). *Designing powerful professional development for teachers and principals.* Oxford, OH: National Staff Development Council.

WILSHIRE, D. K. (1991). *Teachers in transition: An exploratory study of self-directed change and educational planning in professional development.* Unpublished doctoral dissertation. The Pennsylvania State University, University Park.

# CHAPTER 5

# *ACTION RESEARCH*

**W**E ASSERTED in our platform of beliefs that teaching is a complex problem-solving activity and that supervision and evaluation processes should honor that complexity. Action research is a powerful tool for educators to employ in navigating the complex world of teaching and learning. Good teachers are constantly engaged in a process of asking questions about students and their learning and gathering information, albeit in an informal way, to answer those questions. Consider the following example.

Jamie, a third-grade teacher, noticed that Patti, one of her students, exhibited two very different patterns in beginning the school day. On some days, Patti was bubbly, smiley, talkative, and very much on top of the tasks that started the day. On other days, she would come into the room looking very sullen and angry, put her head down on her desk, and ignore both other people and the morning tasks. The inconsistent pattern of behavior puzzled Jamie, so she began to keep track of Patti's morning behavior. After a few weeks of observing the pattern, Jamie was able to relate Patti's behavior to her parents' recent divorce. When Patti stayed at her mom's house, she was bubbly and on track; when she stayed with her dad, she seemed angry, withdrawn, and tired. At the first parent conference a few weeks later, Jamie was able to talk with Patti's parents about the pattern. The parents were grateful and were able to work together to help Patti deal with the divorce more successfully. Although she was not aware of it and would not have labeled it as such, Jamie was involved in the process of informal action research.

Action research is a process that engages teachers in formally asking and answering questions about their own practice. By using this powerful supervisory tool teachers can become more reflective, can enhance their problem-solving capacities, and can facilitate the development of an inquiry stance toward teaching. This chapter introduces you to the process of action research as a supervision activity. The first section discusses the meaning, goals, history, and benefits of action research. The second section describes the action research process. The final section discusses the process of facilitating action research as a component of the teacher supervision and evaluation system.

## GUIDING QUESTIONS FOR PREREADING REFLECTION AND JOURNALING

- Thinking about your practice as a classroom teacher, can you identify any ongoing puzzles, problems, or issues that you struggle(d) to understand and solve? Make a list of some of them.

- As an experienced educator you have been exposed to research in professional classes. What is your attitude about the impact of research on day-to-day teaching? Is there any connection? Would research conducted by teachers seem more credible to you? Why or why not?

- One of your tasks as a teacher is to collect data about your students and their learning. Make a list of all the different types of data, both formal and informal, that you collect routinely about your students during a typical week of teaching.

- Have you ever had the opportunity to work with either another teacher or an outside expert to examine and try to solve problems that you face in your day-to-day work? If so, describe what that experience was like. If not, what would you see as potential advantages and disadvantages of such a process?

# PURPOSE AND BENEFITS OF ACTION RESEARCH

## History and Definition

Action research is not a new phenomenon in education. Some trace its roots as far back as the work of John Dewey near the beginning of the twentieth century (Glanz, 2003). Although Dewey's emphasis on problem solving, reflection, and the scientific method are certainly key components of action research, most experts agree that Kurt Lewin, a social psychologist, brought action research to the social sciences during the late 1930s. In this work, Lewin attempted to have groups of people use scientific inquiry to solve real-life problems that they were facing. "Lewin sought to find ways to involve social actors (school teachers and others) with researchers through group decision making and other elaborate problem-solving techniques as a way of implementing social and cultural changes" (Hollingsworth & Sockett, 1994, p. 3).

Lewin's work influenced many educators, most notably Stephen Corey, a professor at Teachers College of Columbia University, who pioneered the translation of action research into the field of education during the early 1950s. Corey explained his rationale for turning to action research as a school improvement strategy in a 1953 book entitled *Action Research to Improve School Practice.*

> *Our schools cannot keep up with the life they are supposed to sustain and improve unless teachers, pupils, supervisors, administrators, and school patrons continuously examine what they are doing. Singly and in groups, they must use their imaginations creatively and constructively to identify the practices that must be changed to meet the needs and demands of modern life, courageously try out those practices that give better promise, and methodically and systematically gather evidence to test their worth. This is the practice that I call action research. What I will talk about is research that is undertaken by educational practitioners because they believe that by so doing they can make better decisions and engage in better practice. (p. viii)*

During the late 1950s and early 1960s some educators embraced the notion of teacher research, but, following the launch of Sputnik in 1957, the rush toward educational competition with the Soviet Union elevated the academic expert to new heights at the expense of classroom teachers. Teachers were now seen as the problem, not the solution, to school improvement, so action research lay dormant for several decades in the United States.

Fortunately, the tradition of teachers as researchers was kept alive in England during the 1960s and 1970s by Lawrence Stenhouse, John Elliott, and others (see Elliott, 1991). Stenhouse (1975), a curriculum scholar, asked teachers to become engaged in a process of curriculum development that would meld action research, curriculum improvement, and staff development. Elliott developed a classroom action research network in Great Britain that focused on making the day-to-day work of teachers a complex interaction of theory and practice (Hollingsworth & Sockett, 1994). The work of Stenhouse and Elliott also influenced the development of teacher research networks in other European countries and in Australia.

The teacher research paradigm was reborn in the United States during the late 1980s, as a result of its close theoretical connection with the concept of teachers as reflective practitioners. Early in the decade, Donald Schon's (1983) work challenged the prevailing notion that teachers were primarily technicians whose task was to implement the theoretical constructs developed by researchers and other experts. In attempting to deal successfully with the messy world of educational practice.

Schon relied heavily on the wisdom of teacher practice, gained from years of thoughtful experience, and on the capacity of teachers to generate new knowledge about their own teaching. Schon's ideas exerted tremendous influence on the literature in the fields of teacher supervision and preservice teacher education. The concept of teacher as reflective practitioner quickly captured center stage. Problem posing, data gathering, and thoughtful interpretation became critical features of effective teaching practice. The resurgence of the teacher as a primary actor in generating knowledge about teaching resulted in the publication of several books during the 1990s celebrating the concept of action research (see Cochran-Smith & Lytle, 1993; Hollingsworth & Sockett, 1994; Burnaford, Fischer, & Hobson, 2001; Dana & Yendol-Silva, 2003; Glanz, 2003).

Contemporary authors tend to use several terms interchangeably to refer to the process of educational practitioners systematically studying their own practice. Some use "action research," others, "teacher research," and still others, "teacher inquiry." Though these terms differ slightly in meaning, they all share three fundamental assumptions: (1) research starts from where the action is; (2) the practitioner's practical wisdom is a central source of knowledge; and (3) research leads to personal and social change as well as to curricular and instructional change" (Hollingsworth & Sockett, 1994).

We have chosen to use the term action research rather than either of the others. Although teachers might inquire about their practice in many ways (e.g., peer coaching and collegial development groups), action research implies a very specific process for conducting inquiry. It involves problem posing, planning, and systematic data collection and interpretation as well as taking action to improve practice. Thus, research carries a more precise meaning than inquiry. We also prefer the more inclusive term action research as opposed to teacher research. As this text focuses on teacher supervision, we write about teachers using this process as part of the supervision system; however, all educational professionals can engage in research about their practice. Action research is the process of practitioners asking well-defined questions about their practice, systematically gathering and interpreting data to answer those questions, and consequently taking action to improve practice. Action research projects may be carried out individually or as group projects. They can focus on a wide variety of classroom- and school-level questions.

## Types of Action Research

The questions that can serve as the driving force for the process of action research are almost limitless. To help teachers begin the process, we have found it useful to categorize questions into five major types. Most action research questions fall into one of these categories:

- inquiry focused on students
- inquiry focused on teaching practices
- inquiry focused on the teacher

- inquiry focused on curriculum
- inquiry focused on the school as an organization.

Every action research project will most likely touch several of these categories, but focus primarily on one. These five types seem to make sense to teachers and provide an easy starting point for generating potential research questions.

### Action Research Focused on Students

Inquiry focused on students is often a very natural starting point for the action research process. There are so many students with varying needs and individual differences that most teachers have no problem identifying issues or puzzles arising from their daily interactions. Questions that drive action research projects may focus on cognitive, behavioral, social and emotional, or psychomotor domains. They may be targeted at one student or at a small group of students. Examples of action research questions focused on students:

- Why has my 10th-grade social studies student given up and decided to make no effort to succeed?
- What role does my ESL student play in small-group cooperative learning activities?
- What role can his strengths in music and art play in helping my first-grade student learn to read more effectively?
- Are there ways to increase the intrinsic motivation of my two seventh graders who seem to work only when there is an external reward associated with it?
- How do quiet learners prefer to learn?

### Action Research Focused on Teaching Practices

Questions focusing on teaching practices and their efficacy are appropriate for any teacher, but they are often especially attractive to teachers who are in the early stages of their careers and still attempting to refine and broaden their repertoire of teaching strategies they can also be attractive to veteran teachers in a new teaching assignment. Action research projects directed at teaching practice are similar in some ways to self-directed growth projects described in Chapter 4. Both types of projects may focus on teaching practices or curriculum and may require the development of new teaching behaviors or refinement of current practices. There is, however, a fundamental difference between the two. Action research projects are driven by questions or wonderings about some aspect of one's work, whereas self-directed growth projects are driven by goal setting aimed at acquiring new knowledge or skills, refining teaching practices, or redesigning curriculum.

Teachers who engage in action research are driven by not knowing something and wanting to figure it out. Their ultimate aim is to take action, but they either are not sure whether taking action will have a positive impact on their students or are not sure what action to take. In contrast, teachers who engage in self-directed growth projects have already decided that taking a particular course of action is the right thing to do. The self-directed project is aimed at putting that good idea into practice.

To make the distinction clearer, let us return to two vignettes from Chapter 4. Lori Stollar's goal was to learn about differentiated instruction and to provide differentiated learning opportunities for her students. She was already confident that differentiated instruction was the right direction to go in. If Lori's project had been an action research project, she might have been driven by a question concerning the impact differentiated instruction might have on her students. She would still have had to learn how to provide differentiated instruction, but her focus would have been on assessing its impact, not simply learning how to provide it.

Ann Willman wanted to motivate at-risk students to continue reading over the summer, and thereby to maintain their reading skills. She developed an outstanding summer reading program and wrote about it for an educational journal. If her project had been an action research project, her question might have been what impact a summer reading program would have on students' ability to maintain their skills. She might also have asked about the aspects of the program that had the greatest impact on student skill maintenance. She would still have had to implement the summer program to answer these questions, but the focus would have been on assessing its impact.

The difference between the two project types, then, is focus. Self-directed growth projects often have elements of wondering embedded in them. For example, Lori wondered how to motivate students, who needed to be challenged, to choose higher order activities. Ann actually measured the impact of her summer program on students' skills. However, in both projects, the wonderings arose as subcomponents once the project was underway; they did not drive the projects. Action research projects are driven by wonderings. They are front and center in the process. The goal is to begin to answer the questions. It is precisely because of these differences that both self-directed growth and action research should be included as components of a teacher supervision system. The following questions are focused on teaching practices:

- What type of behavioral expectations must I establish in order to use science talks effectively with students?
- Will the use of literature circles increase my students' enjoyment of reading?
- What impact will the use of technology-enhanced lessons have on the attentiveness of my students?
- Which method or combination of methods of parent communication will be most effective—a web site, e-mail, team newsletter, or home–school journals?
- What conflict resolution strategies can I use to help students become more capable of handling conflict situations independently?

***Action Research Focused on the Teacher*** Research questions that focus on the teacher are often targeted at the teacher's beliefs and the congruence between beliefs and practice. The teacher may also focus on work habits, personality traits, career stage development, or some other personal aspect of teaching. Action research focused on the teacher tends to be less common than research on students or on teaching practices. Examining oneself requires a high degree of self-confidence and the willingness to step back and examine oneself objectively. When teachers are comfortable taking this type of risk, research focusing on self as teacher can truly lead to powerful transformations because changes in beliefs, thinking, and practice are required. Examples of questions focusing on the teacher are:

- How do my attitudes about students affect how I intervene when they are behaving inappropriately?
- How well do my assessment practices match my beliefs about how students learn?
- How can I become less defensive and more open to having parent volunteers in my classroom on a regular basis?
- How does my own learning style affect the variety of teaching strategies that I use and do not use in my classroom?
- Can I use a reflective journal as a tool that will help me to grow professionally at this late stage in my career?

***Action Research Focused on Curriculum*** As they begin to explore issues of students, pedagogy, and self, teachers often realize that the curriculum is exerting a significant influence on both students and their teaching practice. For example, the teacher who pursues the question, mentioned earlier, concerning the use of conflict resolution strategies by children may discover that there is little or no time to teach and to practice conflict resolution strategies because the curriculum is filled with content from the first minute of school to the last. Consequently, the teacher may begin an action research project that focuses on the content of his or her curriculum in an attempt to find content that can be jettisoned without harming students.

Curriculum-focused projects can travel beyond the individual teacher's classroom. Teachers do not necessarily share students, teaching philosophies, or personal characteristics, but they do share curriculum. As a result, curriculum is often a fertile ground for collaborative action research. Such curriculum-oriented projects can be threatening for those individuals who are charged with maintaining curriculum coherence across classrooms and buildings. The implications for action resulting from curriculum projects are not limited to a single teacher. They concern multiple teachers, perhaps even the school as a whole. We suggest that the potential scope and implications of an action research project be thought about at the initiation of the project and discussed openly among the teachers and curriculum administrators in order to decrease the potential for surprises and hurt feelings later on. (We will return to this issue in the final section on facilitating the action research process.) The following example questions focus on curriculum:

- How can we incorporate higher level math into our interdisciplinary unit on genetics?

- How can I incorporate more primary sources into our unit on the revolutionary war?

- How can I design the unit on fractions so that it focuses more on a conceptual rather than on a procedural understanding of equivalent fractions?

- How can we revise our middle school reading program so that students become better critical readers of both print and electronic texts?

- How can I redesign the unit on Westward Expansion to make it more inclusive of multicultural views and developmentally appropriate?

***Action Research Focused on the School as an Organization*** Whereas curriculum-focused action research projects may or may not travel beyond the doors of a single classroom, action research projects focused on the school as an organization go beyond the individual teacher by their very definition. Organizationally focused projects often involve collaboration by a group. Collaboration offers several benefits to this type of project. First, the project is larger in scope and generally requires greater effort at data collection. Collaboration makes data collection feasible. Second, having multiple players involved in interpreting the data generally increases the accuracy of the conclusions that are drawn. Third, the implications for action resulting from the project will most likely require the commitment and cooperation of multiple stakeholders. Having multiple stakeholders involved in the entire project makes implementation of resulting changes more likely, especially if the participants come from a variety of roles. Finally, like curriculum projects, organizationally focused projects can be threatening because of their scope. The threat and potential divisiveness of the implications resulting from the project may be reduced if multiple players are involved.

Collaboratively developed action research projects that focus on the school as an organization are potentially very powerful forms of inquiry. Their power lies in their ability to make visible for examination structures, policies, traditions, and procedures that are often taken for granted as "the way we do things around here." Those taken-for-granted ways of doing things sometimes result in inequalities within the system, and they often make innovation extremely difficult by imposing bureaucratic and systemic roadblocks to change. The power of such traditions lies in their invisibility. Collaborative action research strips that power away and may lead to rethinking and change. Examples of organizationally focused action research questions are:

- What are the advantages and disadvantages of grouping students homogeneously for English in our middle school?
- Why do we have such a difficult time attracting a diverse group of parents to participate in our various school activities for parents?
- How can we more effectively meet the needs of new students, especially those for whom English is a second language?
- How can we make our high school a more caring place for all students?
- How can specials be scheduled more effectively so that our primary-level team has more time to work together on curriculum?

## Benefits of Action Research

As mentioned earlier, we believe that action research can be a powerful mechanism for transforming teachers individually and the culture of teaching as a whole. For the individual teacher, engagement in a single action research project is not an end in itself. The project is really a vehicle for adopting an inquiry stance toward teaching on a daily basis.

Possessing an inquiry-oriented stance toward teaching heightens the possibility that teachers will function as adaptive experts as opposed to routine experts. Hammerness, Darling-Hammond, and Bransford (2005) use the label adaptive expertise to refer to teachers who are experts in what they do, but who are open to the possibility of engaging in new practices when those practices have the clear potential to be more beneficial to students. Engaging in new practices requires that teachers give up their expert ways of functioning and learn new behaviors. They are willing to live through the temporary period in which they lose efficiency and feel less like experts because they believe that eventually they will become adept at using the new behaviors that will be beneficial for students. Lori Stollar's commitment, as illustrated in Chapter 4, to learn how to use differentiated instruction is an example of a teacher who is willing to disrupt the status quo in order to serve students more effectively. In contrast, routine experts are those who have developed a very efficient system of teaching practice and adhere to it consistently. They refuse to try out new behaviors because they fear the temporary loss of efficiency and effectiveness. To make this concept clear, we can use the analogy of two general surgeons.

Both surgeons have been practicing for more than 20 years, have done hundreds of gall bladder operations successfully, and enjoy fine reputations. Surgeon A, our adaptive expert, embraces new laser and laparoscopic surgical techniques because she believes that the benefits for patients are too important to ignore. In making this choice, she must be willing to take on the role of neophyte and work diligently to use these new techniques well. Initially, she is not as efficient in performing these new techniques as she was with a scalpel. Eventually, she returns to the same level of efficiency with the new techniques. Surgeon B, our routine expert, refuses to give up his level of expertise and continues to perform surgery only with the scalpel and traditional methods. Like surgery, teaching is a very complicated endeavor. Efficiency is enticing. Giving up efficiency to learn new strategies is difficult. Developing an inquiry-oriented stance should increase the likelihood that teachers will become adaptive as opposed to routine experts. Action research is a powerful tool in the repertoire of a teacher with an inquiry-oriented stance.

"An inquiry-oriented stance actually becomes a professional positioning, where questioning one's own practice becomes part of the teacher's work and eventually a part of the teaching culture" (Dana, Gimbert, & Silva, 1999, p. 2). Teachers who have adopted an inquiry stance approach teaching in a fundamentally different and more productive way (Cochran-Smith & Lytle, 1993). Such teachers continually pose questions about their teaching and its impact on learners and pursue answers to those questions. They do not wait for problems to arise before questioning what they do. They continuously ask themselves five questions:

1. What am I doing,
2. Why am I doing it that way,
3. What impact is it having on learners,
4. How might I do things differently, and ?
5. If I did things differently, what impact might it have on learners?

Teachers who have an inquiry stance also are open to questions from others and to unexpected evidence concerning the impact of their practice on learners. When students, parents, and administrators ask them questions about what they are doing in the classroom, they view the question as an opportunity to learn. They can tolerate the ambiguity of temporarily not knowing the answer, but they are not content to stay in that position. They take action to try to find the answer. They listen to the question carefully, reflect on it, and try to gather good information to begin to answer it accurately. Such teachers do not change their practice simply because someone else raises questions about it, but they do not shut down and become defensive either.

In gathering evidence concerning the effects of their teaching on learners, teachers who have an inquiry stance demonstrate a commitment to following the evidence wherever it may lead. They look for multiple sources of evidence in order to obtain a more comprehensive picture. For example, if they are trying to understand why students as a class did not do well on a test, they might take several actions including asking the students, checking the test against their lesson plans and the textbook to make sure that the content was appropriate, discussing the test results with a colleague who teaches the same material, and analyzing test items to identify exactly where the students had problems. This commitment to follow the evidence implies a willingness on the part of the teacher to change his or her way of doing things if that is what the evidence suggests.

Though they are consistently engaged in learning from their own practice, teachers with an inquiry stance also welcome the opportunity to work with and learn from others. They consistently seek better ways of doing things from external sources. They observe the practices of colleagues, read professional literature, take courses, and attend conferences and workshops. They have the confidence to take risks and to try new approaches. However, they do not adopt the ideas of others uncritically; they treat new ideas as hypotheses whose worth must be tested in terms of their actual impact in the classroom.

In short, an inquiry stance is associated with reflection, self-assessment, and a mindset of continuous improvement. Yet, experience indicates that only a small percentage of teachers adopt an inquiry stance naturally, and that most people need help and support in developing such a stance. Action research offers that support. Undertaking an action research project requires teachers to adopt many of these characteristics and behaviors. The teacher must ask questions, collect and interpret evidence to answer the questions, follow the evidence where it leads, and make changes in practice as a result of what has been learned. By providing practice with these behaviors, an action research project can be the stimulus that leads the teacher to adopt an inquiry orientation. If the teacher works in a school that is marked by a collaborative culture of inquiry and action research, the likelihood of the teacher adopting an inquiry stance is greatly increased. Exercise 5.1 provides practice in questioning one's practice.

---

**EXERCISE 5.1   Questioning Your Practice**

**Part 1 (Individual)** Choose topic a, b, or c below and answer the five questions that mark the practice of teaching with an inquiry stance:

1. What do I do?
2. Why do I do it that way?
3. What impact does it have on learners?
4. How might I do it differently?
5. What impact might it have if I do it differently?

Topic a.   How you assign student grades.

Topic b.   How you group students for instruction.

Topic c.   How you establish classroom rules and procedures.

If you are no longer teaching, answer the questions in reference to your former teaching practice. As you answer each of the five questions, jot down the answers and bring them to class with you.

**Part 2 (Triad)** Link up with two other students who, in part I, answered the questions in reference to the same topic of teaching as you. Discuss the similarities and differences in how you handled that aspect of teaching and also in how you answered the five questions.

**Part 3 (Triad)** With your partners discuss the following questions. Did this activity cause you to wonder about or doubt the efficacy of your practice? Were you able to identify any alter ways for handling that aspect of your practice? Would you take any action to change your practice as a result? Why or why not?

---

The benefits of action research for the school as a whole follow from the benefits for the individual teacher. When teachers are engaged in carrying out action research projects and are given the opportunity to share their work with colleagues, the level of professional conversation in the school and the school culture change dramatically. Drawing on the work of Little (1982) and others, Lieberman and Miller described the types of changes that occur when teachers are encouraged to talk with one another about teaching and to work together to find solutions to common problems. "In the process of encouraging these activities, traditions of practicality, isolation and privacy were replaced by shared ownership of issues and problems of practice, a willingness to consider alter explanations, and a desire to work together as colleagues" (Lieberman & Miller,1994, p. 210). In her investigation of teachers who exhibited an inquiry stance in their teaching, Snow-Gerono (2003) reported changes in school culture as a result of teacher inquiry. Teachers perceived the culture of the school as being marked by greater acceptance of uncertainty as a teacher state of mind and by professional dialog and inquiry as vehicles for reducing that uncertainty.

Creating a more collaborative, inquiry-oriented school culture has a significant impact on the amount of job-embedded learning that occurs for teachers. As noted in Chapter 4, job-embedded learning is a very powerful form of professional development. The work of Susan Rosenholtz (1989), who examined workplace conditions for teachers, provided clear evidence of the impact of school culture on teacher beliefs and development. Teachers in settings where there was little or no organizational support for collaboration reported that professional learning was limited to their first 2 years of experience. In contrast, teachers who worked in schools with a more collaborative culture saw learning from teaching as a never-ending process. Andy Hargreaves' (1994) work on school culture also supports the notion that individualized and balkanized school cultures inhibit and set artificially low ceilings on teacher learning, whereas collaborative cultures allow teacher learning to flourish. The ultimate impact of action research on the school as an organization is the creation of a community of professional learners committed, individually and collectively, to examining and improving their practice for the benefit of students.

Joseph Senese, the assistant principal of Highland Park High School in Illinois, summarized the benefits of action research in his school. The school as an organization benefited from the creation of interdisciplinary learning teams and from the establishment of looping between disciplines. Its culture came to be characterized by teachers engaging in frequent cross-disciplinary communication, more frequent use of data-driven decision making, and much greater sharing of best teaching practices (Senese, 2002).

In addition to benefiting individual teachers and the school as an organization, Calhoun (2002) provides evidence that action research can be beneficial to students as well. She describes a high school collaborative action research project designed by faculty members who perceived that their students were not good readers. Low scores on standardized reading tests validated the teachers' perceptions. The outcome of the action research project was the development of a literacy course aimed at assisting the poorest readers. After participating in the course for one semester, student scores on the same standardized reading test had risen two grade equivalents. The multiple benefits of action research for the school as an organization as well as its stakeholders were summarized succinctly by Smylie, Conley, and Marks (2002):

[In summary, the literature suggests that teacher research can serve as a form of teacher leadership and as a source of influence for school improvement. It suggests that inquiry, particularly inquiry in collaborative contexts, or 'inquiry communities' can create new opportunities for teachers to learn and lead efforts to improve their schools. Moreover, the evidence suggests that the products of teacher research–the knowledge, the findings of inquiry, can provide an impetus and direction for improvement planning and other organizational changes at the school level (pp. 171–172).]

Having discussed the benefits of action research, its definition, its history, and the five types of action research questions, we now turn our attention to the process of conducting action research.

# THE PROCESS OF ACTION RESEARCH

The process of conducting an action research project is cyclic rather than linear in nature. As figure 5.1 indicates activities are interdependent and recursive. Each new step builds upon and stimulates rethinking of what was accomplished during earlier phases of the process. Although we need to describe the steps in a linear fashion as if each were done in isolation, we ask you to keep the cyclic nature of the process in mind. Keep in mind also that although we describe the process in terms of the teacher as researcher, the steps would be the same for any practitioner role.

As you can see from the references that we cite, there are many full-length texts written about the process of action research. Teaching you everything that you would need to know to carry out the process goes beyond the scope of this chapter. Though we provide a fairly thorough description of the process, our intent is to help you understand what activities its various phases entail (declarative knowledge). We believe that this description will not be sufficient to teach you how to carry out all of these activities (procedural knowledge).

**FIGURE 5.1**   Cycle of Action Research

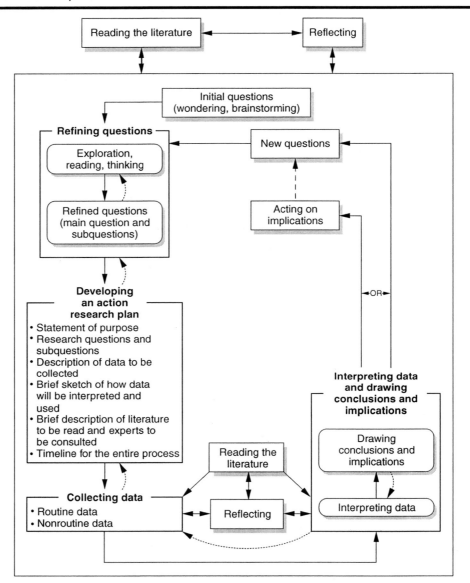

This is especially true with regard to data interpretation, which requires hands-on learning. When practitioners carry out action research projects, they will most likely need to use one or more of the references that we cite in order to develop the requisite skills.

## Identifying and Refining Questions

The action research process begins with a set of questions that arise in the course of the teacher's everyday work. Though most educators use the term question to refer to the driving force behind the action research process, our colleague Nancy Dana (Dana & Yendol-Silva, 2003) uses the term wondering instead. We have found wondering to be a teacher-friendly term. It seems natural to wonder about events that occur in one's teaching.

For some individuals, it also seems less threatening to wonder about one's practice than it does to question it. In our work with teachers, we typically introduce both terms and use them interchangeably depending on the teacher's preference.

Questions do not typically begin as neatly formulated ideas. Thus, the example questions provided earlier represent wonderings that have been refined through a developmental process. Typically, questions begin as a vague statement of discontent and frustration (e.g., I hate teaching measurement like this) or puzzlement (e.g., I don't get it, what is with this third period class?), or as an attempt to navigate between two competing aspects of our teaching that create tensions for us (e.g., I never seem to know whether to push Jennifer just a little bit more or back off and let her see how far she has come). Sometimes wonderings arise from our observations of children, or as Hubbard and Power (1999) suggest, as "glimpses of something out of the corner of your eye that intrigue you" (p. 29).

Sometimes questions land in our laps unexpectedly. Consider the following example. During the first parent conference of the school year, Caroline, a kindergarten teacher, was enjoying her chat with Katy's mom. Katy was a cooperative, bright, and energetic young child. Caroline really liked working with her and was telling her mom what a great year Katy was having. In the middle of listening to the teacher's praise, Katy's mom blurted out, "But I am really worried that she does not seem to be developing any friendships. When I ask her who she plays with, she is not really able to give me any names on a consistent basis." At first, Caroline was really taken aback by this worry. She did not see Katy as a student who lacked friends. She responded, "You know, Mrs. D, I have not really noticed that Katy has any problems with developing friendships, but I will be happy to try to watch for that more closely and see if there is a problem." Over the next few weeks, Caroline observed Katy and was forced to agree with her mom. She did not seem to have any real friend in the class. This parent concern led Caroline to an action research project focused on friendship groups in her kindergarten class.

Although questions sometimes arise unexpectedly, as in Caroline's example, systematically developing questions can be a very useful and enlightening activity. We therefore suggest that teachers begin the action research process by brainstorming a list of initial questions that could serve as the focus for an action research project. Exercise 5.2 provides practice in brainstorming.

### EXERCISE 5.2    Brainstorming Questions

**Direction:**   Brainstorm a list of at least 10–15 questions that might serve as the initial starting point for an action research project that you would be interested in conducting. Try to make sure that your list includes a variety of questions including questions about students, your teaching practice, yourself, the curriculum, and the school as an organization.

Once the teacher has brainstormed a list of questions, the process of refining the questions begins. As depicted in figure 5.1, the refining process includes thinking on one's own, exploring possibilities with colleagues, and even some initial reading of literature in the areas that the questions focus on. This process of refining the questions takes time and should not be rushed. It will, in fact, not be totally complete until the end of the action research process. One important principle to keep in mind is that it is always appropriate for the teacher to refocus and refine the research questions, no matter where he or she is in the action research process. Refocusing and refining the questions typically indicates that the teacher has gained new knowledge and insight and is able to appreciate his or her wondering in more sophisticated and enlightened ways.

Hubbard and Power (1999) suggest three guidelines that can be used in refining a list of initial questions:

1. Ask only real questions, ones to which you do not already have an answer.
2. Avoid closed questions that can be answered yes or no.
3. Eliminate jargon in phrasing the question; instead, try to make the language as plain and clear as possible.

Using these principles the teacher can eliminate some questions and rephrase others, so that they are more plainly stated and more open ended.

At the same time that the teacher attempts to refine the initial list of questions, he or she must begin to narrow the list of possible questions into one overarching question and a set of related questions that will guide the research process. The list of refined research questions can be narrowed by applying four questions developed by Amy Swart, a teacher–researcher in the State College Area School District. She suggests that teachers ask themselves four questions about each of their refined wonderings (A swart, personal communication, february 2001);

1. Is the wondering really important to my teaching, my students, my school, or myself?
2. Can I think of data that I can collect to help me answer this question?
3. Will this research idea fit into my everyday classroom routine?
4. Is my question focused on something that I am really interested in or passionate about?

If the answer to any of these four question is no, then the teacher is advised to eliminate that question from the list. The final step in the refinement process is for the teacher to choose, from what should be a significantly shortened list, the question about which he or she is most passionate.

That question then becomes the focus for the action research process. In many cases, the research question leads to a set of subquestions. Subquestions are questions that will need to be answered along the way toward answering the general research question. Consider the previous example. "The over-arching question might be, what conflict resolution strategies can I use to help students become more capable of handling conflict situations independently? This question raises several related questions that must also be answered: (1) What do I mean by a conflict situation in my classroom?; (2) What conflict resolution strategies are available for students of this age?; (3) How can I teach these conflict resolution strategies effectively?" (4) What does it mean for students to handle a conflict situation independently? This general research question and the four subquestions would then become the driving force for the action research project. Exercise 5.3 provides practice in refining and narrowing questions.

### EXERCISE 5.3  Refining and Narrowing Your Questions

**Part 1** Take the list of wonderings that you developed when you completed Exercise 5.2 and use the three guidelines identified by Hubbard and Power to refine them. The result should be a shorter list of questions phrased somewhat differently.

**Part 2** Apply the four questions suggested by Swart to each of the questions in your refined list that resulted from Part 1. Eliminate any questions to which the answer to one of Swart's questions is no. If all of your potential questions have been eliminated, go back to the one or two that are most important to you and see if you can rework them so that Swart's questions do not result in a no answer.

**Part 3** Choose the one question that is of most interest to you and identify any subquestions that will need to be answered. This question and subquestions will be used in the remaining exercises in this section.

## Developing an Action Research Plan

The teacher develops the action research plan immediately after identifying the research question and subquestions. Its development requires an understanding of data collection, data interpretation, and the role of the existing professional literature. These topics are addressed next.

An action research plan is really a blueprint for the entire action research process. The plan include: (1) a statement of purpose for the research; (2) the research questions and sub-questions; (3) a description of the data that will be collected to answer the questions; (4) a brief sketch of how the data will be interpreted and used; (5) a brief description of the literature to be read and experts to be consulted; and (6) a timeline for the entire process. It is important to remember that the action plan is just that, a plan. Plans can change over time and often do. As the process unfolds, research questions are further refined, and better sources of data become apparent. Nonetheless, the action research plan does offer a very useful tool for moving the process forward. Figure 5.2 provides examples of action research plans at both elementary and secondary levels.

**FIGURE 5.2**  Sample Action Research Plans

---

**Example 1—Kristen Warner (Second Grade)**

---

**Purpose**  The purpose of my action research is to try to advance the reading skills of a student in my classroom. In doing that, I hope that I will also advance my knowledge and skills about the process of teaching reading. Thus, the inquiry is an attempt to help the students with reading and improve my professional development in the area.

**Research Question**  How can I help this struggling reader improve his comprehension?

**Subquestions**  What reading skills does he already have? How does he think about and approach the process of reading? What seem to be the obstacles to his comprehension? What strategies exist to capitalize on his strengths and to overcome his obstacles? How can I involve the Title I teacher and IST teacher in helping him to succeed?

**Data Collection**  Running records of his reading during small group. Observations and anecdotal notes of his reading during silent reading time and the book-look language station. Tape recordings of his reading for later analysis. Interview his first-grade teacher and parents to see what strategies seem to work well with him and are motivating for him. A test of his sight-word vocabulary using flash cards. Keep track of all of the comprehension strategies that we work on in his small reading group.

**Data Interpretation**  I will do a comparison of weekly running records throughout the project to look for improvements in phonemic awareness and comprehension. I will keep track of his scores over time on the sight-word list. I will take notes on the interviews and use the interviews to find ways to motivate him to want to read more and to identify strategies that were effective with him last year. I will analyze the tape recordings to identify any changes in his fluency and oral expression over the length of the project. By the end of the project, I should have a record of any improvements in phonics, oral reading, sight vocabulary, and comprehension as well as a record of the strategies that seemed to lead to the improvement.

**Literature/Experts to Consult**  Books and articles on beginning reading comprehension and guided reading. Title I teacher. IST teacher.

**Timeline**  Weekly running records and sight-word lists. Weeks 1–3—Continue working in reading group and talk with first-grade teacher, parents, IST teacher and Title 1 teacher. Week 4—Review running records and sight-word tests to see where we are making progress and plan future strategies. Weeks 5–7—Continue comprehension strategies, running records, and sight-word work. Week 8—Review all assessment data to date and plan where to go from there.

---

**Example 2—Laura Fisanick (Middle School Science)**

**Purpose**   In general, I am concerned about how to use scientific investigations to improve my students' understanding of science. I have always used hands-on science activities with my seventh and eight graders to help them understand concepts. However, I have seen many students do the activities enthusiastically but not really seem to have a clue about the concepts we are studying. I have recently been introduced to the idea of writing across the curriculum and I am wondering if more intensive writing could improve my students' understanding of the concepts we are investigating in the lab.

**Research Question**   What types of required writing activities help my students understand science laboratory activities better?

**Subquestions**   Does writing make any difference at all? Is writing the hypothesis, procedure, and conclusion enough to impact understanding? Will requiring students to produce a data table and write an explanation to justify the conclusions make a difference in their level of understanding? Will it make a difference if the writing is done individually or in groups?

**Data Collection**   I will divide the students into six groups, pretty equal in ability, for the laboratory activities. We will do four investigations, one each week. For each of the investigations, two groups will write nothing; two groups will write only the hypothesis, the procedure, and the conclusion; and two will write the hypothesis, procedure, a data analysis table, the conclusion, and a rationale for the conclusion (see the table below). During the fourth week, each student will write all the steps individually. I will give a quiz, taken individually, during each of the 4 weeks. The quiz will cover the basic concepts that were the focus of the laboratory activity.

**Design of Action Research Project**

| Week | Groups A and B | Groups C and D | Groups E and F |
|------|----------------|----------------|----------------|
| One | Write nothing | Write partial | Write all |
| Two | Write all | Write nothing | Write partial |
| Three | Write partial | Write all | Write nothing |
| Four | Individual—all | Individual—all | Individual—all |

**Data Interpretation**   For each weekly quiz, I will compare the scores of the groups that wrote nothing with the groups that wrote parts of the information and the groups that wrote all of the information. I will also compare the scores of each group from week to week. Finally, I will compare the scores of each individual student over the 4 weeks. By making these comparisons, I will be able to see what effect each of the experimental conditions has on my students' understanding as measured by my quizzes.

**Literature/Experts to Consult**   I will use readings on writing across the curriculum, writing and thinking, and facilitating laboratory work.

**Timeline**   I am going to do this over a 4-week period in January. My purpose in contracting the timeline is to connect it with our annual science fair. I will tell my students that I am doing my own science fair project at the same time that they are doing theirs. Of course, I will not let them in on all of the details of my experiment until it is over. Once I have interpreted my data, I will share it with my students and explain to them how I am going to use the information to structure lab activities for the remainder of the year.

Though each of the action research plans was well conceived and provided excellent direction for the research process, neither plan was carried out exactly as written. Kristen discovered that one of her student's major comprehension problems was that he really had no general understanding of the central structure of narrative stories. Thus, Kristen ended up doing much more reading aloud to help him recognize this generalized story structure. Consequently, one of her ending questions focused on how to help struggling readers understand story structures.

In Laura's case, her compact timeline resulted in the implementation of her design exactly as specified in the action plan. Her thinking did not change until her data were collected. As she began comparing the various scores, she noticed that some students had much higher scores when they worked as individuals, whereas others did not. In pursuing this intriguing finding, she discovered that all of the students in two groups, B and E, scored as high on the quizzes when they did the work as a group as they did when they worked individually. This led Laura to a new wondering: How did these two groups interact differently than the other four groups? In the end, her project focused as much on group interaction style as it did on writing. Even though her focus shifted during the project, the action plan provided her with much needed direction and support in implementing the project.

## Data Collection

The guiding question in deciding on data collection strategies should always be: "How can I capture the simplest data possible that will still answer my research question?" In planning data collection, the teacher should first look to those data that are available in the normal day-to-day teaching and learning process. We refer to such data as routine data because they exist routinely (although they may not always be captured or saved) even if no action research project is underway.

One type of routine data is classroom artifacts, that is, tangible products that are generated as a normal part of teaching and learning. Generated routinely, artifacts are readily available for use in an action research project. One source of artifacts is student products including homework assignments, worksheets, writing samples, drawings, quizzes, tests, and projects. Another source is teacher materials including unit plans, lesson plans, handouts, worksheets, tests, project rubrics, running records from reading groups, behavior contracts, and anecdotal notes on student behavior. A third source is the communication with parents, other teachers, the principal, counselors, school psychologists, therapists, and others that occur as a normal part of teaching a particular child or group of children. Though such artifacts are not produced every day, their creation is part of routine teaching activity. Because they are so much a part of the teacher's everyday work, classroom artifacts are sometimes unfortunately overlooked in conducting teacher research.

We have labeled the second type of routine data collection as classroom recordings. These data also focus on naturally occurring classroom events are also the focus of these data, but the teacher or a willing colleague must make a special effort to record them. These data can take the form of photographs, audiotapes, and videotapes of classroom activities and interactions. They can also take the form of written records (referred to as field notes for an action research project) or systematic observations (discussed in Chapter 2) made by the teacher or a professional colleague during classroom activities. We have found in our work that the more job-embedded the data collection strategies, the more likely that teachers will see action research as doable. Thus, both types of routine data should play important roles in the data collection process.

We have labeled the second general category of data as nonroutine data because they typically require data collection methods outside the regular classroom. Even if the data are collected in the classroom, as in the case of the student interview questions in Figure 5.4, the activity is not part of the typical classroom routine. The four most common types of nonroutine data are teacher journals, surveys or questionnaires, interviews, and documents.

As suggested in Chapter 4, teacher journals offer a very powerful method for capturing the teacher's thoughts, feelings, and beliefs. "Journals are accounts of classroom life in which teachers record events, analyze their experiences, and reflect on and interpret their practices over time. Journals intermingle description, record keeping, commentary, and analysis" (Cochran-Smith & Lytle, 1993, p. 26). It is important to understand how teacher journals differ from written records, that is, field notes and systematic observation done by the teacher. Written records are observations that are captured in real time, literal descriptions of what is happening written while the events are taking place. Teacher journals, on the contrary, are captured after events have occurred, are filtered through the teacher's memory, and typically mix description, interpretation, and feelings. Both teacher journals and written classroom records are valuable data sources, but they capture different types of data.

Teacher journals may be the most commonly used strategy in action research because they are so versatile. Action researchers use journals as a tool for data collection, for record keeping concerning their activities in the action research process, for reflecting on the data that have been collected, and for formulating new avenues for data collection. Journals can also serve as a primary data source for questions that are focused on the teacher's thoughts or feelings. Such questions are at the centre 8 action research projects focused on the teacher, and they might also be subquestions in projects that are focused on students, pedagogy, curriculum, or the school as an organization.

Surveys are a useful tool for capturing the perceptions of a large number of people. Survey questions can be open–ended or closed–ended. Open-ended questions ("How do you feel about the way the teacher assigns homework?") give those surveyed a great deal of freedom in choosing how to respond. Closed-ended responses ("I believe that the amount of homework assigned by this teacher is: too much/too little/just about right") limit the respondents to particular choices. Closed-ended responses generally require only counting and tabulating on the part of the researcher, whereas open-ended responses require interpretation and sorting into themes or categories. Open-ended questions increase the likelihood that respondents will have the opportunity to address whatever is on their minds. Closed-ended questions increase the likelihood that the action researcher will get the specific information that he or she wants. Thus, closed-ended questions are the more appropriate choice when the researcher is very clear on what kind of information is needed and can develop precise questions, whereas open-ended responses are more appropriate when the researcher is not clear on what kind of information is needed, feels that the respondents need freedom, or is unable to develop precise questions.

Glanz (2003) offers several suggestions for constructing good survey questions. The writer should use as few items as possible and make them as concise as possible. Unclear words such as *meaningful* or *relevant* should be avoided as should leading questions (e.g., "Don't you agree that ..."). Glanz also suggests asking a colleague to look over and take the survey before it is actually used. To these suggestions we would add phrasing survey questions so that they ask respondents about their own attitudes and perceptions rather than general attitudes and perceptions (e.g., "How do you feel about the new bus schedule?" as opposed to "How do parents feel about the new bus schedule"?). Figure 5.3 provides examples of closed- and open-ended questions used to survey third-grade parents in two action research projects focused on parent communication. Christine Portland Mori developed the first set of open-ended questions, and Christy Hermann developed the second set of closed-ended questions.

**FIGURE 5.3** Sample Closed- and Open-Ended Survey Questions

**Open-Ended Survey Questions—Parent Communication**

**Directions** Please answer each of the following questions as honestly as you can by writing in the blank spaces provided. Feel free to add any comments that you feel are important.

1. If a newsletter were sent home, how often would you like to receive one?
2. Would you be willing to read and discuss the newsletter with your child?
3. What type of information would be most useful for you to see in the newsletter?
4. Would you find it beneficial if your child participated in creating the newsletter? In what ways?

5.  What day of the week would you like to receive the newsletter? Why?

*Note:* Christine Portland Mori, a third-grade teacher in Florida, developed these questions.

### Closed-Ended Questions—Parent Communication

**Directions**   Please circle the response that best represents your honest answer to each of the following questions.

1.  Do you have access to a computer?
Yes    No

2.  Where is this computer?
Home Work    Friend/neighbor    Other

3.  Have you or another family member used this computer to visit our Room 19 web site?
Yes    No

4.  What members of your family have visited our web site? (Circle all that apply)
Mother    Father    Sibling    Grandparent    Other

5.  How many total times do you think your family has visited our web site?
Once    2–3 times    3–4 times    4–5 times    >5 times

6.  The Room 19 web site provided me with interesting information.
Not at all    A little    Some    A lot

7.  The information from the web site encourages discussion about school.
Not at all    Rarely    Sometimes    Frequently

8.  My child appears to be enthusiastic and interested in the web site.
Not at all    Rarely    Sometimes    Frequently

9.  My child has talked about writing e-mails and learning to make a web page.
Not at all    A little    Sometimes    Frequently

10.  Having a classroom web page is a valuable addition to my child's education.
Strongly agree    Agree    Disagree    Strongly disagree

*Note:* Christy Hermann, a third-grade teacher in Virginia, developed these questions.

In contrast to surveys, which are useful with large numbers of people, interviews are typically conducted with relatively few individuals to obtain in-depth information. Interviews provide the opportunity to ask probing questions that give the researcher a more in-depth understanding of the respondent's attitude and perceptions. The researcher typically tape records the interview and then either transcribes the tape word for word (a very lengthy process) or takes notes from the tape.

Interview protocols typically begin with open-ended questions to allow the respondents to take the responses in whatever direction they desire. The researcher then uses specific follow-up and probing questions to elicit additional information if needed. For example, an action researcher who is interviewing parents for an action research project on parent-teacher communication would probably start with a very broad question such as "How do you feel about parent–teacher communication this year?" This broad question ensures that the parent will be able to discuss whatever aspects of the process are most important to him or her. If the parent does not touch on areas of interest to the researcher, then the researcher could follow up with specific questions concerning newsletters, the web site, journals, and so on. If the researcher started instead with very narrow questions, it is possible that those issues that are of most interest to the parent might never come up.

We suggest that a protocol for a 30-min interview should contain no more than five to eight general questions. If necessary, specific follow-up questions can be asked during the interview. Figure 5.4 contains a sample set of interview questions that Tara Kauffman and Taryn Little asked their second graders as part of an action research project focused on whether students become too dependent when there are multiple adults in the room. They used the interviews along with their own observations to understand better how students sought help from adults. Notice that some potential follow-up questions were embedded in the set of general interview questions.

**FIGURE 5.4** Sample Interview Questions (Second-Grade Students)

1. What do you do when the teacher gives you work to do and you do not know how to do it?
   *Probes:* If that does not help you figure out how to do it, what do you do?
   If he or she says ("I go to a teacher"), ask "Which teacher and why?"
2. Who helps you with your work in school when you are stuck?
3. How do your teachers help you figure out what to do?
4. What kinds of things can you usually do on your own?
5. What kinds of things do you usually need help with?
6. Tell me about a time when you were stuck and got help?
7. Tell me about a time when you needed help and did not get it?
   *Probe:* How did you handle that?

The final type of nonroutine data is documents that the teacher can analyze. Documents can be an especially useful source of information for action research projects focused on the school as an organization or on the curriculum. For example, official documents such as curriculum guidelines and policy manuals can provide important clues as to why decisions were made in a particular way as can records, such as minutes of meetings or memos and e-mails among committee members. Figure 5.5 provides a summary of the types of data that are useful to consider in planning an action research project.

**FIGURE 5.5** Data Collection Methods for Action Research Projects

**1. Routine data**

**A. Classroom artifacts**

- Student products—homework, worksheets, quizzes, tests, writing samples, drawings, and projects
- Teacher products—unit plans, lesson plans, handouts, worksheets, tests, project rubrics, running records from reading groups, behavior contracts, and anecdotal notes
- Communications—parent, teacher, counselor, and therapist communication such as notes, e-mails, and journals

**B. Classroom recordings**

- Videotapes, audiotapes, and photographs of classroom activities
- Written records—teacher notes and systematic observation of classroom activities

**2. Nonroutine data**

- Teacher journals
- Surveys
- Interviews
- Documents

**EXERCISE 5.4   Matching Data Collection to Research Questions**

**Directions:** Return to the research question and subquestions that you developed in Exercise 5.3. For each question and subquestion, identify at least two or three different types of data that could be collected to answer the question. For each data type that you identify consider the following questions: Who can collect the data? When will the data be collected? What obstacles am I likely to encounter in collecting the data? What will each particular type of data contribute to answering the research questions?

## Reading the Literature

Typically, the issues and problems that drive the action research process are not unique. Other educators are likely to have struggled with the same questions. Thus, a critical component of every action research project is an attempt by the researcher to use the professional literature to deepen his or her understanding of the topic that the research questions address.

The literature can be helpful in refining research questions, in pointing out good sources for data collection, in helping to interpret what the data are saying, and in deciding on courses of future action. Thus, although we discuss reading the literature at this point in connection with the process of collecting and interpreting data, it is an activity, as depicted in Figure 5.1, that can begin as early as the initial development of questions and should continue throughout the action research process.

The action researcher's purpose in consulting the literature differs from that of the academic researcher. The academic researcher wishes to make a contribution to the field and must demonstrate through a literature review what pieces of the large-scale puzzle his or her study will seek to fill. The action researcher is interested in solving a problem or answering a question for himself or herself, not for the field as a whole. In action research, the literature is used as a tool to help the teacher to understand his or her own questions better, to think about them more productively, and to draw on the wisdom and experiences of others in trying to answer them.

We suggest that action researchers consider looking at books, journal articles, and other print documents and also searching for information on the Internet. Obviously, Internet information that has not been reviewed by others or exposed to some other process of external scrutiny and critique must be looked at with a healthy dose of skepticism. The Universal Resource Locators (URLs) of several web sites focused on action research have been included at the end of the chapter in the suggestions for additional reading. General search engines such as Yahoo, Lycos, Webcrawler, Altavista, and Google can also be helpful in finding resources on the Internet. For help with both print and electronic resources, researchers are also advised to contact school librarians and professors in schools and colleges of education. We will say more about locating expert help in the final section.

Perhaps the most valuable tool for locating journals and other print documents is ERIC, the Educational Resources Information Center. ERIC databases include CIJE (the Current Index to Journals in Education) and RIE (Resources in Education). Both provide abstracts and bibliographic information, CIJE for a wide variety of educational journals and RIE for other documents, such as conference papers, curriculum guides, and technical reports. The ERIC system also provides some excellent online searching features such as AskERIC, ERIC Wizard, and ERIC Digests.

We suggest that the action researcher use as much help as possible in locating relevant literature. Expert help can really streamline a potentially cumbersome process, reducing time spent searching or reading sources that are not clearly connected to the research focus. We also suggest that the reading be done frequently for short periods of time and that it be spread out to allow time for reflection.

## Interpreting the Data and Drawing Conclusions and Implications

Of all the components of the action research process, data interpretation is the most difficult to explain. Learning to interpret data is somewhat like learning to do needlepoint or to spackle dry wall; it really requires hands-on activity. In the absence of real data to work with, understanding the process is difficult.

The data interpretation process is heavily dependent both on the kinds of data that have been collected and on the action researcher's understanding of the research questions and what others have already learned about those questions. In action research, data interpretation is an ongoing process. The researcher does not wait to begin the analysis process until all of the data have been collected. As soon as the first piece of data is collected, interpretation can begin. Interpreting data on an ongoing basis has multiple advantages. It allows the researcher to refine the research questions even further and to identify new questions that need to be answered. It provides the opportunity to refine or completely change data collection strategies based on the quality of the data that are being collected. Finally, it often helps the researcher to focus his or her reading on areas that appear to be more important based on the collected data.

The common element across all different types of data interpretation processes is the search for patterns in the data. Though pattern seeking is a hard process to explain without data, it is not unique to action research. Humans are natural pattern seekers; we understand the world by dividing it into categories that are based on patterns that we find. For example, the 4-year-old who can distinguish cats from dogs has learned to do that by finding patterns in what is common to cats that is not common to dogs. Thus, although pattern–seeking is a complex process, it is a natural activity that is not difficult to master.

More specifically, the patterns may be found by counting, tabulating, and graphing (quantitative data), by reading, rereading and, categorizing (qualitative data), or by comparing events such as student test scores or other performances over time. The task of data interpretation is to identify patterns or themes across all of the data sources and to compare them. The process of comparing patterns across data sources is called triangulation. When multiple types of data provide the same patterns, then the action researcher can be reasonably sure that he or she is heading in the right direction. If, however, the data seem to have different stories to tell, the researcher needs to identify additional data collection strategies that can be used to try to understand why these differing patterns exist.

It is really in the data interpretation process that the true artistry of action research can be found. The quality of the interpretations that result from this process can be determined in large measure by the answers to the following questions:

1. Are the questions and subquestions well defined and clear in the mind of the researcher?
2. Were the data collection strategies well matched to the questions?
3. Does the researcher have a deep understanding of the data collection strategies?
4. Is the interpretation process appropriate for each of the types of data?
5. Has the researcher acquired a deep understanding of the focus for the research project through reading the literature and consulting with others?

If each of these questions can be answered in the affirmative, then it is likely that the data interpretation process will yield powerful insights.

Powerful insights in the arena of action research are not always answers to the research questions. Sometimes, the outcome of the data interpretation process is clear answers to the questions posed; often, however, it is a new set of questions. If these new questions are better questions that move the teacher toward a deeper, more sophisticated understanding of the action research focus, then the insights are indeed powerful. Laura, the teacher in the second example provided in Figure 5.2, was led by interpreting the data to new questions about group interaction in science. Her new question, "What kinds of group interaction contribute to excellent work by all individuals in the group?", though different from her original focus on writing, is a very sophisticated question that could lead to powerful changes in how she does group work. Thus, although she does not leave the process with definitive answers to her questions, she leaves with a well-defined question based on a deeper understanding of the nature of her students' performance. Sometimes, the most powerful outcome of the action research process is better questions not answers.

Initially, many teacher researchers are very disappointed by an outcome that consists of new questions instead of answers. They feel that research is supposed to lead to answers and that they have, thus, failed to accomplish their goal. We have found that it is crucial throughout the process to help action researchers understand that the goal is deeper understanding, not definitive answers and that more enlightened questions are evidence of deeper understanding. We agree with the sentiments expressed by Hubbard and Power: "When you analyze your data thoroughly, there is a fair degree of uncertainty in the task. Human relations are complex, so any analysis of what goes on in a classroom teeming with kids will end up with some unknowns and ambiguities. Good research analyses raise more questions than they answer" (1999, p. 117). Once the action researcher has found patterns across the various data sources that provide answers to the research questions or point the way toward more powerful new questions, it is time to draw conclusions and implications.

Conclusions are statements that describe what the researcher has found through the process of data interpretation and the researcher's thoughts about these findings. Remember that the research questions often change as the researcher begins to understand the topic more fully. Conclusions usually provide the best answer to the research question at any give point in time and also identify new research questions that have developed. Implications state what actions the researcher should now take as a result of the conclusions drawn. Turning conclusions into action is the sine qua non of action research. Sometimes, the implications are to keep doing what is already being done or to do it more intensely. Other action research projects result in implications that require the teacher to change the status quo and move in entirely new directions. Wherever the conclusions lead, the action researcher is bound to follow. Putting the implications into practice often leads to a new set of questions that can begin the action research process anew, as depicted in Figure 5.1.

**EXERCISE 5.5   Designing and Refining an Action Plan**

---

**Part 1** Using the research question and subquestions that you have developed in earlier exercises, design an action plan that could be used to carry out an action research project focused on those questions.

**Part 2** Trade action plans with a classmate. Read your classmate's plan. Jot down any questions about aspects of the plan that are not clear to you. Also, note any suggestions that you might have to improve the action plan.

---

Some action research projects end simply with the teacher taking action based on the conclusions to improve personal effectiveness. Other action research projects result in the researcher taking action and also sharing the results of the research either in a paper or in an oral presentation. A paper has little, if any, impact on the culture of the school as a whole, whereas a presentation has the potential to begin the creation of a culture of inquiry within the school organization. The next section provides suggestions for supporting, sharing and celebrating action research.

Action research is a process consisting of interdependent phases including developing focused questions, collecting data to answer the questions, interpreting the data, and acting on those interpretations to improve teaching and learning. Because action research is designed to help teachers grow and to improve their effectiveness in the classroom, we see it as an important component of a district's supervision system.

# FACILITATING ACTION RESEARCH AS A COMPONENT OF THE SUPERVISION SYSTEM

Incorporating action research as a supervision strategy will require that administrators engage in four important activities:
(1) initiating the process;
(2) sustaining the process;
(3) celebrating the process; and
(4) administering the process.

## Initiating the Process

Of all the supervision options that we recommend as components of the teacher supervision and evaluation system, action research is likely to be the least popular, at least initially. Many teachers see research as something that is foreign to them; others believe that action research will take too much time. Though participation may be low initially, we see action research as an important supervision strategy because it can help lead to the development of an inquiry stance on the part of individuals and to the creation of a community of inquiry at the school level. Our experience indicates that if action research is well supported, it will grow in popularity. One of the authors began working with a school district on action research in the 1999–2000 academic year. During the first year, one teacher chose action research as a supervision strategy. Just 2 years later, 27 teachers were involved in action research. This dramatic growth occurred because the district attended carefully to what it needed to do to initiate, support, and celebrate the teacher-research process.

Though many practitioners engage in informal inquiry into their practice on an ongoing basis, most have not been prepared to carry out the formal process of action research. As is evident in the preceding section, conducting action research requires specialized knowledge and skills. Thus, to providing mandatory staff development for teachers as a group before the process begins and to having support available thereafter for individuals as-needed basis are important. Given the benefits of action research noted earlier, the resources that are invested in providing the required staff development are well spent. Figure 5.6 provides an outline for a 3-day staff development workshop, conducted over approximately a 2-week period, to prepare teachers to engage in action research. We suggest that the 3 days be separated in time to allow teachers to have the time to work individually or collectively on various components of the process.

**FIGURE 5.6** Sample 3 Day Staff Development Workshop on Action Research

---

**Day 1—Introduction to action research and initial wonderings**

*Morning—introduction to action research*

- Lecture and discussion to define the meaning of action research and its benefits
- Group participants into groups of five to use a jigsaw strategy. Have each of the five group members read a different example of teacher research (e.g., focus on students, teaching, the teacher, curriculum, and the school as an organization) and share it with the group members
- Discussion to refine understandings of what action research is.

*Afternoon—developing initial wonderings*

- Lecture to discuss different types of wonderings, using the readings from the morning as examples
- Each participant brainstorms a list of initial wonderings
- Group activity to share and refine wonderings
- Introduce questions from Hubbard and Power and from Ruth to refine wonderings

*Assignment for day 2*—Continue to define wonderings and return to next session with a research question and subquestions

**Day 2—Development of action research plan (about 1 week after day 1)**

*Morning—Focus on data collection methods*

- Lecture, discussion, and activities to introduce routine and nonroutine data sources, including examples of each and suggestions for how to interpret each data source

*Afternoon-Focus on action research plans*

- Lecture on action plans, using several examples
- Each participant or group has individual time to develop a draft action research plan
- Draft research plans are shared with two other participants for reactions and feedback

*Assignment—Prepare written action research plan for day 3*

**Day 3—Action research plans and reading the literature (2 or 3 days after day 2) (*Note:* Need access to computers for literature searching)**

*Morning-Finalizing action plans*

- Each participant shares action plan with the whole group and facilitator(s). The group and facilitator(s) also suggest refinements and provide suggestions about local experts who might be able to provide assistance

*Afternoon—Reading the literature*

- Librarian or other expert conducts mini-workshop on electronic databases and searches for both print and electronic information
- Participants have time to begin a search for relevant literature

*Assignment—Read literature; contact expert, if appropriate; begin collecting data*

---

In the school district mentioned earlier in which one of the authors had been involved in facilitating action research, university faculty members conducted the training workshop the first year using action research reports drawn from other districts and facilitating most of the activities personally. Since then, teachers from the district who have engaged in action research have conducted the same workshop with very little help. The growth of in-house facilitators is a tremendous asset to the district in encouraging more teachers to engage in action research.

## Sustaining the Process

Teachers are much more likely to be successful when two conditions are met: (1) they are connected to colleagues who are also engaged in action research; and (2) they can get expert help when they need it. Sustaining the process means first and foremost ensuring that these conditions can be met.

Our experience suggests that most action researchers get discouraged because the project can seem overwhelming at certain points. Refining the questions is difficult. Collecting data sometimes presents unexpected obstacles (even obstacles as basic as a camera or tape recorder that does not work). After several weeks of data collection, there seems to be a mountain of data that needs to be interpreted, and the exact procedures for interpretation are fuzzy. At these and other points, teachers who are engaged in action research really benefit from talking with one another. Often, a colleague who looks at the researcher's dilemma from a fresh perspective can help solve problems. In any case, simply knowing that other teachers are experiencing the same feelings can be a great relief and provide the motivation to keep going.

Therefore, providing the opportunity for those involved in action research to talk with one another is very important. We suggest that weekly group meetings of all the teachers who have selected action research as their supervision option be held throughout the year. Typically, these meetings would be done on a districtwide basis as the number of teachers who are conducting action research in any single building would be small. The meetings would have an open agenda and would allow the action researchers to share problems, successes, and stories with each other. Teachers should be able to attend whenever they feel it would be helpful. Although help from colleagues suffices in some situations, in others researchers need special expertise. Thus, helping teachers to connect with individuals who have relevant expertise is an equally important component of sustaining the process. We have already noted that school librarians can offer valuable assistance in locating relevant information. Professors also have content expertise, and in many cases, expertise in data collection and interpretation strategies. Depending on the project, learning support teachers, reading specialists, school counselors, school psychologists, and school administrators might also be able to offer expertise and assistance. For example, Kristen, the elementary teacher in Figure 5.2, used both the Title 1 reading teachers and the instructional support teachers as experts in helping her deal with her student's reading problems.

Sagor refers to these expert partners as critical friends. "A critical friend is just what the name implies. A person who has your interests at heart and gives you constructive criticism" (Sagor, 2000, p. 46). Critical friends are chosen by and participate at the continued invitation of the action researcher. They are positive and aim to move the project forward. They commit themselves to respond honestly in providing feedback and assistance. Finally, they treat the work and findings as confidential unless the action researcher asks them to do otherwise (Sagor, 2000). Establishing a network of critical friends can be an important strategy to provide ongoing support to sustain the action research process. Initial training in action research and the development of the action research plan get the project moving in the right direction. The opportunity to talk with fellow researchers and the assistance of critical friends are key components in capitalizing on the initial momentum.

## Celebrating the Process

Providing the opportunity to share action research projects and to celebrate their contributions is an important step because sharing projects has multiple benefits at three different levels. First, teachers benegfit as individuals. Conclusions and implications from an action research project can often be helpful to other teachers. When a teacher presents a solution to his or her own dilemma, it often touches on similar dilemmas felt by other teachers. In addition, the information and literature that the researcher has gathered can be very informative for other teachers.

Second, teaching as a profession benefits. Celebrating teacher research respects and honors teachers as professionals who have the capacity to generate new knowledge. Teachers are viewed in a new role. They are no longer simply the implementers of knowledge generated by others. It also implies that teachers have a new responsibility. They are obligated to continually learn from their own practice and that of others.

Finally, the school as an organization benefits. Celebrating teachers who are willing to ask questions about their practice and collect evidence to help answer the questions creates a climate of continuous improvement and ongoing reflection. As teachers hear about the action research of colleagues, they are often inspired to believe that they too can conduct action research, opening the door for collaborative action research in the future.

There are many ways to share action research projects. A common strategy is to hold an annual teacher inquiry conference. All of the teachers who conducted action research during the year present their projects at the conference. In addition, teachers who completed self-directed growth projects can also share their efforts at this conference. Such conferences can be scheduled after school, perhaps accompanied by a dinner, or on Saturday mornings. They can also be incorporated into a regularly scheduled in-service day. Each teacher researcher can be given 20 min to talk about his or her project with an opportunity for other participants to ask questions. Action research projects can also be shared during faculty meetings or team meetings. If this strategy is used, only one action research project is shared at a time. We suggest that in addition to being shared orally, all action research projects be posted on the school district web site in a section for professional staff members. The next section discusses a written format for sharing the project within the district.

## Administering the Process

When action research is incorporated within a system of teacher supervision and evaluation, administrators must perform certain activities to keep track of the process. In the spring, all veteran teachers whose performance is satisfactory or better are asked to choose their supervision activities for the following school year (see Figure 1.3). The administrator identifies the teachers who have opted to participate in action research and informs those who have not had the mandatory initial training when that training will take place.

Training for action research should occur either during the summer or early in the school year. Soon after the initial 3 days of training have been completed, the building administrator meets with each teacher who is conducting action research as a supervisory activity. The teacher brings his or her action research plan to the meeting and shares it with the administrator. The administrator listens to the plan, asks questions, and makes suggestions, if appropriate, to improve the plan. In addition, the administrator talks with the teacher about critical friends who might help with the project and tries to be of assistance in making connections. The administrator also reminds the teacher where and when the districtwide action research group (all those teachers conducting action research) will be meeting.

If the focus of the proposed action research plan is curriculum or the school as an organization, the scope of the project should be discussed at this initial meeting. The degree to which teachers are free to experiment with curriculum differs significantly across school districts. In fact, the definition of curriculum differs across districts. In some districts, curriculum refers only to the goals and objectives; in others, it also refers to materials and even teaching strategies. It is very important, to avoid problems later, that the scope of the teacher's freedom in experimenting with and changing curriculum be discussed at this initial conference.

Teachers need to understand whether their curriculum project may or may not lead to changes in the school curriculum. We have experienced the discouragement of teachers who (unrealistically, given the school district's administrative mindset) expected that their action research project would lead to curriculum change, only to discover that their effort had no impact on curriculum at all. When action research focuses on the school as an organization, the initial meeting needs to address additional questions such as: (1) Is it possible that school policies and procedures can be changed as the result of an action research project?, (2) Who will make the decision about whether policies and procedures need to be changed as the result of the project?, and (3) What process, if any, will be followed in making changes in policies and procedures? Again, clarity at the outset can prevent a great deal of bitterness later on.

At the initial meeting, the teacher and administrator schedule a follow-up meeting to be held approximately halfway through the project. As different projects require different amounts of time, the time that elapses between these two meetings will vary from project to project. The purpose of this meeting is to check on the progress that is being made and to provide additional assistance if necessary. The teacher brings the action research plan to this meeting and discusses any changes that have been made to the initial research plan. In addition to these formally scheduled meetings, we believe that it is useful for the principal to check in with the teacher informally from time to time to see how things are going.

The final step in the process is the sharing of the action research project with the principal and with others. If the sharing is done at an inquiry conference or at a faculty meeting, then the principal becomes part of the audience at that activity. We suggest that in addition to sharing the research project, the teacher write up a revised action plan, using a format like the one in Figure 5.7, and provide that to the principal. This revised action plan can then become a part of the teacher's file, as a record of the teacher's participation in supervision that year. It can also be shared with other professional staff members through posting on the district's web site.

**FIGURE 5.7**  Format for Final Revised Action Plan

**Teacher:**                    **School:**                              **Subject/grade:**

1.  Purpose of the research
2.  Research question and related questions
3.  Data collection and interpretation methods
4.  Literature read
5.  Experts consulted
6.  Timeline of activities
7.  Conclusions and implication

_____                    _____

Teacher signature and date                         Administrator signature and date

# CHAPTER SUMMARY

Action research, as a component of the teacher supervision and evaluation system, is the process of practitioners asking well-defined questions about their practice, systematically gathering and interpreting data to answer those questions, and consequently taking action to improve practice. Action research has a long history in the United States and offers potential benefits to students, individual teachers, and the school culture. There are five types of action research questions: questions about students, about teaching practices, about the teacher, about curriculum, and about the school as an organization.

Developing and refining the research question and subquestions is the initial task of the action researcher. After the questions have been identified, an action research plan can be developed, specifying data collection strategies, literature to be read, experts to be consulted, data interpretation processes, and a timeline

of activities. The process of action research continues with ongoing data collection, data interpretation, and reading of the professional literature. The final step in the action research process is drawing conclusions and implications for practice. The actual process is more cyclic than linear in nature, and the result of the process is often more enlightened and sophisticated questions as opposed to definitive answers.

Four key activities are required to facilitate the process of action research as a supervisory activity. Providing high-quality staff development is an important initial activity. Once the action research process is underway, providing opportunities to interact with fellow teacher–researchers and to consult with experts helps to sustain the momentum of the project. Sharing the results of completed projects and celebrating action research benefits individual teachers, the profession of teaching, and the school culture.

# DISCUSSION QUESTIONS

**1.** Curriculum development is typically a school- or districtwide activity. Thus, it is appropriate to question whether individual teachers should be encouraged to pursue curriculum-focused action research. Where do you stand on this issue? Should individual teachers be encouraged to conduct action research projects focused on curriculum? Why or why not? If teachers are encouraged to conduct curriculum-oriented action research, should any parameters be placed on the scope of their projects? Why or why not? If teachers are encouraged to conduct curriculum-oriented action research, should the results of the projects be used to change curriculum? Why or why not?

**2.** Should individual teachers or groups of teachers who wish to conduct action research projects focused on the school as an organization be required to get permission from the building principal to do so? Why or why not? What parameters, if any, would you place on such projects if you were the building administrator? Explain your answer. Should the results of such projects be used to change policies and procedures? Why or why not? Who should be involved in deciding

whether school policies and procedures should change as a result of action research projects? Why?

**3.** The authors suggest several different vehicles for sharing action research projects including after-school conferences, Saturday conferences, faculty meetings, regularly scheduled in-service days, and posting projects on the Web. What do you see as the advantages and disadvantages of each vehicle? Would you require teachers to share their projects in some form? Why or why not?

**4.** Think about the current staff of teachers that you work with. What percentage do you think would be willing to participate in action research? Why? What factors would make a difference in determining whether more teachers would participate in action research? What strategies might you use to encourage more teachers to become involved in action research? Identify any particular teachers in the faculty who influence the opinions of others. How could you encourage these informal leaders to see the value of action research?

# THEORY-INTO-PRACTICE APPLICATIONS

**1.** Develop a survey of 10 items that could be used to survey parents concerning either a topic of your own choice or their attitude about the possibility of mov-

ing from the current school calendar to a year-round calendar of four 9-week terms with 1-month vacations between the terms.

**2.** Develop an interview protocol for a 30- min interview that you could conduct with a group of middle school students concerning either a topic of your own choice or their reaction to moving from your school district's current school calendar to a year-round calendar of four 9- week terms with 1- month vacations between the terms.

**3.** Refer back to your research question and subquestions from Exercises 5.3 and 5.4. Use the library and electronic databases to compile a bibliography of print and electronic sources that could serve as the starting point for your reading of the literature about these questions.

**5.** Consult one of the online sources of teacher research reports identified in the additional resources section. Read an article that reports action research and share the article with two other students in the class. In sharing, be sure to summarize the key points of the article as well as to point out its strengths and weaknesses.

## CASE STUDY: ACTION RESEARCH

### Introduction

Diane Reed and Amy Warner are two fourth-grade teachers. One of the units that is included in their social studies curriculum is a 4-week unit on explorers. The unit typically engages students in studying three or four famous explorers who had some connection with the "discovery" of the Americas. Diane and Amy were concerned about several aspects of the unit. They felt that the curriculum was much too surface level, resulting in students understanding only a few facts about each of the explorers but not really understanding anything about discovery and exploration at a deeper level. They also worried about the Eurocentric perspective that was portrayed in the unit. The perspectives of the indigenous people, who inhabited the Americas before European explorers "discovered" them, was not represented very well in the unit. This discomfort with the explorers unit led them to undertake a collaborative action research project. They felt that they wanted to try to teach the unit in a manner that really engaged the students in critically thinking about the "discovery of America," but they were worried that fourth graders would not be developmentally ready to handle the topic from a more multicultural and critical perspective. They decided to turn that wondering into an action research project.

### Wonderings

Diane and Amy decided that they would approach the unit very differently and undertake an in-depth study of the "discovery of America" by Christopher Columbus. Their broad wondering was whether the true story of the discovery of America, taken from a multicultural perspective, could be made understandable at a developmentally appropriate level. After doing some thinking about that question, consulting some references on teaching for multicultural understanding, and talking with faculty members from a local university as well as curriculum personnel from the district, Diane and Amy refined this broad wondering into specific questions:

1. Can this unit be taught to fourth graders in a multicultural and developmentally appropriate way?
2. Can fourth graders begin to understand the concept of author bias in historical readings?
3. Will students' understandings of Christopher Columbus and the Taino people (the indigenous people of the Caribbean region) change as a result of a multicultural approach to the unit?
4. Will the students' understandings of "discovery" change as a result of this new approach to the unit?

### Lessons

The unit began with a short pretest. Part 1 of the pretest asked the students to define "discovery." Part 2 consisted of a KWL chart in which the teacher asked the students to list everything they thought they knew about Columbus and everything they thought they knew about the Taino people. As one might imagine, the students knew many facts about Columbus, but were hard pressed to come up with even one fact that was accurate about the indigenous people.

That afternoon the students experienced a rather dramatic illustration. Diane and Amy in their respective classrooms arranged an example of what discovery might have meant to the indigenous people. While the students were out to recess, each teacher took a backpack that belonged to one of her students and placed it on the teacher's desk. (The teacher had pre-arranged with the owner of the backpack that this was going to happen.) When the students came back from recess, the teacher proudly proclaimed that she had "discovered" a backpack and was now going to use it to store her things. The morally outraged fourth graders protested wildly that the backpack belonged to student A. The teacher said that she had discovered it, that it matched her favorite color, and that she could name all of the contents without even looking inside (because she had emptied the students' materials and added her own). This vignette led to a rather lengthy discussion, quite heated at times, about what discovery really means and whether it is possible to legitimately discover something that belongs to someone else.

In terms of the inquiry project, the heart of the unit focused on a series of lessons on author bias. The teachers found three texts about the Columbus expedition. One was unabashedly Eurocentric and positive about Columbus, the great explorer. The second presented a more neutral description of Columbus and the indigenous people, whereas the third portrayed the encounter in a fashion that was much more sympathetic to the indigenous people. The students participated in three sets of activities on each book. First, they conducted a picture walk through each book and counted how many times Columbus and his companions were pictured in the text and how many times the indigenous people were pictured. Second, the students counted how many times Columbus or his companions spoke and how many times the Tainos spoke. Finally, the students gathered information from each text about Columbus and the Taino people.

At the end of the 4-week unit, Diane and Amy had the students return to the KWL chart idea and again list all of the things that they now knew about Columbus and all of the things that they now knew about the Taino people. In addition, each of the students was asked to write a definition of what "discovery" means. There were many other lessons that were taught during the unit, but these are the ones that are most germane to the inquiry project.

## Data Collection

Diane and Amy collected data in multiple ways. The lesson plans that they developed became the data source for deciding if the unit could be taught in a developmentally appropriate way. They kept the written definitions of discovery that were written at the beginning and the end of the unit. They kept the tallies that the students made when they looked at the three books and counted pictures, words, and information. In addition, they also recorded the classroom conversations that were held with students after they had completed each of these three activities on author bias. Finally, they compared the KWL charts from the beginning and the end of the unit.

## Data Interpretation

Diane and Amy used a data interpretation process that was pretty straightforward. They used their own professional judgment to decide if the lesson plans that they had developed had achieved the general goals toward which they were aiming and had appeared to go smoothly and be appropriate for all students. They compared the pre- and postdefinitions of discovery. They compared the amounts of information and the accuracy of the information about Columbus and the Taino people on the pre- and post-KWL charts. Finally, they analyzed both the tallies that the students had created from the three books and also analyzed the conversations that followed. In doing this analysis, they also decided to pay attention to different types of students. They were worried, for example, that students who were better readers would understand the concept of author bias, whereas Title 1 students and other readers who had greater difficulty in reading might have a harder time understanding the concept. They also looked at whether learning support and other special needs students would be able to grasp the concept. So, in essence, they added an additional question during the data interpretation process: Would the understanding of author bias occur for all students or just for certain types of students?

## Findings and Conclusions

The results of the project were unbelievably positive. All of the lessons seemed to be effective, and all students were able to participate in them without any problems or issues. In their postdefinitions of "discovery," almost every student in the room made it a point to state explicitly that it was not possible to discover something that already belonged to someone else. They used the example of Columbus to make that clear.

Secondly, the differences in the pre-and post-KWL charts were amazing. On the initial charts, students were able to list dozens of facts about Columbus. They were able to list almost none about the Taino people. Though, being good fourth graders, they did their best to come up with statements that made sense, such as, "the Taino people wore head dresses, the Taino people shot turkeys with bows and arrows, the Taino people celebrated Thanksgiving with Columbus," and so on. At the end of the unit, students were able to list a large number of facts about the Taino people that were accurate. They were also able to add a variety of information that was critical of Columbus (e.g., he brought new diseases to the Taino people, he was only after their gold, he tricked them, etc.). Perhaps, the most powerful statement made by a student on the post-KWL chart was made by a learning support student who wrote the following about the Taino people, "They had names." That seems like such a simple statement, but in reflecting upon it, Amy and Diane realized that it was extremely significant. Recognizing that they had names humanized the Taino people. It made them real people. Amy and Diane conjectured that it is much harder to demonize and neglect people who have names than it is to ignore those who remain nameless.

In terms of the author bias question, the class discussions and the book tally sheets provided a wealth of evidence that the students really understood the concept of author bias. The students did not actually use those words. Instead, they said, "This author is rooting for Columbus. Columbus talks 25 times and the Taino people do not talk at all." "This other author is rooting for the Taino people. There are 10 pictures of them and four of Columbus." In analyzing the discussions and the sheets, Diane and Amy were also able to show that Title 1 students were able to detect author bias and to talk about it in appropriate and accurate ways. They had clear evidence that all types of students were able to grasp this concept, recognizing author bias, which is a critical lifelong skill for those of us who live in an information society. One of the most powerful pieces of evidence concerning the impact of this unit on students occurred in a current events discussion right after the explorers unit. The current event was the presidential election. One of the students had brought in an article from a generally conservative newspaper. After hearing the article, one of the other students raised her hand and said, "I think this author is rooting for President Bush."

## Discussion Questions

1. Critique this action research project by answering the following questions: (a) How well were the wonderings stated?, (b) Did the data collection strategies match the wonderings?, and (c) Did the conclusions that were drawn seem well supported and reasonable?

2. How would you classify the data that Amy and Diane collected? How much extra work on their part did it take to collect the data that they used?

3. In what ways, if any, does this project challenge or change your own thinking about fourth-grade students and about the teaching of social studies?

4. One of the major justifications for the use of action research as a supervision strategy is that it provides job-embedded professional development. In what ways do you think Diane and Amy grew from conducting this action research project?

5. Was it appropriate for Diane and Amy to add a research question during the data interpretation process? Why or why not?

# REFERENCES

Burnaford, G., Fischer, J., & Hobson, D. (2001). *Teachers doing research: Practical possibilities (2nd ed.)* Mahwah, NJ: Lawrence Erlbaum Publishers.

Calhoun, E. (2002). Action research for school improvement. *Educational Leadership, 59*(6), 18–24.

Cochran-Smith, M., & Lytle, S. (1993). *Inside/outside: Teacher research and knowledge.* New York: Teachers College Press.

Corey, S. (1953). *Action research to improve school practice.* New York: Bureau of Publications, Teachers College, Columbia University.

Dana, N., Gimbert, B., & Silva, D. (1999). Teacher inquiry: Staff development for the 21st century. *Pennsylvania Educational Leadership, 18*(2), 6–12.

Dana, N., & Yendol-Silva, D. (2003). *The reflective educator's guide to classroom research.* Thousand Oaks, CA: Corwin Press.

Glanz, J. (2003). *Action research: An educational leader's guide to classroom research (2nd ed.).* Norwood, MA: Christopher Gordon Publishers.

Hammerness, K., Darling-Hammond, L., & Bransford, J. (2005). How teachers learn and develop. In L. Darling-

Hammond & J. Bransford (Eds.), *Preparing teachers for a changing world: What teachers should learn and be able to do* (pp. 358–389). San Francisco, CA: Jossey-Bass,.

HARGREAVES, A. (1994). *Changing teachers, changing times: Teachers' work and culture in the postmodern age.* New York: Teachers College Press.

HOLLINGSWORTH, S., & SOCKETT, H. (1994). Positioning teacher research in educational reform: An introduction. In S. Hollingsworth & H. Sockett (Eds.), *Teacher research and education reform: The Ninety-Third Yearbook of the National Society for the Study of Education.* Chicago, IL: University of Chicago Press.

HUBBARD, R., & POWER, B. (1999). *Living the questions: A guide for teacher-researchers.* York, ME: Stenhouse Publishers.

LIEBERMAN, A., & MILLER, L. (1994). Problems and possibilities of institutionalizing teacher research. In S. Hollingsworth & H. Sockett ( Eds.), *Teacher research and education reform: The Ninety-Third Yearbook of the National Society for the Study of Education.* Chicago, IL: University of Chicago Press.

LITTLE, J. W. (1982). Norms of collegiality and experimentation: Workplace conditions of school success. *American Educational Research Journal, 19*, 325-340.

ROSENHOLTZ, S. (1989). *Teachers' workplace: The social organization of schools.* New York: Longman.

RUTH, A. (2001). *Finding your wondering.* Personal communication. State College, PA.

SAGOR, R. (2000). *Guiding school improvement with action research.* Alexandria, VA: Association for Supervision and Curriculum Development.

SCHON, D. (1983) *The reflective practitioner: How professionals think in action.* New York: Basic Books.

SENESE, J. (2002). Energize with action research. Journal of Staff Development, 23(3), 39–41

SMYLIE, M., CONLEY, S., & MARKS, H. (2002). Building leadership into the role of the teacher. In J. Murphy (Ed.), *The educational leadership challenge: Redefining leadership for the 21st century. The One Hundred and First Yearbook of the National Society for the Study of Education.* Chicago, IL: University of Chicago Press.

SNOW-GERONO, J. (2003). *Living an inquiry stance toward teaching: Professional development school teachers' perceptions of teacher inquiry.* Unpublished doctoral dissertation. The Pennsylvania State University.

## SUGGESTIONS FOR FURTHER READING AND RESEARCH

CARR, W., & KEMMIS, S. (1986). *Becoming critical: Education, knowledge and action research.* London: Falmer Press.

DANA, N. F, & YENDOL-SILVA, D. (2003). *The reflective educator's guide to classroom research.* Thousand Oaks, CA: Corwin Press.

HOLLY, M. L., ARHAR, J., & KASTEN, W. (2005). *Action research for teachers: Traveling the yellow brick road, (2nd ed.).* Upper Saddle River, NJ: Prentice-Hall.

PARSONS, R. D., & BROWN, K. S. (2002). *Teacher as reflective practitioner and action researcher.* Belmont, CA: Wadsworth.

## ONLINE REPORTS OF TEACHER RESEARCH

Action Research International: http://www.scu.edu.au/schools/gcm/ar/ari/arihome.html

Penn State–State College Elementary PDS Teacher Inquiry: http://www.ed.psu.edu/teacher_inquiry

# CHAPTER 6

# COLLEGIAL DEVELOPMENT GROUPS

**W**ORKING WITH teachers in staff development activities is an important and interesting task as well as somewhat unpredictable. Every group of teachers is idiosyncratic to some degree, and cultures vary significantly across schools and districts. How a new audience of teachers will react to new ideas or even to unfamiliar activities is never guaranteed. Staff development sessions, however, do have one predictable aspect. When the day is finished, and teachers are asked what they found most productive and enjoyable, the majority of teachers will respond, "Having the opportunity to talk and share ideas with colleagues."

Teachers love having time to discuss their work with colleagues, especially when they can really be honest in sharing problems and can receive advice from their colleagues. In addition to being enjoyable, ongoing professional interaction with colleagues can be a very powerful form of job-embedded teacher learning. In keeping with our belief in creating differentiated supervision opportunities for teacher growth, we recommend that teacher supervision and evaluation systems incorporate opportunities for participation in collegial development groups. This participation should be as a major component of the teacher supervision process for veteran teachers who are performing at a satisfactory level or better.

The present chapter provides an in-depth understanding of collegial development groups as a key component of the teacher supervision and evaluation system. The first section defines the term collegial development group, describes three major types of collegial development groups, and explains the benefits of implementing collegial development groups. The second section focuses on study groups, one type of collegial development group, provides suggestions for facilitating group functioning, and ends with a detailed description of the work of one teacher study group at the middle school level. The third section focuses on the second type of collegial development groups, critical friends groups (CFGs). It discusses the use of critical friends groups as a mechanism for facilitating conversation and reflection concerning both student and teacher work. The fourth section focuses on lesson study as a form of collegial development. It describes the process of lesson study as a tool for developing and refining "research lessons," a tool for engaging teachers in job-embedded inquiry and consultation. Lesson study constitutes a wonderful connection to the previous chapter on action research. As the term "research lesson" implies, the process involves focused data collection and analysis, key components of the action research process. The final section focuses on the task of incorporating collegial development groups into the teacher supervision and evaluation system. It discusses the administrator's role in supporting group work and offers guidance on administrator participation in collegial development groups.

# GUIDING QUESTIONS FOR PREREADING REFLECTION AND JOURNALING

- What would you see as the potential benefits of providing opportunities for teachers to meet on an ongoing basis to discuss ideas that are of interest to them? What outcomes might result? What problems might be encountered?

- If you were given the opportunity to sit down with trusted colleagues and talk with them about teaching practices and educational issues, what are some of the topics that you would want to talk about? Why? Would you be willing to take time from your schedule to engage in these conversations? What factors would encourage or inhibit you from doing so?

- Think about the teachers in your building and their expectations for student work. Do they have similar expectations for the quality of student work? How do you know? When was the last time you sat with a group of colleagues and examined a piece of student work together? What do you see as the advantages and disadvantages of doing that?

- How often do teachers in your building work together on planning a specific lesson and then watch the lesson as it is implemented to study its impact on students? Does this seem like a powerful form of professional development to you?

# INTRODUCTION TO COLLEGIAL DEVELOPMENT GROUPS

Professional development for educators has taken on increased importance recently as a strategy to improve the quality of our schools. "Every modern proposal to reform, restructure, or transforms schools emphasizes professional development as a primary vehicle to bring about the needed changes " (Guskey, 1986, p. 5). Unfortunately, the impact of professional development on school change has not been very dramatic.

Clark and Florio-Ruane (2001) assert that historically teacher development efforts have been generally disappointing and ineffective for four interrelated reasons connected with the way most programs are designed and implemented. First, administrators, not teachers, design programs. As a result, teachers do not feel ownership of their own professional development. Second, the programs are designed based on a deficit model, attempting in one way or another to fix the teachers rather than capitalizing on teacher knowledge and wisdom. Third, professional development tends to be universal and standardized, offering the same training to all teachers regardless of the grade level or subjects that they teach. As a result, the important role of context in shaping effective teaching strategies is ignored. Fourth, the programs are short-range interventions focused on particular issues or innovations. They do not provide an ongoing, systematic mechanism for solving the problems that are inherent in the process of teaching and learning.

Clark and Florio-Ruane (2001) suggest that tinkering with the system will not do. They opt for a dramatic shift in the nature of professional development. "This shift is needed to engage teachers as reasoning and responsible professionals in the process of refining their knowledge, skills, and dispositions to teach in new ways that support pupils engaging in higher-order thinking across the content areas, and to empower teachers to assume leadership in the management of schools" (p. 6).

Collegial development groups represent the dramatic shift in professional development that Clark and Florio-Ruane call for. We define a collegial development group as a small (usually 12 or fewer participants) voluntary group of teachers who meet together regularly (at least once a month) on a long-term basis to support one another's personal and professional development through critical analysis of theories and ideas, new and existing practices, and student and teacher work. In reality, some lesson study events involve far more participants than 12, but our focus here is on lesson study within a school as opposed to large-scale lesson study. Lesson study teams within a school would typically fall into the 6–12 -person range. For example, in Highland Elementary School in California, teams of three to six teachers form a lesson study group. At the conclusion of the process, each lesson study group shares its conclusions with other lesson study groups in the school (Lewis, Perry, Hurd & O'Connell, 2006). Collegial development groups are collaborative in that power is shared equally among the participants. Although individuals may act as facilitators or coaches for sessions, either on a permanent or on a rotating basis, the control over the agenda is in the hands of the group as a whole. Though teachers typically direct the group, administrators and other staff members may be involved in the group as equal participants. External resources such as readings, videos, and expert consultants often inform the work of the group.

Collegial development groups address all of the typical shortcomings of traditional staff development discussed above. Because the group members control the agenda, ownership for professional development rests clearly in the hands of teachers. One of the underlying assumptions of collegial development groups is that although all teachers can improve their practice, teachers in general do not need to be "fixed". The vast majority of teachers are intelligent professionals who are thoughtful about their practice and have accumulated a great deal of practical wisdom. Their insights and ideas definitely need to be connected to external resources, but, at the end of the day, teachers are not the problem, they are part of the solution. The small size of collegial development groups gives participants the opportunity to contextualize ideas and practices. Participants can ask what a practice would look like in their particular setting and can choose to pursue topics that would be of interest to them, not to the faculty as a whole. In fact, collegial development groups often arise spontaneously out of the desire of a few teachers to study a particular topic (e.g., Reading Recovery programs, or National Science Foundation approved curricula in math and science). Finally, collegial development groups meet regularly over time. They represent a commitment to ongoing professional development, not to fixing a particular short-term problem.

## Types of Collegial Development Groups

We discuss three major types of collegial development groups: study groups, critical friends groups, and lesson study groups. Typically, study groups are designed by participants to explore and study ideas, innovations, theories, and practices that are currently not widely used in the district. The study and exploration occur through conversations generally stimulated by external sources including readings, videos, and conversations with outside consultants, who may come from a variety of contexts and roles (administrators, other teachers, parents, university professors, counselors, etc.). As noted, participation is voluntary, and group size is limited. Participants choose topics for conversation, and the conversation formats are open- ended and designed by the group. Typically, the responsibility for facilitating conversations rotates among group members.

Critical friends groups are similar to study groups in several ways including voluntary participation, limited group size, and participants having control of the topics and agendas. Critical friends of groups differ from study groups in that the topics are based on practices that teachers are using and in that sessions focus on examining either student work products or teacher thinking and practice. Both teacher and student work are examined through the use of conversation protocols. The protocols regulate the types of activities that occur during conversation and the duration of these various activities. Because pre-established protocols play such a large role in the conversations of critical friends groups, trained facilitators or coaches usually take the lead in facilitating conversations during the first few sessions in which a particular protocol is used. Thereafter, facilitation typically rotates among group members.

As mentioned previously, lesson study groups differ from the other two types of collegial development groups in that the total number of participants in a lesson study process may be very large. In Japan, lesson study events will sometimes draw more than 100 participants. However, a single lesson study team is typically somewhere between three and six teachers. A second major difference between lesson study and the two other types of collegial development groups lies in the focus of the work. Although the focus in study groups and critical friends groups is on conversation, the focus in lesson study is on the design, implementation, and analysis of research lessons that are developed collaboratively by the group, taught by an individual teacher, and observed by other members of the lesson study team. Each of the observers is asked to collect a specific type of data that has been decided upon by the group. The conversation that follows includes all those who have participated in the lesson and focuses on the data that were collected by the observers and the degree to which the intended goals were actually achieved by the lesson. Figure 6.1 summarizes the similarities and differences among these three types of collegial development groups.

## Benefits of Collegial Development Groups

Participating in collegial development groups benefits the individual participants and the overall school culture.  The opportunity to talk with other professionals about one's

**FIGURE 6.1**    Comparison of Study Groups, Critical Friends Groups, and Lesson Study Groups

|  | Study groups | Critical friends groups | Lesson study |
|---|---|---|---|
| Size | 12 or fewer | 12 or fewer | Variable |
| Participation | Voluntary | Voluntary | Voluntary |
| Topic | Chosen by group | Chosen by group | Research lessons developed by the group |
| Focus | Ideas, theories, and practices not in current use | Practices in current use | Design and analysis of research lessons |
| Conversations | Open ended and controlled by participants | Protocols control process | Focused on data collected while the lesson is being implemented and professional judgment |
| Facilitation | Rotates among group members | Initially led by trained facilitators | Led by group members with participation by others including invited guests with particular expertise |

practice helps the individual teacher become more adept at articulating his or her implicit theories and beliefs (Clark, 2001). As discussed in Chapter 2, most teachers have not been asked to articulate their platform of beliefs for others since they were initially interviewed for a teaching job. The result is that their beliefs often operate beneath the conscious level and, therefore, are not open to examination and change. Articulating one's beliefs for others allows one to reexamine and rethink those beliefs, a process that serves as a powerful impetus for teacher growth.

The benefits of articulating beliefs accrue to the listener as well as the speaker. Listening carefully to the beliefs and thinking of colleagues helps teachers develop greater capacity for perspective taking, that is, for seeing the world through the eyes of others (Clark, 2001). The benefits of perspective taking are clear. For example, teachers who are better at seeing school, subjects, and learning through the eyes of their students are more effective teachers. Kegan and Lahey (2001) suggest that a key factor explaining the difficulty many people experience in resolving conflicts is the tendency to believe that our own perceptions are more valid than the perceptions of others without ever attempting to check the validity of others' perceptions. Learning to be better at perspective taking is a powerful step toward developing the capacity for more positive interpersonal relationships with both children and adults.

In the process of articulating their beliefs and listening to others' before, teachers also reaffirm their commitment to putting their beliefs into practice (Clark, 2001). In the messy, busy, and dynamic world of classroom teaching, teachers can easily lose focus on what really matters most. With the pressures of all the curriculum mandates, state accountability systems, and required paperwork and meetings, there is very little time to sit back and reflect. Collegial development groups provide time for reflecting on beliefs and ideals. Group interactions can spur a recognition that beliefs and practices are no longer congruent and stimulate the teacher to make a personal commitment to align them more closely.

Study groups also offer very practical benefits in the form of new teaching strategies, new curriculum resources, and new methods of assessment that can provide solutions to specific problems of practice (Clark, 2001). Colleagues and experts involved in the process alike can point out very useful strategies to improve the teaching–learning process. Useful ideas need not even be new ideas. They can be minor adjustments to old ways of doing things that result in much greater efficiency and/or effectiveness.

When teachers bring specific problems and issues to the group for advice, they engage in a process that is very similar to that of doctors who consult with other specialists regarding patients. The result is typically a better solution to the problem. The opportunity to solve problems with colleagues can improve student achievement. "We know from research on staff development that cooperative, job-embedded learning has the greatest potential for improving teacher performance and, eventually, student learning" (Spillane & Seashore Louis, 2002, p. 93).

Finally, participation in collegial development groups benefits individual teachers by helping them feel a renewed sense of professionalism. The opportunity to participate in collegial development groups communicates to teachers that administrators recognize and respect teachers as thoughtful, knowledgeable practitioners. Having ownership of their professional development helps teachers to see themselves as responsible for their own growth on an ongoing basis. As noted in Chapter 3, self-direction and ownership are fundamental principles of adult learning and development. The interaction with other colleagues also helps teachers to recognize that as a group they do have the ability to make changes in their practice and in the school as an organization.

All three types of collegial development groups provide the three key benefits that were attributed to lesson study groups by Lewis, et al. (2006). First, participants enter the group with a learning stance. They expect to learn important information about their students, their craft, and about their subject matter as a result of participation. Second, the group not only has internal ownership over the process but also reaches out to the external knowledge base. For example, study groups read information that provides access to external expertise. Lesson study groups collect information and ideas from others as they plan research lessons. Critical friends groups use protocols for analyzing books and articles and also use this information in protocols related to student work and teacher practice. Finally, study groups serve the school's work. They assist teachers in managing the demands of external mandates while simultaneously improving the quality of professional service offered to students. These benefits provide a stark counterpoint to the criticism of traditional professional development.

Collegial development groups also have the potential to transform the culture of the school. "Teaching has been described as the second most private act in which teachers engage. In fact, schools have been characterized by some critics of public education as little more than independent kingdoms (classrooms) ruled by autonomous feudal lords (teachers) who are united only by a common parking lot" (DuFour & Eaker, 1998, p. 115). Collegial development groups offer one mechanism for disrupting the privatism, isolation, and fragmentation that have traditionally characterized teaching. They build relationships among teachers and create a sense of professional community (Birchak et al., 1998).

In Chapter 3, we asserted that most schools have a congenial culture rather than a collaborative one. Even teachers who have taught next door to each other for many years do not really know much about each other's teaching. Collegial development groups provide a professional connection that is otherwise lacking. Lesson study groups at Highland Elementary have been shown to help teacher's extend each others' thinking about subject matter and to begin to develop a sense of collective responsibility for student learning (Lewis et al. 2006). When teachers are connected to one another, a strong sense of community begins to develop. The school culture becomes collaborative, not isolated. Collaborative school cultures have been shown to have many beneficial aspects. They increase teachers' sense of creativity (Woods, 1993), motivating teachers to take risks and test new ideas (Rosenholtz, 1989; Helsby, 1999).

Collaborative cultures provide an ongoing support network that can help sustain teachers through difficult periods and setbacks (Nias, 1989). They stimulate increased opportunities for teacher learning (Hargreaves, 1994). The establishment of collaborative school cultures featuring joint work and common planning has been linked to gains in achievement, better solutions to problems, increased confidence among all members of the school community, better guidance for beginning teachers, and a greater variety of ideas, methods, and materials (Little, 1990). Collegial school cultures also result in increased feelings of teacher efficacy. The more collegial the school culture, the higher the teacher sense of efficacy or confidence in their ability to teach even the most difficult children (Chester & Beaudin, 1996). Bandura (1997) argued that a collective sense of efficacy, the groups' shared belief in their ability to positively influence students, is systematically connected with higher student achievement. In studying the impact of lesson study on school cultures, Lewis et al. summarized their findings in the following way. "Their comments also suggest that instructional coherence may emerge across classrooms and how a school-wide culture of learning from practice may be built as groups of teachers conduct and share investigations. Teachers may develop a collective sense of efficacy so that mandates like standards-based instruction feel less overwhelming" (2006, p. 276).

The establishment of a collaborative culture does present some challenges. As a sense of community and collaboration begin to develop, conflict will almost inevitably be more evident. Teachers who have seen the benefits of cooperative learning for their students recognize that an inevitable aspect of working together closely is more conflict. Administrators who wish to establish a collaborative school culture must, therefore, expect and be willing to work through this conflict. Typically, schools are able to avoid dealing with conflict because with little time for teachers to talk, conflicting beliefs and practices are not brought out into the open. When teachers begin to talk honestly in collegial development groups, conflicting views emerge. Though not always comfortable, conflicting viewpoints can be positive for the school culture. Teachers have the opportunity to understand one another, and working through the conflicting values may result in greater movement toward a common vision.

Collegial development groups also provide support for the implementation of new curricular and instructional ideas. The most difficult task for most schools in implementing new ideas is the transfer of the idea to classroom practice. Having the opportunity during the implementation process to share frustrations and successes and to get advice from peers who are struggling with the same innovation is a powerful mechanism for working through the "implementation dip" that accompanies any innovation. "Implementation dip" refers to the phenomenon in which a teacher will not be as smooth or polished in implementing new practices as he or she was in carrying out tried and true methods. Thus, even if the new practices appear to have promise of greater effectiveness, many teachers, who cannot handle the temporary discomfort, abandon the new ideas (Fullan, 2001). When we asked teachers about the obstacles they encountered in their attempts to change, the one major obstacle they mentioned most often was having to implement the changes alone. They often felt unsure about how well they were interpreting the new material. The intellectual work of thinking one's way through new programs is never more difficult than when it is undertaken alone (Hargreaves Earl, Moore, & Manning 2001). Collegial development groups offer the school a vehicle for helping teachers work through the implementation problems together.

In sum, "collegial development groups provide opportunities for individual teachers to interact professionally, develop norms of collaboration, inquire and experiment collaboratively, and, in so doing, foster the establishment of a shared culture. Such groups are forums for teachers to probe deeply into instructional practice, prying at the vary core of professional and personal values and identities" (Gimbert & Nolan, 1999).

# STUDY GROUPS

Our focus in this section is on small in-district teacher study groups that function as part of the teacher supervision and evaluation system. Two valuable types of study groups that will not be discussed are whole-school faculty study groups (WFSGs) and teacher networks that exist across school districts and even states.

WFSGs are created by the administration for purposes of professional development related to school improvement issues; all teachers in the school must participate (Murphy & Lick, 2001). WFSGs can be a powerful form of school improvement, but they are quite different in form, structure, and purpose from the study groups we discuss here. For a detailed explanation of WFSGs, consult Murphy and Lick (2001).

Teacher networks linking teachers across districts and states also offer a powerful form of professional development. Networks are often connected with large-scale projects such as the Bay Area Writing Project and the Foxfire Network or national organizations in various disciplines such as the National Council of Teachers of Mathematics and the

National Council of Teachers of English. These networks are quite different in scope, structure, and purpose from study groups within a school district. For a discussion of teacher networks and their impact on reform, see Lieberman and Grolnick (1996).

As noted earlier, a study group is a small group of teachers within a school or school district who meet voluntarily on a regular basis over time to study and explore ideas, theories, issues, and practices that are not currently in widespread use in the district. Though participants may choose to focus on topics that are of interest only to the group, the topics are most often closely connected to issues within the school or district or to initiatives and programs that the district and/or school is interested in exploring. Obviously, such a connection significantly increases the benefits of the group for the school and district.

## Topics and Norms

Birchak et al. (1998) provide excellent suggestions concerning the organization of study groups. Typically, the first two or three meetings of the group are used to make decisions about logistics and to begin identifying the topic(s) that the group will discuss. The topics that are chosen and the amount of time devoted to the topics vary across study groups. Some study groups choose to focus on a single subject (e.g., brain research), issue or dilemma (e.g., reconciling developmentally appropriate practice with required state tests for third graders), or question (e.g., What are the advantages and disadvantages of block scheduling?). Other study groups focus on a variety of questions or issues over the course of the year. The group usually selects readings and other outside resources that will serve as the focus for discussions. The group develops the format for conversations, and responsibility for facilitating the conversations typically rotates among members.

Among the logistical decisions to be made are when to meet, where to meet, how long to meet, the obligation of each member in terms of attendance, how to choose facilitators, and how to get materials that participants will be reading or viewing. Topic identification usually begins in the first meeting when participants brainstorm potential topics and discuss them briefly. Topic selection usually occurs at the second meeting after participants have had time to think about the topics independently. Exercise 6.1 Provides practices in brainstorming topics.

**EXERCISE 6.1   Identifying Topics for a Study Group**

---

**Directions:**   Brainstorm a list of topics that would be of interest to you if you were going to participate in a teacher study group in your school. In your list of topics, include at least three issues or dilemmas, three questions, and three general subjects.

---

The second meeting of the group is also a good time to determine the norms that will govern the interaction of group members. Having a set of agreed-upon expectations enables the group to operate smoothly and also to keep individual members on track. Without agreed-upon norms, there is a strong possibility that a single, strong-willed individual can take over and dominate the group—a very uncomfortable situation for everyone. Birchak and her colleagues provide an example of initial operating norms that were developed by a teacher study group in Arizona: (1) Take care of yourself; (2) Asking questions is okay; (3) No side conversations; (4) Not too much "homework"; (5) Avoid jargon; (6) Start and end on time; and (7) Everyone is important (1998, p. 36).

Development of the list of norms at the initial group meetings should be left open ended so that additional expectations can be discussed and added to the list as they become necessary. It can be helpful to take time on occasion to revisit the norms as a group and to ask, "How are we doing in living up to the expectations that we developed initially?" If the conclusion is that some of the expectations are not being met very well, the group needs to decide whether to change its behavior or its expectations. Sometimes expectations that seem important at the beginning of the process seem much less critical as time goes on.

## Meeting Structure

In addition to having a shared set of expectations, it is also helpful to have a general structure that can be followed for group meetings. As noted above, the first several meetings are devoted to making basic decisions. These decisions are likely to take at least two and sometimes part of the third meeting. Once these decisions have been made, the group can fall into a common structure for conducting its meetings. In our experience with study groups, we have typically met for 90 min. Following the norms identified above, we insist on rigid starting and ending times. If the group gets into the habit of beginning late, our experience tells us that the starting time will get later and later.

Various meeting structures are possible; we will describe one that we have found effective in different contexts. The first 15–20 min are generally set aside to allow people to share experiences or insights they have had, in the time intervening since the last meeting, that are connected to the topic being studied. If the group has reached the point where some members have tried out ideas and suggestions, this is a wonderful time to share those experiments. We have tried our best not to turn the sharing opportunity into a gripe session although it is sometimes important for people to get things off their chests. If they are not allowed to do that, the entire time is unproductive for them. Keeping the sharing to 20 min ensures that not all of the study group session will be devoted to complaining.

The second part of the meeting is usually devoted to talking about the readings in groups of two to four people. We generally have members of these small groups discuss what parts of the reading inspired, enlightened, confused, angered, delighted, or frustrated them. In our experience, looking at these six types of emotional reactions has proven to be a great catalyst for promoting rich discussion. The small-group part of the activity usually lasts about 30 min.

Following these small-group discussions, we then take time to share reactions and insights as a large group. Sometimes, the large-group session consists of follow-up reporting on the small-group sharing that took place; other times, however, it has little relationship to the small-group discussions. Instead, participants may introduce new ideas or practices that were not directly addressed in the readings but somehow seem related to the general topic. The direction of this discussion is determined to a large extent by the facilitator with the consent of the group members.

We try to reserve the final 15 min of the session for group maintenance tasks. These tasks include periodically discussing how well the group feels it is doing in living up to its own expectations, discussing whether to continue with the current topic or change to a new topic, making sure that everyone knows when and where the next meeting will take place, identifying what will be read or viewed to prepare for the next meeting, and making sure that everyone has access to these materials. On occasion, it is necessary to devote a larger period of time to group maintenance. For example, if the group indicates the desire to switch to a new topic, time must be devoted to identifying the new topic.

The general structure that we have followed and recommended here has worked extremely well in a variety of different study groups; however, you may find that a different structure works best for you. As noted, the decision on structure is best made by the group itself.

## Roles

Birchak and colleagues (1998) identified three important roles for study groups: facilitator, note taker, and timekeeper. The roles may rotate from meeting to meeting or may be permanent. In the case of facilitators, unless there is some compelling reason why one individual should take this role, rotation is preferable. Rotating the responsibility for facilitation seems to motivate everyone to pay more attention to both norms and general structure as each member will be responsible at some point for structuring the meeting and upholding the group norms. Rotating this responsibility also helps to underscore the equality of all participants. In addition, the different styles of facilitation bring both diversity and freshness to group meetings.

The facilitator is responsible for arriving early to make sure the location is available, getting the meeting started on time, following the general structure that was agreed upon, holding the group to its expectations, facilitating discussion and making sure that every member has an opportunity to participate, and taking care of logistics and group maintenance issues at the end of the meeting, including the choice of the next facilitator if the responsibility is rotating.

The designated note taker keeps track of the group's decisions regarding norms, meeting structure, roles, and topic as well as ongoing logistical matters, that make the functioning of the group much more efficient. The note taker can also keep track of the various issues that are discussed and positions that are taken. The goal is simply to have some ongoing record of the group's activities. It is not necessary to keep detailed notes on who said what and why. Birchak and colleagues (1998) suggest that the note taker be responsible for sending out a summary of the notes (no more than one page) within a week of the meeting.

The timekeeper makes the group members aware when it is time to begin and to end the meeting. In addition, if the meeting is structured in parts, as outlined above, the timekeeper makes the group aware of the various transition times. Having an assertive timekeeper can be very useful in keeping the group on track.

Case 6.1 provides an extended example of how a middle school study group might function. Vandeweghe and Varney also provide a detailed description of the evolution of a teacher study group at Rishel Middle School in Denver in their *Phi Delta Kappan* article (2006). The following description of the group's work was written by Heather Leaman, the teacher who was responsible for the initial development of the group. As you will see, the group grew dramatically during its second year as a result of positive reports from first-year participants. In fact, its size during the second year far exceeded what we feel is optimal. Even though this large group seemed to operate very successfully, an alternative would have been to split the group in two, making sure that each of the new groups contained a mix of old and new members. The success of the unusually large second-year group likely resulted from the fact that, due to a variety of factors, attendance at monthly meetings typically was limited to 12 members or less. The group's open attendance policy, established at the initial meetings, solved the problems associated with having too many participants.

# CASE 6.1 MIDDLE SCHOOL TEACHER STUDY GROUP

## Study Group Description

**Year 1** The Cocalico Middle School study group convened at the beginning of the 2000-2001 school year as an alternative to the traditional in-service day professional development opportunities typically offered by the school district. The study group, comprised of 12 teachers of grades 6–8, was designed to meet once per month, for a 1-h session, directly following the close of the school day. This was to allow for the optimum ease of teacher involvement. Teachers volunteered their time for membership in the group and as meeting facilitators.

**Year 2** The second year that the study group was in operation, more teachers were interested in participating. Some heard from other teachers that the group was a beneficial experience for them, and others joined in order to meet newly developed state requirements for ongoing professional development. During the second year, the format and function of the study group remained similar, though group dynamics were changed as the size of the group enlarged.

## Participants

**Year 1** During the first year, there were 12 volunteer participants. Ten of the 12 volunteered as meeting facilitators working either alone or in pairs. The group was comprised of three males and nine females. Of the 12 participants, eight were traditional classroom teachers. The remaining four held positions in guidance, special education, administration, and library media. Most teachers attended 80–100% of the meetings.

**Year 2** During 2001–2002, each of the members from the first year rejoined the group, except for the administrator. Eleven additional teachers joined the study group on a regular basis. These teachers came from a variety of different disciplines including special education and ranged in years of teaching experience from 2 to 29. Most were able to attend 50–100% of the meetings. Again, members volunteered to act as facilitators for each of the meetings. Twelve of the group members held facilitation roles either individually or in pairs during year 2 of the group.

## Organization

The founding member organized the study group. Her role was to inform the teachers at Cocalico Middle School of the group's intentions and to organize the initial meeting for the year. At its initial meeting, the group brainstormed potential topics for discussion, voted on and selected the most popular topics, and decided on facilitators for each monthly meeting. The founding member then served as organizer for the meeting dates, by conferring with the monthly facilitator and e-mailing dates to the remainder of the group. In the future, each facilitator would handle this organizational role. Group members were free to come to as many or as few meetings as their interest and schedule allowed.

The founding member also served as researcher and information gatherer for the facilitators of each topic. Some facilitators had participants read selections prior to the meeting; others chose to read materials for their own background information but not to have participants read it before the meeting. They led the meeting

Participants included the following middle school personnel:

| M/F | Certification | Subject/grade | Experience (years) |
| --- | --- | --- | --- |
| Male | Secondary education | Social studies/8 | 32 |
| Male | Secondary education | Science/7 | 14 |
| Male | Guidance | Grade 6 | 6 |
| Female | Elementary education | Language arts/6 | 29 |
| Female | Library | Library media/6–8 | 26 |
| Female | Secondary | Language arts/7 | 6 |
| Female | Special education | Special education | 18 |
| Female | Family consumer science | FCS/6–8 | 30 |
| Female | Elementary | Social studies/6 | 9 |
| Female | Elementary | Language arts/7 | 2 |
| Female | Administrator | Principal/6–8 | 13 |
| Female | Elementary | Science/6 | 10 |

by presenting and discussing key points in the reading, providing reading materials for other group members at the meeting itself. Some facilitators chose to use research as a basis for discussion, whereas others had topics that worked best with discussion, only. There were no organizational changes for year 2.

## Topics

In both year 1 and year 2, topics ranged from practice-based subjects to those more philosophically oriented. Some concerned problems or issues faced by

- Year 1:
  - Student learning styles
  - Alternatives to yearly administrative observation of teachers (differentiated supervision)
  - Reading of nonfiction materials
  - Viewing video: *Emotional Lives of Boys*
  - Developmentally appropriate practice for middle-level students
  - The role of the school in society
  - Teacher empowerment/leadership
  - National and state assessment

## Typical Session

A typical session began at 3 p.m., the official dismissal time for teachers at the middle school. Meetings occurred in the school library, the most comfortable location in the building, and one where few disruptions occur. As teachers entered, there was time for casual conversation over snacks and juice prior to the start of the meeting. The session facilitator announced the start of the meeting. He or she typically explained how the meeting would be run, either by whole-group discussion or by breaking into smaller groups prior to whole-group conversation. This often depended on the number of participants attending the meeting. Meetings were informal and teachers took turns offering comments and questions regarding the topic. The facilitator determined, individually, how much or how little he or she structured the meeting. Some facilitators prepared outlines to structure the meeting, others made a list of relevant ideas pertaining to their topic, and others allowed for an open discussion session, interjecting and steering the conversation as needed. By the end of the session, most group members had shared either in small groups or within whole-group discussion. Sessions ended at four, though if a topic had been fully discussed, they ended earlier. Typical sessions ran a bit past 4 p.m. with teachers leaving as they needed to. Often, several members stayed behind to finish conversation in pairs or small groups while reorganizing library tables.

the teachers at this particular school, whereas others applied to general education topics. Each year, the initial meeting was designated for topic brainstorming and choosing. The group's first meeting also included readings on the purpose of and theory behind collaboration among educators and the use of study groups as a form of professional development. The second year included introducing new members to the format, purpose, and benefits of the study group, as seen by the previous year's members. The topics chosen by group members included:

- Year 2:
  - Youth culture and critical media analysis
  - Disseminating crisis information
  - ESL and cultural diversity
  - Co-teaching/team teaching/full inclusion
  - Stress management for adults
  - Book talk: *A Breed Apart*
  - Sharing session: classroom teaching techniques

## Participant Reactions

Perhaps the strongest evidence that this middle school study group was beneficial to teachers was the growth in participant numbers from year 1 to year 2. Plans for the third year of the study group again showed an increased number of participants who intend to participate in the coming year. When study group participants were interviewed concerning their experiences, their comments provided concrete evidence of the benefits of participation. The following is a list of comments from study group members:

"There is no other opportunity available in the district where teachers can completely self-direct their learning and professional growth."

"It is a format which allows each of us to share our area of expertise and recognize expertise that other teachers have."

"I like the sense of camaraderie that the study group allows, the sense that I'm not alone in this."

"I got to hear various opinions from people with different experience and backgrounds. Many discussions inspired me to explore an issue after study group or re-think my position on an issue."

"I liked getting to hear other teachers' points of view."

"The benefits were hearing the experiences of the veteran teachers and learning about some of the issues that we as teachers face."

"I liked hearing different ideas and perceptions from teachers of all experience levels."

"It was a way for me to get to know teachers since I'm new to the building."

"I learned a lot about certain issues that I wouldn't normally have delved into, on my own. There's not time."

"It's great adult time to talk about educational issues. There's no time during the day to do this."

"I think staff development should be self-directed and empowering to teachers. Our study group does this."

---

**EXERCISE 6.2    Analyzing Group Structure and Benefits**

**Directions** Jot down your individual answer to the following two questions and then form a triad with two other classmates to discuss what each of you found individually.

1. What similarities and differences did you note between the structure and functioning of study groups as described by the authors and the structure and functioning of the Cocalico Middle School Study Group?
2. What similarities and differences did you notice between the benefits of study group participation identified by the authors and the benefits described in the quotes from the Cocalico teachers?

---

As you probably discovered from completing Exercise 6.2, the area in which there is the greatest congruence between the earlier discussion of study groups and this example is in benefits for participants. Many of the potential benefits that we reported in the initial section of the chapter were echoed in the words of these participants. You also saw a structure that not only resembles the structure we recommended but also deviates from it in several ways. We emphasize again that the group itself must decide on its structure and organization. Successful study groups can be organized in multiple way, and, consequently, successful study groups may look quite different from each other.

# CRITICAL FRIENDS GROUPS

As the first section of the chapter explained, critical friends groups (CFGs) are small groups of teachers who meet voluntarily on a regular basis (usually once a month) to examine their own work and the resulting student learning with the aid of conversation protocols. Typically, CFGs are facilitated by a coach who has been trained to use the various protocols.

Critical friends groups should not be confused with the concept of a critical friend in the action research process. In action research critical friends are individuals, usually external to the school, who collaborate one-on-one with teacher researchers. This is far different from groups of teachers in the same school who meet regularly to discuss teaching practices and student learning.

Critical friends groups, though a relatively recent invention, have grown dramatically. They were initially developed as a result of the work of the Annenberg Institute for School Reform, an outgrowth of Ted Sizer's Coalition of Essential Schools. A group of professional development specialists, known as the National School Reform Faculty of the Annenberg Institute, collaborated to implement a form of professional development that would challenge practitioners and improve student learning through collegial interactions (Dunne, Nave, & Lewis, 2000). Dunn et al. described the outcome of this collaborative effort: "The work of these reformers resulted in a program designed to help practitioners, working in CFGs, identify student learning goals that made sense in their schools, look reflectively at practices designed to achieve those goals, and collaboratively examine student and teacher work in order to meet their objectives" (2000, p. 9). These critical friends groups are facilitated by coaches who are trained through the National School Reform Faculty. The coaches create a collegial culture within the group focused on reflection on teacher practice and student work. The principal vehicles for creating this collegial culture are conversation protocols that direct the activities of group members (Dunne et al. 2000).

Protocols for conversations are guidelines and prescribed steps that everyone understands and agrees to follow. According to Allen (1998), protocols are structured to allot time for different activities and create opportunities for different participants to speak and listen. The intent is to promote the kinds of in-depth conversations that teachers are not used to having in schools. According to the Nation School Reform Faculty (2000), protocols have multiple advantages in structuring collegial interaction. Protocols are vehicles for building the skills and culture necessary for collaborative work. The use of a protocol makes it safe for teachers to ask challenging questions to one another and also ensures that the group members feel a sense of equality in terms of opportunities for listening and speaking. Protocols make it more likely that all group members will have the opportunity to have their issues attended to by the group. They also require participants to engage in thoughtful and reflective listening without feeling the need to respond instantaneously. Similarly, protocols give presenters time to listen carefully to feedback from others without needing to respond or defend. They provide a certain measure of protection to those presenters who are asked to put their dilemmas and problems on the floor for the edification of themselves and others. Finally, protocols have been designed to make maximum use of the limited time that is available for conversations in schools (National School Reform Faculty, 2000).

Before they first participate in the use of a CFG protocol, many teachers express reluctance at having to adhere to a rigid set of guidelines for interaction. They fear that the process will be too constrained and artificial. One of the authors had the same reservations when asked to participate in CFG protocols at a conference. The experience of the author, however, mirrors the experience of most teachers. The conversations were not at all artificial or limiting. They were deep, insightful, and freeing. The resulting conversations were far more reciprocal and substantive than is typically the case. Protocols give group members time to listen carefully without needing to respond.

Although the protocols are quite powerful, they, in and of themselves, do not ensure productive conversations. The presence of a well-trained coach to facilitate the protocols is an important component of a successful critical friends group. It is especially important that a skilled facilitator be present for the first few uses of each protocol. Those who are interested in becoming trained as coaches for critical friends groups should consult the web site of the National School Reform Faculty, http://www.harmonyschool.org/nsrf/default.html, for information on new coaches' seminars. The seminars are given quite frequently at various locations across the country. There are two main types of protocols, protocols for examining student work and those focused on teacher thinking and practice. We now look at each type in turn.

## Examining Student Work

Collaborative examination of student work was the primary task of critical friends groups, and this strategy has been demonstrated to be a powerful mechanism for promoting both teacher development and improved student learning. A variety of protocols can be used for examining student work, including the Tuning Protocol, the Collaborative Assessment Conference, the ATLAS Protocol, and the Slice. Information on these various protocols can be downloaded for educational purposes by nonprofit organizations under certain restrictions from the web site of the Looking at Student Work (LASW) Collaborative (see "Suggestions for Further Reading and Research"). A variety of student products can be examined through these protocols including, writing, drawings, tests, worksheets, and videos.

In all of these protocols, the teacher–presenter brings one or more samples of student work for the group to discuss using the protocol. The student work that is brought to the group can be quite varied, for example, one sample of a single student's work, multiple samples of a single student's work over time, or the work of several students such as contrasting samples of high-quality and low-quality work. After carefully reading the work sample(s), CFG participants, using the protocol guidelines, share their understanding of the student's work and the learning that it represents. The focus of the group's discussion depends on the protocol that is being used. At the end of the discussion of student work, the participants discuss any generalizations that can be made about the work, about student learning, or about teaching practices. The final step in most protocols is an opportunity for group members to reflect on how well the conversation went, how well the protocol functioned, and to suggest improvements for the future. Depending on the amount of time that has been reserved for the group to work together and the specific protocol (protocols require anywhere from 45 to 75 min for each teacher–presenter), one or two teachers may be able to present student work.

David Allen cites three guidelines for facilitators of CFGs that engage in examining student work. Facilitators should be assertive in keeping time so that all of the components of the protocol can be used. Facilitators should seek to protect teacher presenters from inappropriate or hurtful comments and questions (e.g., comments or questions that demean the teacher or the student). Finally, facilitators should try to discourage blanket praise and encourage probing questions that will enable the presenter to view the work in a new light (Allen, 1998).

Useful guidelines for participants of CFGs to keep in mind as they examine student work are available (Cushman, 1996). Participants should stay focused on the evidence that is present in the student work and look for patterns in the work that show what the student was thinking. Participants should also try to identify patterns in their own thinking about student work and attempt to relate these patterns to how they work with students in the classroom. In addition, participants are expected to be respectful of teacher–presenters and of the facilitator's role in maintaining adherence to the protocol.

Figure 6.2 describes one of the protocols for examining student work, the Collaborative Assessment Conference. Although each protocol is somewhat different, the phases in the Collaborative Assessment Conference are very similar to those in other protocols. The time limits are simply suggestions. The actual time will vary depending on the number and types of work samples.

**EXERCISE 6.3  Using the Collaborative Assessment Conference**

Form a group with five other students. Use the collaborative assessment conference protocol to examine a piece of student work that one of you has brought to class. Write a brief reflection that explains how your thinking about the student work was affected by the conversation that took place.

**FIGURE 6.2** Collaborative Assessment Conference (CAC) (Adapted from Blythe, Allen, & Powell, 1998)

**Part 1—Introductory activities (time varies depending on work sample(s))**
>    A. The facilitator convenes the group.
>    B. The presenter provides copies of the work for all of the participants to see or read.
>    C. Participants read the work individually.

**Part 2—Literal description of the student work (10 min)**
> The participants describe what they see literally without interpreting or assessing the quality of the work. The presenter is silent.

**Part 3—Questions raised by the student work (10 min)**
>    A. The participants raise any questions that they have about the work including the assignment, the student, or the conditions under which the work was done.
>    B. The presenter does not respond to the questions at this point but does note them.

**Part 4—Focusing on the student's thinking and understanding (10 min)**
> The group tries to identify what the student was thinking, understood, was puzzled by, and/or was working through in completing the work. The presenter is a silent listener.

**Part 5—The presenting teacher speaks (15 min)**
>    A. The presenter describes what he or she sees in the student work, both a literal description and his or her sense of what the student was thinking.
>    B. In giving his or her perspective, the presenter gives information that he or she feels is important in answering the questions raised by the group.
>    C. The presenter discusses his or her reaction to the comments made by the other participants.

**Part 6—Implications for teaching and learning (10 min)**
> The group discusses any generalizations it can find about student work, student learning, and/or instructional practices.

**Part 7—Reflecting on and closing the CAC (10 Min)**
>    A. The members discuss how the conversation went, how well the protocol worked, and any changes that should be made in the future.
>    B. The participants thank the presenter for sharing the work to help them learn.

## Examining Teacher Practice and Thinking

Though CFGs were originally developed to focus on student work, the underlying intent was to impact teaching practices and to enhance teacher learning. During the last decade the focus has broadened to explicitly address teaching practice and teacher thinking. Several protocols, including the Critical Incident Protocol, the Success Analysis Protocol, and the Consultancy Dilemma, were developed specifically to focus on teaching practice.

The guidelines for the facilitator of CFGs focusing on teacher practice and thinking are essentially the same as those identified above for facilitating the examination of student work. Keeping time, protecting the teacher–presenter, and promoting thoughtful conversation are important tasks for the facilitator. General guidelines for participants require above all that they listen carefully to the presenter and really try to understand his or her point of view, without expressing negative or positive judgments about the teacher's practice or thinking. Participants are also encouraged to ask probing questions that might help the presenter to see components of the situation that were not apparent beforehand. The task of the participant is not to lead the presenter to a particular solution or way of thinking about the issue, but rather to broaden the way that the presenter is thinking, to bring into play additional perspectives that might be helpful, and to more clearly define the issues and questions that need to be addressed.

The various protocols for examining teacher thinking and practice follow the same general format. The teacher–presenter describes the situation, providing brief background and context. The participants ask both literal and probing questions to help them understand the situation better. There is a period of time during which the presenter is silent and participants talk about what the presenter has said and the new insights and questions that it raises for them. The presenter then responds to the participant talk, after which all members identify any generalizations that can be made about teacher thinking or practice. Finally, the group reflects on its work and the effectiveness of the protocol.

Figure 6.3 describes the Consultancy Dilemma Protocol, in which the presenter discusses a dilemma that he or she is facing and asks for the group's input on how to think about it more productively. The dilemmas may focus on

---

**FIGURE 6.3** Consultancy Dilemma Protocol

**(Adapted from Thompson-Grove, 2002)**

**Part 1—Introduction (10 min)**

    A. The presenter describes the dilemma that he or she is facing, including brief contextual background.

    B. The presenter phrases the dilemma as a question that he or she needs to resolve. The question is phrased in terms of what action the presenter might take, not the actions of others.

**Part 2—Literal questions (5 min)**

    The group asks who, what, when, and where questions that have factual answers.

**Part 3—Probing questions (10 min)**

    A. The group asks questions that try to expand the presenter's thinking or help him or her see the dilemma through a new perspective.

    B. The presenter responds to the questions if he or she chooses to do so.

**Part 4—Observed discussion (10 min)**

    The participants talk with one another about the insights and ideas that they have concerning the dilemma while whereas the presenter observes silently. The goal is for the participants to introduce missing points of view, to identify the presenter's hidden assumptions, and to relate the dilemma to situations that they have faced.

**Part 5—Presenter response (10 min)**

    A. The presenter responds to what he or she has heard from the participant discussion.

    B. The group discusses the dilemma and attempts to reframe the original questions so that the presenter sees it in a different light.

**Part 6—Generalizations (5 min)**

    The group identifies any generalizations about teaching and learning that can be drawn from this dilemma.

**Part 7—Reflection on the process (5 min)**

    The group reflects on the quality of the conversation and discusses how well the protocol worked.

- student issues (e.g., how to motivate a group of under-achievers to do their best on the state assessment test);
- instructional issues (e.g., how to decide whether it is worth the effort to insist that students who lack social skills work in cooperative groups or whether to allow them to work individually);
- parent issues (e.g., how to deal with parents who think their fourth-grade son is more advanced than he really is);
- colleague issues (e.g., how to deal with a protégé who sees curriculum in a very different way); or
- administrator issues (e.g., how to get support from the administration in dealing with a discipline problem).

The group's goal is not to resolve the issue but to help the teacher think about it more productively. This dilemma protocol was originally designed by the Coalition of Essential Schools National Re:Learning Faculty Program and was revised by Gene Thompson-Grove of the National School Reform Faculty (Thompson-Grove, 2002). The descriptioning Figure 6.3 was adapted from her work.

---

**EXERCISE 6.4   Using the Consultancy Dilemma Protocol**

---

**Directions:**   Form a group with two other students. Each of you should come to the group prepared to be the presenter for a consultancy dilemma. Use the protocol three times with each of you serving as the presenter once and as the facilitator once. Write a reflection that examines: (1) your perceptions as presenter; (2) your perceptions as the facilitator; and (3) your perceptions as a respondent.

---

As suggested above, there are a variety of specific protocols that can be used to examine both student work and teacher thinking and practice. Our experience, as well as that of hundreds of teachers from across the country, indicates that critical friends groups provide an extremely powerful mechanism for transforming educational practice (Bambino, 2002; Easton, 2002). Incorporating CFGs and study groups as key elements of a teacher supervision and evaluation system dramatically increases the potential of that system for improving teaching and learning.

# LESSON STUDY GROUPS

Although it may seem deceptively simple on the surface, lesson study is a complex process that combines elements of action research and study groups. Participants in lesson study come together to learn more about themselves, their students, and their subject matter through a defined process focused on research lessons. Though the process is focused on the development and analysis of a single lesson (that may be redesigned and implemented several times), the purpose is not, as some have mistakenly believed, the perfection of that individual lesson. The goal is to learn about teaching, students, curriculum, and subject matter much more globally by getting at underlying principles and concepts. As was the case with classroom supervision as noted in Chapter 2, it is possible to go through the steps of lesson study in a rather mechanical way without attending to the underlying intentions and the spirit of the process. Experiencing the process mechanically may lead to a well-designed single lesson, but it is very unlikely that it will lead to any complex learning that is generalizable across lesson, and perhaps, even across subject matter. Thus, before discussing the logistics of the process, it is important to articulate the general principles and key skills that are the heart of the endeavor.

## Principles of Lesson Study

Lewis et al. (2006) identify four principles that should undergird the lesson study process. First, lesson study is about teacher learning, not just about lessons. Some individuals see lesson study as a process of polishing lessons and practicing them so that they will eventually become showcase lessons. It would be much more productive to see research lessons as hypotheses that are tested through an evidence-based action research process. The lesson study team is like a group of researchers who combine their knowledge about teaching, students, and subject matter to develop a hypothesis about what teaching strategies will be most effective in achieving certain goals. The heart of the process is not polishing lessons but rather analyzing the effectiveness of the lesson by examining the data that were collected during the lesson and discussing them with knowledgeable colleagues. The outcome is a deeper understanding of the process of teaching and learning, not a perfect lesson.

A second principle of lesson study suggests that the quality of the lesson study process hinges on skillful observation and subsequent discussion. The process of data collection in lesson study parallels the process of data collection in classroom observation and peer coaching. Specific foci for data collection are chosen as the lesson is being designed. Lesson study team members take responsibility for designing the data collection tools and also for collecting data during the lesson. All members of the team are mutually responsible for collecting data that will guide the analysis of the lesson. Lewis, et al. (2006) suggest that the most profitable lesson analyses are guided by a set of preplanned questions about the lesson that are closely related to the data that were collected. The parallels to effective postobservation conferencing as discussed in Chapter 2 are obvious.

"Lesson study is enhanced by turning to outside sources of knowledge" (Lewis et al., 2006, p. 275). This third principle of lesson study suggests that teachers involved in the lesson study process should consult both the professional literature as well as individuals with particular types of expertise at two distinct points in the process. When the research lesson is planned, team members should conduct systematic research to identify lessons focusing on the same concepts that have been developed by others, especially those with considerable subject matter expertise. They should also examine multiple textbooks to see how the topic is addressed and covered in various ways in these texts. In the post-lesson analysis, expertise becomes a key factor in determining how much participants learn from the process. Inviting outside experts to attend, to pose questions, and to participate in the analysis is a powerful strategy for elevating the level of conversation. If outside expertise is not available in person, connecting to the available literature should be a standard component of the lesson analysis process.

The fourth principle of lesson study as articulated by Lewis et al. (2006) is that the phases or components of the lesson study process should be balanced and integrated. The authors suggest that those who are relatively new to the lesson study process spend many meetings developing and refining the research lesson and spend only one meeting analyzing the lesson after it has been taught. This has the unfortunate effect of making the teaching of the lesson more of a performance than a hypothesis test. More sophisticated lesson study teams spend more time in the lesson analysis phase and also tend to see the process as connected across research lessons. They use findings and ideas from past research lessons as valuable information for planning future research lessons, and they attempt to compare findings across lessons to test the generalizability of the concepts and principles that are discussed. In this way, the lesson study process becomes more cyclic in nature, resembling the cycle of classroom supervision very closely.

## The Lesson Study Process

Given this clear understanding of the principles that underlie the lesson study process, we can now turn our attention to the components of the process itself. In general, there are three major components to the process: collaboratively designing the research lesson; teaching the lesson to a particular group of students while collecting observational data; and the post-lesson analysis conversation.

***Collaboratively Designing the Research Lesson*** This phase of the lesson study process typically occurs over multiple meetings of the lesson study team. In choosing a topic for a research lesson, team members typically choose to focus on lessons that meet one or more of the following criteria: (1) the lesson has proven to be particularly problematic in achieving the desired student learning; (2) the lesson plays a particularly central or key role in the school curriculum; or (3) the lesson focuses on a big idea that is central to developing future knowledge in the discipline. The team members often focus on lessons that achieve both subject matter goals as well as long-term goals for student learning, such as learning to cooperate effectively with others or learning to think critically. Although it is certainly possible to focus lesson study on topics that do not match these criteria, the outcomes for teacher learning are likely to be reduced. Exercise 6.5 provide practice in choosing a research lesson topic.

Once team members select the topic for the lesson, they begin the process of locating resources to help plan the lesson. Typically, they examine a variety of textbooks to examine the similarities and differences in how the topic is handled. They also search the Internet and print literature to identify any example lessons that have been developed and shared by other lesson study teams or by individual teachers. Simultaneously, they begin to search for materials that can be used to help students understand the concept more deeply. Team members also examine their own subject matter knowledge regarding this topic. If necessary, they spend time developing their own knowledge and skills. This may be accomplished through their own research or with the help of an external expert who is willing to help the group.

After example lessons have been identified and potential materials have been collected, the team actually designs the lesson. In designing the lesson, the team pays particular attention to the learning goals for students. Their task is to develop a well-thought-out plan that will enhance student achievement of these goals. Thus, the goals drive the actual development process. In designing the lesson, the team also thinks deeply about effective ways to assess the impact of the lesson on students.

Typically, observational data are used to assess the impact as well as any field notes taken by the observers and any actual student work samples. In particular, the team members focus their data collection efforts on strategies that will help the team understand the thinking that students engage in during the lesson. Team members also develop a list of questions concerning the effectiveness of the lesson that they will discuss during the post-lesson analysis conversation. The final result of the design phase of the process is a well-articulated lesson plan, based on external and internal resources and knowledge, with a list of data collection strategies and analysis questions that can be used to assess the impact of the lesson on student achievement of the specified goals.

**EXERCISE 6.5   Choosing Research Lesson Topics**

It would be best to do this exercise with a teaching colleague, but it can be done individually as well. Think about the curriculum that you teach or have taught most recently and do the following:

1. Identify two or three lesson topics that would fit the criteria identified above.
2. List the specific goals that lessons on these topics are supposed to achieve.
3. Identify resources, print, nonprint, or human, that you could use in planning these lessons.
4. Identify data that could be collected to help determine if these goals were actually achieved by a lesson.

*Implementing the Lesson*   The second phase of the lesson study process is the actual implementation of the lesson with a particular group of students. Typically, one teacher implements the lesson with his/her students while the other team members collect the agreed-upon data. In collecting the data, observers may often engage the students in conversations and ask questions to help them capture students' thinking. Having students articulate what they are doing and thinking is the most valid way to get at student thinking. In collecting data, the goal of the observers is to develop the ability to really see, hear, and understand what students are experiencing as a result of the lesson. Their focus is much more on the students than it is on the teacher. Typically, lessons last only one instructional period, but they may extend over several days depending on the lesson goals.

*Post-Lesson Analysis*   As close to the lesson as possible, lesson study team members meet, often with the participation of others, to engage in a conversation that analyzes the effectiveness of the lesson in meeting the specified goals. One of the lesson study team members agrees to lead the conversation. As noted above, the most effective lesson analysis conversations rely on questions about the lesson effectiveness that were developed by the team members during the lesson design process. The conversation leader chooses an important question about the lesson and poses the question to the group. In the discussion of the question, any pertinent data that were collected by observers are shared. In addition, the teacher shares his/her perceptions that were formed while teaching the lesson. Typically, team members do most of the discussing but also invite nonteam members to participate. The discussion leader monitors the flow of conversation and introduces other questions, as appropriate and as needed, to maintain the flow of the process. If an external expert has been invited to participate in the process, that individual is typically asked to make comments about his/her observations about the lesson. After the key questions and important data have been covered, the discussion leader asks the group to summarize the key insights that have been gained from the lesson analysis. This process may take more than one meeting. The study team members may then decide to redesign or refine the lesson and teach it again in order to gain more insights. If this is the case, the design process begins again. As was the case in the Highland Elementary lesson study process, the study team members may also share their insights and conclusions with other lesson study teams or with the entire school faculty.

Additional details concerning the lesson study process may be found in Lewis (2002a, and 2002b) and on the web sites identified under "Additional resources." As noted earlier, lesson study seems simple on the surface, but it is quite complex. Lewis et al. (2006) suggest that the deceptive simplicity of the process has encouraged some neophytes to engage in the process without the benefit of those who have more expertise and experience in the process. Such efforts typically do not produce the type of in-depth, generalized teacher learning that can be acquired through participation in well-designed lesson study processes. Those wishing to begin lesson study would be well advised to work with those who are already knowledgeable in the process.

# FACILITATING COLLEGIAL DEVELOPMENT GROUPS AS A TEACHER SUPERVISION PROCESS

## Logistical Considerations

As collegial development groups are teacher driven, the administrator's role will vary from group to group depending on the wishes of the teachers and the administrator. As we have seen, collegial development groups make several logistical decisions; some of these decisions may require administrative help.

One decision that must be made is when and where the group will meet. Most groups meet at a regular time and place convenient for group members. Some schools do allow collegial development groups to meet during scheduled staff development days or to substitute collegial development group meetings for mandatory in-service day attendance. This is particularly true in the case of lesson study groups. In schools where participation in whole faculty study groups or critical friends groups is mandated, the district provides time for these groups to meet. Voluntary collegial development groups typically meet on their own time.

A second logistical decision concerns resources the group needs—materials for lessons, books, copies of journal articles, videotapes, and/or advice from external consultants as well as, in the case of critical friends groups, either an external facilitator or training for a teacher to be a facilitator. Books, videotapes, and other materials can often be acquired through school or district staff development funds. Within schools, in addition to discretionary funds that administrators might have, librarians often have small amounts of money to purchase professional literature for the school library and may, thus, be an alternative source of support. If none of these resources are available, teachers buy their own books and copy materials on their own.

As with action research, school administrators can be a valuable asset in connecting teacher study groups to external consultants. Teachers in other buildings, administrators, specialized support staff, teachers and administrators from centralized educational service agencies, and faculty from higher education can play valuable roles in teacher study groups. Regardless of the type of expertise that is needed, the administrator often has external contacts that can be useful in finding the appropriate resources. With CFGs, where there is a need to either employ an external facilitator or provide training in facilitation for one or more teachers, we feel that providing training is the better option. Training develops in-house expertise that can be used in a variety of ways to support collaborative group activities

A final logistical issue that should be addressed concerns the administrator's participation in collegial development groups. Although administrators are not typically participants in teacher-initiated collegial development groups, they sometimes do participate in or even create such groups. When the administrator participates in the group, he or she does so as an equal participant with no greater authority or power than anyone else. The administrator must agree to respect the confidentiality of the group activity and not to use any information from the group in any negative way. It is critical that the group members trust the administrator and that they not feel threatened by his or her presence. We suggest that an administrator only participate in a teacher-initiated collegial development group when invited to do so by the teachers. We also suggest that before any administrator is invited to participate, the members of the group have an open discussion of the pros and cons. An invitation should not be extended if any participant expresses reluctance.

There are occasions when an administrator wants to create a study group with teachers for purposes of exploring an issue, question, or topic. Because administrators are more often exposed to the big picture, administrators can sometimes recognize an opportunity for exploration that is not so obvious to teachers. Recognizing and acting on such an opportunity can be very useful for the school as a whole. Thus, we do not want to preclude the administrator's creating a study group, but we suggest that the administrator exercise caution. More specifically, we suggest that the administrator explain the intended focus for the study group and invite interested teachers to participate. Once the group members have been identified, the administrator should allow the teachers to drive the process.

By giving up the leadership role, the administrator emphasizes the teacher-directed nature of the activity and the equality of group members. Even if the administrator does not participate in the collegial development groups, he or she still plays a role in documenting collegial development group work as a teacher supervision process.

## Administering the Process

As with action research, the process of documenting collegial development group participation begins in the preceding spring At that time all veteran teachers who are performing at or beyond a satisfactory level complete a form that indicates their supervision option for the upcoming year (see Figure 6.4). Also, during the spring, teachers have the opportunity to propose establishing collegial development groups.

In late September or early October, the administrator meets individually with each teacher who has opted for collegial development group participation and asks the teacher to identify what type of group the teacher will be participating in and what the teacher hopes to gain from participation. The administrator may or may not be involved in the group as noted above. At the midway point of the school year, the administrator and teacher meet again to discuss how the group is going and any professional development that has taken place for the teacher.

At the end of the year, the administrator and teacher meet once again to discuss the teacher's participation in the group and its effect on the teacher's professional development. This final meeting is structured around a district-created survey that is completed by all members of each collegial development group (see Figure 6.5 for an example). The teacher brings the completed survey to the final meeting. One copy of the survey form is placed in the teacher's personnel folder, simply as a record of his or her participation in the

**FIGURE 6.4**   Documenting Participation in Collegial Development Groups

---

**Spring of Previous School Year**   Teachers choose supervision option for next year.

**Late September/October**   Administrator and teacher meet to identify collegial development group that teacher will attend and expected impact on professional development.

**January**   Administrator and teacher meet to discuss collegial development group experience to date.

**April/May**   Teacher completes participant survey. Administrator and teacher meet to discuss the teacher's experiences and perceptions using the participant survey as the focus for the meeting.

---

**FIGURE 6.5**  Sample Collegial Development Group Participant Survey

---

Name _____          School _____

1. Type of collegial development group
   Study group   CFG   Lesson study
2. How many teachers participated in your collegial development group?
3. How many times did your collegial development group meet?
4. How many meetings of the group did you attend?
   *Study group participants answer questions 5 and 6, and then skip to question 12, and continue from there .*
   *CFG participants skip to questions 7, 8, and 9, and then to 12, and continue from there.*
   *Lesson study participants skip to question 10 and continue from there.*
5. If the group was a study group, which topics, issues, and questions were discussed?
6. What readings or other resources were used in your study group work?
7. How many meetings used protocols for examining student work?
8. How many meetings used protocols for examining teacher thinking and practice?
9. How important was the facilitator in carrying out the group's work?
   Very important   Somewhat important   Relatively unimportant   Not important
10. How many lessons were developed and taught by the group?
11. What roles did you play in each of the lessons?
12. Would you choose to participate in a collegial development group again?
    Yes   No   Unsure
13. Why did you answer question 12 as you did?
14. How much impact did the collegial development work have on your professional development?
    Great impact   Some impact   Not much Impact   No impact
15. If there was impact on your professional development, describe the impact specifically.
16. How much impact did the collegial development group have on your classroom teaching practice?
    Great impact  Some impact Not much impact No impact
17. If there was impact on your teaching, describe it specifically.
18. How could the work of the collegial development group be improved so that it has more impact on your development and teaching?
19. Please add any comments that you feel would be helpful.

---

supervision process for the year. A second copy goes into a central file of surveys completed by participants in collegial development groups. The administrator who provides oversight for the teacher supervision and evaluation system, usually an assistant superintendent, summarizes all of the survey results in a document that describes the work of the various groups and the impact on teacher development. This yearly summary serves as an important data source in examining the impact of collegial development groups on teacher development.

## CHAPTER SUMMARY

Collegial development groups are small groups of teachers who meet voluntarily on a long-term basis to support one another's personal and professional development through critical analysis of theories and ideas, new and existing practices, and student and teacher work. Study groups, which employ open-ended conversation formats, focus on issues, questions, and ideas that are not currently widely used in the school district. Critical friends groups employ conversation protocols to facilitate inquiry into existing practices. A variety of CFG protocols have been developed to examine student work and also teacher thinking and practice. Lesson study groups design, implement, and analyze research lessons together through data that are collected during the observation. All three types of collegial development groups can enhance the professional development and classroom practice of individual teachers and transform the culture of the school as a whole.

Study groups can be very useful in developing awareness of innovative practices as well as studying issues that schools are faced with. Implementation of study groups involves identifying topics of interest, establishing group norms, developing a meeting struc-

ture, and identifying important group roles. Critical friends groups grew out of the work of the Coalition of Essential Schools as a strategy for teacher collaboration around student work. Conversation protocols, facilitated by a trained coach, and shared norms for participation guide the activities of CFGs. Lesson study groups immerse teachers in developing curriculum-based research lessons that are aimed at enhancing teacher learning about students, teaching, and subject matter through a process that combines elements of action research and collegial development groups.

When collegial development groups are integrated as a component of the teacher supervision and evaluation system, administrators can support their work by providing resources and helping with logistical decisions. The administrator may participate in collegial development groups as an invited, equal participant.

## CASE 6.2 CRITICAL FRIENDS GROUP PROTOCOL

The work of study groups and critical friends groups is difficult to capture in a case study format as the case study material would essentially take the form of a transcript of a group conversation. Instead of providing a transcript or a set of summarized notes from a collegial development group, we have decided to walk you through a collaborative assessment conference as our case study material. Although you can complete pieces of the protocol individually, you will need to work with colleagues or classmates to comprehend the protocol fully and gain a sense of what it would really feel like.

*Please do not read beyond this paragraph unless you are in the process of completing the case study protocol.* To really experience the protocol, you must experience it as it truly unfolds, one step at a time. Decide now whether you will work individually or work with a group of colleagues. Then, complete the phases of the protocol one step at a time. If you read ahead to the latter stages of the protocol first, the initial stages will be meaningless for you.

As you will recall, a collaborative assessment conference protocol is used when the presenter (the teacher who brings the work to the group) has a sample of student work that he/she wants to understand better. Typically, the presenter is confused, frustrated, or stymied by the work and hopes that examination of the work by others will provide new insights and perspectives that will enable the presenter to help the student more effectively.

### The Protocol: Phase 1—Reading the Work

The protocol begins with the presenter providing copies of the work for participants to read. The participants read the work silently and individually with no background information provided. The task of the participants, and your task in this case study, is to read the work and be able to describe what you see. As you read, you may make notes if that is helpful to you. The work that you are reading could represent the work of any student at any educational level: elementary, middle, high school, undergraduate, or graduate.

The goal of this phase of the protocol is to be able to accurately describe what one sees in the work, not to make judgments about it. Descriptions can be very far ranging, from noticing that the words are spelled correctly, sentences are complete, or punctuation is wrong to more complex descriptions that identify the main ideas that are being expressed, describe the student who provided the work sample, and/or describe the type of work or assignment the sample represents.

### The Student Work Sample

This week I began teaching the Animal Unit in science. The lessons I taught involved more thinking on the students' part compared to the ones I taught in the past. I feel that the lessons where I have to do more of the talking without a hands-on experiment are more difficult for me. Usually the experiment itself is engaging enough so that the students are paying attention to me. Without a fun experiment to watch, it is my job to engage the students for the entire lesson. Lessons that involve more thinking and listening force me to be extra prepared with relatable examples, questions that will evoke student responses, and ways to refocus student attention back on me. I have been developing more questions that prompt student thought because my mentor informed me that I was answering a lot of my own questions. She said that if I ask a question and no one raises his or her hand immediately or no one answers correctly, I end up answering it myself. By preparing quality questions and examples ahead of time, I feel that students will understand what I am talking about.

Right now I am working on trying to understand the big ideas of each lesson that I teach and the unit as a whole. When I plan lessons, I need to ask myself, "What should the students take away from the lesson that I am teaching?" Since I started the Animal Unit, relating previous information to the new material we are learning has been very difficult. In preparation for my science lessons for next week, I am going to read ahead in the unit to find out where lessons are going. By reading ahead I will be able to tell the students how the information we are learning will come into play in the future.

Even though I have observed my mentor in the classroom all semester, it is still an adjustment for me to teach in a student-centered curriculum. I was raised in a textbook-centered curriculum that called for reading a chapter and answering the questions at the end. The schools in this district have students creating their own questions and reflecting upon what they have read. I think this puts an enormous amount of responsibility on the teacher instead of the text. The teacher is forced to come up with questions to see if the students understand instead of relying on textbook developed questions. Often times, I find myself frustrated with the units and how they are set up.

As a beginning teacher I have been trying to teach everything that was in the unit plan. I thought that if the information was included in the unit plan, then it must be important. If it was not important, the unit would have left it out. As I was including so much information in my lessons, I was rushing to get everything done. I think this is why I have not been trying to dig into student thinking and not trying to understand and reinforce all of their ideas. I was trying to get through the material instead of taking my time. As a result, I have been neglecting student thought. This seems like a tremendous amount of responsibility for a new teacher. I think a more textbook-centered curriculum would be helpful to me and to my students.

## Phase 2—Describing the Work

In this section of the protocol, group members share what they have seen in the work. This sharing continues for a period of about 10 min. The presenter is silent during this descriptive period. The facilitator begins the process by asking the group, "What do you see in the work?" Participants are encouraged to share only descriptions and to avoid judgments about the work or the student at this point. If anyone states a judgment about the work, the facilitator will ask: "What evidence from the work do you have to support that judgment?"

If you are completing this case study individually, take a few minutes now to jot down all the statements that you can make in describing the student work that you have just read. If you are working with colleagues, as we hope you are, begin the process of sharing your descriptions of the work. Stop the descriptions after about 10 min.

## Phase 3—Questions Raised by the Work

During this phase of the protocol, participants spend about 10 min discussing questions that the work has raised for them. These questions can be about the work sample itself, about the student who created the work sample, about the assignment or task that resulted in the student work sample, about the context in which the student is working, or about any other areas of inquiry that arise. During this time period, the presenter is silent but may make notes about any questions that are asked. No one answers the questions here. The goal is simply to raise as many questions as possible.

If you are working individually, take some time now to jot down as many questions as possible that the work sample raises for you. If you are working with colleagues, begin sharing the questions that group participants have about the work. Stop after about 10 min.

## Phase 4—Focusing on the Student's Thinking and Understanding

In this phase of the protocol, group members attempt to collectively identify what the student was thinking, understanding, and feeling as he/she was creating this student product. Participants might focus on what the student understands/does not understand, what the student is puzzled or confused by, what the student is feeling, what issues the student is attempting to work through, and so on. The facilitator begins this 10-min phase by asking the group, " What do you think the student is working on?"

If you are working individually, take some time now to jot down what you think this student understands, thinks, and/or feels. What issues is he/she puzzled by or working through? If you are working collectively, take the next 10 min to share your thoughts about these same issues.

### Phase 5—The Presenter Speaks

During this part of the protocol, the presenter, who brought the work to the group, speaks for the first time. The presenter is silent up until this point because the goal of the protocol is for the presenter to gain new insights into the student by listening to what other participants see in the student work. If the presenter felt that he/she had a really good handle on the student, then a collaborative assessment conference would not be the appropriate protocol to use. During this phase, the presenter typically does three things: (1) makes the context of the work clear and explains why this piece of work is puzzling and of special interest; (2) describes what he/she sees in the work and responds to any questions that were raised by others; and (3) notes any particularly surprising, unexpected, or helpful comments that were made by other group members in the earlier stages of the protocol. This phase usually last about 10 min. As the presenter here has not been privy to the earlier conversations among your group members, she can only engage in (1) and (2) above.

Susan, a student teaching supervisor, brought this student work to the group. It represents a journal entry of Jessica, an elementary student teacher, teaching at the fourth-grade level. Writing at least one reflective journal entry each week is a requirement of the student teachers in Susan's program. Jessica wrote this particular entry during the sixth week of a 14-week student teaching experience. Jessica had just begun teaching science and was experiencing difficulty in several aspects of her teaching. Sifting out important from extraneous information was very difficult for Jessica. As noted in the journal entry, she has a very difficult time identifying the big or important ideas for students to learn. As a result, her lessons tend to be packed with lots of information, covered at a very quick pace. There is little time to explore student thinking and limited time for checking to see whether students are really understanding the concepts.

Susan's primary reason for bringing this particular journal entry to the group is her growing frustration in working with Jessica. She believes that Jessica is truly struggling with understanding what the big ideas are and needs a great deal of support from her mentor and from Susan to plan lessons that are effective in promoting student understanding. Susan is also conflicted emotionally herself. She resents Jessica's whining about teaching in a student-centered curriculum and not having a textbook to rely on.

As Susan sees it, teaching should be student centered. Science should be taught in a hands-on, engaging manner and encourage students to think, weigh evidence, and make claims that are clearly supported by scientific observations. Susan believes that teaching science by having students read the chapter and answer end-of-chapter questions is totally inappropriate. She also resents the fact that Jessica seems upset by the planning burden that student-centered teaching places on a new teacher. Susan feels that planning creative lessons is the essence of teaching. Because she is resentful of Jessica's feelings about the curriculum, Susan worries about losing her ability to work effectively with Jessica. So she has brought this particular piece of work to the group in the hope that she might gain some new perspectives on Jessica and also develop a greater sense of empathy and support for Jessica's struggles.

### Phase 6—Implications for Teaching and Learning

In this final phase of the protocol, participants engage in a open discussion, lasting about 5–10 min, concerning any thoughts or insights that they have gained about their own teaching, student learning, or ways to support learners and teachers in the future. The protocol ends with the group reflecting on the use of the protocol and how to improve its work in the future. The questions for discussion that follow will provide an opportunity for you and your group to reflect on the protocol.

## DISCUSSION QUESTIONS

**1.** What are the strategies your school district typically uses to implement innovative practices? How successful are these strategies? What would be the impact if potential initiatives were introduced through study group activities that provided readings and an opportunity for discussion among staff members? Explain your thinking. Do you see any role that critical friends groups could play in supporting the implementation of innovative practices in your school district? Explain your thinking.

**2.** In addition to acquiring the services of a trained facilitator, what other preparation work, if any, would need to be done before implementing critical friends groups in your school? Why would this preparation be important? What variables would you examine in order to determine whether your school was ready to implement CFGs?

**3.** If you were a building principal and had the authority to do so, would you be willing to try to free up time on a monthly basis for collegial development groups to meet on district time? Why or why not? What are some strategies you might use to free up time for monthly meetings?

**4.** As you see it, what is the relationship between peer coaching, self-directed teacher growth, action research, and collegial development groups? How are they similar to each other? How are they different? What unique contribution, if any, does each of them offer to individual teachers and to the school as an organization?

**5.** The authors suggest that one of the obstacles that must be faced in creating collegial development groups is the possibility that conflicting philosophies will be brought out into the open, instead of remaining hidden. How would you deal with this type of conflict? What steps might you take or ask teachers to take to make sure that the differences in philosophy become a productive tension?

**6.** Discuss the following questions in reference to the critical friends group protocol included at the end of the chapter:

a. What was it like for you to read the student work without having any context or background information? Why is the lack of background information an important component of the protocol?

b. What did you notice about the descriptions of the work and the questions about the work that were raised by you and your colleagues?

c. How did hearing the presenter's explanation of why she brought this student work to the group affect your interpretation of the work? How would the protocol have played out differently if the presenter's perspective had been given before you read the work?

d. What do you see as the value of this critical friends protocol? Can you think of any situations in which using a protocol like this might be or might have been helpful to you?

e. If you were Jessica's supervisor, what would you do to help and support her? Why?

## THEORY-INTO-PRACTICE APPLICATIONS

Numbers 1 and 2 refer to the web site of the "Looking at Student Work Collaborative": http://www.lasw.org/index1.html.

**1.** Visit the virtual protocol for the online collaborative assessment conference: http://www.lasw.org/vp.html. Go through all of the steps of the protocol and note your reactions to the different phases of the protocol. In what ways did the protocol facilitate or inhibit conversations? How is your assessment of the student work different now from what it had been before participating in the protocol? Share your reactions with two classmates. What similarities and differences did you find? What accounts for these differing reactions?

**2.** Visit the protocol section of the web site: http://www.lasw.org/methods.html. Read through the steps of each protocol that is described in detail. Identify two protocols that you see as being particularly useful and two that you see as not being very useful. Explain the reasons for your choices. Can you adapt the protocols that you see as less useful to make them more helpful?

**3.** Develop and administer a survey that could be used to assess the interest of teachers in your school district in participating in collegial development groups. Make sure the survey includes a brief explanation of what collegial development groups are as well as items that focus on whether teachers would choose to participate, their reasons for participating or not participating, topics that they would like to address in study groups, and preferences for when the groups might meet.

**4.** Implementing collegial development groups does not occur overnight. Work with a partner to develop a 5-year plan for preparing, implementing, and evaluating the impact of collegial development groups in your school. In the plan, be sure to address the resources required as well as professional development activities that would be needed to implement the groups successfully. In developing the evaluation plan, identify evaluation strategies for assessing impact on individual teachers, on the school as a whole, and on students. Share your plan with a school administrator who might be able to help you implement it.

**5.** Visit the following web site: www.lessonresearch.net. Then using the resources available there as well as the information in this chapter, develop a 20-min PowerPoint presentation for teachers at your school about the lesson study process.

# REFERENCES

ALLEN, D. (Ed.). (1998). *Assessing student learning: From grading to understanding.* New York: Teachers College Press.

BAMBINO, D. (2002). Critical friends. *Educational Leadership, 59*(6), 25–27.

BANDURA, A. (1997) Self-efficacy: Toward a unifying theory of behavior change. *Psychological Review, 84,* 191–215.

BIRCHAK, B., CONNOR, C., CRAWFORD, K., KAHN, L., KASER, S., TURNER, S., & SHORT, K. (1998). *Teacher study groups: Building community through dialogue and reflection.* Urbana, IL: National Council of Teachers of English.

BLYTHE, T., ALLEN, D., & POWELL, B. (1998). *Looking together at student work: A companion guide to assessing student learning.* New York: Teachers College Press.

CHESTER, M., & BEAUDIN, B. (1996). Efficacy beliefs of newly hired teachers in urban schools. *American Educational Research Journal, 33*(1), 223–257.

CLARK, C., (2001). Good conversation. In C. Clark (Ed.), *Talking shop: Authentic conversation and teacher learning.* New York: Teachers College Press.

CLARK, C., & FLORIO-RUANE, S. (2001). Conversation as support for teaching in new ways. In C. Clark (Ed.), *Talking shop: Authentic conversation and teacher learning.* New York: Teachers College Press.

CUSHMAN, K. (1996) What does a critical friends group do? *Horace 13*(1) 1–2.

DUFOUR, R., & EAKER, R., (1998). *Professional learning communities at work: Best practices for enhancing student achievement.* Bloomington, IN: National Education Service.

DUNN, F, NAVE, B., & LEWIS, A. (2000). Critical friends groups: Teachers helping teachers to improve student learning. *Phi Delta Kappa Research Bulletin, 28,* 9–12.

EASTON, L. B. (2002). How the tuning protocol works. *Educational Leadership, 59* (6), 28–31.

FULLAN, M. (2001). *Leading in a culture of change.* San Francisco, CA: Jossey-Bass.

GIMBERT, B., & NOLAN, J. (1999). *School–university communities: Creating and sustaining student-directed classroom learning environments through collegial inquiry, conversations, and collaborative reflection.* Unpublished manuscript. Penn State University.

GUSKEY, T. (1986). Staff development and the process of teacher change. *Educational Researcher, 15*(5), 5–12.

HARGREAVES, A. (1994). *Changing teachers, changing times: Teachers' work and culture in the postmodern age.* New York: Teachers College Press.

HARGREAVES, A., EARL, L., MOORE, S., & MANNING, S. (2001) *Learning to change: Teaching beyond subjects and standards.* San Francisco, CA: Jossey-Bass.

HELSBY, G. (1999). *Changing teachers' work.* Bristol, PA: Open University Press.

KEGAN, R., & LAHEY, L. (2001). *How the way we talk can change the way we work.* San Francisco, CA: Jossey-Bass.

LEWIS, C. (2002a). Everywhere I looked—Levers and pendulums. *Journal of Staff Development, 23*(3), 59–65.

LEWIS, C. (2002b). Does lesson study have a future in the United States? *Nagoya Journal of Education and Human Development, 1,* 1–23. Also available at www.lessonresearch.net.

LEWIS, C., PERRY, R., HURD, J., & O'CONNELL, P. (2006). Lesson study comes of age in North America. *Phi Delta Kappan, 48*(4), 273–281.

LIEBERMAN, A., & GROLNICK, M. (1996). Networks and reform in American education. *Teachers College Record, 98*(1), 7–45.

LITTLE, J. (1990). The persistence of privacy: Autonomy and initiative in teachers' professional relations. *Teachers College Record, 91*(4), 509–536.

MURPHY, C., & LICK, D. (2001). *Whole-faculty study groups: Creating student-based professional development* (2nd ed.). Thousand Oaks, CA: Corwin Press.

National School Reform Faculty. (2000). *Protocols: Looking at work collaboratively.* Bloomington, IN: National School Reform Faculty.

NIAS, J. (1989). *Primary teachers talking: A study of teaching as work.* New York: Routledge.

ROSENHOLTZ, S. (1989). *Teachers' workplace.* New York: Longman.

SPILLANE, J, & SEASHORE LOUIS, K. (2002). School improvement processes and practices: Professional learning for building instructional capacity. In J. Murphy (Ed.), *The educational leadership challenge: Redefining leadership for the 21st century. One Hundred and First Yearbook of the National Society for the Study of Education.* Chicago, IL: University of Chicago Press.

THOMPSON-GROVE, G. (2002). *The consultancy dilemma: A revised protocol from the National School Reform Faculty.* Bloomington, IN: National School Reform Faculty.

VANDEWEGHE, R., & VARNEY, K. (2006). The evolution of a school-based study group. *Phi Delta Kappan, 88*(4), 282–286.

WOODS, P. (1993). *Critical events in teaching and learning.* Bristol, PA: Open University Press.

# SUGGESTIONS FOR FURTHER READING AND RESEARCH

CHARLES, L., CLARK, R., ROUDEBUSH, J., BUDNICK, S., BROWN, M., & TURNER, P. (1995). Study groups in practice. *Journal of Staff Development, 16*(3), 49–53.

*Journal of Staff Development, 23*(3)—Summer 2002. Entire issue devoted to school culture.

MURPHY, J. (Ed.). (2002). *The educational leadership challenge: Redefining leadership for the 21st century. One Hundred and First Yearbook of the National Society for the Study of Education.* Chicago, IL: University of Chicago Press.

ROUTMAN, R. (2000). *Conversations: strategies for teaching, learning, and evaluating.* New York: Heinemann.

ROUTMAN, R. (2002). Teacher talk. *Educational Leadership, 59*(6), 32–35.

SARANSON, S. (1971). *The culture of the school and the problem of change.* Needham Heights, MA: Allyn & Bacon.

WATANABE, T. (2002). Learning from Japanese lesson study. *Educational Leadership, 59*(6), 36–39.

# ADDITIONAL RESOURCES

The web site of the "Looking at Student Work Collaborative": http://www.lasw.org/methods.html.

The web site of the National School Reform Faculty: http://www.harmonyschool.org/nsrf/default.html.

The web site of Mills College on lesson study: http://www.lessonresearch.net/index.html.

The web site at Teachers College on lesson study: http://www.tc.edu/lessonstudy.

The web site of Research for Better Schools on lesson study: http://rbs.org/lesson_study.

# CHAPTER 7

# STANDARDS FOR EFFECTIVE TEACHING AND TEACHER EVALUATION

THIS CHAPTER represents a marked departure in many ways from the previous five chapters, which dealt with different components of the supervision process. Each of those chapters provided a detailed description of a particular process aimed at enhancing teacher development. Now, in Part IV, we turn our attention to questions regarding what standards should be used to evaluate teaching and how to design and implement an evidence-based or data-driven teacher evaluation system. As explained at length in Chapter 1, teacher evaluation and teacher supervision are two complementary but separate organizational functions aimed at ensuring that all students receive high-quality classroom instruction.

This chapter and Chapter 8 also represent a departure in another sense. Each of the chapters on supervision recommended supervision processes that are currently in use in school districts across the country exactly as described in the chapters. Although there are teacher evaluation systems that contain components, sometimes multiple components, of what we are recommending in this chapter, we are not aware of any districts that use all of our recommended teacher evaluation standards or practices. As authors, we had to make a decision as to whether we should describe what currently is or what we believe, based on current research, should exist. As teacher evaluation does not receive sufficient attention and resources and, consequently, despite the best efforts of administrators to do it well, is not as effective as it could be, we felt a professional obligation to describe evaluation systems as we believe they should exist. Any school that implements our suggested evaluation strategies will be on the cutting edge of teacher evaluation. We also feel the need to say that although we have separated this chapter from the following chapter in order to explain the ideas more clearly and to make the reading more manageable, the concepts in the two chapters are obviously interrelated. The procedures that are used for teacher evaluation must be connected to principles of effective evaluation and to standards for evaluating teacher performance. Thus, there is some conceptual overlap between the two chapters.

Recent work in the area of teacher evaluation by Peterson (2000) and Danielson and McGreal (2000) has influenced our conceptions greatly. We have attempted to mesh their somewhat related but still disparate frameworks into a state-of-the-art evaluation process that will likely challenge the thinking of those administrators who use traditional teacher evaluation methods. High-quality teacher evaluation is not for the faint of heart. It requires a clear, coherent vision of what the system should look like and the subsequent commitment of resources to make that system a reality. As Danielson and McGreal (2000) suggest, designing new evaluation systems is a major event. Improving teaching and student learning is not cheap.

This chapter contains two major sections. The first section identifies a series of eight principles that should be used as the foundation for the development of an effective teacher evaluation system. The second section addresses some of the substantive standards of effective teaching that might be used as the foundation for judgments of teacher quality.

## GUIDING QUESTIONS FOR PREREADING REFLECTION AND JOURNALING

- Think about your experiences being evaluated as a teacher. What was the stated purpose of the evaluation? How well did the process match the purpose?
- Given your own experiences with evaluation, what are some important beliefs that you have about how effective teacher evaluation should be carried out?
- If you were given the opportunity to design a teacher evaluation system, what standards would you use in judging a teacher's effectiveness?

## BASIC PRINCIPLES OF TEACHER EVALUATION

The literature on teacher evaluation identifies several different purposes that might be accomplished by a teacher evaluation system (Danielson & McGreal, 2000; Peterson, 2000). These purposes include assuring adequate instruction for all learners, documenting the quality of teaching practices that currently exist, instituting accountability procedures that will satisfy key stakeholders including parents and taxpayers, and improving the quality of instructional practices. Many district policy manuals for teacher evaluation identify the primary goal of teacher evaluation as improving the quality of teaching for all teachers. Unfortunately, this goal is rarely achieved in practice. Though there are isolated exceptions, teacher evaluation typically does not improve teaching or enhance student learning (Peterson, 2000).

Why is this the case? Some scholars and practitioners would argue that teacher evaluation fails to improve practice because the procedures that are used are faulty. Although many evaluation procedures undoubtedly have shortcomings, this is not the reason. As we explained in Chapter 1, the process of teacher evaluation is incompatible with the goal of improving instruction beyond a minimal level of competence.

When the teacher's performance is marginal or unsatisfactory, teacher evaluation can often force the teacher to improve to the point where his or her performance is at least minimally competent (see Chapter 11). However, only a handful of teachers in any school fall into this category. The vast majority of veteran teachers are competent or excellent practitioners. Although the teacher evaluation process may help these teachers recognize a need for or an opportunity for growth, the supervisory processes, explained in Chapters 2 through 6, provide the support, structure, and motivation required to capitalize on this recognition.

Growing and improving require that teachers take risks, try new behaviors, and reach out in new directions. When teachers are being evaluated, most of them are far from innovative. They are much more likely to stand by their tried-and-true ways of teaching in order to put their best foot forward. We believe that well-designed evaluation can accomplish two fundamental goals: (1) enabling teachers and administrators to document the quality of teaching that currently exists and, in doing so, identify both areas of strength and potential areas for growth; and (2) ensuring that all teachers within the system teach at a minimum level of competence or better.

A well-designed system of teacher evaluation must be based on a set of coherent beliefs. Identifying core beliefs or principles makes it more likely that all stakeholders within the system will have a clear understanding of the values that underlie teacher evaluation. In designing the evidence-based teacher evaluation system presented in this text, we have relied on eight core principles of teacher evaluation derived from our platform of beliefs about supervision and evaluation (Chapter 2), the research on effective teacher evaluation, and our knowledge about schools as organizations. These principles are elaborated below.

*Principle 1: Teacher evaluation should be broad and comprehensive in nature, accounting for all of the duties that teachers are expected to perform.*

Imagine yourself looking through the view finder of a camera with a high-powered telephoto lens. As you get ready to take the picture of your family with its seven members (including pets), you adjust the lens to its most powerful telephoto setting. The result is a splendid closeup of your son's belly button, with the rest of the family completely out of the picture. This metaphor exemplifies much of current practice in teacher evaluation. Most systems of teacher evaluation in school districts are too narrow and restricted in scope. These systems rely very heavily on administrative observations of, at most, a few lessons that the teacher teaches during the course of the year. These observed lessons are often not carefully selected for any specific purpose. Most often, observations occur whenever the administrator can find the time to do them, sometimes during the last week of school or while the teacher is giving a test. The result is a very restricted view of the teacher's performance, captured through only one data source.

Not only does reliance on a limited number of observations fail to consider the noninstructional responsibilities that teachers are expected to fulfill, but it also provides a very restricted range of even the teacher's instructional performance. As discussed in Chapter 1, most teachers teach a wide variety of classes, lessons, and students. As you saw in Exercise 1.2, devising an observation schedule that will capture this wide variety of instructional activities is a very complex task. Effective teacher evaluation systems provide multiple opportunities to capture the teacher's instructional performance and are carefully constructed to collect a wide variety of data concerning the classes, lessons, and students that the teacher teaches. In addition, effective teacher evaluation systems are designed to collect accurate and reliable data concerning the teacher's ability to carry out noninstructional duties such as contributing to the school as an organization, interacting with professional colleagues, working cooperatively with families, and growing personally and professionally. Effective teacher evaluation systems are like artistic photographers; they use a combination of cameras and lenses to capture as much of the action as possible while still allowing the focus to be as close and precise as possible.

*Principle 2: Effective evaluation systems make use of a wide variety of data sources to provide an accurate and reliable portrait of teacher performance.*

Let us continue with the photography analogy a little bit longer. Assume that your spouse is unavailable for whatever reason and pleads with you to capture your 6-year-old's singing debut in the annual school concert. As a loving spouse you take your mission seriously. You use your highly sophisticated 35-mm camera to capture as much of the concert as possible. You are so excited to show your spouse the results of your labor that you take the film for 1-h processing, then drive straight home with the pictures. Your spouse dutifully praises the pictures, but you note a sense of disappointment. When you ask what is wrong, your spouse explains your son's singing was more important than his appearance. Your spouse wanted a videotape, not a still photograph. Let us analyze your performance. You accepted your assignment lovingly, carried it out enthusiastically, and produced artistic results. However, the data source that you used is not capable, no matter how skillfully employed, of capturing the variety of data that were necessary to achieve the desired objective.

A similar problem is evident in the teacher evaluation systems that are used in many school districts. Most teacher evaluation systems are inadequate in that they rely almost totally on administrative observation and rating as the only data source for capturing teacher performance. In truth, the problem in teacher evaluation is even worse than our analogy. A 35-mm camera is a wonderfully sophisticated tool to collect data. It captures data of high quality, unfortunately, a limited type of data. Reliance on administrator observation and rating is problematic not only because it captures a limited source of data, but also because the data that it produces do not appear to be of very high quality. Over the last several decades, many research studies have been conducted to examine the efficacy of administrator judgments in accurately and reliably capturing the quality of teaching performance. The results of such research have been pretty dismal (Peterson, 2000).

According to Medley and Coker (1987), "to this day almost all educational personnel decisions are based on judgments, which according to the research, are only slightly more accurate than they would be if they were based on pure chance" (p. 243). Peterson (2000) puts it even more bluntly, claiming that 70 years of research on principals' ratings of teachers show that they do not work well. He goes on to say: "Findings challenge the assumption that an observer can enter a classroom, use an observation framework of supposedly desirable performances, count or rate the teacher, and draw conclusions about the quality of teaching that can be defended for purposes of teacher evaluation" (p. 22).

School districts are faced with a serious challenge concerning data sources for teacher evaluation. They must broaden these to include, along with administrator observations, sources such as peer observations, videotapes, reviews of teacher products and artifacts, student products, student learning data, parent input, student input, teacher portfolios, teacher documentation of professional growth, and peer input. Chapter 8 explains the use of these alternative data sources as well as processes to improve the quality of administrator observations.

*Principle 3: Well-qualified, trained administrators are the appropriate personnel to make summative judgments concerning teacher performance.*

Most school administrators have not been adequately prepared to evaluate teachers. State certification guidelines for school administrators typically require either one or no course in teacher supervision and evaluation. Courses in supervision may or may not deal specifically with the process of teacher evaluation, depending on the supervision textbook that is used. In developing an effective teacher evaluation system, school districts should assume that they will have to provide staff development that will equip administrators with the knowledge and skills necessary to engage in teacher evaluation productively.

The role that administrators should play in the evaluation process has been debated in the literature. Some authors, such as Peterson (2000), suggest that teachers are probably better judges of teacher performance than are administrators. They recommend that teacher evaluation systems be reconstructed to minimize administrator judgment of teacher quality. As an alternative, they recommend the use of peer teacher panels (staffed by teachers who do not know or associate with the teacher being evaluated). Although we appreciate Peterson's work and have been influenced by it, we do not recommend that teachers assume the primary responsibility for assessing teacher performance. We can see how peer assessment can be an integral part of a teacher evaluation system and, as Peterson (2000) points out, such an approach has been used successfully in Toledo. However, we cotend that the vast majority of districts are not ready for this approach, that most teachers are unwilling to take on this evaluative role, and that many parents, community members, and school board members would not see peer evaluation as sufficiently rigorous.

Further, we argue that administrators, if properly prepared for the role, can do an excellent job of teacher evaluation. Administrators know the local context, both school-wide and districtwide, understand the mission and goals of the school and the district, and have the opportunity to see a wide range of teacher performance, both instructional and noninstructional. Furthermore, they are individuals in formal leadership positions who have accepted the mantle of teacher evaluation.

We believe that the poor record of administrator observations as a teacher evaluation tool in the past stems from a lack of appropriate preparation, from confusion about the appropriate purposes of teacher evaluation, and from faulty procedures rather than from any inherent difficulties in the role of administrator or personal shortcomings of individual administrators. In short, we assert that well-prepared administrators should be responsible for making summative judgments concerning teacher quality using a wide variety of data sources to look at the teacher's performance broadly and comprehensively. This does not imply that the roles of the teacher and administrator should remain exactly as they are defined by most current systems of evaluation. We believe that the role of the teacher being evaluated can be expanded greatly and that the role of the administrator can be streamlined to make it more effective. We will say more about redefining teacher and administrator roles in Chapter 8. When administrators are entrusted with the responsibility for summative evaluation, they must be prepared to carry out the task effectively. Thus, staff development, ongoing consultation, and monitoring of administrator performance are critical tasks for any teacher evaluation system.

*Principle 4: Ongoing professional development focused on the teacher evaluation system must be provided for all professionals in the organization.*

Administrators must be well prepared so that they will have the knowledge and skills that will enable them to be viewed as credible, reliable evaluators. Teachers too need professional development to prepare them to engage effectively in the teacher evaluation process. At a minimum, all teachers must be provided with training that will help them to understand the process, including the substantive standards by which their performance will be judged and their own role in the process. If carrying out their role requires knowledge or skills beyond those required to successfully carry out their job duties, then staff development must be provided to help teachers acquire that knowledge and those skills. Providing this type of staff development is a minimal requirement to show that the teacher's due process rights have not been violated. If adequate training is not provided and a teacher is given an unsatisfactory rating, that rating may well be overturned by an arbitrator or in the courts.

Providing staff development for teachers is especially important if teachers are to be given the role that we suggest they play in the teacher evaluation process. As described in Chapter 8, we believe that the teacher should have responsibility for gathering data to document his or her teaching performance. To carry out this new role effectively and gather the most accurate, reliable evaluation data, teachers will need help in understanding the data sources that may be used and how to interpret each of them. Staff development is a must.

The staff development process should consist of both training and job-embedded types of professional development. Under a training model, external experts are brought into the system to teach new skills and knowledge. Following the work of Joyce and Showers, training should include five elements: theory, demonstration, practice, feedback, and coaching (Fullan, Joyce, & Showers, 2001). Job-embedded development would include opportunities for teachers to work and talk with colleagues as they are involved in the process of putting these new skills in practice. Specifically, this might mean that all of those teachers who are involved in the formal evaluation process in a given year are provided with opportunities to work with self-selected colleagues in gathering the data that will be used in the evaluation process. Release time might be provided during the school day for consultation, or teachers might be paid for before or after schoolwork.

Job-embedded staff development for administrators might be delivered in a slightly different way. If the system is designed, as we suggest, to include teacher portfolios, administrators could examine the same portfolio and then discuss their interpretations of its quality. If multiple administrators observe nontenured teachers and marginal teachers, as we suggest in Chapters 10 and 11, those administrators who observe the same new teachers could be given time to talk in order to compare notes. Additionally, time should be provided on a regular basis during administrative team meetings to talk about the evaluation process. Rather than holding these discussions in the more threatening atmosphere of the entire administrative team, principals should be given the opportunity to consult with a smaller, self-selected group of administrative colleagues. Opportunities for this type of sharing should be built into administrative meetings and summer retreats. Finally, central office personnel should monitor the performance of principals in conducting teacher evaluations. We suggest that each year central office personnel choose two or three teacher evaluation portfolios for each building principal, read both the portfolios and the principal's evaluation of them, and provide specific, detailed feedback concerning the quality of the evaluation decision.

Finally, professional development should be ongoing. Too often professional development is provided at the initiation of a system of teacher evaluation, but then disappears. This approach ignores much of what we know about change and professional development. Fullan (2001) suggests that professional development may be even more important after implementation has begun than it is before implementation. Until staff members begin to implement the system, they are often not aware of the areas in which professional development is most important. A second problem with providing intense staff development during early implementation and then withdrawing it concerns staff turnover. Teachers and administrators leave and must be replaced. When staff development stops early in the process, newcomers often receive far less staff development than veterans. Eventually, the school district ends up with a situation in which the majority of teachers and administrators neither fully understand nor support the teacher evaluation system.

*Principle 5: The process used to develop and assess the teacher evaluation system should be participatory and open to representatives from various stakeholder groups.*

Though it is administrators and teachers who are most directly involved in the teacher evaluation process once the system has been developed and operationalized, many stakeholders within the school have a legitimate interest in teacher evaluation. Parents certainly have an interest in making sure that their children receive high-quality instruction. School board members often have questions and concerns about processes for holding professional staff members accountable. Finally, other community members are much more willing to provide financial support for school districts when they feel assured that processes are in place to monitor the quality of teacher performance. Thus, it is a good idea to involve representatives from the various stakeholder groups in the process of developing and implementing the teacher evaluation system and procedures. These stakeholders should also be involved in ongoing assessment of the system after it has been fully implemented. Too often schools develop a policy, implement it, and forget it. Chapter 12 provides extensive guidance concerning the formation of a supervision and evaluation committee with multiple stakeholders as well as procedures that the committee might follow in carrying out its various tasks.

*Principle 6: The process used to evaluate teacher performance should emphasize the use of professional judgment informed by a deep understanding of both the research on teaching and the specific teaching context.*

Professional judgments about the quality of teacher performance cannot be made arbitrarily. The basis for judgments must be clearly understood by all those involved in the system. One of the most viable ways to ensure that the process for making judgments is understood is to involve teachers and other stakeholders in developing the criteria. The committee described under Principle 5 becomes the vehicle for carrying out this task. All scholars who write about teacher evaluation agree that the basis for judgments about quality should be agreed upon and understood clearly by everyone involved; however, there is no agreement about the criteria that should be used. Although we will take up this topic in greater detail in the next section, we need to address the issue here briefly.

Historically, the model that has been used as the basis for making judgments about the quality of teaching has been a discrepancy model. The district identifies some description of effective teaching, usually drawn from research studies, and uses this description or model as the criteria for excellence in teaching. Then evaluators judge and rate the teachers' teaching in terms of the amount of discrepancy between the research model and observed teaching performance.

Peterson (2000) suggests that there are four major problems with discrepancy-based teacher evaluation: (1) there is no comprehensive list of effective teacher behaviors; (2) even if such a comprehensive list existed, not everyone would agree on it; (3) different contexts require different types of teaching performance: (4) different teaching styles can be equally effective. The first two points that Peterson suggests refer to the fact that there are multiple research-based models that could be used as the basis for a discrepancy evaluation process, not a single one. The multiple models are all effective for reaching different educational goals, for example, teaching creative writing versus teaching how to use a microscope versus teaching to develop tolerance for diversity. As all researchers do not agree on the most important goals of education, various researchers tout different models as being effective.

Peterson's third and fourth points refer to the notion that context makes a difference in what works in teaching. What is effective teaching of one subject, at one grade level, and for one type of learner may turn out to be totally inappropriate for a different subject, grade level, or type of learner. Any teacher who has used the exact same lesson plan with two different classes understands that the same teaching behaviors can produce very different outcomes with different students, even when the grade level and subject remain constant.

One explanation for the widespread use of discrepancy-based procedures for judging teacher performance is the understandable desire of school districts to simplify the complexity of the world of teaching. Having a neat checklist of behaviors to observe makes the process very easy to understand, and it also appears to be very objective and precise. Unfortunately, it is neither objective nor precise. The lack of objectivity can be seen in the fact, noted above, that there are many other models of ideal teaching behavior that could have been adopted as the desired list of behaviors. Thus, the very choice of the ideal model represents a subjective judgment on the part of the system developers. The lack of precision is apparent from the general and somewhat ambiguous form in which the ideal teaching behaviors are listed, for example, "treats students equitably." Such broad statements are open to multiple interpretations and do not really have any concrete meaning until they are put into the hands of evaluators. Does equitable treatment mean treating everyone the same or treating everyone differently according to his or her needs? When such general descriptors are used, it is the evaluators' interpretation of "treats students equitably" that becomes the basis for judgment, not some research-based ideal relationship. Exercise 7.1 looks at translating general statements into specific behaviors.

---

**EXERCISE 7.1  Translating General Statements into Specific Behaviors**

---

**Part 1** The four phrases below, which are based on research on teaching, are often found in descriptions of effective teaching models. In your own words, define what each of these descriptors looks like in practice.

1. The teacher establishes a positive classroom climate.
2. The teacher uses appropriate questioning techniques.
3. The teacher adapts instruction to accommodate individual differences.
4. The teacher assesses student progress regularly.

**Part 2** Form a triad containing one elementary teacher, one middle school teacher, and one high school teacher. Compare your descriptions of these four effective teaching behaviors. Based on your written descriptions, how confident are you that each of you would reach the same conclusion concerning the effectiveness of an observed lesson?

---

As Exercise 7.1 makes clear, discrepancy models are motivated, in part, by a desire to replace professional judgment with a checklist of behaviors. Although understandable, this attempt is misguided. You, likely, have already discovered in Exercise 7.1 that the professional judgment and interpretation of the observer are a necessary ingredient in applying generalized criteria to any specific teaching performance. We assert that professional judgment concerning the quality of teaching performance is the sine qua non of effective teacher evaluation. We recommend avoiding the use of a generalized checklist of desired teaching behaviors. Instead, we suggest that the processes for making professional judgments about the quality of teaching be informed by a deep understanding of both the research on teaching and the context in which the teaching takes place. Thus, decisions are based on the practices that the teacher employs and the outcomes (defined broadly) that result for the particular group that he or she is teaching. The next chapter provides suggestions for making qualitative judgments about teachers' performance as well as questions, based on standards, that can be used to guide the process of data gathering to make those judgments more accurate.

*Principle 7: The teacher's due process rights must be protected by the teacher evaluation system.*

As we suggested in Chapter 1, teacher evaluation is a process that is closely intertwined with legal issues. All school administrators hope that the teacher evaluation process will demonstrate that all of the teachers in the school district are performing at a very high level of competence. Unfortunately, not all teachers are high performers. Some teachers demonstrate marginal or even unsatisfactory levels of performance. Every teacher evaluation system must have procedures that can be used to remediate the performance of marginal and unsatisfactory teachers and also procedures for firing teachers who continue to perform at unsatisfactory levels. Chapter 11 focuses exclusively on marginal teachers and how to work with them effectively. If it becomes necessary to rate a teacher "unsatisfactory" and to attempt to dismiss that teacher, the district must show that the teacher was given due process. These due process rights are explained in Chapter 11.

*Principle 8: The procedures used for the evaluation of veteran teachers who are performing at a satisfactory or higher level should differ from those procedures used to evaluate preservice teachers, novice teachers, or veteran teachers whose performance is marginal or below.*

In Chapters 9–11, we explain in detail how the procedures for the supervision and evaluation of preservice, novice, and marginal teachers should be different from the procedures provided for veterans who demonstrated satisfactory performance or better. In general, novice, preservice, and marginal teachers should be evaluated much more frequently than adequately performing veterans and should be given much greater direction and less freedom in gathering evaluation data.

The reason for the restricted freedom of preservice and novice teachers is that these teachers simply do not have enough experience yet to make some of the important decisions on their own. They require more guidance and support from colleagues and administrators. Giving them a great deal of freedom without close guidance and support would be developmentally inappropriate. The same holds true for marginal teachers. Although such teachers do not lack experience, they are sometimes not knowledgeable enough or thoughtful enough to make sound judgments about their teaching performance. Thus, they too require much greater guidance and direction from others. In summary, the eight principles underlying a standards- and evidenced-based system of teacher evaluation are listed in Figure 7.1.

Operationalizing these eight principles of high-quality teacher evaluation requires the development of a set of standards by which teacher performance can be judged as well as a system of procedures for collecting, compiling, and using the data to make an evidence-based summative judgment. The next section focuses on the standards for evaluation. Chapter 8 focuses on procedures for developing an evidence-based teacher evaluation system.

**FIGURE 7.1** Eight Principles for High-Quality Teacher Evaluation

1. Teacher evaluation should be broad and comprehensive in nature, accounting for all of the duties that teachers are expected to perform.
2. Effective teacher evaluation systems make use of a wide variety of data sources to provide an accurate and reliable portrait of teacher performance.
3. Well-qualified, trained administrators are the appropriate personnel to make summative judgments concerning teacher performance.
4. Ongoing professional development focused on the teacher evaluation system must be provided for all professionals in the organization.
5. The process used to develop and assess the teacher evaluation system should be participatory and open to representatives from various stakeholder groups.
6. The process used to evaluate teacher performance should emphasize the use of professional judgment informed by a deep understanding of both the research on teaching and the specific teaching context.
7. The teacher's due process rights must be protected by the teacher evaluation system.
8. The procedures used for the evaluation of veteran teachers who are performing at a satisfactory level or beyond should differ from those procedures used to evaluate preservice teachers, novice teachers, or veteran teacher whose performance is marginal or below.

# STANDARDS FOR EFFECTIVE TEACHING

## The Search for the Universal Model of Effectiveness

Historically, teacher evaluation in the United States has been a search for the perfect, research-based model of teaching that can serve as the benchmark for evaluating the performance of individual teachers. We concur, in general, with Danielson and McGreal's (2000) account of the history of the search for the effective teaching model. During the 1950s, the focus in assessing teacher quality was on finding teacher characteristics and personality traits that would be universally effective in positively affecting student learning. The search for characteristics and traits proved fruitless (Peterson, 2000). However, the remnants of this paradigm can be seen in many current teacher evaluation documents that typically include questions concerning the teacher's personality and appearance.

Propelled by the development of numerous systematic observation instruments that could be used to record and code interactions between teachers and students, the focus during the 1960s turned to appropriate models of teacher–student interaction. Again, however, researchers were forced to conclude that there was no interaction style that was universally effective. Context makes a difference (Flanders, 1976). As a result, systematic observation records were not deemed a definitive method for evaluating teacher performance.

The impact of teacher effectiveness research, including research on specific teaching behaviors such as questioning, teacher expectations, and management styles, on the process of teacher evaluation became apparent in the mid-to-late 1970s. Teachers were evaluated on the amount of congruence between their behaviors and the behaviors called for in whatever model of instruction was popular. This focus on teacher effectiveness models continued throughout the 1980s with the widespread implementation of models of direct instruction such as that developed by Madeline Hunter. The focus on direct or explicit instruction (see Rosenshine & Stevens, 2001) was expanded during the latter part of the decade to include popular instructional initiatives such as cooperative learning and critical thinking. The early portion of the decade of the 1990s saw the continued proliferation of popular models of instruction including those focused on multiple intelligences, authentic assessment, and brain research. The 1990s also saw the rise of a countermovement to these popular, generic instructional models.

The work of Lee Shulman and his associates at Stanford focused on content-specific pedagogy for teaching specific disciplines (see Shulman, 1988). Shulman asserted that educational supervisors were too focused on questions of generic pedagogy at the expense of questions concerning how to teach subject matter content. Through his work, the term pedagogical content knowledge entered the educational dictionary. Pedagogical content knowledge refers to the teacher's understanding of the content in terms of how to teach it successfully to specific groups of learners. Thus, the task of the teacher evaluator was now complicated by the need to identify a model of teaching that could incorporate both generic and subject-specific competencies. The search for the universal model of effective teaching was further complicated during the late 1990s and the early 21st century by the turn to national and state standards and to models of teaching for understanding (Wiggins & McTighe, 2005). This brief historical overview illustrates the point made earlier under Principle 6. The search for a single model of instruction that can be used as the universal model of competence by which all teaching is judged is futile.

"There are as many kinds of good teachers in our schools as there are varieties of good apples in our supermarkets. Unfortunately, we tend to honor only one kind of teacher at a time" (Cruikshank & Haefele, 2001, p. 26). To honor the variety of effective teaching that takes place in a school district, the teacher evaluation process must rely on professional judgment, informed by an underlying set of standards for excellent teaching, rather than on a single checklist or even a single rubric for effective teaching.

In contrast to checklists that rate teachers on the basis of their fidelity to particular models of instruction, a standards-based approach to effective teaching specifies a given number of capabilities, applicable in a variety of contexts, that teachers are expected to possess. For each standard, stated in broad terms, there are multiple indicators that can be identified in a teacher's performance to show evidence that the teacher possesses that capability. These indicators, in contrast to specific behaviors required by a model of teaching, may be demonstrated using a variety of teaching models or approaches that are appropriate for the goals of the lesson, the subject, and the particular group of learners. For example, a teacher may show a deep understanding of content through an inquiry-based lesson, a well-designed lecture, or through a culminating assessment tool that evaluates student understanding.

Experts have developed a variety of standards for teaching developed by experts that can guide the process, we assert that the standards of effective teaching that are used to evaluate teaching should be developed locally if schools have that option. Some schools are bound to evaluate teachers using a form supplied by the state. Typically, schools can either obtain approval for use of their own set of standards or, at least, take time to flesh out and elaborate upon state standards. If neither of these is permissible, then districts must use the exact standards and criteria developed by the state education agency. If local development of standards is not allowed, the data sources and procedures described in Chapter 8 can still be used to arrive at the rating on the state form.

Development of standards of effective teaching locally, as we define it here, may take the form of either creating the district's own set of standards or modifying standards developed by external sources. Some would argue that developing standards locally is simply reinventing the wheel and that it is more efficient to adopt (without adaptation) a set of standards developed by the "experts."

We believe that the advantages of local development of standards outweigh the disadvantages. First, local development makes it much more likely that staff members will feel ownership of the system and view the teaching standards as credible and useful. Second, developing standards creates shared meanings, assumptions, and values about excellent teaching that can be used to advance the quality of teaching across the district. Finally, the process of local development of standards also engages educators naturally in a process of self-reflection and can provide a vehicle for true professional learning (Danielson & McGreal, 2000). We recommend that the committee of stakeholders described under Principle 5 take responsibility for developing the standards in consultation with the stakeholder groups that they represent. There are many predeveloped sets of standards for excellent teaching that can serve as the starting point for the development of local standards. The next section reviews four sets of standards created by experts.

## Existing Standards for Assessing Teaching

There are literally hundreds or thousands of sets of teaching standards in existence, if one counts all of the standards developed by states and local school districts. We have chosen to focus on four sets of previously identified standards. Experts in the field of teacher evaluation developed three; the fourth was developed by the National Board for Professional Teaching Standards (NBPTS). Our rationale for choosing each of these sets of standards as examples is stated in the discussion of each example. An additional sets of standards, developed by the Interstate New Teacher Assessment and Support Consortium (INTASC), is included in Chapter 9 as they were developed primarily for the assessment of preservice and novice teachers. Our purpose in presenting these examples of standards is to provide the reader with a variety of options to choose from. These examples are also the basis for a hybrid set of standards that we have developed and present later. Readers should note that although we have done our best to present the essential components of four sets of standards, each is elaborated in much greater detail in the original works cited.

Edward Iwanicki of the University of Connecticut is a respected scholar in the field of teacher evaluation. He wrote the chapter on teacher evaluation for the highly touted *Handbook of Research on School Supervision.* Iwanicki's (1998) set of model standards for teacher evaluation focuses on 14 indicators of teacher effectiveness separated into five domains: planning, management of the classroom, instruction, assessment, and professional responsibilities. The reader will note that the majority of Iwanicki's standards focus on those aspects of performance that are readily assessed through classroom observation alone. We decided to include these standards because we view them as very strong in terms of their focus on instruction. They are, however, limited in that they do not stress some important areas such as diversity, individual differences, or the use of technology. Figure 7.2 lists the 14 specific standards.

One of the most popular current models for teacher evaluation is the one developed by Charlotte Danielson (2007). She suggests that her framework is based on the research on teaching and is compatible with the INTASC and NBPTS standards. The standards included in her framework appear to accommodate a variety of approaches to data gathering in addition to focused classroom observations. We have included Danielson's work because we see it as a well-conceived set of standards for assessing teaching and because it serves as the basis for many school-based evaluation models and also for the Praxis III assessment system developed by Educational Testing Service.

Danielson conceptualizes teaching in four domains: planning and preparation, the classroom environment, instruction, and professional responsibilities. Included in these four domains are 22 teaching components, shown in Figure 7.3. In addition to the 22 components, the author also suggests several themes, which, though not explicitly stated, are inherent in the standards. These themes are equity, cultural sensitivity, high expectations, developmental appropriateness, accommodating students with special needs, and appropriate use of technology. Although the author uses the label "components of professional practice," we believe that they can be called standards of teaching. Danielson has also developed rubrics that can be used to assess teacher performance on each of the standards.

**FIGURE 7.2**  Iwanicki's (1998) Recommended Standards

1. The teacher effectively plans instruction.
2. The teacher promotes a positive learning environment.
3. The teacher maintains appropriate standards of behavior.
4. The teacher engages the students in meeting the objectives of the lesson.
5. The teacher effectively manages routines and transitions.
6. The teacher creates a structure for learning.
7. The teacher develops the lesson effectively, using appropriate instructional techniques.
8. The teacher presents appropriate content.
9. The teacher uses appropriate questioning techniques.
10. The teacher communicates clearly, using precise language and acceptable oral expression.
11. The teacher monitors student learning and adjusts teaching when appropriate.
12. The teacher performs noninstructional duties.
13. The teacher assumes responsibility for meaningful professional growth.
14. The teacher assumes leadership for school improvement and professional growth.

**FIGURE 7.3** Danielson's (2007) Standards

1. Demonstrating knowledge of content and pedagogy
2. Demonstrating knowledge of students
3. Setting instructional outcomes
4. Demonstrating knowledge of resources
5. Designing coherent instruction
6. Designing student assessments
7. Creating an environment of respect and rapport
8. Establishing a culture for learning
9. Managing classroom procedures
10. Managing student behavior
11. Organizing physical space
12. Communicating with students
13. Using questioning and discussion techniques
14. Engaging students in learning
15. Using assessment in instruction
16. Demonstrating flexibility and responsiveness
17. Reflecting on teaching
18. Maintaining accurate records
19. Communicating with families
20. Participating in a professional community
21. Growing and developing professionally
22. Showing professionalism

The third set of standards for teacher evaluation comes from the work of William Ribas, a practicing school administrator in Massachusetts and the author of a recent text on teacher evaluation (Ribas, 2005). Ribas offers 10 teacher performance standards for evaluating teachers (Figure 7.4). We selected Ribas' ideas for inclusion because they are strong in their emphasis on instruction and also because they were developed by a practicing administrator. The reader will note that Ribas' standards are similar to those offered by Iwanicki in that both seem focused primarily on classroom observation as the data gathering tool.

**FIGURE 7.4** Ribas' (2005) Standards for Teacher Performance

1. The teacher demonstrates competency in subject area(s).
2. The teacher plans instruction effectively.
3. The teacher provides effective assessment of student learning.
4. The teacher communicates effectively with students.
5. The teacher uses appropriate instructional techniques.
6. The teacher applies classroom management techniques to establish a positive and productive learning environment.
7. The teacher maintains and models appropriate standards of behavior, mutual respect, and safety.
8. The teacher promotes high standards and expectations for student achievement.
9. The teacher promotes equitable opportunities for student learning.
10. The teacher demonstrates continuing concern for professionalism.

The National Board for Professional Teaching Standards developed the final set of standards that we will present here. The NBPTS developed five core propositions about teaching that serve as the basis for assessing teachers who seek national board certification. The five core propositions are elaborated in a set of supporting statements (National Board for Professional Teaching Standards, 1999). We include the NBTPS standards because they represent an excellent example of broadly stated standards with clearly stated sample indicators of performance. Figure 7.5 presents the five core propositions and supporting statements.

## Suggested Evaluation Standards

The four sets of standards presented above, augmented by the INTASC standards in Chapter 9, provide a rich variety of examples that a local evaluation committee can draw on in developing evaluation standards. Moreover, the four sets of standards have many more similarities than differences. By studying these examples along with evaluation criteria from a variety of school districts, we have developed a hybrid set of eight standards that captures the important commonalities.

Specific statements that indicate teacher performance that meets the standard further elaborate the eight standards given in Figure 7.6. These indicators are not exhaustive. They

**FIGURE 7.5** National Board for Professional Teaching Standards (1999)

1. Teachers are committed to their students and their learning.
   A. Teachers recognize individual differences in their students and adjust their practice accordingly.
   B. Teachers have an understanding of how students develop and learn.
   C. Teachers treat students equitably.
   D. Teachers' mission extends beyond developing the cognitive capacity of their students.

2. Teachers know the subjects they teach and how to teach those subjects.
   A. Teachers appreciate how knowledge in their subjects is created, organized, and linked to other disciplines.
   B. Teachers command specialized knowledge of how to convey a subject to students.
   C. Teachers generate multiple paths to knowledge.

3. Teachers are responsible for managing and monitoring student learning.
   A. Teachers call on multiple methods to meet their goals.
   B. Teachers orchestrate learning in group settings.
   C. Teachers place a premium on student engagement.
   D. Teachers regularly assess student progress.
   E. Teachers are mindful of their principal objectives.

4. Teachers think systematically about their practice and learn from experience.
   A. Teachers are continually making difficult choices that test their judgment.
   B. Teachers seek the advice of others and draw on education research and scholarship to improve their practice.

5. Teachers are members of learning communities.
   A. Teachers contribute to school effectiveness by collaborating with other professionals.
   B. Teachers work collaboratively with parents.
   C. Teachers take advantage of community resources.

**FIGURE 7.6** Nolan and Hoover's Evaluation Standards and Example Indicators

1. The teacher possesses a deep understanding of the content that he or she teaches.
   A. Understands the central concepts and processes of inquiry in the discipline
   B. Represents content accurately for students
   C. Links content with student experiences
   D. Keeps current with new developments in the subject matter field(s)

2. The teacher develops long-range and daily plans that are appropriate for students and consistent with district curriculum and state standards.
   A. Develops clear, achievable learning goals
   B. Plans lessons in a justifiable sequence
   C. Makes planning decisions based on students' prior knowledge and skills
   D. Employs activities that are consistent with long- and short-term goals
   E. Seeks out a wide variety of resources, including technological resources, in planning instruction

3. The teacher uses a wide variety of instructional strategies including effective questioning to engage students in learning and promote deep understanding of content.
   A. Uses a variety of instructional strategies that are developmentally appropriate
   B. Employs activities aimed at in-depth, not just surface-level understanding
   C. Uses a variety of ways of presenting content including examples, analogies, demonstrations, and hands-on, minds-on activities
   D. Captures "teachable moments" to maximize student engagement
   E. Helps students recognize the importance and relevance of subject matter
   F. Communicates clearly and effectively with students
   G. Uses effective questioning to promote and assess student understanding of content
   H. Incorporates technology into instruction as appropriate

4. The teacher assesses student understanding frequently, provides feedback to students, and uses assessment to plan instruction.
   A. Uses a variety of formal and informal assessment techniques including tests, quizzes, projects, checklists, rubrics, anecdotal records, and so on.
   B. Assesses student understanding on an ongoing basis during instruction
   C. Designs or selects assessment tools that are congruent with curriculum goals and developmentally appropriate
   D. Provides high-quality feedback to students in a timely manner
   E. Reteaches lessons, if needed, based on assessment data
   F. Maintains accurate records of assessments and handles records confidentially

5. The teacher creates a positive classroom environment that is well organized and conducive to student learning and manages student behavior effectively.
   A. Creates a classroom atmosphere that is respectful and nurturing for students
   B. Establishes routines and procedures to organize the classroom environment to support learning activities
   C. Focuses management on engaging students in productive learning activities
   D. Employs effective transitions to maximize instructional time
   E. In dealing with inappropriate behavior, focuses on interventions that help students learn to control their own behavior

6. The teacher understands and responds to a wide variety of student diversity, including cultural differences and special-needs students.
   A. Differentiates instruction to accommodate the needs and strengths of all learners
   B. Provides opportunities for students to examine events from multiple points of view

    C.  Works with support personnel to accommodate the needs of students with exceptional needs

    D.  Sets high expectations for all students and respects the dignity of each student

7.  The teacher is a lifelong learner who seeks opportunities to reflect on his or her practice and grow professionally.

    A.  Uses reflection to asks questions about and improve his or her teaching

    B.  Uses feedback from students, colleagues, and others to improve his or her teaching

    C.  Seeks and takes advantage of opportunities for professional development

    D.  Uses professional organizations and journals as resources for growth and development

    E.  Acts as a resource to colleagues when appropriate

8.  The teacher interacts professionally with families and colleagues and contributes to the school as an organization.

    A.  Interacts tactfully and ethically with colleagues and families

    B.  Communicates regularly with families concerning their children's performance

    C.  Understands and respects different family beliefs, traditions, and values

    D.  Carries out noninstructional duties effectively

    E.  Works for the good of the school community at large

---

are simply examples and are certainly not intended as a checklist of behaviors. The focus in teacher evaluation should be on the eight general standards, and not on the specific indicators, as there are many potential indicators for each standard. We offer these synthesized standards as an additional example that local committees can consider. These standards will also serve as the example that we will use in explaining how to implement the evaluation procedures that we recommend. It is important to remember, however, that the standards used in a school district's evaluation system, though informed by expert examples, should be developed locally for the reasons articulated earlier.

Some authors, including Danielson and McGreal (2000), advocate the development of a rubric that can be used to measure teacher performance for the purpose of summative evaluation. Although this approach seems attractive on the surface, we agree with Peterson, who sees it as appearing to be far more objective than it really is (Peterson, 2000). We also perceive a real danger in that the rubric can easily become a sophisticated checklist that is used by administrators to rate how well the teacher's behavior matches teaching in its ideal form. Though Danielson and McGreal (2000) are adamant that their rubric be used as a guide to professional judgment, not as a checklist, we have already witnessed it being used as a checklist in some districts. Peterson, on the contrary, does not appear to support the use of any explicit standards for judging the quality of teacher performance. He favors reliance on professional judgment informed by a great deal of knowledge about teaching and learning. Although we agree that evaluators need a deep understanding of pedagogy, we believe that the absence of explicit standards of effective teaching makes the process too arbitrary and too dependent on the personal whims of the evaluator. We also believe that explicit standards generally result in more informed judgments.

Rather than using a rubric, we prefer to rephrase the effective teaching standards as a set of questions that can drive the process of summative teacher evaluation. Questions reduce the danger of a checklist mentality and are a natural force for driving data collection procedures. We recommend that local supervision and evaluation committees begin by identifying a set of standards with sample indicators and then rephrase the standards as

**FIGURE 7.7** Evaluation Questions Derived from Standards

**Question 1** In what ways does the evidence demonstrate that the teacher possesses a deep understanding of the content that he or she teaches?

**Question 2** In what ways does the evidence demonstrate that the teacher develops long-range and daily plans that are appropriate for students and consistent with district curriculum and state standards?

**Question 3** In what ways does the evidence demonstrate that the teacher uses a wide variety of instructional strategies including effective questioning to engage students in learning and promote deep understanding of content?

**Question 4** In what ways does the evidence demonstrate that the teacher assesses student understanding frequently, provides feedback to students, and uses assessment to plan instruction?

**Question 5** In what ways does the evidence demonstrate that the teacher creates a positive classroom environment that is well organized and conducive to student learning and manages student behavior effectively?

**Question 6** In what ways does the evidence demonstrate that the teacher understands and responds to a wide variety of student diversity, including cultural differences and special-needs students?

**Question 7** In what ways does the evidence demonstrate that the teacher is a lifelong learner who seeks opportunities to reflect on his or her practice and grow professionally?

**Question 8** In what ways does the evidence demonstrate that the teacher interacts professionally with parents and colleagues and contributes to the school as an organization?

questions. Figure 7.7 contains the evaluation questions derived from our set of standards. The evaluation process described in Chapter 8 is based on these questions.

# CHAPTER SUMMARY

Teacher evaluation is an important organizational function that requires a substantial commitment of time, energy, and resources on the part of all district personnel. Its fundamental purposes are to (1) enable teachers and administrators to document the quality of teaching that currently exists and, in doing so, identify both areas of strength and potential areas for growth, and (2) ensure that all teachers within the system teach at or beyond a minimum level of competence.

A high-quality system of teacher evaluation is built on a solid set of principles concerning effective evaluation and a well-designed set of standards of effective teaching. The principles of effective evaluation address (1) the comprehensive nature of teacher evaluation; (2) the use of a wide variety of data sources in making judgments of teacher effectiveness; (3) the need for credible, well-trained evaluators; (4) the importance of providing staff development concerning evaluation processes; (5) the importance of stakeholder participation in developing the evaluation system; (6) the need to protect the teacher's right to due process; (7) the use of differen-

tiated procedures for evaluating preservice, novice, veteran, and marginal teachers; and finally (8) the central role that professional expertise and judgment must play in the evaluation process.

When stakeholders understand and agree on these key principles, they can use them to develop the standards of effective teaching by which teacher performance will be judged and the procedures to be used in making that summative judgment. Evaluation standards should be created locally or adapted from standards developed by experts in the area of teacher evaluation. Standards developed by Iwanicki, Danielson, Ribas, and the National Board for Professional Teaching Standards offer beginning points for local evaluation criteria. In addition, the authors have also developed a set of standards that can be used to inform the work of the local committee. Local development enhances both ownership of the system on the part of stakeholders and the credibility of the evaluation standards. The standards are rephrased as questions that can drive the process of collecting evidence to document the teacher's performance.

# DISCUSSION QUESTIONS

**1.** Principle 3 of effective teacher evaluation states, "Well-qualified, trained administrators are the appropriate personnel to make summative judgments concerning teacher performance." Should school administrators be required to demonstrate proficiency in teacher evaluation before they are actually allowed to engage in summative evaluation? If so, how would you have them demonstrate their competence? Through a paper-and-pencil test? Through some sort of performance task? Through some combination of the two? Through some other method?

**2.** This chapter suggests that there is no model of teaching that is universally effective. Though no model of teaching may be effective in all contexts,

certain teaching behaviors may be effective across contexts and students. What teaching behaviors have you found that are universally effective?

**3.** This chapter provides five sets of standards for teacher performance. What do you see as the strengths and weaknesses of each set?

**4.** The authors advocate strongly for the development of local standards of effective teaching. Would you be willing to put the time and effort needed to develop a local set of standards of effective teaching? Why or why not? If so, what stakeholders should be involved in that process?

# THEORY-INTO-PRACTICE APPLICATIONS

**1.** Interview three to four teachers and one administrator from the same school concerning the degree to which the principles of evaluation outlined in the first section have been operationalized in their teacher evaluation system. You will first need to develop a set of questions that capture the principles. After conducting the interviews, compare the responses that you receive. Based on the responses, write a paper describing the actions you would take to strengthen that teacher evaluation system. Share your findings with the school district.

**2.** Examine Figure 7.6, the synthesized set of standards for teacher performance created by the authors. Take each of the eight general standards and identify

additional descriptors for each standard that could be used as indicators that the teacher's performance meets the standard.

**3.** If you are currently teaching, you can complete this activity in reference to your own teaching. If you are not currently teaching, pair up with someone who is and complete the activity in reference to their teaching. Take each of the eight evaluation questions in Figure 7.7 and make a list of all the evidence that you could gather yourself to demonstrate your effectiveness as a teacher in reference to each evaluation question. Now make a list of evidence that an administrator could gather for you through classroom observation.

# REFERENCES

CRUIKSHANK, D., & HAEFELE, D. (2001). Good teachers, plural. *Educational Leadership, 58*(5), 26—38.

DANIELSON, C. (2007) *Enhancing professional practice: A framework for teaching!* (2nd ed.) Alexandria, VA: Association for Supervision and Curriculum Development.

DANIELSON, C., & MCGREAL, T. (2000). *Teacher evaluation to enhance professional practice.* Alexandria, VA: Association for Supervision and Curriculum Development.

FLANDERS, N. (1976). Interaction analysis and clinical supervision. *Journal of Research and Development in Education, 9,* 47—57.

FULLAN, M. (2001). *The new meaning of educational change* (3rd ed.). New York: Teachers College Press.

FULLAN, M., JOYCE, B., & SHOWERS, B. (2001). *Student achievement through staff development.* Alexandria, VA: Association for Supervision and Curriculum Development.

IWANICKI, E. (1998). Evaluation in supervision. In G. Firth and E. Pajak (Eds.), *The handbook of research on school supervision.* New York: Macmillan Reference Library.

MEDLEY, D., & COKER, H. (1987). The accuracy of principals' judgments of teacher performance. *Journal of Educational Research, 80,* 242—247.

National Board for Professional Teaching Standards (1999). *What teachers should know and be able to do.* Arlington, VA: National Board for Professional Teaching Standards.

PETERSON, K. (2000). *Teacher evaluation: A comprehensive guide to new directions and practices.* Thousand Oaks, CA: Corwin Press.

RIBAS, W. (2005). *Teacher evaluation that works: The educational, legal, public relations, and social-emotional standards and processes of effective supervision and evaluation* (2nd ed.). Westwood, MA: Ribas Publications.

ROSENSHINE, B., & STEVENS, R. (2001). Teaching functions. In M. C. Wittrock (Ed.), *Handbook of research on teaching* (4th ed.). New York: Macmillan.

SHULMAN, L. (1988). A union of insufficiencies: Strategies for teacher assessment in a period of educational reform. *Educational Leadership, 46*(3), 36–41.

WIGGINS, G., & MCTIGHE, J. (2005). *Understanding by design* (2nd ed.). Alexandria, VA: Association for Supervision and Curriculum Development.

# SUGGESTIONS FOR FURTHER READING AND RESEARCH

DARLING-HAMMOND, L., WISE, A., & PEASE, S. R. (1983). Teacher evaluation in the organizational context: A review of the literature. *Review of Educational Research, 53,* 285–328.

MARZANO, R., PICKERING, D., & POLLOCK, J. (2001). *Classroom instruction that works.* Alexandria, VA: Association for Supervision and Curriculum Development.

The website of the National Board for Professional Teaching Standards: http://www.nbpts.org.

# CHAPTER 8

# PROCEDURES FOR EVIDENCE-BASED TEACHER EVALUATION

**C**HAPTER 7 initiated our discussion of effective teacher evaluation systems by describing standards for effective teacher evaluation as well as standards for effective teaching. These standards form the conceptual underpinning for the development of an evidence-based system of teacher evaluation, and the questions that are developed from the locally developed standards for effective teaching become the driving force for evidence-based teacher evaluation. This chapter focuses on the development of procedures that can be used to operationalize those principles. We use the term "evidence based" very deliberately. We advocate strongly that teacher evaluation procedures be developed that are aimed at generating a wide variety of evidence that can be used to answer the evaluation questions (similar to those depicted in Figure 7.7) that are developed from the local standards for effective teaching.

## GUIDING QUESTIONS FOR PREREADING REFLECTION AND JOURNALING

- Describe the role you played in the evaluation process as the teacher being evaluated. Would you change it in any way?
- What data sources do you believe are most appropriate and helpful in making accurate judgments about the quality of a teacher's performance?
- What responsibilities, if any, should teachers have for gathering evidence concerning the effectiveness of their teaching?

In a similar vein to the exercises at the beginning of Chapters 1 and 3, the purpose of Exercise 8.1 is to give you an opportunity to bring to the surface some of your attitudes about teacher evaluation and to discuss them with classmates. The purpose is not to find correct answers, but rather to identify the important issues involved in the process of teacher evaluation. Many of the concepts embedded in the exercise will be discussed later in this chapter.

**EXERCISE 8.1   Exploring Your Attitudes About Teacher Evaluation**

**Part 1 (Individual)**    Circle the response that best indicates your attitude about each of the following statements:

1. As administrators are ultimately responsible for upholding district standards, they alone should be involved in evaluating a teacher's performance.

Strongly agree        Agree        Unsure        Disagree        Strongly disagree

2. A teacher's performance can be evaluated fairly by in-class observations and informal out-of-class contacts and monitoring alone.

Strongly agree        Agree        Unsure        Disagree        Strongly disagree

3. Announced Classroom observations are more accurate measures of teacher performance than ones that are prearranged.

Strongly agree        Agree        Unsure        Disagree        Strongly disagree

4. Comparing a teacher's present teaching performance against a research-based model of effective teaching is the most appropriate way to evaluate teacher performance.

Strongly agree        Agree        Unsure        Disagree        Strongly disagree

5. Because teachers are ultimately responsible for promoting student learning, they should be evaluated on the basis of how much students actually learn.

Strongly agree        Agree        Unsure        Disagree        Strongly disagree

6. Promptness in handling paperwork, record keeping, and involvement in extracurricular activities should be considered in evaluating teacher performance.

Strongly agree        Agree        Unsure        Disagree        Strongly disagree

7. Rapport with students and parents, personal appearance, and teacher personality traits should be considered in evaluating teacher performance.

Strongly agree        Agree        Unsure        Disagree        Strongly disagree

8. Teacher participation in professional development outside of the school environment should be considered in evaluating teacher performance.

Strongly agree        Agree        Unsure        Disagree        Strongly disagree

**Part 2 (Group)**    Form a group with three other people and attempt to reach group consensus on each of the eight statements. What concepts could the group easily agree on? Why? What concepts were most difficult to agree on? Why? Given your experience in completing this activity as a group, what appear to be some of the issues that must be addressed in designing a teacher evaluation system?

# TEACHER EVALUATION PROCEDURES

The set of evaluation procedures described here is based on the principles of effective evaluation and standards of effective teaching that were described in Chapter 7. We also assume that the procedures will be employed in a differentiated system of teacher supervision and evaluation similar to that depicted earlier in Figure 1.3. The procedures are generally consistent with the teacher evaluation system recommended by Danielson and McGreal (2000), and employ scaled down versions of the procedures required of candidates for certification by the National Board for Professional Teaching Standards (NBPTS) (see http://www.nbpts.org).

Keep in mind that the procedures listed here focus on the evaluation of veteran teachers whose performance is satisfactory; the modifications that must be made when evaluating novice teachers or veteran teachers whose performance has been identified as marginal are explained in Chapters 10 and 11. In addition, Lawrence (2005) also discusses procedures for evaluating the marginal teacher. The remainder of this section addresses the roles that various stakeholders should play, the wide variety of data sources that can be used, a process for compiling data sources into a picture of teacher performance, and a format for summative teacher evaluation.

## Stakeholder Roles

We agree with Peterson (2000), who suggests that teachers can and should play a greatly expanded role in the teacher evaluation process. In most current evaluation systems, teachers play a very passive role. The teacher teaches while the administrator collects all the data, makes summative judgments about the teacher's performance, and announces those judgments to the teacher. We believe the administrator should have the responsibility for making the summative judgments about the quality of the teacher's performance, but the teacher should play a very active role in compiling the data that are used as the basis for those summative judgments. Focused administrator observation and informal monitoring of the teacher's out-of-class behavior in meeting professional obligations should be mandatory data sources for all teachers. Other data sources should be used at the teacher's discretion in consultation with the administrator. The remaining data sources used in the evaluation process come from a menu of data possibilities including teacher materials (e.g., lesson plans, unit plans, tests, projects, etc.), videotapes, student input, parental input, documentation of professional growth activities, and student learning data. The use of each of these data sources is discussed below. The teacher assumes responsibility, in collaboration with the administrator, for choosing the data sources that will be used to address each evaluation question (standard), collecting the data, and compiling the data into a portfolio that addresses the evaluation questions.

The role that we have outlined here for the teacher provides greater autonomy and responsibility for the teacher and also requires more work on the teacher's part. Some teachers who are comfortable with the once-a-year evaluation visit by the principal for purposes of summative evaluation may react negatively to this extra work, complaining that it takes away from the time that they can devote to students. We see two counterarguments to this complaint. First, the vast majority of the data collection process is embedded in the day-to-day work of teaching. Collecting the evaluation data will not take time away from teaching. Second, though the reflective process of compiling the portfolio takes additional time, this time can actually benefit students. The process requires the teacher to make a comprehensive assessment of his or her work, and such assessments typically result in new insights into what works well and what can be improved. Students would be the beneficiaries of both of these types of insights. As we see it, taking the time periodically to formally assess one's practice and its impact on clients is a legitimate responsibility of every professional.

The role of the administrator also changes from that of directing the entire process to that of making summative judgments about the teacher's performance and communicating those judgments to the teacher both orally and in written form. The administrator also plays a role in helping the teacher decide what data sources should be used and in collecting the chosen data. If requested by the teacher, the administrator can consult with the teacher in assembling the teacher portfolio that will be the basis for summative judgments. Although the administrator may assist the teacher, if requested, in collecting and compiling the data, he or she must remain objective in assessing the degree to which the data answer the evaluation questions and whether the evidence shows that the teacher has met district standards or not. In making such summative judgments, the administrator must keep the best interests of students in mind at all times.

The role of the other stakeholders in the evaluation process is determined to a large degree by the procedures that are established by the school district. If the district follows our advice in allowing the inclusion of other data sources (in addition to mandated administrator observation and out-of-class monitoring), the role of the other stakeholders is left to teacher and administrator discretion. As noted, possible data sources include teacher materials, videotapes, student input, parental input, documentation of professional growth, and student learning data. Across all of the veteran teachers who are being evaluated in any given year, it is likely that all of these data sources will be used to some degree. Thus, we envision an expanded role, not only for teachers but also for parents, students, and peers in the process of teacher evaluation.

## Data Sources

***Administrator Observation***   As noted earlier, research has suggested that administrator ratings are not very accurate in assessing teacher quality (see Peterson, 2000). How then can we justify mandating administrator observations as a source of evidence? The answer is because our conception of appropriate administrator observation procedures differs markedly from the traditional process. We conceptualize administrator observations as a series of visits directed at collecting observable evidence that can be used to address the evaluation questions developed by the district. Observation is not as a single event where the administrator observes and rates the teacher's performance simultaneously.

As noted in Chapter 2, observations are different from judgments. We suggested focusing on observations during the lesson and then making judgments based on those observations jointly in the postobservation conference. The evaluation procedures used in most schools do not allow for the separation of observations and judgments. The evaluator typically employs a checklist to record judgments about the teacher's effectiveness. Clearly, the judgments are based on what the administrator is observing; however, the summative evaluation focuses on the judgments, not the observations. Observing lessons and making split second judgments of teaching effectiveness is an enormously complicated task. No model of general educational evaluation advocates simultaneous data collection and judgment making. Every evaluation model separates data collection from data assessment. We believe that the failure to separate the observation process from the judgment-making process in teacher evaluation explains the poor track record of administrator observation in assessing teacher performance.

If the standards for assessing teacher quality are rephrased in the form of questions, instead of statements, then the questions can direct the administrator to collect data that would provide the types of evidence specified in the standards. Over the course of the year, the administrator would make several observations directed at collecting such evidence. At the beginning of the evaluation process, the teacher and administrator would discuss which questions can best be answered through classroom observation and which can be best addressed by other data sources. The questions identified in this discussion would become the foci of the administrator's observations throughout the year. For example, Question 3—focusing on instructional techniques—can be observed much more easily than Question 7—focusing on lifelong learning. The actual judgment-making process concerning teacher performance would be suspended until all of the data have been compiled in the teacher's portfolio.

We also believe that administrator observations should be a combination of announced and unannounced visits. Announced visits allow the administrator an opportunity to see the teacher's optimal performance. If the teacher cannot perform well when the administrator's presence has been announced in advance, it is usually a clear indication that the teacher does not possess the required instructional skills to be an effective teacher. Unannounced observations give the administrator a much better chance of seeing typical teacher performance. By collecting evidence during both unannounced and announced visits, the administrator is, therefore, likely to capture a much more comprehensive picture of teacher performance.

***Teacher Materials***   Teacher materials can provide an excellent window into areas of teacher performance that cannot be tapped in other ways; for example, unit plans and lesson plans can provide clear evidence of teacher planning and preparation. Teacher tests, homework assignments, and other projects that have been used to assess student learning can provide excellent insights into both teacher goals for student learning and the teacher's thinking about assessment. The teacher's use of technology as both a teaching tool and a resource finding tool can also be captured through web pages, Web Quests, PowerPoint presentations, instructional movies, digital photos, and so on.

The use of teacher material in teacher evaluation is not just a simple matter of keeping materials in a box or capturing them electronically. Collection is the first step in the process. However, the more critical step is sorting through those materials to match them to the district's evaluation questions. Matching is a time-consuming activity that prompts reflection on the part of the teacher and should enable the teacher to gain greater insight into both his or her own teaching and the evaluation criteria.

***Videotapes*** As mentioned in Chapter 2 and discussed in detail in Chapter 9, videotapes of lessons can be very powerful sources for documenting, studying, and evaluating teacher performance. When the responsibility for much of the data collection process is turned over to the teacher, the teacher can use videotape to capture key classroom events that the administrator cannot witness. Videotapes can take a variety of foci. They might be used to capture optimal performance, or they might be used to show the teacher's ability to reflect on and correct a lesson that did not go so well. A combination of administrator observation and videotapes that focus on collecting data to answer a particular evaluation question generally provides a more powerful form of evidence than either data source alone. We suggest that the teacher and the administrator use the evaluation planning conference to discuss what videotape evidence to collect, how videotapes and observations can be used together, and who might assist with videotaping lessons.

A video camera that is stationary in the back of the room with a wide-angle lens can capture a wide variety of data. However, a mobile camera in the hands of an administrator or colleague can be much more accurate and precise in gathering the specific kind of evidence that is useful in the evaluation process. For example, a teacher who is attempting to demonstrate his or her ability to respond to student needs during group work would obtain much better data if the camera followed the teacher from group to group, instead of focusing on a fixed space. The evaluation planning conference can be a great resource in deciding not only what videotaped evidence to collect but also who might be best able to capture that evidence.

### EXERCISE 8.1   Deciding on Videotape Evidence

Assume that you are a middle school principal and one of the science teachers you evaluate has asked you to videotape two different lessons, one whole-group lecture and one small-group experiment, to capture evidence concerning Question 5—the creation of a positive classroom learning environment. What aspects of the teaching and learning process would you focus your mobile camera lens on to capture this evidence?

***Student Input*** Student perceptions of the classroom environment and of their interactions with the teacher can be a very valuable source of evidence concerning teacher effectiveness. Note that students should not be asked to rate the teacher's effectiveness. Students do not have the experience or the knowledge needed to make such judgments. What students can provide is evidence concerning their feelings, perceptions, and experiences. Such data can be collected through focus group interviews with small groups of students or through surveys. Surveys are more appropriate for older children who can read well and are not driven to please the teacher. Younger children (K-3) may not read well enough for a written survey and may answer questions in a positive way just to please the teacher. In administering surveys, it is important that students be given assurances that their opinions will remain anonymous. Figure 8.1 contains several example questions that might be used. School districts may find it useful to develop a standard set of items for student input and to allow teachers to use those items and to add, delete, or modify as they see fit. Consultation with the administrator or colleagues can also be a productive step in assembling the survey items or interview questions.

**FIGURE 8.1**   Sample Questions for Student Input

*Student survey*
*Teacher*
*Central High School*

**Directions**   As part of his or her teacher evaluation process, your teacher is interested in your perceptions of this class. The purpose of this activity is to help us understand what you experience as a student working with your teacher. There are no right or wrong answers. You are asked to complete the survey without attaching your name or any other identifying information to it. Circle the response that is most accurate for you.

1. In this class, the amount of learning that I have accomplished is

More than I expected          About what I expected          Less than I expected

2. In this class, my opportunities to interact with the teacher are

Too frequent          Not frequent enough          Just about right

3. The teacher in this class motivates me to work hard and do well.

Yes          Not sure          No

4. The amount of feedback I receive in this class about my learning is

Too much          Not enough          Just about right

5. I feel that the pace at which material is covered in this class is

Too fast          Too slow          Just about right

6. I feel that the teacher in this class is interested in me as an individual.

Yes          Not sure          No

7. The way the teacher teaches matches how I learn best.

True          Not sure          False

8. I understand the rules and expectations in this class.

True          Not sure          False

9. I am treated fairly in this class.

True          Not sure          False

10. The teacher's explanations are usually clear to me.

True          Not sure          False

Please use the back of this form to explain any of your answers, if you feel that is necessary, or to add any additional comments.

**Parental Input**   As with student input, if the teacher opts to include parental input as a source of data, parents should also not be asked to judge the teacher's effectiveness. Though parents do have a great deal of experience, they have neither the professional knowledge necessary nor the opportunity to see the teacher's performance on a regular basis. Questions should, thus, be phrased in terms of their own or their child's interactions with the teacher and the feelings and perceptions resulting directly from those interactions. Because parental interviews are very difficult to schedule and almost always end up with a very skewed sample of parents (usually those who are most positive and/or most negative), it is preferable to use surveys to gather parental input.

Because parents, especially parents of high school students, do not always have a full picture of their child's classroom experiences, a useful technique for increasing the amount of information they have is to suggest that they sit down with their child and discuss the specific items on the survey form. Note that the directions accompanying the sample survey in Figure 8.2 make this suggestion.

Again, questions are to be answered anonymously and are phrased in terms of their own perceptions. As with student surveys, it is useful for the school district to develop a standard set of items and to allow the teacher to add, delete, and modify items. The teacher may find it valuable to consult with the administrator and colleagues in choosing the items to use. Finally, the rate of return from parent surveys, though often quite low, seems to be improved when the surveys are sent out by and returned to the school principal.

**FIGURE 8.2**   Sample Questions for Parental Input

*Parental survey*

*Teacher*

*Central Elementary School*

**Directions**   As part of his or her teacher evaluation process, your child's teacher is gathering parental input. The purpose of this activity is to help us understand what your child has experienced as a student working with this teacher and also what you have experienced as a parent working with this teacher. We suggest that you take some time before completing the survey to talk with your child about his or her experiences and feelings. There are no right or wrong answers. You are asked to complete the survey without attaching your name or any other identifying information to it. Circle the response that is most accurate for you.

1. The teacher has kept me adequately informed of my child's performance.

True          Not sure          False

2. The teacher has responded to my questions/concerns promptly.

True          Not sure          False

3. The teacher has responded to my questions/concerns in a helpful way.

True          Not sure          False

4. The teacher has helped me to feel that we are partners in the educational process.

True          Not sure          False

5. My child's motivation to learn in this class is

Greater than I expected          About what I expected          Less than I expected

6. My child's performance in this class is

Better than I expected          About what I expected          Less than I expected

7. The amount of work that my child is asked to do for this class is

Too much          Just about right          Not enough

8. My child respects this teacher.

True          Not sure          False

9. My child feels cared about by this teacher.

True          Not sure          False

10. I feel comfortable in interacting with this teacher.

True          Not sure          False

Please use the back of this form to explain any of your responses, if you feel that is necessary, or to add additional comments.

**Documentation of Professional Growth**   The most successful and impressive school districts that we have encountered in our work are those where a culture of continuous improvement exists. In such school districts, almost all professional personnel, both administrators and teachers, when asked to describe the district, have responded, "We are good here, and we keep getting better all the time." In other words, preserving the status quo is not an option in these districts. All professionals can choose how to grow, but they cannot choose not to grow. Thus, one important question that a high-quality teacher evaluation system should pose is: What evidence suggests that the teacher is a lifelong learner who seeks to enhance his or her teaching ability?

For purposes of teacher evaluation, teachers can be asked to document their own professional growth over time. Learning can take many forms including enrollment in graduate courses; attendance at workshops, conferences, and inservices; participation in supervision activities such as peer coaching, action research, and collegial development groups; service on district curriculum and school improvement committees; and participation in professional educational organizations. Clearly, not all professional development activities should be expected to have a direct impact on classroom performance. Some activities serve the function of helping the teacher to grow personally, renewing the teacher's enthusiasm, and/or helping the teacher be a better colleague and better member of the school community. However, over a 3-year period, it is also reasonable to expect that some professional growth will be translated into enhanced classroom performance. Thus, in addition to documenting all professional growth experiences, teachers should be asked to identify those experiences that have affected their classroom performance and to document or, at least, describe what the impact has been.

**Student Learning Data**   One potentially valuable source of information that can contribute to the picture of teacher performance is information about student learning (Iwanicki, 1998; Peterson, 2000). We deliberately use the term student learning instead of the more common student achievement. Too often student achievement is construed solely as information about student learning that is gleaned from standardized achievement tests, especially in the era of *No Child Left Behind*. Although test scores provide one data source about student learning, they do not provide a comprehensive picture.

Standardized achievement data are very similar to the closeup picture of your son's belly button in the photography analogy used in chapter 7. They ignore a great many interesting aspects of student learning. Among the additional forms of data that can demonstrate student learning are the following: assessment measures implemented by the teacher at the beginning and end of a unit of instruction; performance on end-of-the-unit and end-of-the-semester tests; performance on other end-of-the-unit measures such as projects, speeches, research papers, drawings, performances, and other teacher documentation such as running records, checklists, rating scales, and anecdotal notes. In contrast to using standardized test scores alone or value-added assessment (VAS) data based only on standardized test scores, using a wide variety of these data sources can provide a very comprehensive and detailed picture of the learning of an individual student or of a group of students.

There are some important ideas to keep in mind when using student learning as a measure of teacher performance. Student performance is not a direct measure of teacher performance. The teacher cannot control the student's behavior. Students always have the final say. They make the decision about how much effort they will put into learning. Sometimes this decision reflects directly on the quality of the teacher's performance; other times, it says very little about the teacher's performance. The difficulty encountered by those who wish to use student learning as a proximal measure of teacher performance is that the relationship between student effort and teacher performance is often not very clear. Unless student learning data are coupled with other data sources such as administrator observations, teacher materials, and videotapes, it is impossible to ascertain to what degree there is a relationship between student learning and teacher performance.

When using student learning as a data source, it is best to look at students as a group as opposed to looking at individuals. It is also very important to look at student learning over time as opposed to a single year. If the data show very high or very poor student performance across different types of students over the 3-year evaluation period, then it is much safer to assume that there is some direct connection to the teacher's performance.

Because of the need for caution in interpreting student learning data and because we believe that the teacher should have some choice of the data sources, we would not require the inclusion of student learning data. This being said, it is our hope that teachers would choose to include student learning data. After all, impacting student learning positively is the teacher's primary mission.

## Compiling the Data: The Evaluation Process

Although the formal evaluation process occurs only once every 3-years for veteran teachers who are performing well, the process of compiling data is ongoing. The teacher is responsible for continuously gathering data concerning his or her performance. If the teacher takes this task seriously, a large amount of data will be collected over the 3-year period. The question then becomes how to compile these data into a manageable and informative package.

In late September of the year of formal evaluation, the teacher and the administrator who will be responsible for the summative evaluation meet to formally plan for the data compilation process. During this conference, the two professionals should note the data that the teacher has already collected and identify additional data that will be collected during this third year of the cycle. A matrix can be valuable first step in deciding what additional evaluation data to collect. A matrix depicts the evaluation questions on one axis and then all of the possible data sources on the other. Figure 8.3 provides a sample of part of such a matrix. As it is intended only as an illustrative example, it does not include all evaluation questions or all potential sources of evidence.

**FIGURE 8.3** Sample Evaluation/Evidence Matrix

| Evidence | Question 1: Planning | Question 4: Instruction | Question 5: Classroom climate | Question 7: Lifelong learner |
|---|---|---|---|---|
| Administrator observation | xx | xx | xx | |
| Student input | | xx | xx | |
| Parent input | | | xx | |
| Teacher materials | xx | xx | | xx |
| Professional growth documentation | | xx | | xx |
| Student learning | | xx | | |

At the September conference, the administrator and the teacher discuss very specifically which evaluation questions will require observation data from the administrator. At the end of the conference, the administrator should have a clear picture of his or her role in data collection and should make a tentative observation plan for gathering the data through announced and unannounced visits.

During the months of October and November, the teacher continues to compile data for which he or she is responsible (teacher materials, documenting growth, etc.). The administrator also collects data through classroom observations. In early December, a second conference is conducted at which the teacher and the administrator review progress in data collection and make plans for collecting student input and parental input if these data sources are to be used. If the teacher is at the secondary level and teaches in a block schedule or teaches semester courses, student and parental data must be collected at this point in the year. Otherwise the data can be collected in February or early March to allow more time for students to be working with the teacher.

Data collection continues until the end of March, at which point all relevant data have been collected. At the beginning of April, the administrator turns over all observational data to the teacher who now has all of the data that will be used in making the summative evaluation. The reflective process of compiling a comprehensive picture of teacher performance now begins. We believe that a teacher portfolio provides the best vehicle for compiling the data sources. As noted earlier, portfolio development requires work on the part of the teacher, but this work can lead to growth as the teacher gains insights into the quality of his or her performance (Bullock & Hawk, 2004). Figure 8.4 depicts the timeline for the evaluation process.

**FIGURE 8.4**   Formal Evaluation Timeline—Veteran Teachers

---

**September**   Evaluation planning conference by teacher and administrator to develop data collection plan.

**October/November**   Data collection by teacher and administrator as specified in the plan.

**December**   Midterm conference to check on the progress of data collection to date and to arrange for collecting student and parent input if chosen as a data source.

**March 31**   Data collection stops and all data are given to the teacher for compilation.

**May 1**   Teacher evaluation portfolio is given to the administrator.

**June 1**   Final evaluation conference is conducted and summative rating is given.

---

Teachers should view portfolio development as the process of constructing an argument to support a case they are trying to make. The process is analogous to that used by a trial lawyer. Just as a lawyer tries to convince the jury or judge, a teacher tries to convince administrator of the case of teaching excellence (i.e., the administrator) of the correctness of his or her case, namely that he or she is an excellent teacher. The contents of the portfolio are the pieces of evidence that make the argument. In developing the portfolio, the teacher uses the district's evaluation questions as a guide to sift through the data that have been collected and find those data that provide the most compelling evidence to answer the question. The evidence that is most compelling is definitely included in the portfolio.

The teacher then uses the "value-added principle" to decide whether to include additional data for that question (Bird, 1990). This principle requires the portfolio developer to look at each new potential piece of evidence and ask the question: "Will this piece add anything to the argument that I am trying to make?" If the answer is yes, then the evidence is included; otherwise, it is discarded. The process continues until all of the pieces of evidence for each evaluation question have been examined.

We recommend that the portfolio begin with a table of contents that lists each of the district's evaluation questions together with the data sources that have been included in the portfolio to address each. Each evaluation question and its data sources comprise one section of the portfolio. At the end of each section, the teacher provides a reflective statement of no more than one page that summarizes what the data sources demonstrate about the teacher's performance in reference to the evaluation question. Figures 8.5 and 8.6 contain a sample table of contents and a sample reflective statement for one evaluation question, taken from the portfolio of a third-grade teacher.

**FIGURE 8.5** Sample Table of Contents for Evaluation Portfolio

*Teacher*
*Administrator*

**Question 1** In what ways does the evidence demonstrate that the teacher possesses a deep understanding of the content that he or she teaches?

*Evidence A* Lesson plan and videotape of inquiry lesson on simple machines
*Evidence B* Web Quest developed as part of social studies unit on Japan
*Reflective statement*

**Question 2** In what ways does the evidence demonstrate that the teacher develops long-range and daily plans that are appropriate for students and consistent with district curriculum and state standards?

*Evidence A* Unit plan for Japan unit
*Evidence B* Daily lesson plans on fractions and decimals
*Evidence C* Administrator observation of writers' workshop activities (October 7)
*Reflective statement*

**Question 3** In what ways does the evidence demonstrate that the teacher uses a wide variety of instructional strategies including effective questioning to engage students in learning and promote deep understanding of content?

*Evidence A* Administrator observation of learning stations during language arts (November 14)
*Evidence B* Photographs of "cave paintings" completed by students
*Evidence C* Videotape of student discussion on equivalent fractions
*Reflective statement*

**Question 4** In what ways does the evidence demonstrate that the teacher assesses student understanding frequently, provides feedback to students, and uses assessment to plan instruction?

*Evidence A* Student pre- and post-test scores on basic geometric shapes
*Evidence B* Student story draft with teacher comments and revised student story
*Evidence C* Parental survey items concerning providing feedback
*Evidence D* Homework assignment on metric conversion (March 15) and videotaped lesson on metric conversion (March 17)
*Reflective statement*

**Question 5** In what ways does the evidence demonstrate that the teacher creates a positive classroom environment that is well organized and conducive to student learning and manages student behavior effectively?

*Evidence A* Letter to students and parents from September
*Evidence B* Videotape of morning meeting on October 28
*Evidence C* Administrator observation of learning stations (November 14)
*Evidence D* Parental survey items on motivation, respect, and caring
*Reflective statement*

**Question 6** In what ways does the evidence demonstrate that the teacher understands and responds to a wide variety of student diversity, including cultural differences and special-needs students?

*Evidence A* Adapted prewriting story map activity for learning support student
*Evidence B* Parental survey items concerning respect, caring, and comfort level
*Evidence C* Record of instructional support process and adaptations made for student X
*Reflective statement*

*(Continued)*

**FIGURE 8.5** (*Continued*)

---

**Question 7** In what ways does the evidence demonstrate that the teacher is a lifelong learner who seeks opportunities to reflect on his or her practice and grow professionally?

*Evidence A* Completion of staff development workshops on *Math Their Way* and literature circles

*Evidence B* Comparison of previous unit on Japan with the current Japan unit

*Evidence C* Self-directed growth project on Web Quests completed last year

*Reflective statement*

**Question 8** In what ways does the evidence demonstrate that the teacher interacts professionally with families and colleagues and contributes to the school as an organization?

*Evidence A* Mentoring of a new third-grade teacher this year

*Evidence B* Parental survey items on comfort in interacting and responses to parental concerns

*Evidence C* Service on new math textbook committee last year and writing assessment committee 2 years ago

*Evidence D* Attendance at PTA meetings in October and March as third-grade representative

*Reflective statement*

---

**FIGURE 8.6** Sample Reflective Statement

---

**Evaluation Question 1—Content Knowledge**

I have chosen to include two pieces of evidence to demonstrate the depth of my content knowledge. The inquiry-oriented lesson on simple machines consists of a "science talk" with my students concerning levers and force and a follow-up activity in which the students use Lego kits to work through some of the ideas that surfaced in the science talk.

During the science talk, my understanding of content is demonstrated by my use of questioning to probe the student misconception that force can only be applied in a downward direction and the subsequent activity with the Legos, where force is applied in an upward fashion. This misconception needs to be confronted or the students will not be able to develop an appropriate understanding of the three types of levers and the relationship between the fulcrum and the direction of the force. If I did not understand the content well, the importance of the misconception concerning the direction of force would not have been clear to me, and students would have been unable to understand the concept of the three classes of levers, which is an important objective in this unit.

The Web Quest on Japan represents a real demonstration of growth of understanding on my part, not only in terms of my understanding of Japanese culture, but also in terms of my understanding of the uses of the Internet for students. The Web Quest groups students in teams of four. Each team has a meteorologist, a geographer, a political scientist, and an economist. After spending a week in expert groups learning what each of the roles means, the teams visit each of the various regions (using books and predetermined web sites) of Japan and obtain information about weather, government, the economy, and the physical geography of the region. Each piece of information must be validated by at least two sources, electronic or print. The group then uses the information to develop a travel brochure for each region of Japan. The development and implementation of this web site demonstrates that I have a deep understanding of the political, geographic, meteorological, and economic conditions of each region of Japan. It also demonstrates a real understanding of the print and electronic resources available in studying Japan and a facility in using technology with my students. Finally, it demonstrates a deep understanding on my part of the importance of teaching students about the wide variety in the quality of information one can find on the Internet. Asking students to validate each piece of information through two sources helps them to begin to understand the need to validate information through multiple sources, a critical technological literacy skill.

Taken together, these two artifacts demonstrate a deep understanding of the subject matter that I teach to my third-grade students.

## Making the Summative Evaluation Judgment

As noted in Figure 8.4, the portfolio is given to the administrator by May 1st, and he or she makes a summative judgment concerning the teacher's performance based on the evidence. The administrator conveys this judgment to the teacher in a final evaluation conference held near the beginning of June. At the final evaluation conference, the teacher signs the summative rating and has the opportunity to attach a written reply to the evaluation if he or she has a different opinion. In addition, the teacher has the right to appeal the summative rating to the central office administrator designated for that role. In the event that the administrator knows of evidence that should have been included in the portfolio but was not, the administrator has the right to add that evidence and to use it as a basis for making the summative judgment. This addition of evidence by the administrator should happen only in very rare instances as the administrator has been involved throughout the formal evaluation process in consulting with the teacher regarding data sources. The summative judgment by the administrator consists of two distinct components, reflected in the summative evaluation form depicted in Figure 8.7.

**FIGURE 8.7**  Sample Summative Evaluation Form

**Question 1**  In what ways does the evidence demonstrate that the teacher possesses a deep understanding of the content that he or she teaches?

_____ Evidence is clear that the standard is met.  (Level 1)

_____ Evidence is not clear concerning whether standard is met. (Level 2)

_____ Evidence is clear that standard is not met. (Level 3)

*Narrative statement*

**Question 2**  In what ways does the evidence demonstrate that the teacher develops long-range and daily plans that are appropriate for students and consistent with district curriculum and state standards?

_____ Evidence is clear that the standard is met.

_____ Evidence is not clear concerning whether standard is met.

_____ Evidence is clear that standard is not met.

*Narrative statement*

**Question 3**  In what ways does the evidence demonstrate that the teacher uses a wide variety of instructional strategies including effective questioning to engage students in learning and promote deep understanding of content?

_____ Evidence is clear that the standard is met.

_____ Evidence is not clear concerning whether standard is met or not.

_____ Evidence is clear that standard is not met.

*Narrative statement*

**Question 4**  In what ways does the evidence demonstrate that the teacher assesses student understanding frequently, provides feedback to students, and uses assessment to plan instruction?

_____ Evidence is clear that the standard is met.

_____ Evidence is not clear concerning whether standard is met.

_____ Evidence is clear that standard is not met.

*Narrative statement*

**Question 5**  In what ways does the evidence demonstrate that the teacher creates a positive classroom environment that is well organized and conducive to student learning and manages student behavior effectively?

(*Continued*)

**FIGURE 8.7** (*Continued*)

_____ Evidence is clear that the standard is met.

_____ Evidence is not clear concerning whether standard is met.

_____Evidence is clear that standard is not met.

*Narrative statement*

**Question 6**   In what ways does the evidence demonstrate that the teacher understands and responds to a wide variety of student diversity, including cultural differences and special-needs students?

_____ Evidence is clear that standard is met.

_____ Evidence is not clear concerning whether standard is met.

_____ Evidence is clear that standard is not met.

*Narrative statement*

**Question 7**   In what ways does the evidence demonstrate that the teacher is a lifelong learner who seeks opportunities to reflect on his or her practice and grow professionally?

_____ Evidence is clear that the standard is met

_____ Evidence is not clear concerning whether standard is met.

_____ Evidence is clear that standard is not met.

*Narrative statement*

**Question 8**   In what ways does the evidence demonstrate that the teacher interacts professionally with families and colleagues and contributes to the school as an organization?

_____ Evidence is clear that the standard is met.

_____ Evidence is not clear concerning whether standard is met.

_____ Evidence is clear that standard is not met.

*Narrative statement*

**Final summative rating**

_____ Satisfactory _____ Needs improvement _____ Unsatisfactory

| | |
|---|---|
| (Teacher signature and date) | (Administrator signature and date) |

In the first summative evaluation component, the administrator provides a clear response to each of the evaluation questions used by the district. The administrator's answer to eachs evaluation question falls into one of the three levels.

- A Level 1 assessment indicates that the evidence shows clearly that the teacher meets the evaluation standard.

- A Level 2 assessment indicates that the evidence is not clear whether the teacher meets the evaluation standard. This judgment may mean that the evidence that has been captured is not very good evidence or is not clearly connected to the standard. In this case, the administrator should go back to the teacher and attempt to find better evidence that can be used to make that determination. The judgment may also mean that the evidence is appropriate but does not provide clear support of the teacher's performance meeting the standard.

- A Level 3 assessment indicates that the evidence is clear that the teacher's performance does not meet the evaluation standard.

The administrator should also provide a brief narrative statement that explains and justifies his or her answer to each of the evaluation questions. In addition, the narrative statements can be used to praise positive areas of performance and to point out potential

**FIGURE 8.8** Sample Narrative Statement for Question 1

The evidence presented in the portfolio along with my classroom observations indicates that Ms. X clearly meets the criteria for Standard 1. She consistently uses information about potential student misconceptions to plan lessons that promote deep student understanding. The science talk on levers is an excellent example of a lesson that promotes deep understanding. I commend her highly for her thoroughness in planning for, teaching toward, and assessing student understanding. In addition, Ms. X typically finds external resources in the form of books, articles, Internet web sites, and so on to augment her content knowledge. The Web Quest that she developed on Japan required a comprehensive understanding of e-resources and collaboration with colleagues in other district buildings and beyond.

---

areas for future growth for the teacher. Figure 8.8 contains a sample narrative statement for evaluation Question 1 on teacher content knowledge. The sample evaluation statement is an assessment of the evidence described by the teacher in Figure 8.6.

The second component of the summative evaluation is an overall rating of the teacher's performance. Determining the overall rating is a complex process requiring the application of certain guidelines, aided by professional judgment. This rating should be confined to three categories: satisfactory, needs improvement, or unsatisfactory. Some readers will object that this lumps teachers whose performance is outstanding with those whose performance is merely adequate. Although accurate, this criticism does not undermine the validity of our recommendation. Unless the evaluation process is used to determine merit pay or some other form of differentiated compensation or recognition, there is no need to make distinctions among competent veteran teachers. Remember, evaluation is not the mechanism that promotes growth beyond competence toward excellence. Evaluation simply documents the quality of teaching that exists and ensures that all teachers perform at a satisfactory level. These three categories are all that is required to meet these objectives. Moreover, although the overall rating does not distinguish satisfactory from excellent performance, the narrative answers to each of the evaluation questions would certainly be different when describing these two different levels of performance.

One common difficulty arises in translating the answers to the evaluation questions into a summative rating. No defensible, generalizable guideline exists for determining how many evaluation standards must be clearly met in order to achieve a satisfactory rating. In some cases, one single area of deficiency may be so critical that it renders the teacher's total performance unsatisfactory. For example, a teacher who possesses content knowledge, plans well, interacts with others well, can use a wide variety of strategies, and so on, but cannot organize the classroom environment so that students become engaged in learning activities is not performing at a satisfactory level. On the contrary, a deficiency in one or two standards may be more than compensated for by outstanding performance in other areas.

Relating the individual evaluation standards to an overall summative rating requires expertise and professional judgment on the part of the evaluator. This is the point where initial and ongoing professional development for administrators as well as consultation with other principals and central office personnel can be critical. When in doubt concerning what summative rating to give, an administrator should share the teacher's portfolio and his or her responses to the evaluation questions with fellow administrators to get their opinions. Such consultation can help the administrator who is responsible for the summative rating to make a more informed decision. It can also help to ensure that administrators are reasonably consistent in making summative judgments. The administrator, not needing to make a snap judgment, can take the portfolio home, study it, and even gather more information, if needed, to make an accurate judgment.

Danielson and McGreal (2000) suggest that the district may want to set a maximum number of Level 2 or 3 assessments that a teacher can obtain and still receive an overall rating of satisfactory. We would recommend that, unless the evidence makes a strong case to the contrary, any teacher who has a Level 3 assessment in one or more standards or a Level 2 in two or more standards should receive a needs improvement rating, at best.

The overall summative rating determines the veteran teacher's placement in the teacher supervision and evaluation system for the following years. A satisfactory rating allows the teacher to continue in the supervisory growth options for the following 2 years, returning to formal evaluation during the third year. A needs improvement or unsatisfactory rating places the teacher in the intensive assistance category until a satisfactory rating is regained or the teacher is dismissed. In the context of a differentiated supervision and evaluation system, when an administrator is in doubt concerning which of the overall ratings to give, he or she should go with the lower rating. The lower rating assures that the teacher will receive greater direction and more structured support and also protects children's interests to a greater degree. As the process of assigning an overall rating is complex, we strongly recommend that the teacher supervision and evaluation committee take up the question of how to develop the overall summative rating, revisit it periodically over time, and make adjustments as necessary (see Chapter 12).

## CHAPTER SUMMARY

Although administrators remain solely responsible for making the summative judgment about the quality of teacher performance, teachers can play a greatly expanded role in collecting data on which to base that judgment. In addition to administrator observation and informal monitoring, teacher materials, videotapes, student input, parental input, documentation of professional growth, and student learning data can serve as valuable data sources to be included in the teacher's evaluation portfolio.

The formal evaluation of competent veteran teachers occurs once every 3 years. During the formal evaluation year, the teacher and administrator work together to compile the data concerning teacher performance. The data are then reduced to a portfolio that addresses each of the district's evaluation questions. The administrator uses the portfolio to assess the teacher's performance in each standard area and to develop a global summative rating of the teacher as satisfactory, needs improvement, or unsatisfactory.

## DISCUSSION QUESTIONS

**1.** Some experts suggest that teachers should be responsible for making summative judgments concerning the teaching performance of other teachers. Other experts assert that summative judgment making should remain the task of administrators. What is your view on this issue? What do you see as the advantages and disadvantages of each position?

**2.** What role should performance of noninstructional duties play in the evaluation of teacher performance? Why? How should it be related to classroom teaching performance? Why? What strategies or procedures can an administrator employ to document the teacher's performance in noninstructional areas?

**3.** The authors advocate a system of evaluation that gives a satisfactory rating to all teachers whose performance is satisfactory or beyond, whereas many systems in use in school districts distinguish among satisfactory performers, using labels such as commendable, outstanding, or superior. What do you see as the advantages and disadvantages of each of these two approaches? If you were creating an evaluation system, which would you choose? Why?

**4.** What guidelines would you set for the process of determining an overall summative rating from the ratings on individual evaluation standards; for example, how many Level 3 assessments would be sufficient to result in a rating of unsatisfactory or needs improvement? Why?

# THEORY-INTO-PRACTICE APPLICATIONS

**1.** Work with a group of colleagues at different instructional levels (elementary, middle, and high school) to develop a standard set of items that could be used across settings to elicit student input and parental input concerning teacher performance.

**2.** Work with a small group of colleagues to develop an interview protocol or survey that could be used to assess the willingness of teachers to be involved in the process of compiling the data that will be used in the evaluation of their performance. Be sure to ask not only about general willingness but also about specific types of involvement, for example, collecting materials, making videotapes, compiling a portfolio, and so on. In the introduction to the survey or interview, provide several statements that point out both the potential

benefits of teacher involvement in the process as well as the extra work that will be required.

**3.** Develop a PowerPoint presentation that could be used to introduce the teachers and administrators at your school to these procedures and processes for teacher evaluation. In the slides be sure to include not only the procedures but also the concepts and rationales that support the various procedures.

**4.** Do an Internet search to identify school districts across the country that utilize some or all of the evaluation procedures that are advocated in this chapter. Which procedures seem to be commonly employed? Which are rarely employed? What implications can you draw from this Internet search?

# REFERENCES

BIRD, T. (1990). The school teacher's portfolio: An essay on possibilities. In J. Millman & L. Darling-Hammond (Eds.), *The new handbook of teacher evaluation: Assessing elementary and secondary school teachers* (pp. 241–256). Newbury Park, CA: Sage Publications.

BULLOCK, A., & HAWK, P. (2004). *Developing a teaching portfolio: A guide for preservice and practicing teachers* (2nd ed.). Upper Saddle River, NJ: Merrill/Prentice Hall.

DANIELSON, C., & MCGREAL, T. (2000). *Teacher evaluation to enhance professional practice.* Alexandria,

VA: Association for Supervision and Curriculum Development.

IWANICKI, E. (1998). Evaluation in supervision. In G. Firth and E. Pajak (Eds.), *The handbook of research on school supervision.* New York: Macmillan Reference Library.

LAWRENCE, C. (2005). *The marginal teacher: A step by step guide to fair procedures for identification and dismissal* (3rd. ed.). Thousand Oaks, CA: Corwin Press.

PETERSON, K. (2000). *Teacher evaluation: A comprehensive guide to new directions and practices.* Thousand Oaks, CA: Corwin Press.

# SUGGESTIONS FOR FURTHER READING

MILLMAN, J., & DARLING-HAMMOND, L. (1990). *The new handbook of teacher evaluation: Assessing elementary and secondary school teachers.* Newbury Park, CA: Sage Publications.

SCRIVEN, M. (1988). Duty-based teacher evaluation. *Journal of Personnel Evaluation in Education, 1*(4), 319–334.

STANLEY, S., & POPHAM, J. (1988) *Teacher evaluation: Six prescriptions for success.* Alexandria, VA: Association for Supervision and Curriculum Development.

# CHAPTER 9

# SUPERVISION AND EVALUATION
# OF THE PRESERVICE TEACHER

**P**ART **V** of this book focuses on special cases in teacher supervision and evaluation. Many of the concepts and skills that were discussed in the preceding chapters on supervision and evaluation are applicable to all teachers. However, supervisors who work with preservice teachers, novice teachers, and marginal teachers need to modify some of the techniques to meet unique challenges. In this chapter, we take an in-depth look at the first of the cases: university supervisors and cooperating teachers collaborating to assist preservice teachers in gaining practical knowledge and skills to enter the profession.

Preservice teachers or teaching interns are unique in that they view the classroom through the eyes of a student, on the one hand, and through the new lens of an aspiring educator, on the other hand. They have attained a substantive knowledge base in their coursework, but they still need to acquire practical or applied learning through firsthand experience in a school setting. Closely related to the dual role as student and as teacher is the developmental journey in which preservice teachers engage—from focus on self to concern for their students' learning and well-being.

Supervision and evaluation of preservice teachers requires that university personnel, cooperating teachers from a wide variety of settings, and preservice teachers themselves work closely together in a triad. We discuss five supervisory activities that are powerful at nurturing the development of preservice teachers into competent and reflective practitioners. Those activities are the preobservation conference and the post observation conference (which were introduced in Chapter 2), structured videotape analysis of teaching, reflective electronic growth portfolios, and online professional learning communities. Although we explore those supervisory practices in the context of preservice teacher supervision, any of them can be added to a supervisor's repertoire to assist novice or experienced teachers as well.

Evaluation of preservice teachers is an extremely important function. The summative evaluation decisions that are made by the supervisor and the cooperating teacher determine who gains entry into the teaching profession. In discussing the evaluation of preservice teachers, we identify several issues that complicate the evaluation process, emphasize the importance of well-defined criteria for assessing performance, and recommend procedures for carrying out this significant task. We end the chapter with a brief discussion of failure in student teaching and some suggestions for dealing with preservice teachers who are not succeeding.

# GUIDING QUESTIONS FOR PREREADING REFLECTION AND JOURNALING

- What type of specialized knowledge or specific strategies might be helpful to you in the role of university supervisor or cooperating teacher dealing with preservice teachers?

- If you have worked with a preservice teacher in the past, take a moment to reflect on and jot down the unique rewards and challenges of such a supervisory role. Share your perceptions with the group.

- Describe the roles or responsibilities (or both) that you believe a university supervisor and a cooperating teacher should assume to effectively communicate and collaborate with one another and with the preservice teacher as members of a triad.

- How was your performance as a preservice teacher evaluated? What role did the university supervisor play? What role did the cooperating teacher play? What role did you play? How could the process have been improved?

# WHY ARE PRESERVICE TEACHERS A SPECIAL CASE IN SUPERVISION AND EVALUATION?

Although the cycle of supervision and the activities embedded in the cycle are similar to those employed with experienced teachers, several factors make supervising preservice teachers a unique challenge. First, preservice teachers have gained formal, academic knowledge through their teacher training programs, but they need to develop "practical knowledge"—learning that is grounded in actual teaching experience. Such learning can be achieved only by assuming responsibility for making daily on-the-job decisions and professional judgments (Cochran-Smith, 2000). For example, preservice teachers may be able to *compose* sound lesson plans that take into account content standards and curriculum requirements, but can they *implement* those plans effectively, adapting on the spot to deal with students' prior knowledge (or lack thereof) and individual differences among their students?

Bransford, Derry, Berliner, Hammerness, and Beckett (2005) compare a preservice teacher's knowledge and skills to that of an engineer building a bridge. Although the engineer must certainly be well grounded in the principles of physics needed for a safe structure, he or she must also take into account variables such as nature of the terrain, availability of materials for construction, and the aesthetics of the design. Likewise, teachers must possess not only the declarative or technical knowledge, but also the "capacity to be adaptive experts who can take nonroutine aspects of the context into account in making sound teaching decisions" (p. 78).

The role of university supervisors and cooperating teachers is to guide the preservice teacher's formal entry into these real-world classroom experiences by modeling effective teaching, providing scaffolding or developmentally appropriate feedback and support when necessary, fostering a climate conducive to inquiry and reflection, and challenging each preservice teacher to grow as a professional.

The second factor contributing to the challenge of supervising preservice teachers lies in the unique transition that they are making from university student to classroom teacher. Typically, during the transition, the teacher candidate passes through three distinct developmental phases: survival, task, and impact (Fuller, 1969). The survival phase is characterized by egocentric concerns about one's own competence or well-being. Preservice teachers in the survival phase are struggling to meet the myriad demands of the job. They have concerns about whether they will be able to keep up with the day-to-day planning and grading, whether their students will like them, and whether they can be successful after their years of study. Those concerns are exemplified by a preservice teacher's comment in a recent online journal: "I seem to have no energy and even less confidence. Some days I wonder what the hell I am doing up in front of a class."

In the task phase, the concerns of preservice teachers focus more on gaining command of the content to be taught or on refining their skills (e.g., concerns about classroom management or about matching instructional strategies and assessments to lesson goals). An elementary preservice teacher reflected: "I am not pleased with the students' behavior when they join me on the carpet at circle time. I am going to experiment. I have prepared 3 × 5 cards with their names and taped them to the floor. I am going to have them come forward and sit on their cards so that I can control who is sitting next to whom."

The impact phase occurs if and when preservice teachers have achieved enough competence and confidence to focus on their students and to reflect on ways to improve their teaching behaviors so as to have a positive impact on students' learning. A math teacher's journal reveals his concern about his students' deeper understanding of key concepts:

> *I honestly feel that, for a Friday afternoon, the student-centered activity kept the class focused on their learning far more than a lecture or individual seatwork assignment would have. I know they enjoyed the activity. The question I ponder is will they retain the material more by working together in groups and discussing the problems with one another? I know I could have covered more content through lecture, but would they have truly understood? I think explaining math to others is one of the most effective strategies for strengthening reasoning abilities. Are my students really thinking more?*

Although the various areas of concern are not necessarily discrete (e.g., a preservice teacher may have a concern at each of the phases, depending on the circumstances), supervisors who possess an awareness of the three developmental stages can more effectively facilitate the preservice teacher's progress from personal concerns to task considerations to an emphasis on their students. Exercise 9.1 provides practice in distinguishing among the phases of preservice teacher concerns.

### EXERCISE 9.1 Phases of Preservice Teacher Concerns

**Directions** Read the following excerpts from preservice teachers' reflective journals. For each excerpt, decide whether the preservice teacher's reflection is predominantly at the survival **(S)**, task **(T)**, or impact **(I)** level of concern.

1. Several of my students have less than desirable home situations with little stability. They bounce from parent to parent. With no enforced bedtime, they come to school exhausted and find it difficult to stay focused and on task. I am searching for ways to minimize the way their lives outside of school affect their performance in school.

2. Writing five different lesson plans per day is so much more work than I ever imagined it would be. I feel as if I never see my boyfriend throughout the week!

3. Because the students in my second placement are far more diverse in their abilities (from gifted to many with special needs), I need to be more attentive to designing differentiated instructional opportunities.

4. I have a terrible cold and felt as if I were just robotically going through the motions of teaching today.

5. I find it interesting how my students' reading abilities transfer over to their writing abilities. Those who are poor readers struggle to express themselves in writing. I am trying to spend more time working one-on-one with them.

6. I am currently planning two units, one on motion in science and one on geometry in math. I am enthusiastic because there are so many opportunities for me to incorporate hands-on, minds-on activities. I have spent a lot of time looking through outside resources.

7. The past week has been very frustrating for me because of classroom management. I am sure I am always going to be tested and have behavior problems, but at least now I have some practice thinking on my feet.

8. The pace of the lesson really began to drag as we were working on the punctuation exercise. My suspicions were confirmed when one of the students gave me this sentence he wrote as an example of an interrogative statement, "When is this activity going to be over?"

---

The third factor that contributes to the challenge of supervising preservice teachers is the need to work closely as part of a triad. Whether representing the university or the school district, supervisors must engage in ongoing communication, collaboration, and coordination of the team's effort. They must bridge any gap between the philosophical perspectives of the university and of the public schools. Historically, the individuals engaged in higher and in basic education have viewed themselves as separate entities working in isolation (theory versus practice; "ivory tower" versus "life in the trenches") rather than as educators with a common purpose within a seamless K–16 system (Holmes Group, 1990). Moreover, many studies have highlighted "differences in understanding among cooperating teachers, college supervisors, and student teachers about each other's roles, expectations, decision making, and the process for policy formation" (McIntyre & Byrd, 1998, p. 411). True collaboration between university-based and school-based supervisors requires a partnership marked by shared knowledge and goals, respect for one another's expertise, and equity in decision making.

For those teacher education institutions operating within the context of a well-functioning professional development school (PDS) model as outlined by the Holmes Group, the triad may be more likely to function as a genuine partnership or "professional community" with a common knowledge base and collective aims, particularly to enhance the educational experiences of all students. A well-functioning PDS effectively links a university faculty's research skills with the practical knowledge and expertise of teachers. Meanwhile, the school site becomes a center for learning "for the development of novice professionals, for continuing development of experienced professionals, and for the research and development of the teaching profession" (Holmes Group, 1990, p. 1).

When an ongoing PDS relationship exists, university faculty and cooperating teachers create a shared sense of purpose concerning the education of preservice teachers. They know each other well. Typically, they have common understandings of teaching and learning, and they have close personal relationships with one another based on mutual respect and trust. In addition, preservice teachers typically spend extended periods of time involved in field experiences in the PDS context. The cooperating teacher and supervisor therefore have a much longer period of time to work with the preservice teacher. All of these factors make supervision and evaluation of preservice teachers much easier in a professional development school.

In the absence of a PDS model, some type of collaborative forum—such as an in-service opportunity or a continuing education seminar for cooperating teachers—is a necessary first step in creating a mutual understanding about the roles, expectations, and procedures involved in supervising and assessing preservice teachers. The research shows that providing training for cooperating teachers has multiple benefits. For example, preservice teachers who worked with trained cooperating teachers had attitudes toward student teaching that were more positive and received significantly more feedback on their teaching than student teachers who worked with untrained cooperating teachers (McIntyre &

**FIGURE 9.1** Suggested Goals for a University Supervisor/Cooperating Teacher Seminar

1. To build a bridge between the university and the school setting by exploring the collaborative roles, responsibilities, shared expertise, and decision making of supervisory partners

2. To join in an open and informed exchange concerning the collective goals and challenges of supervising preservice teachers

3. To explore and reach an understanding about performance indicators or criteria for success to which all preservice teachers should aspire

4. To construct a common knowledge base about effective supervisory practices that encourage continuous reflection by preservice teachers and personal inquiry into their teaching and its impact on students' learning

5. To distinguish between actions designed as formative or supervisory and those designed for summative evaluation to judge competence according to performance indicators of success

6. To review and practice data collection and interpretation during live or videotaped classroom observations/lessons and to assist preservice teachers in making use of the data to refine teaching practice

7. To outline and role play a plan for conducting preobservation or planning conferences and postobservation conferences

8. To review artifact collection as part of creating a working or process portfolio to reflect on progress toward performance indicators

Byrd, 1998). Moreover, trained cooperating teachers also demonstrated greater use of active listening skills, use of a wider variety of models of instruction, and increased self-confidence and self-direction (Guyton & McIntyre, 1990).

Figure 9.1 offers a set of goals for an inservice or continuing education seminar designed to build communication and collaboration between university supervisors and cooperating teachers.

## SUPERVISING PRESERVICE TEACHERS: FACILITATING PRACTICAL KNOWLEDGE AND REFLECTION

One of the major challenges facing university supervisors and cooperating teachers today is how to effectively integrate reflective opportunities into preservice programs (Brookfield, 1995; Colton & Sparks-Langer, 1992; McIntyre & O'Hair, 1996). The ability to systematically reflect on one's teaching—that is, to take a self-analytical approach—is an ability that is learned through experience and time. Few individuals are capable of critical reflection at the beginning of their student teaching field experience or internship. University supervisors and cooperating teachers must understand that providing preservice teachers with direct feedback about their lessons is helpful and supportive initially, but that continuing to supply all the answers is counterproductive. Instead, they should overtly and explicitly model reflective decision making. If preservice teachers remain in a passive role in their triad, they have little chance of evolving into reflective practitioners. As Nolan (1997) explains, "The supervisor's role is not to make judgments and communicate those to the teacher but rather to collect observational and inferential types of data that can be used to enable the teacher to make better judgments about his or her own teaching performance and its impact on learners" (pp. 104–105). The ultimate goal is to empower preservice teachers so that they assume greater personal responsibility for solving classroom dilemmas and for making informed decisions about their practice without direct supervisory intervention.

What, then, are effective tools that supervisors can use to encourage preservice teachers to deliberate on their teaching? Five of the most effective means are the preobservation or planning conference, the postobservation conference, the structured videotape analysis of teaching, reflective electronic portfolios, and online discussion groups to build professional learning communities.

## Engaging in the Preobservation Conference

In Chapter 2, we addressed the importance of the preobservation conference as part of the supervision cycle. Here, we refer to it again as a particularly useful strategy for encouraging reflection and uncovering a preservice teacher's oftentimes implicit planning and decision-making processes. With an emphasis on fluency and rehearsal, the preobservation conference becomes a wonderful opportunity for university faculty and cooperating teachers not only to tap into the preservice teacher's planning decisions but also to offer guidance through the use of probing questions, relevant suggestions, and modeling.

Fluency occurs as the supervisor and the preservice teacher reach a shared understanding about the detailed planning in which the preservice teacher engaged before implementing the lesson to be observed. Among the many aspects for discussion are the learning objectives, their connection to the curriculum or content standards, the instructional strategies and activities that would be most appropriate for meeting the learning objectives and standards, the teaching materials necessary for the lesson, and the ways of formatively assessing students' progress. Rehearsal takes place when the preservice teacher role plays parts of the upcoming lesson that seem particularly unclear or problematic. Figure 9.2 presents sample questions that a supervisor or cooperating teacher might use when conducting a preobservation or planning conference.

Preobservation conferences with preservice teachers can also increase the usefulness of written lesson plans. Most universities and school districts require preservice teachers to turn in their tentative plans to their cooperating teachers at least a day in advance for suggestions and approval. In many cases, the cooperating teacher simply reads and initials the

**FIGURE 9.2**  Structured Questions for a Preservice Teacher's Preobservation Conference

1.  What, specifically, do you want your students to learn and be able to do?
2.  Where do those learning goals fit into the curriculum and content standards?
3.  If students ask you why they need to learn this, what would your answer be?
4.  How will you introduce the lesson? How will you tap into your students' prior knowledge or explore misconceptions about the topic?
5.  Why do you think that the instructional strategies and learning activities that you have planned will be effective in teaching this material?
6.  How can you adapt the lesson to meet the diverse needs and abilities of your students?
7.  How did you structure the learning to make it meaningful or relevant to the students' personal experiences or to connect it to other learning?
8.  Where did you find the resources for this lesson? In what ways did you go beyond the teacher's guide or textbook?
9.  How will you formatively assess if the students learned what you intended?
10. How can I help you in the planning process? Let us walk through a portion of the lesson together.

plan without discussing it with the preservice teacher. A potential problem with that approach is that, on the basis of past experience, the cooperating teacher may automatically fill in any gaps.

For example, Jim, a cooperating teacher, is reading Nicole's plan for third-grade math. Nicole states that she will have the students break into groups for an activity without any indication of how she will do so. As Jim reads, he unconsciously fills in the gap by thinking how *he* would place students into small groups. He brings his experience to his interpretation of Nicole's plan.

Jim later watches the lesson that he approved and is surprised by what he sees. When Nicole says, "Now we need to break into groups," Patty, one of her students, asks, "Miss S, can we please pick our own groups? We never get to do that!" Nicole responds, "Well, if you promise to behave and stay on task, I don't see why not." The students join in a chorus of promises to be good. Ten minutes later, Nicole is still searching for appropriate groups for Meghan, Jeff, and Danny, who have not been included by any of the others and who adamantly refuse to work together.

We believe that a cooperating teacher who understands the nature of preservice teacher supervision can use the written plan as a valuable preconferencing tool. Discussion of the plan can promote fluency and rehearsal, turning a requirement into a useful learning experience. By asking probing questions, the cooperating teacher can tap into the preservice teacher's thought processes. In the preceding example, if Jim had asked Nicole how she intended to place students into groups, the lesson could have been far more productive.

Recognizing that a well-designed preconference can be time consuming, we are not suggesting that cooperating teachers conduct preobservation conferences before every lesson. However, early in the semester, such conferences are useful tools for examining philosophies, for sharing strategies related to best practice, and for providing ongoing feedback. Preservice teachers are often unsure of their abilities. Consequently, they are grateful for the opportunity to rehearse potentially troublesome aspects of their lessons. Moreover, because the lesson has not yet been implemented, they have no reason to be defensive about their decisions—as they might be during the postobservation conference, when they sometimes feel obligated to rationalize why a lesson did not go well.

One additional consideration arises concerning preobservation conferences with preservice teachers. The supervisor and the cooperating teacher should feel less bound to establish an agreed-upon "contract" in the preobservation conference than supervisors or peer coaches working with veteran teachers do. Student teachers are often unable, especially at the beginning of the semester, to identify foci for data collection. In that circumstance, it is appropriate for the cooperating teacher and university supervisor to identify foci for the student teacher. Gradually, they can turn that responsibility over to the student teacher as that student teacher becomes more knowledgeable and confident.

We typically begin our observations of preservice teachers using wide-angle techniques (as discussed in Chapter 2). We use those initial observations to identify specific areas to pursue in greater depth. In addition, even when the student teacher has been allowed to choose the focus for a particular observation, we make it clear that the supervisor and the cooperating teacher always have the right to collect other data that they feel will be helpful to the student teacher.

## Engaging in the Postobservation Conference

The general importance of the postobservation conference as part of the supervision cycle was discussed in Chapter 2. During the postobservation conference, the supervisor or the cooperating teacher and the preservice teacher share and discuss interpretations of the data, compare lesson aims with actual results, assess the overall effectiveness of the lesson in terms of student learning, and come to consensus on future teaching goals.

Several considerations that are not germane to supervising veteran teachers become important in postobservation conferences with preservice teachers. Those considerations relate to the fact that few preservice teachers are capable of participating in a nondirective or collaborative conference at the beginning of their field experience (see Chapter 2). At that point in their practice, they have had little opportunity to discuss their own teaching behaviors or to interpret data collected during instruction. As mentioned earlier, most are overwhelmed by survival concerns: They seem to require assurance that their performance is acceptable before they can engage in deep or productive reflection about their actions. Thus, in the beginning, the university supervisor and the cooperating teacher may need to take an essentially directive approach in postconferencing.

Still, we cannot underestimate the importance of setting the stage for preservice teachers to gradually assume a more active and collaborative role in reflecting upon and analyzing the effectiveness of their lessons. We suggest that supervisors make clear their expectation that preservice teachers will become increasingly capable of self-direction. "Self-direction" includes making sense of observational data and subsequently using the data to make good decisions about teaching performance.

How, then, do university supervisors and cooperating teachers guide preservice teachers through the developmental process of assuming responsibility for making self-reflective judgments? A good starting point is to provide help in the data collected during observations. Many preservice teachers are unfamiliar or inexperienced with systematic data collection instruments. The supervisor should first explain the various types of data collection instruments and the meaning of the symbols used. Upon receiving such explanations, some preservice teachers are capable of interpreting the data; others are not. For the latter, the supervisor needs to develop a well-designed sequence of activities that will lead the student teacher to become more independent in interpreting data.

As a starting point, supervisors can model "think-aloud" interpretations of the data. For example, as the preservice teacher listens, the supervisor explains, "I noticed that students in the back of the room were off task three times as often as those in the front. I wonder why that would be. Could I be too far removed from them? Are they bored?" The next step would be to provide the preservice teacher with additional data, and to request a think-aloud interpretation. The supervisor listens and asks guiding questions about patterns in the data. This "scaffolding process" provides preservice teachers with the knowledge and skills to become more self-analytical.

Once preservice teachers understand how to interpret the data, many will be able to use the data to decide whether they accomplished their lesson objectives or whether they might change their teaching behaviors. Others may struggle with this aspect of the postobservation conference as well. The supervisor must match the level of support to the preservice teacher's level of development.

The mildest form of support is collaborative: asking questions that prompt the preservice teacher to think about the data productively. For example, the supervisor might ask, "As you notice your position in the room relative to the location of increased off-task behavior, what does that tell you?"

If the collaborative strategy does not provide enough direction, the supervisor can once again model a think-aloud, this time offering options from which the preservice teacher may choose: "I notice that the amount of off-task behavior is far greater in the back of the room. I also see that you never stray more than a few steps away from the front whiteboard during the entire lesson. During the next lesson you must either make a conscious effort to monitor and maintain eye contact with all of your students, particularly those in the back, or spend more time walking around the perimeters of the classroom. Which of those options seems most comfortable for you?"

If the preservice teacher affirms understanding, but has difficulty choosing an option to follow or does not follow through with suggestions, then the supervisor must more strongly direct the preservice teacher's behavior during the next supervision cycle. The supervisor can now give a clearly articulated explanation of why the suggested behavior is appropriate: "I noticed that the students in the back of the room continue to be nonengaged in the lesson. According to the new data, you spent the vast majority of the time in the front of the room at the center of the whiteboard. It seems to me that the strategy of monitoring the back row from the front of the room is not working. Tomorrow I want you to move about the room during the entire class period. Spend at least as much time in the back of the room as at the front. I believe that your physical proximity will be an effective nonverbal management technique." The supervisor then monitors to ensure that the student teacher follows through with the directive.

Figure 9.3 spells out a sequence of four levels of supervisory support commensurate with the student teacher's level of independence in data interpretation and informed decision making. Note that two separate but related factors are involved: the student teacher's ability to interpret data independently, and the student teacher's ability to decide how to proceed instructionally once the data have been interpreted.

**FIGURE 9.3**  Levels of Supervisor Support

---

*Level 4*
- Student teacher can interpret data and decide how to proceed independently.
- Supervisor asks questions about data and about future instruction.

*Level 3*
- Student teacher cannot interpret data, but can decide how to proceed after data are interpreted.
- Supervisor models data interpretation process and then asks questions about future instruction.

Or

- Student teacher can interpret data, but cannot decide how to proceed after data are interpreted.
- Supervisor asks questions to elicit data interpretation, then models possible options about how to proceed based upon data interpretation. Supervisor asks student teacher to choose from the options provided.

*Level 2*
- Student teacher cannot interpret data and cannot generate ideas about how to proceed.
- Supervisor models data interpretation process. Supervisor subsequently models how to identify options about how to proceed. Supervisor asks student teacher to choose from the options provided for future instruction.

*Level 1*
- Student teacher cannot interpret data, cannot identify options for how to proceed, and has difficulty choosing options and following through.
- Supervisor models data interpretation process. Supervisor also models how to identify options about how to proceed. Supervisor directs student teacher to implement one of the options identified and monitors to make sure that the implementation occurs.

---

To summarize, we suggest that, to help preservice teachers become better decision makers, university supervisors and cooperating teachers conduct postobservation conferences using a four-level model. First, collaboratively ask supportive questions and hypothesize strategies for future lessons, encouraging the preservice teacher to reflect with supervisor guidance. If that is not sufficient, proceed down the levels by modeling the thinking process and providing options from which the preservice teacher might choose to change behavior. If that level of support does not work, then direct the preservice teacher, but continue to model teacher thinking about why a choice is the most appropriate course of action from the standpoint of learning theory and best practice. The ultimate goal over the course of the field experience or internship is for the supervisor to gradually withdraw support as the preservice teacher proceeds up the hierarchy and becomes capable of making decisions independently.

The question that we as university supervisors keep firmly in our minds is, "Are our preservice teachers better able today to reflect on data and to make good teaching decisions than they were during the last supervision cycle?" If we can answer affirmatively, then the postobservation process has been successful. If we cannot answer affirmatively—that is, if we observe no growth over time—then we feel professionally obligated to let those individuals know that they are not ready to assume the challenges and obligations of a classroom. We address the choice to withhold recommendation for teacher certification later in this chapter in the section on evaluation.

## Using a Videotape Analysis

In addition to direct observation, another effective means of encouraging reflection and refining practice is to have preservice teachers create and view teaching videotapes and then address open-ended questions about the lessons (Hoover, 1994a). The analyses can take place individually through the use of focused writing prompts or in small groups through discussion sessions. Depending on the situation, the small group may include the preservice and cooperating teachers or the supervisory triad.

Videotaped analyses give teachers a means to document their teaching visually, opening a window into their implicit thought processes, including teaching decisions that may have been made on the spot and of which they were unaware. Videotapes offer an in-depth, uninterrupted, concentrated picture of instruction, interaction with students, and students' interactions with one another. The analyses, whether conducted individually or collaboratively, present an opportunity for teachers to articulate rationale, to examine whether actual teaching behaviors match stated aims, and most important, to explore how actions affect students. James Stigler, who directed the video component of the Third International Mathematics and Science Study (TIMSS), notes (as reported in Willis, 2002):

> Teaching is a performance ... it occurs in real time, in a real classroom, with real students. If you want to improve teaching, you need to find ways of studying the process. Video is the best way of representing that process so you can study it. You could observe live classrooms—that's an important experience, and we should keep doing it—but video allows you to come back, observe the lesson with a group, talk about it, analyze it, and do the kind of work that can actually improve your teaching. (p. 8)

In conducting a videotape analysis, we instruct preservice teachers to first identify a focus area—a question, concern, or goal they have about some specific aspect of the teaching–learning process. We ask them to provide their rationale for choosing that particular focus, explaining why it is meaningful to them.

After the preservice teachers explore their own beliefs and knowledge about pedagogy as related to the particular focus, they decide on the kinds of data that would be most helpful. (See Chapter 2 for systematic data collection techniques.) Once they decide on a data collection strategy, they record the data while viewing the videotape. (Supervisors and cooperating teachers should previously have modeled various ways to collect and interpret data during pre- and postconferences before the videotape assignment.)

Once the data have been collected either individually through writing or in collaborative discussions with the cooperating teacher or university supervisor (see Figure 9.3 for levels of supervisor support), student teachers then search for patterns in the data, attach meaning to the patterns, and hypothesize future teaching options based upon the findings. The videotape analysis concludes with a discussion that summarizes what they have learned and that sets future goals based on their discoveries.

Amanda's case illustrates a preservice teacher's use of a videotape analysis to promote reflection. Amanda is a high school English teacher who espouses creating a learning environment that welcomes students' active participation in discussions about the literature they are reading. Thus, she focuses on her ability to facilitate classroom discussion that provokes higher level thinking.

Amanda videotapes a lesson in which she can focus on students' contributions to a classroom discussion about a series of short stories they recently read. She decides it would be helpful to collect data that examine the types of questions that she asks (convergent or divergent), but she is also interested in capturing data on how she responds to their initial answers. She is interested in the effect that both her question posing and her responses to student answers have on the quality and depth of student involvement and thinking.

After viewing the tape once for a general impression of the lesson, she views it a second time. This time, she uses the selective verbatim technique to record a list of questions that she asks. Her next step is to label as convergent or divergent the questions that she recorded. In analyzing the data, Amanda feels satisfied that she asks mostly open-ended questions (60% were divergent) that spark substantive answers from her students.

Amanda then views the videotape a third time. She once again employs the selective verbatim technique, but this time she records her responses to student answers. She is less pleased with her ability to sustain a discussion. In other words, she uncovers a pattern in which she asks a question, a student responds, and she then immediately offers feedback and opinion, perhaps curtailing further elaboration by the students themselves. Based on that revelation, Amanda sets a goal to temporarily withhold teacher judgment and to encourage students to respond to one another's thinking without first looking to her for affirmation of the "right answer."

To maximize the usefulness of videotaped lessons, we must also acknowledge their limitations. First, if the camera remains stationary on a tripod in the back of the classroom, it might fail to capture significant interaction, especially among the students. Waiting until the cooperating teacher, supervisor, or another student teacher can videotape the lesson, moving the camera as appropriate, is preferable.

Second, preservice teachers sometimes become preoccupied by their teaching persona as revealed on the videotape. (Rarely do teachers have the opportunity to see themselves as their students do.) Moreover, they can be overwhelmed by the complexity and number of classroom interactions that occur during a lesson. We therefore recommend that preservice teachers view their tapes once through to come to terms with the teaching context and with themselves in action before they collect data (as in Amanda's case). Hopefully, external factors will be less distracting the second time through, and the preservice teacher will be able to concentrate on collecting data about the unfolding lesson and the students' learning.

**FIGURE 9.4** Prompts for Reflecting Upon on a Videotaped Lesson

1. Now that you have collected data, what patterns do you notice as you analyze them?
2. What meaning might we attach to those patterns in terms of what you know about educational theory and in terms of your goals for student learning?
3. Explore how you ideally view yourself in connection with this focus area and what the data revealed to you about your concrete actions and teaching behaviors.
4. Did you make any unexpected discoveries about yourself and your teaching while viewing the video? Explain.
5. What discoveries did you make about your students? Their learning?
6. What specific goals will you set based on the data we collected and analyzed? Explain why those goals are logical outcomes of viewing the tape.

Viewing a videotape, especially in collaboration with others, can be time consuming, but it can yield valuable insights into one's practice. Figure 9.4 offers some possible prompts for writing an individual analysis or facilitating a discussion during collaborative analysis of a tape.

## Encouraging Continuous Reflection Through Electronic Growth Portfolios and Online Professional Learning Communities

Preconferences, postconferences, and videotaped analyses are all methods of focusing directly on in-class lessons. Reflection, however, is a continuous process that often occurs outside the classroom as well. Writing based upon carerful analysis of teacher or student artifacts can be a powerful tool to encourage systematic deliberation long after a lesson has been planned and implemented.

Emig (1977) explained that writing is a means of discovery or a learning strategy because of its active nature and because of the permanence of the written word. Through writing, individuals capture their often-disordered thought processes and then rethink and revise them over time. Given the complex and fast-paced nature of the many interactions that preservice teachers have with subject matter, colleagues, and students during the school day, preservice teachers need an opportunity to stop, review, record, and reevaluate their ideas. Reflective writing provides the opportunity.

Fulwiler (1986) describes writing as a means to stop "the more chaotic and undisciplined breadth of my often random thought" and to "frame and focus on fewer possibilities, gaining depth, continuity, and understanding" (p. 6). Holly (1989) concurs, advocating writing as a way for preservice teachers to examine particular teaching situations after the fact, to record questions, to confirm or disaffirm hypotheses, and eventually to clarify ideas to help reach decisions about best practice. She explains, "There is no 'Book of Teaching'; the teacher writes it along the way, drawing on learning from others, from theories and practices presented during teacher preparation; and beyond these, from the everyday realities of the classroom" (p. 9). Reflection about artifacts related to effective teaching standards can become a preservice teacher's personal guide to learning from teaching.

Although some preservice teachers still use traditional paper portfolios, we advocate Web-based electronic portfolios such as LiveText or TaskStream as alternatives that have become an effective means for preservice teachers to illustrate their inquiry into teaching and their professional growth. In creating their electronic portfolios, preservice teachers can be encouraged to use "exemplars," or artifacts specifically selected to demonstrate their knowledge, skills, and disposition concerning a particular standard of effective teaching. In addition to the exemplars, however, preservice teachers can also be asked to include "contrasting evidence," or artifacts from earlier in the field experience. Contrasting the two artifacts through a written reflection can effectively document growth toward meeting that particular standard. For example, in demonstrating planning that includes both knowledge of the subject matter and students' developmental levels, a preservice teacher could include as an exemplar a fifth-grade math lesson on metric measurement. In this particular lesson, the students worked in pairs to demonstrate their understanding by using balance scales and completing a laboratory report that required them to make and test predictions. The contrasting evidence could be an earlier science lesson from the beginning of the semester, one where so much content was included in the lesson that lecturing and passive learning predominated and students had little opportunity to engage in formative assessment.

In conjunction with the use of electronic portfiolios, we also recommend building community through the use of Web-based discussion groups, such as those made possible through Blackboard or Web-CT. Darling-Hammond, Hammerness, Grossman, Rust, and Shulman (2005) advocate learning in professional communities where teachers share their ever-evolving understanding about the nature of good teaching. These discussion boards or online chat sessions provide the opportunity for preservice teachers themselves or all participants in the supervisory triad to virtually "join voices" in an online dialog. They can readily share ideas and progress, address one another's questions and concerns, collaboratively problem solve, and celebrate accomplishments and successes.

Kathleen, one of our student teachers, commented on her participation in an online discussion group: "I have learned so much from my peers. Sometimes when I am reading online, I picture all of us back on campus sitting in a circle discussing issues."

Other participants concurred. Lorena added, "If I ever have a question or concern, right away the others offered opinions to get the thoughts running through my head and get me on my way to solving the problem."

Raeann noted, "I am able to adapt so many of the great ideas that people write about. I love to tap into everyone else's creativity. What a rich pool we have to work from! This is especially helpful because we don't have the years of experience behind us."

In short, online communities have the potential to encourage preservice teachers, cooperating teachers, and university faculty to form a community of learners who offer one another camaraderie, support, a wealth of teaching ideas, and an opportunity for reflection without the barriers posed by time and distance (Hoover, 1994b).

In summary, cooperating teachers and university supervisors can nurture reflective practice more effectively when they are privy to the implicit thought processes that form the basis for preservice teachers' decision making. Preconferences, postconferences, videotape analyses, reflective electronic portfolios, and online communities are research-based methods that provide supervisors with a window on the reflective processes of preservice teachers. All of those tools for supervision are designed to guide the teacher beyond personal concerns to a focus on instruction and student learning.

# EVALUATION OF PRESERVICE TEACHER PERFORMANCE

In addition to encouraging student teachers to become highly skilled reflective practitioners, cooperating teachers and university supervisors share the responsibility for summatively evaluating performance and assigning what the preservice teacher perceives as a high-stakes grade. Thus, all university supervisors and cooperating teachers must understand the evaluative components of the student teaching experience.

## Issues and Considerations

In Chapter 1, we explained that teacher supervision and evaluation are two separate but complementary functions. In subsequent chapters, we described a system that separates the supervision of veteran teachers from summative evaluation by timing and by type of procedure. Unfortunately, separating evaluation from supervision is much more difficult in the case of preservice teachers.

Because the student teaching experience lasts only one semester, timing cannot be used to differentiate the two functions. Evaluation and supervision must occur simultaneously. Different procedures for supervision and evaluation can be used to some extent (e.g., midterm and final evaluation conferences that are separate from day-to-day supervision), but the student teacher is likely to have a watchful eye on the evaluative aspects of the relationship throughout the entire process.

Thus, university supervisors and cooperating teachers face the daunting task of encouraging preservice teachers to take risks, to experiment, and to reflect as part of an ongoing process while they simultaneously make summative decisions about whether those preservice teachers are attaining professional standards of performance. On one hand, they must nurture trust and work collaboratively to promote preservice teachers' professional growth; on the other hand, they must make summative and perhaps life-altering judgments about the competence of those preservice teachers.

The importance of evaluation cannot be overestimated. "Evaluation of student teachers is an integral part of the teacher education program. Gatekeeping or control of entry to the profession is one of the major functions" (Guyton & McIntyre, 1990, p. 225). The university supervisor and the cooperating teacher don the hats of gatekeepers to the profession, protecting the interests of the countless number of children on whom the teacher candidate could have an impact. Those educators are required to make a professional judgment about whether the preservice teacher has acquired the knowledge, dispositions, and skills needed to function independently in carrying out assigned duties in the classroom.

The evaluation task is further complicated by the fact that the university supervisor and the cooperating teacher must also assign a grade for the student teaching performance. Some teacher education programs assign student teaching marks on a pass/fail basis, but most institutions still assign letter grades (Guyton & McIntyre, 1990). Whereas the evaluation of veteran teachers requires simply a judgment of satisfactory or unsatisfactory, evaluators of most student teachers must make fine distinctions between levels of satisfactory performance to arrive at appropriate grades. "Final evaluations, in particular, purport to distinguish among competent and incompetent, effective and less effective, talented and less talented, outstanding, average, and below-average students regarding their potential as teachers" (Guyton & McIntyre, 1990, p. 225). Moreover, many student teachers have the clear impression, whether correct or incorrect, that failure to achieve an "A" in student teaching means that the candidate will never get a teaching position. Acquiring an "A" becomes the central quest for many student teachers, contributing to the perception of the entire process as a high-stakes evaluation experience.

Fortunately, some factors also mitigate the difficulties involved in the evaluation of preservice teachers. First, the responsibility for evaluation is shared by the university supervisor and the cooperating teacher. If a PDS relationship exists, or if the university conducts a cooperating teacher training program, the supervisor and the cooperating teacher are likely to be on the same page concerning the evaluation process. Having a partner with whom to work in making evaluation decisions can lighten the load considerably. The shared nature of the evaluation process also makes it imperative that the standards of performance and the evaluation procedures be clear to all members of the triad. When shared understandings exist, the load is lightened.

Second, because the cooperating teacher has the opportunity to observe the student teacher's work on a daily basis, the triad members have a great deal more information concerning the student teacher's ongoing performance than is typically available in the evaluation of veteran teachers. The cooperating teacher (if not the supervisor) also brings content expertise and a deep understanding of the curriculum, the school context, and the students to the process. This knowledge is a powerful asset in making appropriate judgments concerning the efficacy of the student teacher's performance. Evaluation procedures that place a high value on the cooperating teacher's judgments in assessing the student teacher's performance take advantage of that powerful knowledge source.

Third, the cooperating teacher and the university supervisor have a teacher–student rather than an evaluator–evaluatee relationship with student teachers. Student teachers typically see the other two members of the triad as being responsible for helping them to grow. Student teachers also respect the professional competence of those established educators and trust them to have their best interests at heart. This trusting, respectful relationship can make evaluation a more comfortable process. The triad can then view the standards of performance as goals toward which the student teacher is aiming with the ongoing support and assistance of the cooperating teacher and the university supervisor.

A final consideration in evaluating preservice teachers is that it can provide an opportunity to teach the student teacher about professional self-evaluation. The student teaching experience represents the first time that the student teacher's professional performance is evaluated in a rigorous manner. Although the supervisor and the cooperating teacher will make the final assessment of performance, the student teacher should be given the opportunity to collect evaluation data and to engage in self-evaluation with guidance and support. In subsequent evaluations of professional competence, the teacher is unlikely to ever again experience this same level of support and guidance.

With these basic considerations in mind, we now focus on evaluation standards and evaluation procedures.

## Standards of Performance

Teacher education programs are required by state and national accrediting agencies to have an explicit set of standards by which preservice teacher performance is assessed. The assessment process is ongoing throughout the entire teacher education program and culminates with the evaluation of the preservice teacher's performance in student teaching.

The performance standards for student teaching typically serve as the criteria for graduation with a recommendation for a teaching certificate. Thus, the standards are developed by teacher education program faculty in consultation with partners from basic education. Higher education faculty typically have a better handle on the program's philosophical underpinnings and can ensure that evaluation criteria match the program's philosophy. Cooperating teachers can ensure that the criteria make sense in the everyday life of the classroom and also that the meanings of the criteria are clear to all who will be engaged in evaluating student teachers.

The standards should acknowledge the complexity of teaching and the role of teacher decision making. At the same time, they should offer a universal road map of clearly identified competencies. Competencies provide for accountability; as performance indicators, they acknowledge what preservice teachers should know and be able to demonstrate in facilitating their students' learning.

**FIGURE 9.5**   INTASC Standards

| | |
|---|---|
| *Principle 1* | The teacher understands the central concepts, tools of inquiry, and structures of the discipline(s) he or she teaches and can create concrete learning experiences that make these aspects of subject matter meaningful to students. |
| *Principle 2* | The teacher understands how children learn and develop and can provide learning opportunities that support their intellectual, social, and personal development. |
| *Principle 3* | The teacher understands how students differ in their approaches to learning and creates instructional opportunities that are adapted to diverse learners. |
| *Principle 4* | The teacher understands and uses a variety of instructional strategies to encourage students' development of critical thinking, problem solving, and performance skills. |
| *Principle 5* | The teacher uses an understanding of individual and group motivation and behavior to create a learning environment that encourages positive social interaction, active engagement in learning, and self-motivation. |
| *Principle 6* | The teacher uses knowledge of effective verbal, nonverbal, and media communication techniques to foster active inquiry, collaboration, and supportive interaction in the classroom. |
| *Principle 7* | The teacher plans instruction based on knowledge of subject matter, students, the community, and curriculum goals. |
| *Principle 8* | The teacher understands and uses formal and informal assessment strategies to evaluate and ensure the continuous intellectual, social, and physical development of the learner. |
| *Principle 9* | The teacher is a reflective practitioner who continuously evaluates the effects of his/her choices and actions on others (students, parents, and other professionals in the learning community) and who actively seeks out opportunities to grow professionally. |
| *Principle 10* | The teacher fosters relationships with school colleagues, parents, and agencies in the larger community to support students' learning and well-being. |

As noted, each institution must develop its own set of assessment standards. The standards will be compatible with the philosophical framework and knowledge base that underlie the teacher education program. In developing their standards, institutions can use the sample evaluation standards that we included in Chapter 8; they can also look to the broad set of standards developed specifically to guide the assessment of preservice teachers. A consortium of 37 states, INTASC (Interstate New Teacher Assessment and Support Consortium, 1992), developed a list of 10 entry-level performance standards for licensing new teachers. These broad standards, listed in Figure 9.5, provide a good starting point for the development of institution-specific performance standards.

A broad set of principles is only a beginning because evaluation standards for student teaching must be capable not only of distinguishing between incompetent and competent performance, but also of distinguishing among various levels of competent performance so that grades can be assigned. Therefore, the indicators used to summatively assess the performance of student teachers should be clear, precise, and explicit so that the cooperating teacher and the supervisor are using the same assessment lenses. Specific indicators of performance are preferable to broad or global measures. When rating instruments are compared, those that use analytic methods with specific criteria seem to be more reliable than profile or global scales (Guyton & McIntyre, 1990). Exercise 9.2 provides practice in developing performance indicators based on the INTASC standards.

**EXERCISE 9.2   Developing Performance Indicators**

**Part 1**   Break into pairs or triads. Each group is assigned one of the 10 INTASC principles. In your pair or triad, develop for your assigned principle a set of five specific indicators that you could use to judge a student teacher's performance.

**Part 2**   Discuss with your partner or partners how those indicators would have to be adjusted, if necessary, to be useful at the elementary, middle school, and high school levels. Could any of the indicators be useful at all levels without adjustment?

**Part 3**   Engage in a whole-class discussion in which you share the indicators that the groups developed for each principle and the modifications that were made for the various grade levels.

In addition to including specific indicators of performance, standards for evaluation of student teachers must include some explanation of how performance on those indicators should be translated into a final grade. This translation is a complex process that requires sophisticated, professional judgment and teamwork on the part of the cooperating teacher and the university supervisor. Various institutions use various strategies. Some include an overall rating of effectiveness on their summative evaluation form. This rating (e.g., outstanding, good, average, below average, unsatisfactory) can be roughly equated with a final grade. Other institutions assign point values to specific indicators and then obtain a final grade by totaling the points. Still others describe in words the performance that earns each letter grade. Finally, some institutions use a combination of these methods.

Figure 9.6 provides examples of specific standards for assessing performance based on INTASC Principle 5. The example is excerpted from a standards document that covers all 10 INTASC principles and that is used to assess the performance of student interns in the PDS context in which one of the authors works. Notice that the INTASC principle has been divided into three statements describing desired teaching performance and that each is followed by a list of specific behaviors that provide evidence of the desired performance.

In using the evaluation criteria, the cooperating teacher and the university supervisor rate the student teacher's performance in terms of how consistently the desired teaching performance is demonstrated (i.e., how consistently the performance corresponds to the description associated with each of the three main statements). The focus is on the broad statements of desired performance and not on the specific behaviors that provide evidence of the performance. Thus, each performance descriptor is followed by the phrase "as evidenced by all or many of the following." Not every specific behavior need be exhibited for the student teacher to receive a rating of "consistently."

Figure 9.7 shows a description of the process used in that same PDS context by supervisors and cooperating teachers for assigning a final grade. Admittedly, these standards for final grades are very demanding. They are probably somewhat more demanding than the standards used in most teacher education programs. We believe that high standards of performance should be required for entry into the teaching profession and that grades from student teaching, if they are used, really should distinguish among various levels of performance. Only student teachers whose performances are truly outstanding deserve an "A."

Several aspects of the grading process illustrated in Figures 9.6 and 9.7 are noteworthy. Professional judgment is clearly an important part of the process. Three factors go into the description of the final grade: a description in words of how the intern would be expected to perform as a beginning teacher; ratings on the individual standards of performance; and an overall assessment rating—outstanding, effective, acceptable, or unsatisfactory (i.e., failing). Finally, the grade is based on the performance that the intern exhibits in the later stages of the experience, not on improvement or effort. Student teachers who

**FIGURE 9.6** Sample Student Intern Evaluation Standards

---

**Creating a Nurturing and Productive Learning Environment (Based on INTASC Principle 5)**

---

A. *The intern strategically plans and implements a* positive environment *conducive to learning, as evidenced by all or many of the following:*
 1. Supporting an atmosphere that is caring, respectful, and nurturing
 2. Acknowledging students' rights and responsibilities as members of a democratic classroom
 3. Creating an environment that promotes student inquiry and intellectual risk taking
 4. Developing a community of learners who participate in decision making and work collaboratively
 5. Acknowledging, valuing, and exhibiting students' work and achievements
 6. Other

*Check one only*

| Consistently | More often than not | Sporadically | Rarely | Never | Not observed |
|---|---|---|---|---|---|
|  |  |  |  |  |  |

B. *The intern plans and implements* classroom procedures *that facilitate learning in an orderly environment, as evidenced by all or many of the following:*
 1. Organizing the classroom physical arrangement to support instructional activities
 2. Establishing routines and procedures for recurring events and for the handling of materials, equipment, and supplies
 3. Establishing and enforcing safety procedures
 4. Communicating clear and appropriate expectations for all learners
 5. Using instructional time effectively
 6. Using transitional time productively and efficiently
 7. Other

*Check one only:*

| Consistently | More often than not | Sporadically | Rarely | Never | Not observed |
|---|---|---|---|---|---|
|  |  |  |  |  |  |

C. *The intern manages* student behavior, *as evidenced by all or many of the following:*
 1. Knowing and following the school's disciplinary procedures and expectations
 2. Identifying patterns of conduct that are classified as major or minor misconduct within the unique social setting of the school
 3. Communicating clear standards of conduct to students, parents, and other relevant persons
 4. Involving students, when appropriate, in the development of rules and consequences
 5. Upholding rules and expectations
 6. Implementing lessons that minimize inappropriate behavior by engaging students in productive learning activities
 7. Helping students learn to control their behavior by using a variety of short-term and long-term interventions that maintain student dignity and self-esteem
 8. Working with others to develop and implement strategies to improve student behavior as appropriate
 9. Other

*Check one only*

| Consistently | More often than not | Sporadically | Rarely | Never | Not observed |
|---|---|---|---|---|---|
|  |  |  |  |  |  |

FIGURE 9.7 Description of Criteria for Final Grade for Student Interns

Student teaching is a performance-based, process-oriented course that focuses on the intern's teaching capability demonstrated by performance in multiple domains of planning, teaching, reflecting on teaching, and assuming a professional identity. Because the course is process and performance oriented as opposed to product-based, assessment of the intern's performance is complex. Assessment cannot be reduced to a finite, precise numerical measurement as is often possible with test or paper-based courses. Capturing both the science and the art of teaching requires self-reflection on the part of the intern and sophisticated professional judgment on the part of the cooperating teacher and the university supervisor.

Stated simply, the intern's grade is determined by the intern's teaching capability as demonstrated by performance in the later stages of the internship experience. Thus, the grade is neither effort-based nor improvement-based. It is based on teaching capabilities actually demonstrated by the intern.

A grade of "A" indicates outstanding achievement by the intern. An "A" grade will be assigned when it can be stated confidently that the intern is capable of beginning the first year of teaching demonstrating true excellence as a novice teacher with minimal support. Typically, an intern who earns a grade of "A" would be rated as outstanding in the overall assessment category and as consistently demonstrating desired capabilities across all or almost all domains.

A grade of "B" indicates extensive achievement by the intern. A "B" grade will be assigned when it can be stated confidently that the intern is capable of beginning the first year of teaching as a good novice teacher, provided some support is given. Typically, an intern who earns a grade of "B" would be rated as effective in the overall assessment category and as demonstrating the desired capabilities more often than not across all or almost all domains.

A grade of "C" indicates acceptable achievement by the intern. A "C" grade will be assigned when it can be stated confidently that the intern is capable of beginning the first year of teaching as an adequate novice teacher, provided considerable support is given. Typically, an intern who earns a grade of "C" would be rated as satisfactory in the overall assessment category and as demonstrating the desired capabilities sporadically across all or almost all domains.

Achievement below the "C" level, because of its potential negative impact on children in the internship setting, will result in a failing grade.

try hard but who do not perform well should not be certified as teachers. Student teachers who improve markedly but who still perform at less than effective levels should be graded according to the achieved level of performance, not according to the degree of improvement. The final level of performance is the best indicator of teaching ability.

The availability of specific standards that delineate the criteria to be used in assessing performance and the equating of assessment with a final grade are tremendous assets in carrying out the evaluation of preservice teachers. Once the evaluation criteria are in place, a set of procedures can be implemented to evaluate the student teacher's performance.

## Evaluation Procedures

Because preservice teachers differ markedly from veteran teachers in terms of their readiness to take on the tasks of self-evaluation, the procedures used to evaluate their performance should be substantially different from those used to evaluate veteran teachers.

***Roles*** The preservice teacher's inexperience in assessing personal teaching performance means that the university supervisor and the cooperating teacher must direct the evaluation process (Peterson, 2000). If the supervisor and the cooperating teacher work closely together, they can potentially develop a comprehensive portrait of the preservice teacher's abilities to teach and to reflect on the teaching and learning processes.

As noted earlier, the cooperating teacher has the opportunity to see most of the preservice teacher's teaching and also has intimate knowledge of the curriculum, the school context, and the students. The university supervisor sees much less of the actual teaching, but has the opportunity to see all of the written assignments that the preservice teacher completes (e.g., videotape analyses, reflective journals, and unit plans). The supervisor, therefore, has an excellent opportunity to see how the preservice teacher *thinks* about teaching. In addition, the supervisor can help the cooperating teacher to understand how this particular preservice teacher's performance compares to typical preservice teacher performance.

Together, the supervisor and the cooperating teacher are responsible for making a summative judgment about the preservice teacher's performance. This summative judgment is communicated both in the final grade earned by the preservice teacher and in letters of recommendation that are written for prospective employers.

Although the primary responsibility for making the summative judgment rests with the supervisor and the cooperating teacher, the preservice teacher has a role to play. The preservice teacher should be responsible for using the specific standards of performance developed by the teacher education program to assess personal performance and also for collecting artifacts and assembling them into a personal portfolio that documents teaching and reflection. Recently, the National Council for Accreditation of Teacher Education (NCATE) revised its standards to embrace performance assessment as the central focus of its review process. For that reason, portfolios now play a major role as a means of authentic assessment of preservice teachers' mastery of program goals or standards (Bullock & Hawk, 2001).

***Data Sources*** In contrast to the multiple potential data sources available for evaluating veteran teachers (Chapter 8), the sources available for evaluating preservice teachers are limited by the relatively short time period involved. The two most useful data sources are observations by the cooperating teacher and the supervisor, and artifacts collected primarily by the preservice teacher. The artifacts fall into three categories: teaching artifacts, student artifacts, and student teaching assignments. Teaching artifacts are any products that are produced as a normal part of the teaching process, including unit plans, daily lesson plans, tests, handouts, project assignments and rubrics, audiovisual materials, technology-related instructional materials, and letters or communications with students, parents, and others. Student artifacts include copies of student tests, projects, essays, and other materials produced by students. The preservice teacher should obtain permission from students to include copies of their work in the teacher's portfolio. Student teaching assignments include reflective journals, videotape analyses, and any additional projects that preservice teachers are required to complete during the experience. These artifacts are quite similar to the teacher materials described as a data sources for evaluating veteran teacher (Chapter 8).

The student teaching artifacts are typically assembled into a student teaching portfolio. This portfolio has several uses. It serves as a data source for summative evaluation of the student teaching experience. Although the cooperating teacher and the supervisor have seen a great deal of the preservice teacher's teaching and reflection, they have not seen everything. The portfolio may include artifacts that neither one has seen before. Such artifacts can affect the summative evaluation judgments of the cooperating teacher and the supervisor. If portfolios are collected for all of the preservice teachers in an institution, they or pieces from them can also serve as the performance-based assessment for NCATE and other accrediting agencies. Finally, the portfolio can showcase the preservice teacher's abilities for prospective employers.

Portfolios can be print-based or electronic. Electronic portfolios are becoming increasingly popular and will likely become the method of choice in the not too distant future. They offer the advantage of allowing the user to view the portfolio content in a variety of sequences. They allow the developer to include videotape excerpts and sound recordings to augment the evidence presented. Finally, they demonstrate that the preservice teacher possesses the technological skills necessary to develop the portfolio. That factor alone may give the preservice teacher an advantage in obtaining a teaching position in a district that is technologically oriented. But whether the portfolio is electronic or print-based, it is a vehicle for personal deliberation and reflection that documents and reflects on the preservice teacher's progress toward specific standards of performance.

The portfolio should not be seen as an end-of-semester assignment. Collecting evidence for the portfolio is an ongoing task. The cooperating teacher and the supervisor should help the preservice teacher create the portfolio by periodically reviewing the artifacts that the preservice teacher has selected for inclusion, by asking what each artifact adds to the portfolio and by pointing out useful artifacts that the preservice teacher may have failed to include. Support given to a preservice teacher in collecting, assembling, and reflecting upon artifacts for a portfolio that demonstrates professional performance shows natural blending of supervision and evaluation.

*Evaluation Process* To separate evaluation from supervision to some degree, we suggest that summative evaluation be concentrated in two major events: a mid-semester and an end-of-semester evaluation conference. In a student teaching context in which preservice teachers handle two separate placements, each lasting half the semester, the midterm conference marks the end of the first placement. Otherwise, it simply marks the halfway point of the semester.

Each member of the triad comes to these conferences with the rating sheet of specific standards of performance already completed. They also come with a list of strengths that the preservice teacher has demonstrated and a list of areas for improvement. If the preservice teacher has demonstrated the ability to perform well and to reflect effectively about teaching, the conference can appropriately begin with the preservice teacher's self-evaluation. The supervisor and the cooperating teacher can then augment that analysis with their comments and feedback. If, on the contrary, the preservice teacher is not performing well or is not particularly accurate in self-assessment, the supervisor or the cooperating teacher should take the lead in providing feedback while inviting comments from the other two members of the triad.

After the ratings on the specific standards and the individual lists of strengths and areas for improvement have been discussed, the three partners should agree on a list of strengths and a list of goals for future improvement. Those strengths and goals should be written out and given to all three members of the triad. In the case of the mid-semester conference, the list of goals can focus on supervisory activities during the second half of the experience. At the final conference of the semester, the goals and strengths help to provide closure on the experience, to celebrate the student teacher's accomplishments, and to point the way for future improvement during the first few years of teaching.

When the time comes to assign a grade, the university supervisor and the cooperating teacher share the grade and the rationale for it with the preservice teacher. (It is imperative that the supervisor and the cooperating teacher discuss the grade beforehand and agree about it.) After the conference, the cooperating teacher and the university supervisor typically write letters of recommendation that may be placed in the candidate's personnel file.

# FAILURE IN STUDENT TEACHING

In concluding the discussion of summative evaluation of preservice teachers, we feel it necessary to make a few comments about failure in student teaching. Some preservice teachers are not ready for teacher certification at the end of the student teaching experience, and yet 15% of teacher education programs never fail a preservice teacher. Another 50% fail fewer than 1% of candidates (Guyton & McIntyre, 1990).

Failure at student teaching does not necessarily mean that a candidate should never become a teacher. Although some failing preservice teachers have weaknesses that cannot be overcome, others have the potential to be successful if help is provided. We have both worked with preservice teachers who failed their first student teaching experience, entered an improvement-oriented process, and then successfully completed student teaching, in a subsequent semester, sometimes in spectacular fashion.

We prefer to think of failure at student teaching as an indication that the preservice teacher is not developmentally ready to be certified rather than that the door to certification is permanently shut. It is important that each teacher education program offer remedial opportunities. Those opportunities should be designed to improve the unsuccessful preservice teacher's previously demonstrated shortcomings before the student is allowed to try the experience again. In the absence of remediation, it is unfair, perhaps even cruel, to let the preservice teacher pay the tuition necessary to try the experience gain.

The decision to fail a student teacher or to induce a student teacher's withdrawal from the program is never easy. When in doubt about whether a student teacher's performance is so far below expectation that it warrants failing, the factor to which we give the most weight is our honest answer to the question "How would I react if this person were assigned to teach my child next year?" If the honest answer is that we would be in the principal's office complaining that this person should not be teaching our children, we do not recommend the student teacher for certification. If that person is not good enough to teach our children, then that person is not good enough to teach other people's children either.

No surprise should be involved for a preservice teacher who does not succeed. That individual should have received ample feedback from the cooperating teacher and the supervisor that serious problems were connected with the teaching performance. As soon as the cooperating teacher and the supervisor start to think that the preservice teacher might not complete the experience successfully (no matter how early in the semester), they should make the seriousness of their concerns clear to the preservice teacher and their supervision should become very directive. Problems should be pinpointed, and the preservice teacher should be given help to overcome them. When problems persist, we have found it useful to draw up a contract with the preservice teacher. The contract lists the problems, indicates that all three members of the triad are aware of them, and stipulates that the problems must be overcome by a specified date. The contract further states that if the specified improvement does not occur, the preservice teacher will be asked to withdraw from the student teaching experience because the teaching performance is detrimental to the students. All members of the triad sign the contract.

In the presence of serious problems, we prefer not only to be directive early on, but also to give the preservice teacher an opportunity to withdraw from student teaching rather than take an "F" in it. If the preservice teacher refuses to withdraw (a prerogative available under most university policy), we follow through with the failing grade. Most preservice teachers will choose withdrawal over failure. Although the withdrawal can be quite traumatic for all members of the triad, it often brings relief to the struggling preservice teacher. The individual is aware of the shortcomings and has usually been working diligently to overcome them, to no avail. When withdrawal occurs, the person is frustrated, exhausted, and emotionally drained. Withdrawal provides an opportunity to rest, to take a deep breath, and to gain much-needed perspective. Typically, the chance to rest and to gain some distance from the experience result in a more enlightened decision about whether to pursue a remediation program and reattempt student teaching or to consider an alternative career choice.

# CHAPTER SUMMARY

Supervisors of preservice teachers working as part of a triad face the challenge of meeting both the requirements of the university education program and the expectations of the public school contexts into which the preservice teachers are placed. The roles of university faculty and cooperating teachers require a shared understanding of the goals and processes involved in supervision and evaluation, a genuine recognition of and appreciation for one another's expertise, open lines of communication, and genuine collaboration. Preservice supervisors face the challenge of encouraging reflection and professional growth while serving as gatekeepers to the profession: they make the final determination regarding the preservice teacher's effectiveness in meeting clearly identified performance standards. Structured planning or preconferences before an observation, postobservation conferences based on collecting and interpreting data, videotape analyses of teaching, reflective electronic portfolios, and online discussion groups are powerful supervisory tools. Their use encourages preservice teachers to become reflective practitioners who move beyond their personal concerns to inquire into their practice and to focus on their students' learning.

The evaluation of preservice teachers is complicated by the difficulty in separating supervision from evaluation and by the need to assign a high-stakes grade to preservice teachers. Mitigating factors include the nature of the relationships between the preservice teacher, the cooperating teacher, and the university supervisor, and the fact that two evaluators have the opportunity to capture a comprehensive picture of the preservice teacher's performance.

Standards for the evaluation of preservice teachers are developed by institutions of higher education in consultation with partners from basic education. The standards are heavily influenced by the INTASC standards for the evaluation of new teachers. In contrast with the situation for veteran teachers, the data sources applicable to preservice teacher evaluation are restricted. The supervisor and the cooperating teacher direct the evaluation process with the assistance of the preservice teacher, who compiles a print or electronic portfolio to document his or her performance.

The major events in the evaluation process are three-way midterm and end-of-term evaluation conferences. At those conferences, the preservice teacher is assessed in terms of specific standards of performance and helped to develop lists of strengths and goals for improvement. Grades are also assigned.

Despite the best efforts of all members of the triad, some preservice teachers fail to complete the experience successfully. The supervisor and the cooperating teacher should apprise the preservice teacher of serious deficiencies early in the process and should make it clear that failure to remediate the deficiencies will result in the need to withdraw from the experience.

# DISCUSSION QUESTIONS

**1.** What stumbling blocks can stand in the way of genuine collaboration, sharing of philosophies and of understandings about supervision of preservice teachers, and appreciation of the other's unique expertise between university supervisors and cooperating teachers? What, if anything, can be done to remove or reduce those stumbling blocks?

**2.** What conflicts arise when university faculty and cooperating teachers engage in the dual role of "supervisor" (facilitating self-directed professional growth) and "evaluator" (judging summative performance of preservice teachers)? How can those conflicts be minimized?

**3.** What strategies might be helpful in facilitating the movement of a preservice teacher from self-concern to task concerns to impact concerns?

**4.** In addition to preobservation and postobservation conferences, videotape analyses, frequent written or online journals, and portfolios, can you think of, or have you had experience with, other methods that might be effective in promoting meaningful reflection among preservice teachers? What are those methods and how might they be implemented most effectively?

**5.** Some teacher education programs assign pass/fail grades. Others assign letter grades. What are the advantages and disadvantages of each approach? Which would you prefer as a preservice teacher? As a supervisor or cooperating teacher? As a prospective employer? Why?

# THEORY-INTO-PRACTICE APPLICATIONS

**1.** Engage in a "think-pair-share." Begin by brainstorming a list of ways that you can potentially benefit from agreeing to serve as a cooperating teacher. Next, join with a partner and share your ideas. Create one list of advantages on which you both agree. Take turns sharing that list with the whole group, combining ideas to synthesize a class list of ways in which supervising a preservice teacher can have a positive impact on you and your students.

**2.** In cooperation with the university's teacher training program and your school district, team with a preservice teacher to conduct a planning conference or preconference. Use the questions in Figure 9.2 as a guide. Be prepared to discuss your supervisory experience with the class.

**3.** Engage in firsthand practice with the power of using a videotape to analyze and reflect on teaching: Record a lesson that you teach, select a focus for data collection, collect the data, and answer the questions in Figure 9.4. Pair up with a partner and share what you learned from the activity. Alternatively, write a reflective journal entry that describes the experience and the impact that you experienced.

# REFERENCES

BRANSFORD, J., Derry, S., BERLINER. D., HAMMEMESS, K., & BECKETT, K. L. (2005). Theories of learning and their roles in teaching. In L. Darling-Hammond & J. Bransford (Eds.), *Preparing teachers for a changing world: What teachers should learn and be able to do* (pp. 40–87). San Francisco, CA: Jossey-Bass.

BROOKFIELD, S. D. (1995). *Becoming a critically reflective teacher.* San Francisco, CA: Jossey-Bass.

BULLOCK, A. A., & HAWK, P. P. (2001). *Developing a teaching portfolio: A guide for preservice and practicing teachers.* Upper Saddle River, NJ: Merrill/Prentice Hall.

COCHRAN-SMITH, M. (2000). The future of teacher education: Framing the questions that matter. *Teaching Education, 11*(1), 13–24.

COLTON, A. B., & SPARKS-LANGER, G. (1992). Restructuring student teaching experiences. In C. D. Glickman (Ed.), *Supervision in transition* (pp. 155–168). Alexandria, VA: Association for Supervision and Curriculum Development.

DARLING-HAMMOND, L., HAMMERNESS, K., GROSSMAN, P., RUST, F., & SHULMAN, L. (2005). The design of teacher education programs. In L. Darling-Hammond & J. Bransford (Eds.), *Preparing teachers for a changing world: What teachers should learn and be able to do* (pp. 390–441). San Francisco, CA: Jossey-Bass.

EMIG, J. (1977). Writing as a mode of learning. *College Composition and Communication, 28*(2), 122–128.

FULLER, F. F. (1969). Concerns of teachers: A developmental conceptualization. *American Educational Research Journal, 6*(2), 206–266.

FULWILER, T. (1986). Seeing with journals. *The English Record, 37*(3), 6–9.

GUYTON, E., & McINTYRE, J. (1990). Student teaching and school experiences. In W. R. Houston (Ed.), *Handbook of research on teacher education.* New York: Macmillan.

HOLLY, M. L. (1989). *Writing to grow: Keeping a personal-professional journal.* Portsmouth, NH: Heinemann.

HOLMES GROUP. (1990). *Tomorrow's schools: Principles for the design of professional development schools.* East Lansing, MI: Holmes Group.

HOOVER, L. A. (1994a). Reflective writing as a window on preservice teachers' thought processes. *Teaching and Teacher Education, 10*(1), 83–93.

HOOVER, L. A. (1994b). Using computers to support group-oriented inquiry during student teaching. In J. Willis, B. Robin, & D. A. Willis (Eds.), *Technology and teacher education annual* (pp. 652–656). Boston, MA: Allyn & Bacon.

INTERSTATE NEW TEACHER ASSESSMENT AND SUPPORT CONSORTIUM. (1992). *Model standards for beginning teacher licensing and assessment: A resource for state dialogue.* Washington, DC: Council of Chief State School Officers.

McINTYRE, D. J., & BYRD, D. M. (1998). Supervision in teacher education. In G. R. Firth & E. F. Pajak (Eds.), *Handbook of research on school supervision.* New York: Macmillan.

McINTYRE, D. J. & O'HAIR, M. J. (1996). *The reflective roles of the classroom teacher.* Belmont, CA: Wadsworth.

NOLAN, J. F. (1997). Can a supervisor be a coach? In J. Glanz & R. Neville (Eds.), *Educational supervision: Perspectives, issues, and controversies* (pp. 100–108). Norwood, MA: Christopher Gordon.

PETERSON, K. (2000). *Teacher evaluation: A comprehensive guide to new directions and practices.* Thousand Oaks, CA: Corwin Press.

WILLIS, S. (2002). Creating a knowledge base for teaching: A conversation with James Stigler. *Educational Leadership, 59*(6), 6–11.

# SUGGESTIONS FOR FURTHER READING AND RESEARCH

COCHRAN-SMITH, M., & ZEICHNER, K. (2005). *Studying teacher education: The report of the AERA panel on research and teacher education.* Mahwah, NJ: Lawrence Erlbaum.

DARLING-HAMMOND, L., WISE, A., & KLEIN, S. (1999). *A license to teach: Raising standards for teaching.* San Francisco, CA: Jossey-Bass.

GIROUX, H. A. (1988). *Teachers as intellectuals: Toward a critical pedagogy of learning.* Granby, MA: Bergin & Garvey.

GOODLAD, J. I. (1990). Better teachers for our nation's schools. *Phi Delta Kappan, 72*(3), 185–194.

PATTERSON, R., MICHELLI, N., & PACHECO, A. (1999). *Centers of pedagogy: New structures for educational renewal.* San Francisco, CA: Jossey-Bass.

RATHS, J., & LYMAN, F., (2003). Summative evaluation of student teachers. *Jouranl of Teacher Education, 54*(3), 206–216.

SCHON, D. A. (1987). *Educating the reflective practitioner.* San Francisco, CA: Jossey-Bass.

STEPHENS, D. (2004). School/university partnerships: Rhetoric, reality, and intimacy. *Phi Delta Kappan, 85*(9), 703–707.

# 10

## ERVISION AND EVALUATION THE NOVICE TEACHER

**W**HEN PRESERVICE teachers have graduated and obtained their first positions, they continue on the path toward becoming professional educators. Novice teachers are our second special case in supervision and evaluation. Many school districts have formal induction programs designed to meet the needs of these new teachers.

Well-crafted induction programs provide a positive transition from teacher preparation to longer-term career development by assigning an experienced colleague or a team as mentor(s). Supervision of nontenured teachers by mentors not only affects the retention of promising new teachers by providing a support system but also helps ensure that they develop into competent and enthusiastic practitioners who realize their full potential.

Mentoring is a professional skill that requires training and practice. It can include meeting regularly with novices, in-class peer-coaching cycles, modeling best practice, and assistance in developing a portfolio. Standards-based portfolios provide a tangible record of the novice teacher's professional growth toward identified teaching competencies. We recommend that portfolios be used as a supervisory tool to spark reflection, meaningful dialog, and collaboration during the first year and as part of the novice teacher's evidence-based evaluation during the second and third years.

Evaluation of novice teachers is a tremendously important activity because the decision to grant or not grant tenure represents a golden opportunity to ensure that only excellent teachers are employed by the school district. Because earning tenure is a 3-year process in most states, we describe an evaluation plan that requires increasing participation in the process by the novice teacher over a 3-year period. The plan can be easily adapted to districts that have a longer or shorter probationary period.

When evaluating novice teachers, the administrative team plays a more central role in deciding which data to collect and in gathering the data than it does when evaluating veteran teachers. The goals of the probationary period are to make a well-documented and evidence-based decision on tenure and to socialize the novice regarding the teacher evaluation process and the standards employed in the district.

## GUIDING QUESTIONS FOR PREREADING REFLECTION AND JOURNALING

- Think back on your experiences as a novice teacher. Brainstorm a list of components that you believe are essential to assisting beginning teachers as part of effective teacher induction. Share and compare your list with a partner.

- Think back to someone who served as a capable mentor for you. Discuss what you believe are the most important responsibilities of a mentor.

- What types of specialized knowledge or specific strategies might be helpful to you in the role of mentor working with a novice teacher?

- As a mentor, how might you encourage new teachers to be more consciously reflective about their teaching and their students' learning during their often overwhelming first year?

- How was your performance evaluated prior to earning tenure? What role, if any, did you play? What role, if any, did your mentor play? What role did administrators play? What changes could have been made in the evaluation process to make it more helpful to you?

# WHY ARE NOVICE TEACHERS A SPECIAL CASE IN SUPERVISION AND EVALUATION?

Beginning in the early 1980s, the initial 3 years of teaching became a focus for study and research. Data on teacher retention reveal that beginning teachers are particularly vulnerable. Approximately 33% of new teachers leave the profession within the first 3 years, and almost 50% leave within 5 years (Ingersoll, 2003; Ingersoll & Kralik, 2004). Furthermore, school administrators reported spending inordinate amounts of time addressing novice teacher problems (Odell, Huling, & Sweeny, 2000).

In exploring the reasons behind such dismaying data, researchers discovered that many first-year teachers experience a period of culture or reality shock. No longer under the direct guidance and watchful eyes of a cooperating teacher and a university supervisor, they can find themselves feeling isolated and alone on the job. Other professionals are gradually immersed into their responsibilities. For example, novice lawyers are not expected to tackle the most difficult cases, and first-year engineers are seldom given responsibility for the most challenging projects; they gradually work up to assuming a full load. Teachers, on the contrary, are immersed into the totality of professional responsibilities from their very first day on the job. They typically have the same student loads and daily teaching responsibilities as their experienced counterparts. In the worst-case scenario, because they lack seniority, they are handed a less-than-desirable schedule of classes, often with the least motivated or most needy students. It is no wonder that novice teachers frequently describe their first year as a time of being overwhelmed, trying to keep one step ahead of their students in planning and paperwork, and generally feeling a high degree of stress and frustration.

This transitional time between preservice preparation and a novice teacher's earning tenure has been identified as the "missing piece of the teacher development continuum" (Odell et al., 2000, p. 3). Recognizing the need to be particularly sensitive to the novice teacher's plight, in 1996 the Association of Teacher Educators (ATE) and Kappa Delta Pi (KDP) joined forces to create the National Commission on Professional Support and Development for Novice Teachers "to continue and extend the important focus on mentoring and teacher induction that both ATE and KDP have shared for two decades" (Odell & Huling, 2000, p. xi). Thus by 2003, 79% of new teachers reported participating in some form of teacher induction (Alliance for Excellent Education, 2004).

# SUPERVISING NOVICE TEACHERS THROUGH MENTORING

To ensure a smooth transition into the profession, supervision of the novice professional requires a concentrated effort on the part of both the administration and the experienced faculty serving as mentors. A delicate balance must be maintained between nurturing novice teachers to promote their personal well-being, on the one hand, and nudging them to learn and improve their teaching performance, on the other hand. Research clearly shows that well-designed induction programs that include a strong mentoring component promote the retention of the majority of promising new educators (Ganser, 2002).

For our purposes, we define "induction" as an active and productive transitional period between preservice preparation and longer-term career development, usually the 3 years required for novices to attain tenure (Mager, 1992). Ideally, during the induction period, novice teachers are provided the support and systematic, ongoing professional development that they need to be successful. We define "mentoring" as "the professional practice that occurs in the context of teaching whenever an experienced teacher supports, challenges, and guides novice teachers" in their craft (Odell & Huling, 2000, p. xv). Formal mentors are typically assigned during the first year. In contrast to the situation with preservice teachers where university supervisors and cooperating teachers find themselves assuming the roles of both supervisor and evaluator, typically principals evaluate the non-tenured teacher, whereas mentors function in a more supervisory role. Although induction programs can encompass varied professional development opportunities for novice teachers, this chapter focuses on mentors as supervisors and administrators as evaluators.

## The Role of Mentors: Meeting the Needs of Novice Teachers

The needs of beginning teachers are never universal. Some novices follow the traditional route of preservice teacher preparation programs, but requirements and experiences can vary widely from university to university. An increasing number are pursuing a second career after years of experience in another occupation. Moreover, because of teacher shortages in some disciplines, still others may enter the classroom with emergency or provisional certification (Johnson & The Project on the Next Generation of Teachers, 2004). Yet, despite differences in background, experiences, and education, novices to the classroom tend to share a developmental journey.

Having researched novice teachers for over 15 years as part of the Santa Cruz New Teacher Project in California, Moir (1999) described the typical first year as a metaphorical roller-coaster ride with ups and downs from beginning to end. She finds that most novices journey through five phases: anticipation, survival, disillusionment, rejuvenation, and reflection. The *anticipation phase* occurs before the school year actually begins. During this time, new teachers share an idealized view of their role and an almost romanticized commitment to making a difference in the lives of their students. Then, the oftentimes overwhelming first month on the job bombards them with the practical realities of the *survival phase*, especially in respect to managing their time, developing daily lessons, and implementing effective classroom management techniques. Many struggle to keep their heads above water. The roller coaster dips even deeper during the *disillusionment phase*. Two months of nonstop time commitment and stress are compounded by new challenges such as preparing report cards, communicating with parents during conferences, and undergoing a first formal evaluation by an administrator. Time away over the holiday break typically contributes to a *rejuvenation* phase or slow improvement in attitude as novices regroup and recommit themselves, returning to the classroom with a sense of accomplishment in having survived the first semester. They now possess a more realistic perspective about the day-to-day life of a teacher. Finally, the *reflective phase* begins during the last weeks of school, when novices can breathe a sigh of relief, look back on their accomplishments, and determine their goals for the second year in a new anticipation phase tempered by actual experience.

How, then, does a mentor who is aware of these developmental phases respond to meet the needs of the novice teacher, simultaneously nurturing and nudging during the crucial first year? We suggest the role include the following responsibilities:

1. Serve as an active listener who provides support to reduce novice teachers' feelings of isolation, anxiety, and disillusionment.

2. Assist novices in transferring the knowledge, skills, and dispositions acquired during their preservice experience into their first year of teaching. Most novices come into the first year with a solid foundation in what they need to know and be able to do; they need the confidence to build on this foundation and apply their knowledge and skills.

3. Acquaint novices with "pragmatics," including district policies, procedures, paperwork, and resources, including those available in the community.

4. Familiarize novices with the grade level or content standards and curriculum and assist them in aligning curriculum and instruction with those standards.

5. Share their practical experience with novices to help them expand their repertoire of instructional strategies and assessments to meet the varied needs of students with different learning styles and abilities.

6. Facilitate the development of the novice teacher's professional identity, a journey that moves the novice beyond self-concerns—"from surviving to thriving" as teachers (Ganser, 1996).

7. Engage them in opportunities that cause them to reflect upon their teaching and its impact upon student learning.

Research from Harvard's Project on the Next Generation of Teachers reveals that a majority of induction programs meet only the first three of these mentor responsibilities. Indeed, few induction programs are designed to promote school-based professional development on questions about curricular and instructional issues and best practice related to students' learning (Johnson & Kardos, 2002).

Although the humanistic and pragmatic goals furthered by the first three responsibilities are important, a well-designed mentoring program must also spur novice teachers' growth beyond current levels of performance and enhance their reflective abilities. Because of their developmental levels and emotional roller-coaster ride, many novices can only experience such growth in collaboration with others: "On their own, beginning teachers often develop 'safe' practices that enable them to survive. Induction programs should help them develop 'best' practices and become learners through their teaching" (Feiman-Nemser, Carver, Schwille, & Yusk. 1999, p. 7). Mentors are the collaborative guides during this crucial initial stage of career-long professional development.

## Mentor Selection and Professional Development

The first step in successfully meeting novices' needs through mentoring is for school district leaders to identify the criteria they deem as important in selecting mentors who will serve as positive role models. Strong candidates are likely to demonstrate a commitment to the continuous development of their own practice, sensitivity to the viewpoints of others, and a willingness to volunteer the time to carry out their responsibilities (Schwille, Nagel, & DeBolt, 2000). The National Foundation for the Improvement of Education (NFIE) (1999) organizes the qualities of effective mentors into the following categories:

1. Professional competence and experience—regarded by colleagues as outstanding teachers, possess excellent knowledge of content and pedagogy, and collaborate well with others.

2. Character—willing to serve as role models; eagerly share information and ideas.

3. Communication and interpersonal skills—listen attentively, ask questions that prompt reflection, and maintain confidentiality.

Once mentors are selected, the district must provide them with professional development. Although the individuals may be exemplary educators within their subject/specialty areas and grade levels, in order to be most effective as supervisors, they need training in the knowledge and skills of classroom supervision similar to that provided for peer coaches (see Chapter 3). Connecticut's Beginning Educator Support and Training (BEST) Program, for example, requires a minimum of 20 hours of initial mentor training in the state's teaching standards, portfolio assessment, and coaching strategies (Alliance for Excellent Education, 2004). In fact, if the district has established a strong peer-coaching program, we recommend that only the individuals who meet the requirements and who have participated in peer coaching training be considered as candidates for mentoring novice professionals. If no peer-coaching preparation is available, then mentors must receive more extensive professional development. Figure 10.1 gives a sample 3-day professional development training session for mentor teachers.

After initial training, follow-up support includes scheduling time for mentors to meet periodically throughout the school year to share experiences, discuss dilemmas, and offer one another advice and feedback. Additionally, we recommend that mentors receive some type of incentive in the form of a stipend, modified course load, or credit toward recertification.

Mentors are, in essence, instructional leaders who guide novices through their critical first-year classroom experiences. Once mentors are selected and trained, school districts must willingly devote the resources needed for mentors to work collaboratively with novice teachers. We suggest mentors be provided with the time and institutional support to

• meet regularly with novice teachers to discuss not only their progress, questions, and frustrations, but also curricular, instructional, and assessment issues;

• observe the novice teachers at least three times each semester during the first year, engaging in a form of "expert/novice" coaching;

• invite the novice teachers into their own classrooms to observe at least twice per semester, modeling best practice in identified goal areas the novices might be struggling with;

• confer regularly about the selection of artifacts to be included in a first-year teaching portfolio to demonstrate progress toward the district's identified teaching standards.

By scheduling joint planning time for the mentor and inductee, the principal facilitates regular meetings. Those meetings between mentor and novice provide a forum for an open exchange of ideas about research-based best practice and can be individualized as needed.

**FIGURE 10.1**   Sample Format for 3-Day Mentor Workshop

*Day 1/morning*

- Complete introductory exercises. First, as an icebreaker, have mentors recall their first year of teaching and share some of their most vivid memories. If possible, categorize these recollections. Then complete Exercise 10.1, "A Letter from Mentor to Novice."
- Provide an overview of the goals and objectives of mentor training.
- Present the differences between supervision and evaluation and discuss mentor as supervisor versus principal as evaluator.
- Introduce the knowledge base on the seven essential skills of classroom-based supervision (see Chapter 2).

*Day 1/afternoon*

- Build readiness: Explore novice teacher development, including the research-based phases and needs and concerns of novice teachers (see Figure 10.2).
- Build readiness: Examine salient issues of collaboration, including trust building, maintaining confidentiality, and active listening/interpersonal communication skills (see Chapters 2 and 3).

*Day 2/morning*

- Build readiness: Conduct an espoused-platform conference with one another as a starting point for weekly conferences (return to Chapters 2 and 3 for relevant exercises to use here and below).
- Conduct a preconference that promotes inquiry and reflection—role play.

*Day 2/afternoon*

- Become familiar and experiment with a variety of nonjudgmental data collection instruments. (Suggested resource: Association of Supervision and Curriculum Development's "Improving Instruction Through Observation and Feedback" videotape series—Tape 2, or the district may choose to create their own set of videotaped lessons for practice with data collection.)
- Practice data analysis and interpretation: What is data-driven decision making? What is a directive informational approach to conferencing?
- Conduct a postconference and cycle evaluation—role play.

*Day 3/morning*

- Build readiness: Review of the supervision cycle as a format for in-class observations and conferences.
- Look at standards-based teaching practice from the district perspective: Discuss a common vision and seek a shared understanding of what the district values/identifies as good teaching (see Chapter 7).

*Day 3/afternoon*

- Discuss the uses of a standards-based portfolio with artifacts and reflective captions to document professional growth toward achieving those standards and the mentor's role in facilitating the novice's portfolio development. Complete Exercise 10.2.
- Address questions.
- Closure: Return to Exercise 10.1. Revise the draft of the letter written at the beginning of the training session.

The National Foundation for the Improvement of Education (1999), states that data "dramatically demonstrate that the efficacy of mentoring is linked to the amount of time that a mentor and protégé work together" (online). For example, NFIE reports that 36% of protégés who work sporadically with mentors show substantial improvements in instructional skills; however, this figure jumps to 88% for those who work with mentors once a

**EXERCISE 10.1    A Letter from Mentor to Novice Teacher**

---

*At the beginning of the mentor workshop:* Write a draft of a letter personally welcoming to the school district the novice teacher assigned to you. Consider the following questions as guides to help you shape your thoughts. The new teacher will receive the letter before coming to meet with you for the first time.

1.  Briefly discuss your career experiences in teaching thus far. When did you begin teaching? What grade levels/subjects have you taught? What extracurricular interests do you devote time to? How long have you been working in this district?
2.  Think back to why you chose teaching as your career path. Share your reasons for entering the profession. What still excites you about your work after all these years? What constitutes your very best teaching?
3.  What advice do you wish a mentor had shared with you when you began in teaching?
4.  What are you hoping will be an outcome of your working closely together this first year?

*At the conclusion of the mentor workshop:* Now that you have participated in the training, return to the rough draft. Based on our discussions, make any changes you feel are necessary in preparation for sending the letter.

---

week. Common planning time and electronic mail can be used to keep the lines of communication open between scheduled meetings.

A mentor engages in classroom supervision or coaching by conducting a series of cycles that encompass building readiness, observing, collecting and analyzing data, and conferencing with novices about the teaching/learning process (refer to Chapters 2 and 3). Depending on the developmental level of the novice teacher, the mentor varies the amount of direction provided, seeking always to increase the novice's is independence and to decrease the mentor's own directiveness.

Quality mentors not only listen and offer advice and suggestions, but also lead by example. They view themselves as models of reflection, problem solving, data-driven decision making, and risk taking, but they clearly convey that no teacher has all the answers and that they, too, are continually learning about their teaching. They invite novices to observe them on a periodic basis, and they walk the novice through the stages of their own teacher thinking, including preplanning, lesson implementation, and post-teaching reflective inquiry. Finally, mentors play a major role in helping novices understand the standards that guide the district's vision of teaching excellence. They provide the novice with guidance in choosing appropriate artifacts that demonstrate growth over time. Kardos and Johnson (2007) refer to an environment that fosters substantive interaction about teaching and learning among novices and experienced teachers as an "integrated professional culture," and they report that such a culture lends itself to a school's becoming a true learning organization.

Figure 10.2 lists some possible needs of beginning teachers. This list could serve as a basis for weekly discussions, in-class observations, or district-sponsored professional development scheduled for beginning teachers.

# USING A PROFESSIONAL PORTFOLIO TO SUPPORT NOVICE TEACHER SUPERVISION

In the preceding section, we explored ways for the novice teacher and mentor to collaborate. In this section, we turn our attention specifically to the use of a professional portfolio. Although we presented portfolios as a key component in the evaluation of veteran teachers and preservice teachers, it is important to note that in the special case of novice teachers,

**FIGURE 10.2** Possible Professional Development Topics for Beginning Teachers

1. Effective time management
2. Classroom management: proactive approaches to minimize discipline problems
3. Meeting the needs of special-needs students in an inclusion classroom
4. Differentiating instruction in response to students' diverse needs, abilities, and learning preferences
5. Assessing student learning through a variety of strategies and using data from assessment to inform future instruction
6. Positive interpersonal communication with parents; preparing for parent conferences
7. Educational technology and technological support available within the district
8. Instructional resources available in the school and community
9. Developing a shared understanding of the district standards for evaluation and evaluation procedures, especially those used during the probationary period
10. Creating a portfolio that reflects individual progress toward meeting the standards

the value of a portfolios can be significantly undermined if it is used as a high-stakes means of assessment during the tenuous initial year. Because attaining tenure is a multi-year process, we recommend that, during the first year, the portfolio be used solely as a supervisory tool and a source for sharing and discussion.

We have discussed the movement in education toward standards-based assessment and evaluation. A teaching portfolio not only functions as a written record of progress toward achieving performance-based standards but also provides an ideal means of fostering teacher growth for a variety of reasons.

First, the ongoing nature of creating a portfolio recognizes professional learning as a developmental process that occurs over time (Wolf & Dietz, 1998). Second, self-selection of artifacts and composing the accompanying reflective statements give the teacher ownership and encourage self-assessment. Third, the artifacts presented in the portfolio serve as a purposeful, tangible "body of evidence" or product that demonstrates the novice's ability to meet the predetermined standards. This evidence is important because, as Shulman notes, "a significant obstacle to improving instructional effectiveness is that teaching is like dry ice at room temperature—it evaporates in front of our eyes and leaves no visible traces. In most cases, there is little tangible evidence of the teaching that took place" (cited in Wolf, Whinery, & Hagerty, 1995, p. 30). Fourth, according to Danielson (1996), "assembling items for a portfolio is a powerful vehicle for professional reflection and analysis" (p. 39). The collaboration of mentor and novice in examining potential artifacts that revolve. around a particular standard can serve as a springboard for meaningful dialog about teaching and learning. Bartell, Kaye, and Morin (1998) suggest that substantive conversations concerning the portfolio "offer the richest opportunity to grow, learn, and develop teaching expertise," and serve as "the point at which crucial questions are posed, reflections are shared, ideas are tested, and new challenges are put forth" (p. 131). Those authors see these functions as particularly important for novice teachers,

> [A teacher's entry into the profession marks a period in which habits of mind are formed and approaches to practice are tried, tested, refined, and developed. This journey can be a lonely one, or it can be guided and informed by others in a well-designed plan to induct new members into the profession (p. 136).] Finally, a portfolio sharing session at the conclusion of the first year, one that including inductees, mentors, and administrators, can serve as a well-deserved celebration of achievement and validation of professional growth.

## The Professional Portfolio: Artifacts and Reflective Statements

During their first year under the guidance of their mentors, novice teachers can practice collecting artifacts to address each of the district's standards or performance indicators.

Novices may need to be reminded that artifact collection should be based on *quality* of documentation rather than on *quantity* within the portfolio. Novices may require more modeling than their experienced colleagues about which artifacts to include as evidence that would logically support progress toward a particular standard. Figure 10.3 lists artifacts that can be included to address the eight standards introduced in Chapter 7. We recommend that mentors frequently review a list of artifacts such as this one with the novices.

A possible drawbacks to artifact collection can be the time added to an already overwhelming novice schedule. That problem can be greatly lessened if artifacts are reviewed during regularly scheduled mentor/inductee meetings. We suggest that artifact collection can be facilitated and the meetings made more productive if novices keep a "collection folder" in a prominent place on or near their desks. As they create, disseminate, or collect materials during the course of their regular teaching day, they can slip an extra copy of anything they feel particularly relevant or noteworthy into the portfolio-in-progress file. Then when they meet with their mentors, they can sort through and discuss how the potential artifact connects

**FIGURE 10.3**  Some Suggested Artifacts to Support Performance Standards

1. In what ways does the evidence demonstrate that the teacher possesses a deep understanding of the content he or she teaches?

   *Suggested documentation:*
   - Lesson plan and accompanying videotape
   - Instructional materials created for students' use
   - Examples of real-world connections to content

2. In what ways does the evidence demonstrate that the teacher develops long-range and daily plans that are appropriate for students and consistent with district curriculum and state standards?

   *Suggested documentation:*
   - Sample unit outlines
   - Correlational charts connecting standards and curriculum content
   - Daily lesson plans

3. In what ways does the evidence demonstrate that the teacher uses a wide variety of instructional strategies and appropriate resources to engage students in learning and promote deep understanding of content?

   *Suggested documentation:*
   - Overview of instructional strategies incorporated within a unit
   - Individual plans with highlighted instructional activities
   - Examples of technology integrated into instruction
   - Videotape of student discussion (e.g., morning meeting, literature circles)
   - Mentor or administrator observations

4. In what ways does the evidence demonstrate that the teacher assesses student understanding frequently, provides feedback to students, and uses assessment to plan instruction?

   *Suggested documentation:*
   - Sample record-keeping forms, assessments, and grading rubrics
   - Student artifacts, including graded projects or student work
   - Lesson plans or videotapes of lessons created in response to assessment data

5. In what ways does the evidence demonstrate that the teacher creates a positive classroom climate that is well organized and conducive to student learning and manages student behavior effectively?

   *Suggested documentation:*
   - Mentor or administrator observation forms
   - Classroom artifacts and/or pictures of classroom environment
   - Videotape of a lesson
   - Individualized or group anecdotal records, behavior contracts, or behavior modification plans

*(Continued)*

**FIGURE 10.3**    (*Continued*)

---

6. In what ways does the evidence demonstrate that the teacher understands and responds to a wide variety of student diversity including cultural differences and special-needs students?

   *Suggested documentation:*
   - Teaching materials, behavior plans, or assessments adapted for learning support or inclusion students
   - Lesson content; examples or illustrations representing a wide variety of cultures or ethnic groups

7. In what ways does the evidence demonstrate that the teacher is a lifelong learner who seeks opportunities to reflect on his or her practice and grow professionally?

   *Suggested documentation:*
   - Professional development certificates or graduate course syllabi
   - Examples of adaptations to plans or instruction based on mentor and/or administrator feedback

8. In what ways does the evidence demonstrate that the teacher interacts professionally with parents and colleagues and contributes to the school as an organization?

   *Suggested documentation:*
   - Samples of parent communication
   - Service on committees or leadership roles in professional development
   - Record of extracurricular involvement

---

to the performance standards, addressing why each would or would not make a positive contribution as evidence of professional growth. These ongoing, guided discussions can help to keep the performance-based goals in the forefront of their thinking. Novice teachers can also make the process of assembling a portfolio an ongoing, job-embedded part of daily planning and deliberating about teaching, rather than an overwhelming obstacle that they feel pressured to pull together near the conclusion of their first year.

Novices also need practice in writing accompanying reflective statements that summarize what the artifacts demonstrate about their progress in relation to evaluation standards. Figure 10.4 provides an example of a first-year teacher's reflective statement in response to a standard on professional growth.

**FIGURE 10.4**    Actual Reflective Statement Excepted from a Novice Teacher's Portfolio

---

**Question 8** In what ways does the evidence demonstrate that the teacher interacts professionally with parents and colleagues and contributes to the school as an organization?

This question was the toughest for me to select artifacts to include. It is my feeling that if I am contributing to the good of the community at large, no one should notice! However, for communication with parents I chose to include samples of parent e-mails I received and responded to, a copy of my parent newsletter, and my web page. These artifacts illustrate one of the most important parts of my duties—keeping my parents informed and included in the school lives of their children. Many of my parents could not remember to write me a note, but would remember to e-mail me when they got to work. This exchange kept the dialog open at all times. The same is true for my web page. Important dates, assignments, and projects are available to see online 24 h a day at the convenience of the parents.

The second part of these responsibilities involves my record of noninstructional duties. I am teaching two summer in-service courses for my colleagues: Web Page Design and Using KidPix. This will give me a chance to interact with staff outside the normal parameters of the school day. I was also selected for the Technology Leadership Committee, which will increase my technology skills and allow me to share these skills with others. I am helping with Title 1 reading summer school this year to give at-risk readers a jumpstart into first grade. Finally, I helped with the elementary school musical, Kamp Kaos. All of this came from some good advice from my principal ... become a part of the school and the faculty, and it becomes part of you. These opportunities to contribute have given me a sense of belonging, and I can honestly say made me feel I am a part of the school community.

---

Special thanks to Mr. Jeff Clifton of Dillsburg Elementary School.

Finally, Exercise 10.2 provides mentors with an opportunity to role play the process of helping novices select portfolio artifacts and write reflective statements.

### EXERCISE 10.2   Helping a Novice Create a Portfolio

**Part I**   Work in pairs. Assume the roles of mentor and inductee. Pretend that you are involved in a weekly meeting. The inductee, a second-grade teacher, has asked the mentor to look at an artifact and accompanying reflective caption that he/she has prepared for inclusion in the portfolio. Look at the two evaluative questions below and role play a discussion that might ensue. If you were the mentor, how would you respond? What feedback would you give?

**Question 5**   In what ways does the evidence demonstrate that the teacher creates a positive classroom environment that is well organized and conducive to student learning and manages student behavior effectively?

**Question 6**   In what ways does the evidence demonstrate that the teacher understands and responds to a variety of student diversity including cultural differences and special-needs students?

To illustrate the preceding standards, I have included part of a short-term behavior modification plan I created for one of my inclusion students, an autistic child who has trouble with routines and procedures. Providing her with a daily schedule chart, broken into small, manageable steps, allows me to clearly communicate my expectations and allows her to organize and to practice exactly what is expected of her at the beginning of the day. I have placed the following schedule on overhead transparencies, one for each day. She has a dry erase marker. As she completes each step, she crosses out the responsibility. This will help reinforce the expected daily routine. If she is able to remain on task and complete the list, she is rewarded with her choice of a prearranged sensory stimulation activity, such as bouncing a ball, drawing a picture, or listening to taped music. My hope is that the beginning of each day will become more manageable for her and she will eventually internalize the list.

---

**Morning activities**

1. When I get off the van, I go into school.
2. I go into Mrs. H's room and put my book bag at my desk.

**Erase #1 and #2**

3. I put my lunch in the refrigerator.
4. I hang my coat in my locker.

**Erase #3 and #4**

5. I stand for the pledge to the flag.
6. I sit in my seat, listen carefully, and take part in the day's calendar.

**Erase #5 and #6**

7. If I have erased steps 1-6, I may set the timer for 5 min and choose a sensory activity.
8. When the timer goes off, I put whatever I am doing away.

**Erase #7 and #8**

I then join my classmates at special.

---

**Part II.**   Switch roles with your partner. Repeat the role-play, using the artifact and reflective caption to follow. This time the inductee assumes the role of a sixth-grade science teacher.

**Question 4**   In what ways does the evidence demonstrate that the teacher assesses student understanding frequently, provides feedback to students, and uses assessment to plan instruction?

One of the artifacts that I included in support of my progress toward achieving Standard 4 is the following culminating performance-based project that I assigned at the conclusion of the unit on the changing earth. The formative assessments I used throughout the unit led me to the conclusion that the content of this chapter can be particularly difficult for students to understand; most of them had very little prior knowledge. Thus, I wanted to engage in a hand-on demonstration of what they learned rather a than paper-and-pencil assessment. I also built in enough class time for working on the travel brochure to assure that I could individually conference with each student to give suggestions and feedback. Finally, I created a checklist to assure that both the students and I were clear about the criteria for success. It illustrates the emphasis I put on student responsibility for engaging in self-assessment.

**"Traveling Through the Changing Earth"**

For this project you will become a travel guide. Your task is to create a travel brochure and to vacation through Unit B, "The Changing Earth."

Name: _____ Core: _____ Date: _____

Parent signature:_____

### Requirements

- Each chapter needs to have a separate section in your travel brochure. You need to write at least two complete paragraphs for each main concept from the unit. Within these paragraphs, you need to use *at least five* vocabulary words from each chapter.
  - Chapter 1—Tectonic Plates and the Theory of Continental Drift
  - Chapter 2—Impact of Tectonic Plates on Mountain Building
  - Chapter 3—Earthquakes
  - Chapter 4—Volcanoes
- For chapters 3 and 4, include specific earthquakes and volcanoes that we discussed. As you are creating a travel brochure, you will want to make a trip out of visiting these earthquake and volcano sites as a part of your brochure. Include a map of some kind to show the sites.
- You need to have at least one picture for each section of your brochure.
- Include a final section with some kind of a question-and-answer format. You need to include at least three questions from each chapter.
- Spelling, grammar, and punctuation will be graded.

The possibilities for designing your brochure are endless! Have fun and be creative! You will have 4 days in class to work on this assignment. You will conference with me individually on either Wednesday, January 16th, or Thursday, January 17th. Your brochure is due on Friday, January 18th.

There is a checklist on the back to help you as you are working on your brochure. Make sure you have included all of the requirements and that you have demonstrated your knowledge about The Changing Earth. This is a chance for you to use your talents and show me what you have learned in a style of your own. Always remember, if you have any questions, ask.

| Check when finished | Requirements |
|---|---|
|  | You included at least five vocabulary words from each chapter. |
|  | You wrote two complete paragraphs for each of the four chapters. |
|  | You included references to at least three earthquakes and volcanoes that we studied. |
|  | You designed a map to illustrate the sites of the earthquakes and volcanoes. |
|  | You included at least four other pictures, one to illustrate each chapter. |
|  | You conclude with a question-and-answer section with at least three questions from each chapter. |
|  | You used in-class time wisely and used the feedback that I provided in our conference, carefully checking spelling, punctuation, and grammar. |

**Part III** Come together as a whole group. Ask volunteers to share their role plays for both scenarios. Compare your feedback and advice.

Special thanks to Mrs. Alison Fleagle of Northern Middle School.

# SUPERVISION AFTER THE FIRST YEAR: NOW WHAT?

Many induction programs come to an abrupt halt at the conclusion of the novice's first year. Although we understand that the formal mentoring may end, we strongly advocate that a substantive program of support and professional development to meet the needs of the nontenured teacher continue. Our concrete recommendations are these

1. *Provide funding to support at least one of the cohort's mentors continuing on with the group the second year as a "lead mentor."* The responsibility of the lead mentor would be to organize and coordinate informal support sessions, based on the needs and interests expressed by the group. These meetings could vary in time and location. For example, the group might be given released time for a luncheon meeting on site in September, gather after school over pizza in November, be provided time to network during a January in-service day, and join together for a breakfast session before school in March. In providing this continued assistance to novice teachers, the district is making a worthwhile investment toward a positive climate of community, collaboration, and continuous growth.

2. *Continue to provide professional development opportunities specifically tailored to meet the needs of the novice.* With their first year behind them and a great deal more practical experience, second-year teachers are ready for more sophisticated models of teaching that the district endorses, such as developing differentiated assessment tasks for each unit of instruction that will assess student learning using a variety of learning preferences/products.

3. *Assuming that the group makes good progress toward tenure, set aside the third year for an overview of the district's supervision and evaluation system and of the differentiated growth options available to teachers after attaining tenure.* Opportunities to sit in as an observer on self-directed activities, action research teams, or collegial development groups would be a positive first step toward their understanding the expectation of continuous learning and assuming personal responsibility for their own future self-directed growth.

# EVALUATION OF NOVICE TEACHERS

The probationary period before the novice teacher earns tenure may be the only time when it is financially feasible for school districts to separate supervision from evaluation by using different personnel for each. The previous sections of the chapter described the role of the mentor teacher in carrying out the tasks associated with supervision of novice teachers. We now turn our attention to the administrative function of evaluating novice teachers.

## Basic Issues and Considerations

The multi-year period between the initial hiring of a teacher and the granting of tenure to that individual represents a critical period in the process of teacher evaluation. On the one hand, a great deal of effort has been put into selecting the best candidate for each teaching position. All parties to the process want to see the novice succeed. On the other hand, once tenure is granted, dismissing a teacher who is not performing well becomes much more difficult. The granting of tenure confers a presumption of competence on the part of the teacher; if a district attempts to dismiss a tenured teacher, this presumption of competence must be disproven by the district (Lawrence, 2005). Thus, the tenure decision is the golden opportunity to make sure that only the very best teachers are employed by the school district.

The decision to grant tenure should be taken very seriously, should be based on multiple sources of data accumulated over the entire probationary period, and should involve the professional judgments of multiple administrators. One administrator illustrate the importance of the tenure decision in the following statement:

> I think we have been too casual about the tenure decision, and we have paid a price for that easygoing attitude. It's clear to me now that the tenure decision is the last opportunity we have to enforce high performance standards on our teaching staff. Once they receive tenure, they have to be a blatant failure before we can get rid of them. Every time we make a mistake, it means lots of problems down the road. Students get shortchanged; parents eventually complain; and administrators wind up spending an inordinate amount of time and energy trying to rescue the unsalvageable. I think we can avoid most of these problems by treating the tenure decision for what it is, the single most important personnel decision we make. Before we assume a million dollar obligation to a teacher and limit our future instructional flexibility, we need considerable assurance that our decision to grant tenure is the right one. (Bridges, 1992, p. 51)

Evaluating novice teachers is a bit more complicated than evaluating veteran teachers for two reasons. First, veteran teachers can be evaluated on performance alone. When someone has been teaching for 5, 10, 15, or 20 years, he or she has had the opportunity to learn from experience and to smooth out the rough spots in his or her teaching repertoire. Novice teachers, on the contrary, must be evaluated with one eye on current levels of performance and one eye on their potential for future improvement. As noted earlier, the initial year of teaching is a roller-coaster ride for many professionals (Moir, 1999). The level of performance that is manifested during the first year is likely to improve with time, provided that the types of supervisory support structures that have been identified in this chapter are in place. This is not to suggest that poor or unsatisfactory performance should be tolerated during the first year. It should not. However, a performance that is merely satisfactory may be acceptable if the administrators believe that the difficulties encountered are a result of inexperience or initial adjustment problems. In such cases, a novice's performance may be expected to become excellent by the end of the probationary period. If improvement fails to occur, we recommend that tenure not be granted. The complexity of evaluating performance and potential simultaneously is one of the reasons for our suggestion, later in the chapter, that multiple administrators observe novice teachers.

The second factor that complicates the evaluation of novice teachers is the need to socialize the novice into the process of teacher evaluation in the local school context. Not only must novices be taught the procedures that are used for evaluation, but they must also be helped to internalize the values and high standards that are embedded in the process. Novice teachers need to be given more direction and less choice in the evaluation process than veteran teachers (Peterson, 2000).

An important goal of evaluation for novice teachers should be to enable them gradually to become more skillful in understanding the district's evaluation standards, in evaluating their performance, and in collecting data independently to support that evaluation process. Thus, the probationary evaluation period should provide scaffolding to help the novice acquire this capability in a developmentally appropriate way. During the initial teaching year, responsibility for collecting evaluation data rests entirely on the shoulders of the administrators. The novice practices developing a portfolio as suggested, but this portfolio is not evaluative. It serves a supervision function. During the second and third years of the probationary period, responsibility for gathering evaluation data begins to shift. By the end of the third year, this responsibility is shared equally by the teacher and administrators. As noted in Chapter 8, administrators are always responsible for the summative evaluation decision, but the novice is asked to engage in self-evaluation throughout the entire 3-year period.

# EVALUATION STANDARDS

The standards used to evaluate the performance of novice teachers are identical to those used for evaluating veteran teachers. The eight evaluation standards and accompanying questions introduced in Chapter 7 are appropriate for first-year teachers provided that the evaluator focuses on both current performance and potential for improvement, as discussed earlier. These standards, also serve as the organizer for the first-year supervisory portfolio. However, guidelines for the summative evaluation out of novices teachers differ to some degree from the guidelines we suggested for the summative evaluation of veteran teachers.

At the end of the first year of teaching, any novice who receives a Level 3 rating— "the evidence is clear that the standard is not met"—should receive an unsatisfactory rating unless the administrators believe that there is some compelling reason to give a needs improvement rating. In the absence of a compelling rationale to the contrary (e.g., the novice was teaching particularly difficult or needy groups of students who would have posed a challenge for experienced teachers), the novice would not be allowed to return for a second year of teaching. Nonrenewal of a probationary teacher is legally much easier than the dismissal of a tenured teacher. The probationary teachers does not enjoy the same due process rights:

> *[Since non-tenured teachers are not normally held to have a property right in the renewal of their contacts, they do not, except under very unusual conditions, have a constitutional right to due process under conditions of non-renewal. Some states have extended minimal components of due process to probationary teachers. Most common are the right to a statement of the grounds for non-renewal and the right to respond (Strike & Bull, 1981, pp. 320–321).]*

By the end of the probationary period, all novice teachers who do not receive a Level 1 rating— "the evidence indicates the standard is clearly met"—on all evaluation standards should be rated unsatisfactory and not granted tenure. Employing this high-level standard of summative evaluation should ensure that only those who really deserve it earn tenure.

# EVALUATION PROCEDURES

The procedures for evaluating novice teachers differ considerably from those used to evaluate veteran teachers because of the developmental level of the novice teacher. As the novice gains experience and internalizes the district's evaluation process, the procedures employed become increasingly more consistent with those used to evaluate veteran teachers.

**Roles**   We recommend that the responsibility for novice teacher evaluation be shared by the administrative team as opposed to resting solely with the principal. Many states require that novice teachers be observed four times per year for purposes of evaluation during the probationary period. Typically, the principal responsible for the teacher's evaluation conducts these four observations. Several districts that we have worked with augment the four principal observations with two additional observations each year by a central office administrator. Thus, the novice is observed six times each year, four times by the building principal and twice by a central office administrator. In some cases, the central office observations are done each year by a different central office administrator (e.g., superintendent, assistant superintendent, curriculum director). We endorse this process. Involving multiple administrators lightens the evaluation burden of the principal, and the multiple perspectives make an accurate tenure decision more likely.

During the first year of teaching the role of the novice teacher in reference to evaluation is to work with the mentor teacher to learn about the process of portfolio development and to participate in the observation process conducted by the administrators. During the second year, the teacher continues to participate in the observation process and begins the development of a portfolio that will be used as a key data source in the third-year summative evaluation. In the final year of the probationary period, the novice teacher continues participation in administrative observation and completes the development of the evaluation portfolio.

**Data Sources**   In keeping with the developmental readiness of the novice teacher, the number of data sources employed in the summative evaluation process expands each year during the probationary period.

The sole data source used for evaluation during the first year is administrator observations. In making their classroom observations, administrators should focus on collecting data that can be used to answer the evaluation questions used by the district. The processes of judgment making should be separated from observation, as suggested in Chapter 8. When multiple administrators are involved in making decisions, they should confer with one another about the focus that each will take in observing and should share observation data.

During the second year, teacher materials and videotaped lessons, which may eventually become part of the third-year evaluation portfolio, should be added to administrator observations as data sources.

During the third year of the probationary period, administrator observations again play a key role in the evaluation process. In addition, the novice teacher assembles a portfolio that includes teacher materials and videotaped lessons as well as at least one, but potentially several, of the remaining data sources that are used for veteran teacher evaluation. These data sources, described in Chapter 8, include student input, parental input, student learning data, and documentation of professional growth. We believe that it is appropriate to include both student learning data and parental input as third-year data sources before a tenure decision is reached.

**Evaluation Process**   Early in his or her first year, the novice receives a detailed explanation from the principal of the evaluation processes during the probationary period and the standards that are used. This orientation is followed, as suggested above, by discussions about evaluation with the mentor teacher. Once the evaluation procedures and standards have been explained, the administrative team can begin the process of classroom observation. Classroom observation serves as the only evaluative data source during this first year. In keeping with our suggestions in Chapter 8, half of the observations should be prearranged, whereas the other half remains unannounced. Prearranged observations would be preceded by a conference. All observations would be followed by a conference.

Preobservation conferences for purposes of evaluation differ from preobservation conferences for supervision. The focus in evaluation preconferences is to gain insight into the novice's thinking about teaching and learning. This insight is achieved by talking through the plan for the lesson and getting the novice to explain what the learning activities will look like and why they have been designed as they have.

As noted in Chapter 9, preobservation conferences offer unique windows into true teacher thinking because the teacher need not defend or rationalize behavior because the lesson has not yet occurred. That window can be particularly important in the evaluation process as the high stakes can induce the novice to become defensive during postobservation conferences and rationalize his or her behavior when parts of the lesson went badly. During the entire evaluation process, preconferences may offer the only completely honest view into the novice teacher's thinking.

An additional difference between evaluative and supervisory preconferences lies in the fact that in evaluative preobservation conferences there is no establishment of a contract for data collection. The novice teacher does not have the opportunity to direct data collection. Data collection is driven by the district's evaluation standards and controlled by the administrative team.

Postobservation conferences for evaluation purposes also differ from supervisory postobservation conferences. Evaluative postobservative conferences provide evaluative feedback to the teacher and help the teacher understand how the administrator saw the lesson. The supervisor attempts to involve the teacher in interpreting the data and making decisions about future instruction in order to understand the novice's ability to reflect on his or her teaching and act on that reflection. The evaluator goes further, sharing his or her perceptions of the lesson, providing positive judgments about aspects of the lesson that were effective, and offering suggestions for improvement. As the primary intent of the conference is to provide feedback to the teacher concerning the effectiveness of the lesson in meeting district evaluation standards, evaluative postobservation conferences would typically be classified as directive informational conferences (see Chapter 2) although elements, especially the data interpretation process, may be collaborative or even nondirective. Supervisory postobservation conferences would normally be nondirective or collaborative in their entirety.

After all administrative observations have been completed, the participating administrators review all of the data that have been collected and rate the novice teacher in terms of the district's evaluation standards. The summative evaluation ratings are then shared with the novice in an end-of-the-year summative evaluation conference typically held in late May or early June of the first year. In states that require summative evaluation during each semester of the probationary period, summative conferences would be held in January and June.

The second year of probationary evaluation also begins with a conference between the principal and the novice teacher. This conference is used to accomplish several tasks. Summative evaluation ratings from the first year are discussed in terms of areas needing improvement during the second year. Plans for administrative observations during the second year are also discussed. Finally, the teacher and principal discuss the process of collecting teacher materials and videotaped lessons that may become part of the second-year teaching portfolio. The novice should be encouraged to collect artifacts to address each of the district's evaluation standards and to also consider including artifacts that were collected during the first year of teaching.

Administrator observations during this second year follow the format discussed above. If a different central office administrator occupies the central office observation role, he or she is responsible for reviewing all observation records and the summative evaluation ratings from the first year.

The novice teacher, engaged in artifact collection throughout the school year, meets approximately halfway through the year with the principal to review the artifacts. At this meeting, the administrator provides feedback and guidance concerning the collection of artifacts for the rest of the year. By the beginning of May, the novice teacher gives the completed portfolio to the administrator. The portfolio includes teacher materials and videotaped lessons as well as reflective statements concerning the novice teacher's perception of his or her performance on each of the district's evaluation standards.

Participating administrators then use their observation records as well as the artifact portfolio to complete the summative evaluation rating of the teacher's performance. They share their ratings with the novice teacher at the end of the school year. If any questions are raised at this point about the novice teacher's competence, that is, a Level 3 assessment in any evaluation standard, the teacher should definitely receive an unsatisfactory rating, and his or her contract should not be renewed. If a novice has a Level 2 rating in any standard ("The evidence does not make clear that the standard has been met"), he or she should receive a "needs improvement" rating and be told that failure to move to a Level 1 rating during the final probationary year will result in not earning tenure. Although making negative decisions early in the tenure process may seem harsh, such decisions protect students, provide novices with honest feedback, raise the standards of effective teacher performance, and may prevent much more serious problems later on (Bridges, 1992).

During the final year of the probationary period, the evaluation procedures are essentially the same as those for any veteran teacher whose performance is being evaluated. The only difference lies in the administrator observations. In the case of tenured teachers, the teacher and a single administrator work together to identify areas of the evaluation standards that will serve as the focus for the administrator's observations. In the case of novice teachers, two administrators independently gather evidence concerning all of the evaluation standards.

The year begins with a conference between the principal and the novice teacher. They discuss which data sources, in addition to administrator observations, teacher-materials, and videotaped lessons, will be used as evidence of the teacher's performance. At least one additional data source must be included, but more than one may be included if the teacher and administrator agree. At the end of March of the third year, the novice teacher begins the process of assembling the evaluation portfolio. This portfolio may include any artifacts that were collected during the first and second years, as well as new third year data. In keeping with the procedures used by veteran teachers, the novice compiles evidence to address each evaluation standard and writes a reflective statement for each, describing how the evaluation data show that the standard has been met. The evaluation portfolio is given to the principal by May 1 of the final year of probation.

The principal then uses the evaluation portfolio and all administrative observation data to compile a draft summative evaluation of the novice teacher. This draft evaluation is shared with all administrators who have participated in observing the teacher. The administrative team discusses the data and agrees on a summative evaluation rating as well as a decision about tenure. As suggested above, only novice teachers who have received a Level 1 rating on all standards should be granted tenure. If there is disagreement among administrative team members, we suggest that the opinion of the principal, who will be responsible for working with the teacher if tenure is granted, be given more weight in making the final decision. Following the administrative team discussion, the principal completes a final summative evaluation and shares it with the teacher in a summative evaluation conference.

Figure 10.5 summarizes the 3-year evaluation process for novice teachers.

**FIGURE 10.5**   Evaluation Process for Novice Teachers

*Year 1*

- The principal and a central office administrator conduct administrative observations focused on the evaluation standards.
- A Level 3 rating on any standard results in an unsatisfactory rating.

*Year 2*

- The building principal and a central office administrator conduct administrative observations focused on the evaluation standards.
- The novice teacher creates a portfolio consisting of teacher materials and videotaped lessons to address evaluation standards.
- A Level 3 rating on any standard results in an unsatisfactory rating; a Level 2 rating on any standard results in a rating of needs improvement.

*Year 3*

- The building principal and a central office administrator conduct administrative observations focused on the evaluation standards.
- The novice creates a portfolio consisting of teacher materials, videotaped lessons, and at least one other data source to address district evaluation standards.
- The evaluation team discusses the draft summative evaluation compiled by the principal before reaching agreement on a summative rating and tenure status.
- The novice teacher must obtain a Level 1 rating on all standards to obtain a satisfactory rating and earn tenure.

## CHAPTER SUMMARY

Induction programs for novice teachers provide a support structure for the transition between teacher preparation programs and long-term career development. They are designed to increase retention and encourage reflection and professional growth. In part, they achieve their goals by replacing isolation with the collaborative support and guidance of an experienced mentor teacher. We recommend a strong commitment of time and resources to programs for mentor development; it is especially important that mentors acquire supervisory knowledge and skills.

A key part of induction programs is the novice's creation of a professional portfolio based on clearly identified standards of professional practice. The portfolio serves as a purposeful, tangible record of performance-based growth over time. In the first year, the artifacts and reflective captions serve a supervisory function a starting point for substantive

conversations and collaboration between the novice teachers and their mentors. Ultimately, portfolios are among the data used to evaluate novice teachers for decisions concerning tenure.

The evaluation process for novice teachers is directed, in large measure, by the administrative team. Ideally, several administrators observe the novice teacher during the 3-year probationary period in order to document his or her performance in reference to the district's evaluation standards. The novice builds a modified evaluation portfolio during the second year and expands it to a full-blown evaluation portfolio during the final probationary year. As the granting of tenure is an extremely important personnel decision that potentially binds the district to the teacher for many years, only novices who clearly meet or exceed all district evaluation standards should be granted tenure.

## DISCUSSION QUESTIONS

**1.** Before reading this chapter, you brainstormed a list of essential components to an effective teacher induction program. Return to that list now. Have your perceptions changed? In what ways might you revise this list to ensure that beginning teachers are success-

fully socialized into the school district and the profession? Explain.

**2.** As a mentor, in what specific ways would you structure your interactions with the novice teacher assigned to you to facilitate "striking the right balance" between providing direct assistance and allowing the novice to construct his or her own knowledge and learn from mistakes?

**3.** What are the advantages and disadvantages of using a portfolio as part of the supervisory/evaluative process in working with novice teachers? How might you structure the portfolio process to overcome the disadvantages?

**4.** A well-structured induction program should provide positive aspects for the experienced mentor as well as the novice teacher. Discuss the benefits that could arise from a successful mentoring relationship.

**5.** Under what circumstances, if any, would you be willing to allow a novice teacher who was rated as clearly not meeting a district evaluation standard during the initial year of teaching to continue teaching into the second? What conditions, if any, would you impose on that continuation?

**6.** Under what circumstances, if any, would you be willing to grant tenure to a novice teacher who had not received a Level 1 rating on all of the district's evaluation standards? What justification can you provide for granting tenure in this situation?

## THEORY-INTO-PRACTICE APPLICATIONS

**1.** Visit the mentor chat room at http://teachers.net/mentors/beginning_teachers/.
Here is a sample first-year teacher's call for help retrieved from the online site:

> *Post: Did anyone else have a rough first year?*
>
> *Posted by Languageteacher*
>
> *Hello to all! I am new here and hoping that this site will be very useful to me as I continue my teaching career. As suggested by my title I have had a rough go at being a first-year teacher. Somehow the "Well, the first year is always rough" line of advice isn't cutting it for me anymore. I feel like I have no one to talk to. Already having been stung by the rumor mill a couple of times, I don't wish to speak to my colleagues or my mentor about any more of my thoughts. Having taught for a year has left me with low patience, low self-esteem, paranoid, and wondering why I even chose to study languages and become a teacher in the first place. I know that I shouldn't be feeling so sorry for myself and I'm sure that no one wants to listen to someone else complain; however, I know that I'm not the only one out there. If anyone has it in his heart to help me, please email me. I would like to begin some sort of personal correspondence regarding the daily battles of being a high school teacher.*
>
> *Thank you, Languageteacher*

**1.** First analyze the possible sources of this first-year teacher's frustration. Using Moir's (1999) stages of the first-year teacher, how would you characterize the developmental level of concern? Work with a partner to determine how you might respond in light of what we covered in this chapter.

**2.** Now, peruse other postings online at this web site. Find a first-year teacher who is asking for advice or assistance. Draft a response to the request. Copy and be ready to share with classmates both the novice's request and your reply. What did you learn about both novice teachers and yourself from this assignment?

**3.** Arrange to observe or watch a videotape of a lesson taught by a novice teacher. Use a wide-angle lens approach to collect observational data during the lesson. Use the recorded data and your perceptions to plan two different types of postobservation conferences, a supervisory postobservation conference with you as the mentor and an evaluative postobservation conference with you as the principal responsible for evaluating the novice teacher. In each plan, describe the goals for the conferences as well as the role that the novice and you will take in (a) analyzing data, (b) drawing conclusions, and (c) making decisions about future instruction.

**4.** Work with two other students to obtain copies of the novice teacher induction plans and mentor teacher training programs from each of the districts where you currently work or worked in the past. Examine the plans in terms of what you have learned from this chapter. Identify the strengths and weaknesses of each plan and suggest ways to improve each plan by capitalizing on the existing strengths and improving areas of weakness. If possible, share your analysis with those district personnel who are responsible for overseeing the mentoring program.

# REFERENCES

ALLIANCE FOR EXCELLENT EDUCATION. (2004). *Tapping the potential: Retaining and developing high quality new teachers.* Washington, D C: Alliance for Excellent Education.

BARTELL, C. A., KAYE, C., & MORIN, J. A. (1998). Portfolio conversations: A mentored journey. *Teacher Education Quarterly,* 25 (Winter) 129–138.

BRIDGES, E. (1992). *The incompetent teacher: Managerial responses.* Philadelphia, PA: The Falmer Press.

DANIELSON, C. (1996). *Enhancing professional practice: A framework for teaching.* Alexandria, VA: Association for Supervision and Curriculum Development.

FEIMAN-NEMSER, S., CARVER, C., SCHWILLE, S., & YUSKO, B. (1999). Beyond support: Taking new teachers seriously as learners. In M. Scherer, (Ed.), *A better beginning: Supporting and mentoring new teachers,* pp. (3–12). Alexandria, VA: Association of Supervision and Curriculum Development.

GANSER, T. (1996). Preparing mentors of beginning teachers: An overview for staff developers. *Journal of Staff Development, 17*(4), 8–11.

GANSER, T. (2002). The new teacher mentors. *American School Board Journal, 189*(12), 25–27.

INGERSOLL, R. (2003). *Is there really a teacher shortage?* Seattle, WA: Center for the Study of Teaching and Policy.

INGERSOLL, R., & KRALIK, J. M. (2004). *The impact of mentoring on teacher retention: What the research says.* Retrieved January 13, 2006, from http://www.ecs.org/clearinghouse/50/36/5036.htm.

JOHNSON, S. M., & KARDOS, S. M. (2002). Keeping new teachers in mind. *Educational Leadership, 59*(6), 12–17.

JOHNSON, S. M., & THE PROJECT ON THE NEXT GENERATION OF TEACHERS. (2004). *Finders and keepers: Helping new teachers survive and thrive in our schools.* San Francisco, CA: Jossey-Bass.

KARDOS, S. M., & JOHNSON, S. M. (2007). On their own and presumed expert: New teachers' experience with their colleagues. *Teachers College Record, 109* (12). Retrieved 4/4/2007, from http://www.tcrecord.org/contentasp?content=12812

LAWRENCE, C. E. (2005). *The marginal teacher: A step-by-step guide to fair procedures for identification and dismissal, (3rd ed.)* Thousand Oaks, CA: Corwin Press.

MAGER, G. M. (1992). The place of induction in becoming a teacher. In G. P. DeBolt, (Ed.), *Teacher induction and mentoring: School-based collaborative programs,* (pp. 3–34). Albany, NY: State University of New York Press.

MOIR, E. (1999). The stages of a teacher's first year. In M. Scherer, (Ed.), *A better beginning: Supporting and mentoring new teachers,* (pp. 19–23). Alexandria, VA: Association of Supervision and Curriculum Development.

National Foundation for the Improvement of Education. (1999). *Creating a teacher mentoring program.* Washington, DC: NFIE.

ODELL, S. J., & HULING, L. (2000). Introduction: Leading the teaching profession toward quality mentoring. In S. J. odell & L. Huling (Eds.), *Quality mentoring for novice teachers,* pp. xi–xvi. Washington, D C: Association of Teacher Educators.

ODELL, S. J., HULING, L., & SWEENY, B. W. (2000). Conceptualizing quality mentoring: Background information. In S. J. Odell & L. Huling (Eds.), *Quality mentoring for novice teachers,* (pp. 3–14). Washington, DC: Association of Teacher Educators.

PETERSON, K. (2000) *Teacher evaluation: A comprehensive guide to new directions and practices.* Thousand Oaks, CA: Corwin Press.

SCHWILLE, S. A., NAGEL, A. L., & DEBOLT, G. P. (2000). Mentor selection and mentor/novice matching. In S. J. Odell & L. Huling (Eds.), *Quality mentoring for novice teachers,* (pp. 57–66). Washington, DC: Association of Teacher Educators.

STRIKE, K. & BULL, B. (1981). Fairness and the legal context of teacher evaluation. In J. Millmen (Ed.), *Handbook of Teacher Evaluation.* Beverly Hills, CA: Sage.

WOLF, K., & DIETZ, M. (1998). Teaching portfolios: Purposes and possibilities. *Teacher Education Quarterly, 25* (Winter), 9–22.

WOLF. K., WHINERY, B., & HAGERTY, P. (1995). Teaching portfolios and portfolio for teacher educators and teachers. *Action in Teacher Education, 17(1),* 30–39.

# SUGGESTIONS FOR FURTHER READING AND RESEARCH

Where is the novice teacher to turn at 2 A.M. when his/her mentor is asleep? Try these web sites that offer 24-h guidance and encouragement:

- "Beginning Teachers' Tool Box." *http://www.inspiringteachers.com*
- "Teachers." http://www.teachers.net/mentors
  Source: KELLY, L. (1999). Web wonders. *Educational Leadership, 56*(8), 83.

Association for Supervision and Curriculum Development. (1999). *Videotape: Mentoring to improve schools.* Alexandria, VA: ASCD.

Association for Supervision and Curriculum Development. (2002). Videotape series: *Improving instruction through observation and feedback.* Alexandria, VA: ASCD.

BRADFORD, J. J. (1999). How to stay in teaching (when you really feel like crying). *Educational Leadership, 56*(8), 67–69.

COSTANTINO, P. M., & DELORENZO, M. N. (2002*). Developing a professional teaching portfolio: A guide for success.* Boston, MA: Allyn & Bacon.

CUSHMAN, K. (1999*).* Educators making portfolios: First results from the national school reform faculty. *Phi Delta Kappan, 80*(10), 744–750.

DARLING-HAMMOND, L. (2000). *Solving the dilemmas of teacher supply, demand, and standards: How we can ensure a competent, caring, and qualified teacher for every child.* New York: National Commission on Teaching and America's Future.

FEIMAN-NEMSER, S. (2003). What new teachers need to learn. *Educational Leadership, 60* (8), 25–29.

GANSER, T. (2000). Teams of two: Insider ideas on building and supporting a mentor program. *Journal of Staff Development,* 21(1), 60–63.

GORDON, S. P. (1991). *How to help beginning teachers succeed.* Alexandria, VA: ASCD.

GRATCH, A. (1998). Beginning teacher and mentor relationships. Journal of Teacher Education, 49(3), 220–227.

LYONS, N. (Ed.). (1998). *With portfolio in hand: Validating the new teacher professionalism.* New York: Teachers College Press.

LYONS, N. (1999). How portfolios can shape emerging practice. *Educational Leadership, 56*(8), 63–66.

MURRAY, M. (1991). *Beyond the myths and magic of mentoring: How to facilitate an effective mentoring program.* San Francisco, CA: Jossey-Bass.

PAINTER, B. (2001). Using teaching portfolios. *Educational Leadership, 58*(5), 31–34.

ROWLEY, J. B. (1999). The good mentor. *Educational Leadership, 56*(8), 20–22.

SCHERER, M. (1999). *A better beginning: Supporting and mentoring new teachers.* Alexandria, VA: ASCD.

SMITH, T. M., & INGERSOLL, R. M. (2004). What are the effects of induction and mentoring on beginning teacher turnover? *American Educational Research Journal, 41*(3), 681–714.

VILLANI, S. (2002). *Mentoring programs for new teachers: Models of induction and support.* Thousand Oaks, CA: Corwin Press.

# CHAPTER 11

# SUPERVISION AND EVALUATION OF THE MARGINAL TEACHER

**M**ARGINAL TEACHERS are those with experience and tenure who have been identified as questionably competent or below satisfactory in one or more performance-based standards. Consequently they have received a needs improvement or unsatisfactory summative evaluation rating. They represent the third and final category among special cases.

In contrast to the cases of preservice and novice teachers where supervision and evaluation are two separate and independent functions, evaluation and supervision of marginal teachers are closely intertwined. Because the competence of the veteran teacher is in question, evaluation takes center stage. Supervision processes come into play as part of an improvement plan aimed at remediating difficulties the teacher is experiencing. Though the goal of the process is improvement of performance, the procedures that are followed must also comply with legal requirements for teacher dismissal if that option proves necessary.

The chapter is divided into five sections. The first section discusses the rationale for including marginal teachers as a special case in supervision and evaluation. The next section describes legal aspects of the process, with emphasis on the legal definition of incompetent teaching, and the procedures for notifying the teacher that because of marginal performance he or she will be placed in the intensive assistance track. Following notification of deficiencies, remediation can begin. The third section explains the remediation process. It encompasses distinct aspects of supervising marginal teachers, including assembling a support team and creating an individually tailored intensive assistance plan. The fourth section explains the role that administrators play in the ongoing evaluation of the marginal teacher as well as appropriate evaluation procedures and data sources. After the marginal teacher engages in an individually tailored intensive assistance plan, administrators must make a summative judgment. Has the teacher's performance returned to a satisfactory level, should the teacher should be continued in intensive assistance, or should the teacher be dismissed? The final section takes up the issue of dismissing veteran teachers whose performance is not improved by the intensive assistance process.

## GUIDING QUESTIONS FOR PREREADING REFLECTION AND JOURNALING

- Do you know any teachers whose performance you would rate as marginal or perhaps incompetent? What specific problems or issues lead you to say that the teacher is marginal or incompetent? What, if anything, has been done to help this teacher improve?

- Think about the teacher referred to in the previous question. If you were a teacher serving on a support team to assist him or her, what strategies might you employ to help him or her to improve? What, if anything, would lead you to suggest that he or she is beyond improvement and should be encouraged to stop teaching?

- Many educators believe that the process of dismissing tenured teachers is so expensive, time consuming, and emotionally draining that the outcome is not really worth the effort. Where do you stand on this question? Should districts and individual administrators be willing to pay the price of dismissing teachers whom they see as incompetent? Why or why not?

### EXERCISE 11.1   The Case of Mr. Matthews

**Directions**   Read the following scenario. Decide what you would do next. Then discuss your ideas about next steps with a partner. Be ready to share your solutions with the class.

This is your first year as principal of a suburban high school. In looking through the files of your teaching staff in August, you note that all 60 teachers have received satisfactory summative ratings for the past 5 years. Moreover, teacher evaluation has been synonymous with teacher observation. One of your scheduled observations for December is of Mr. Matthews, a 10th-grade social studies teacher. He has been teaching social studies in the school district for the last 15 years and has completed a Master's degree in social studies education at a local university.

The form the district uses for teacher observation is simple. It has lines for some basic background information such as teacher's name, the grade, subject, and time of the observation, and space for an open-ended narrative. Your assistant principal, who has been in the district for 4 years, informs you that each principal has the freedom to capture the unfolding lesson in any way he or she chooses as long as there is a lesson summary. The form concludes with an area to list commendations and recommendations.

When you observe Mr. Matthews, you notice that he uses a traditional, teacher-centered approach that includes reading round robin from the textbook (15 min of class), followed by individual seatwork (20 min of the class). From the data you gather, he does not seem particularly demanding in terms of his expectations for student behavior. For example, it takes him almost 5 min to start the class, 5 min are wasted in the transition from whole-class reading to the seatwork assignment, and students pack their backpacks early and spend the last 5 min socializing. In addition to this waste of learning time (15 min out of the allocated 50), you find it particularly troubling to note the fact that several students had their heads down for most of the class. Three students were also passing notes across the room during the seatwork assignment. When students misbehaved, there seemed to be no negative consequences. Mr. Matthews either was unaware of what was happening in the room or chose to ignore it.

In the postobservation conference, Mr. Matthews remarks that he felt the lesson went fairly well except for those few students who never seem interested in anything. You share the data and convey your concerns. The district has a set of standards for effective teaching as part of its supervision and evaluation plan, and you give Mr. Matthews a copy. He appears surprised that such a document exists, remarking that this is the first time he has ever laid eyes on it. You suggest that he review it and compare his teaching actions to the standards and that you then return for another observation. Under recommendations you list (1) more active involvement by students; (2) more time directed toward learning; and (3) more awareness of and response to student inattentiveness.

Meanwhile, you do some further checking about Mr. Matthews and find no history of parental complaints. You also note that the vast majority of his students in previous years have received As or Bs. Although Mr. Matthews is certainly not a leader among the faculty, he appears to enjoy a congenial relationship with his colleagues and is active in the union. You also discover a pattern where he appears to use sick leave on most in-service days devoted to professional development. Two months later, you observe Mr. Matthews again and note no change in the reading/seatwork approach to instruction, time wasted during transitions, or degree of student inattentiveness. He comes to this postobservation conference on the defensive, bringing along a union representative. What do you do now?

# WHY ARE MARGINAL TEACHERS A SPECIAL CASE IN SUPERVISORY PRACTICE?

What are the characteristics of a marginal teacher? Danielson and McGreal (2000) describe *marginal teachers* as "those who, in the professional judgment of an administrator, are experiencing difficulty in meeting one or more of the district's standards for effective teaching" (p. 118). Kaye (2004) provides a similar definition, suggesting that marginal teachers are those whose performance cannot be documented as incompetent but borders on incompetence and prompts evaluators to believe that the teaching must be improved. Lawrence (2005) suggests that the marginal teacher seems "unable or unwilling to improve his or her teaching performance and thus has a negative impact on students" (p. 2). Raths and Lyman (2003) define teaching incompetence as "acts of omission or commission on the part of the teacher that either interfere with learning or fail to advance it" (p. 211). In keeping with the suggestions that we made in Chapter 8, we define a marginal teacher as any veteran teacher who receives a summative evaluation rating of either unsatisfactory or needs improvement. Though an unsatisfactory rating is far more ominous and signals the presence of potentially more intractable problems, either rating means that the veteran teacher will automatically be placed in the intensive assistance mode of the district's teacher supervision and evaluation system for the subsequent year. The teacher remains in that mode until either receiving a satisfactory summative evaluation or being dismissed.

One of our fundamental tenets is the separation of the supervision and evaluation functions for veteran teachers who are performing well. The poor performance of the marginal teacher and the potentially negative consequences that may result make this separation of evaluation and supervision inappropriate. The teacher's due process rights require that attempts at improving the marginal teacher's performance (i.e., the supervision function) be directly connected to the deficiencies identified through summative evaluation (Strike & Bull, 1981). In working with marginal teachers, the evaluation process identifies deficiencies in performance and examines the teacher's behavior systematically over time to determine whether the deficiencies have been corrected. The supervision process aims at correcting or ameliorating those deficiencies that have been identified by evaluation. Thus, although involving different participants and procedures, the supervision process derives its aims explicitly from summative evaluation outcomes. Supervision could be correctly seen as a subset of the evaluation process. Figure 11.1 provides a visual overview of the intertwined processes of evaluating and supervising marginal teachers that will be described in the following sections.

# THE PARADOXICAL PROCESS: LAYING THE GROUNDWORK FOR REMEDIATION OR DISMISSAL

As suggested in Chapter 8, the process of dealing appropriately with marginal teachers begins well before the identification of those teachers. First, the district must lay the groundwork by involving all stakeholders in a process to identify and adopt standards of effective teaching (see Chapter 7) based on clearly communicated and commonly understood performance indicators of competence. These standards are a necessity in making expectations for satisfactory performance clear, explicit, and consistent. With such standards in place, the reason for a Level 3 rating ("Evidence is clear that standard is not met") can be well documented by the administrator, and, thus, the marginal teacher cannot object on the grounds of being treated in an arbitrary, capricious, or subjective manner. Rather,

**FIGURE 11.1** Working with the Marginal Teacher

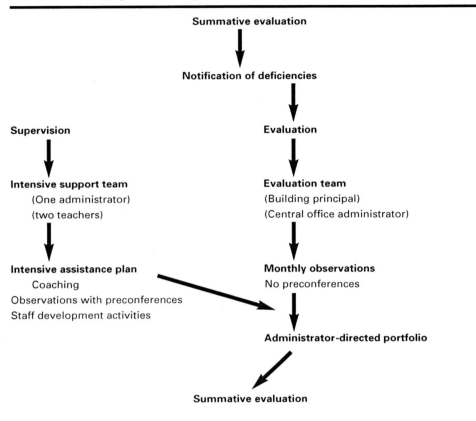

this documentation, as related to the standards, serves as evidence supporting the decision and enabling the marginal teacher to see the rationale for the rating.

Second, teachers must understand the steps of the evaluation process, including how a teacher will be identified as marginal. We have suggested, in Chapters 7 and 8, that evaluation questions be based on performance standards and that every third year teachers be evaluated using both observational data that administrators have collected over time and a portfolio of teacher-selected data sources. If on reviewing these data, the administrator decides that it is unclear whether the teacher has met one or more standards or that the teacher's performance clearly does not meet a standard, then that teacher is considered marginal and a candidate for intensive assistance.

The identification of a teacher as unsatisfactory or needing improvement and the consequent placement of the teacher in an intensive assistance mode of supervision and evaluation marks a significant event. It informs the teacher that there are serious issues surrounding his or her competence and that improvement is required. It also signals to the administrator that consideration must now be given to the teacher's due process rights and to the legal issues involved in dismissing a veteran teacher. Dismissal is not the goal of the intensive assistance process. The goal is to remediate the deficiencies, have the teacher return to a satisfactory level of performance, and eventually enable the teacher to grow toward excellence through the supervision components of the supervision and evaluation system.

Remediation as a goal makes sense from a variety of viewpoints—ethical, organizational, legal,s and economic. As we state in our platform of beliefs, all teachers should be treated ethically, fairly, and respectfully. The primary reason for investing time and effort in remediating the performance of marginal teachers is thus moral and ethical. It is simply the right thing to do. Dismissal, though the appropriate course of action if necessary, would have a devastating impact on the teacher and his or her future career whereas successful remediation will give the teacher a renewed sense of competence and confidence. Successful remediation may also have a positive impact on the school as an organization. It sends other teachers two messages. First, poor teaching performance is not acceptable. Second, the district is prepared to help teachers improve their performance and will work hard at doing so.

From a legal point of view, veteran teachers are entitled to a substantial attempt at remediation before any dismissal notice will be honored by the courts (Zirkel, 1996). The district will be forced to show in any dismissal hearing that such attempts were made. Economically, the school district has already invested a great deal of money in a veteran teacher over the years in terms of salary, fringe benefits, and professional development costs. It makes much more economic sense to attempt to salvage that investment rather than to throw it away. Every individual involved in the evaluation and supervision of marginal teachers should understand that the desired outcome of the process is the return of the veteran teacher to a level of satisfactory performance or beyond.

> *Unfortunately, however, successful remediation is not always possible. "Rarely is a teacher's poor performance due solely to a single cause like effort, skill, or ability. More commonly, unsatisfactory performance stems from other sources as well such as personal disorders, family problems, and inadequate past supervision. Under these conditions, efforts to improve the performance of such teachers represents a formidable challenge" (Bridges, 1992, p. 12).*

Because it is not possible to predict whether remediation will be successful, administrators involved in the evaluation and supervision of marginal teachers live in a paradoxical world. They must always act on the belief that remediation is achievable and do everything possible to achieve that goal. Research shows how critical teacher expectations are in influencing student performance (Good & Brophy, 2007). We suggest that administrator expectations are just as powerful in influencing teacher performance. At the same time, however, administrators must be aware of the legal ramifications and requirements of an unsuccessful remediation attempt leading to a decision to dismiss the teacher. They must collect all of the documentation necessary to support a possible charge of incompetence, but they must not do so in such a way as to lead the teacher to believe that remediation is not achievable.

## Legal Considerations

As noted earlier, granting a teacher tenure confers certain due process rights on the teacher and also confers a presumption of competence that will need to be disproven in any dismissal hearing. The importance of due process cannot be underestimated:

> *Tenure or permanent contract creates an expectation of continued employment. When tenured teachers are dismissed, they are denied the opportunity to practice their livelihood. In the language of the Fourteenth Amendment, teachers cannot be deprived of such a property interest without due process. (Hazi, 1998, p. 970)*

Thus, both the due process rights that the teacher enjoys and the legal definition of incompetent performance must be clearly understood. A veteran teacher may be dismissed for a variety of reasons specified in school codes that have nothing to do with poor teaching performance, for example, moral turpitude, insubordination, willful misconduct, and so on

(Owen, 1999). However, the focus in this chapter is on incompetent teaching as teaching incompetence would be identified through the supervision and evaluation process. The due process rights that tenured teachers enjoy vary to some degree because of differences in state statutes as well as differences in local contracts and bargaining agreements.

In general, however, all tenured teachers enjoy fundamental due process rights in the event of a dismissal proceeding. The action for dismissal must be based on clearly formulated and publicly announced policies. The policies must be general in scope; that is, they must apply to all teachers, not just to this individual. The policies must be regularly applied; they cannot be applied to some individual and not others. Finally, tenured teachers are entitled to a well-established set of procedures that must be followed in any attempt to dismiss the teacher (Strike & Bull, 1981). Figure 11.2 presents a set of recommended procedures that, if followed carefully, should ensure that tenured teachers' due process rights are not violated.

In working with marginal teachers, administrators must keep these due process procedures in mind, especially the first 5, which are directly connected to the teacher evaluation process. The procedures must be afforded to the teacher, and the administrator retain documentation that the teacher was afforded all the components of due process. Courts are much more likely to rely on the professional judgment of administrators in the substantive aspects of evaluation; however, judicial review of the dismissal decision is likely to be much more restrictive when dealing with the procedural aspects of the dismissal (Strike & Bull, 1981). The final four procedures, connected to the dismissal hearing, although also important, are not under the direct control of the administrator. If the administrators have done a good job in laying the groundwork for the unsatisfactory evaluation, the dismissal hearing is likely to proceed much more smoothly.

Although the courts are likely to defer to the professional judgment of administrators in regard to the substantive aspects of evaluation, it is useful to understand how the courts have generally defined incompetence. Most states list incompetence as a reason why a tenured teacher may be dismissed but do not define it very clearly. As a result, the legal definition of incompetence has been developed largely through court decisions on the issue.

**FIGURE 11.2** Recommended Procedures to Protect Procedural Due Process Rights of Tenured Teachers

Provide teachers with the following:

- An understanding of the general evaluation process used for all teachers including standards, processes, and observation forms or procedures. Copies of all observations and other documentation used to evaluate performance.
- A statement of concerns or deficiencies that must be remediated as well as a timeline for required improvements.
- Documentation of assistance provided to help the teacher improve.
- Additional documentation used to make the judgment of unsatisfactory performance leading to the dismissal proceedings.
- A written notification of an unsatisfactory evaluation and the reasons for that evaluation.
- A response that is heard in a meaningful way.
- A hearing at which the teacher may be represented by an attorney, has the right to confront and cross-examine witnesses, and the opportunity to present evidence.
- A decision after the hearing, based on the evidence and legal rules, as well as a statement of the reasons for the decision.
- A written record of the hearing (Strike & Bull, 1981; Lawrence, 2005).

As noted by Owen (1999), the courts have not confined incompetence to poor instructional methodology alone. "Incompetence involves much more than bad teaching. It includes lack of substantive knowledge and deficiencies in personality, composure, judgment and attitude, poor preparation, and lack of classroom control" (Owen, 1999, p. 1). Incompetence typically manifests itself in a pattern of recurring instances, rather than in a single incident and has proven to be irremediable (Strike & Bull, 1981; Bridges, 1992). Among the specific behaviors that have been accepted by the courts as indicators of incompetent performance are the following: failure to maintain discipline, failure to treat students properly, failure to impart subject matter effectively, failure to demonstrate mastery of subject matter, failure to accept teaching advice from superiors, failure to produce intended or desired results in students, poor teaching methods, and poor communication (Strike & Bull, 1981; Bridges, 1992; Owen, 1999).

These court accepted definitions of incompetence are quite broad and require appropriate documentation to demonstrate that the alleged deficiencies do exist and have proven irremediable over time. In relating them to the standards of effective teaching identified in Chapter 7, it is clear that an unsatisfactory rating due to deficiencies in any one or more of those standards could be defensible grounds for dismissing a teacher as long as appropriate documentation is provided. With these legal considerations in mind, we can now turn our attention to the process of actually working with the marginal teacher so that remediation of poor performance will occur and dismissal will be unnecessary.

## Beginning the Process: Initial Notification

The first step in the process of working with the marginal teacher is informing the teacher that he or she has received an unsatisfactory or needs improvement summative rating and placement in the intensive assistance mode of supervision and evaluation for the upcoming year. The teacher is informed of this action orally in the summative evaluation conference with the principal. A written statement, in the form of a letter, follows this oral notification. This letter describes the specific areas of concern or deficiencies that lead to the summative rating. The statement describes any appeal process that is open to the teacher as a part of the teacher evaluation process. It also specifies the timeline that will be followed in beginning the intensive assistance process. Figure 11.3 is an example of a statement that might be used to inform a teacher that he has received a needs improvement rating and will be placed in the intensive assistance mode.

**FIGURE 11.3**  Sample Notification of Deficiencies and Placement in Intensive Assistance

Dear Mr. Matthews,

As you are aware from the summative evaluation conference that was held on June 2nd of this year, you have received a summative evaluation rating of "needs improvement." The purpose of this letter is to explain the concerns that led to the needs improvement rating, to inform you of your right to appeal the rating to the superintendent, and to begin the process of assisting you to improve your teaching performance.

**Explanation of Rating**  As part of the typical teacher evaluation process, the principal observed two different lessons to collect data focusing specifically on your use of instructional strategies (Standard 3) and creation of an appropriate classroom learning environment (Standard 5). The principal conducted the first unannounced observation on December 6th. Issues of ineffective instructional strategies, inefficient use of learning time, and failure to intervene to engage students in learning activities resulted from this observation. Based on data collected during this observation, the principal recommended that you use varied instructional strategies that elicit more active student involvement in the learning process (students passively read

*(Continued)*

FIGURE 11.3 (*Continued*)

round robin from the textbook and then individually completed a worksheet). He also recommended that you use instructional time more efficiently (15 min of class time were wasted) and move about the room more to monitor student behavior (you remained in the front/center portion of the room for the entire period, seemingly unaware of or choosing to ignore students' unengaged behavior).

A second unannounced observation to collect data with the same focus occurred 2 months later on February 12th. In this observation, you failed again to actively involve students (you lectured for 10 min and then assigned students to read silently from the textbook for the rest of the period). During assigned reading, you sat at your desk either ignoring or unaware of off-task behavior. As was the case with the first observation, class began 5 min late, ended 5 min early, and was interrupted by a 5-min transition between the two parts of the lesson. In the postobservation conferences, you gave no indication whatever that these two classes were atypical of your teaching performance.

No other data provided evidence of effectiveness in using a variety of instructional techniques and in creating a positive classroom learning environment Further, you suggested that these techniques you are currently using have been working effectively for 15 years and continue to be effective.

The evaluation data provide no evidence that you use a variety of instructional strategies. The observed strategies involved students minimally in learning activities and resulted in many students not being attentive to instruction. As a result of this evidence, you were rated as clearly not meeting Standard 3 of the district's evaluation standards ("The teacher uses a wide variety of instructional strategies to engage students in learning and promote deep understanding of content").

The evaluation data also indicate that your use of instructional time and management of student behavior need to be improved. In both observations, valuable learning time was lost in beginning the class, in making transitions between activities, and in bringing the lesson to closure. Additionally, students who remained off task for substantial periods of time received no negative consequences for their behavior. As a result, you also received a Level 3 rating ("Evidence is clear that standard is not met") for Standard 5 ("The teacher creates a positive classroom climate that is well organized and conducive to student learning and manages student behavior effectively").

Based on these deficiencies, you received a summative evaluation of needs improvement. As a result, you are assigned to the intensive assistance mode of supervision and evaluation for the coming year.

**Right of Appeal**   According to the district's approved teacher supervision and evaluation system, you have the right to appeal this summative rating and consequent placement in intensive assistance in writing to the Superintendent of Schools. Such an appeal must be sent to the superintendent within 7 days of receipt of this letter. The superintendent will then issue a ruling on the appeal within 14 days.

**Next Steps**   It is your responsibility to contact me to set up a meeting within 7 days of receiving this letter (if you choose not to appeal the rating) or within 7 days of the superintendent's ruling on an appeal (if the ruling upholds the needs improvement rating). The purpose of the meeting is to begin the process of correcting the problems identified above by establishing goals for improvement, a timeline for improvement, and the development of a support team that will work with you to improve your performance. In order for you to receive a satisfactory summative evaluation in the future, it will be necessary to obtain Level 1 ratings on all district performance standards. I am hopeful that if we all work together diligently, you can overcome these difficulties and provide evidence in the future that your teaching performance matches or exceeds all district evaluation standards.

---

The meeting between Mr. Matthews and the principal that follows the receipt of the letter marks the beginning of the supervision and evaluation process for the subsequent school year. As a result of that meeting, the teacher should understand the procedures that will be used to assist him or her to improve (supervision) as well as the process that will be used to evaluate his or her performance.

# SUPERVISION OF THE MARGINAL TEACHER: INTENSIVE ASSISTANCE

In discussing preservice and novice teachers (Chapters 9 and 10), we recommended that whenever appropriate, the teachers be active participants in the supervisory process and be encouraged to share ownership of the process. However, in circumstances where an experienced, tenured teacher is in danger of receiving or has received a summative unsatisfactory rating for consistently marginal performance in any area, the administrator must forgo shared ownership in favor of a directive approach to supervision. The supervisor (in this case either the principal or members of the intensive assistance support team) controls both the process and the products of supervision.

The supervisor has a legal responsibility to make clear to the teacher exactly where the problems are and how the problems can be resolved. Immediate and precise communication is required, both face to face and in writing, to set specific improvement targets within a prescribed but realistic time frame. The specific improvement targets are described in an intensive assistance plan, implemented by an intensive support team. Key supervisory components in working with marginal teachers include supervisor-directed preobservation and postobservation conferences as well as the development of the intensive assistance plan.

## Conducting Preobservation and Postobservation Conferences

Working with the marginal teacher should closely resemble work with preservice teachers with effective veteran teachers. Preobservation conferences for the marginal teacher differ from those for veteran teachers in two ways. First, the teacher does not decide what observational data will be collected. The data are driven by the improvement targets or goals listed in the notice of deficiency. It would be unethical and unwise legally to allow the teacher to decide what to focus on as improvement in the targeted areas is a must.

Second, rehearsal becomes a much more significant aspect of the preobservation conference. Because marginal teachers often have great difficulty planning appropriate instruction, talking through the instructional plan in great detail before the lesson occurs provides a golden opportunity to identify rough spots in the lesson and take steps to remediate them. If poor planning is the issue, the marginal teacher should be required to submit written lesson plans to the principal or support team for at least one lesson per day. This strategy makes the teacher's planning (a mental process that is not explicit or observable) to become explicit for the supervisor and open to remediation. Discussing the written lesson plans would then be a central component of preobservation conferences.

Postobservation conferences with marginal teachers also differ from those with veteran teachers who are performing well. The supervisor takes a much more directive approach in modeling the data interpretation process, identifying subsequent instructional actions to be taken by the teacher, and monitoring to ensure that the teacher follows through on the recommended courses of action. The supervisor assumes that the teacher needs to learn or relearn how to think about instruction in an effective way as well as to develop new behaviors and skills. Thus, modeling, directing, and monitoring are very appropriate supervisory behaviors. If improvement begins to occur, the supervisor can begin to allow the teacher to assume more responsibility during the postobservation conference.

## Assembling a Support Team and Developing an Intensive Assistance Plan

***The Support Team*** A unique challenge for supervisors working with a marginal teacher lies in creating an individualized support team and an intensive assistance plan targeted to assist the teacher in meeting the standard(s) in question. Lawrence (2005) pointed out that this intensive assistance for the marginal teacher is essential because it (1) gives the teacher an opportunity to improve; (2) demonstrates the supervisor's willingness to offer support; and (3) is a necessary part of due process procedures.

The assistance to the teacher may be provided by the building principal alone if there is no established mechanism for involving others in the process or may be provided by a support team assembled to help the marginal teacher improve, provided that the establishment of such a team is permitted by state law and by the local teacher contract. Though there may be cases where the use of a support team is not a good idea, in general, support teams can be helpful (Lawrence, 2005).

When a principal must provide assistance alone, he or she continues the paradoxical life described earlier. At the same time that the principal is collecting data to make an accurate summative judgment of the teacher's performance, he or she is also engaged in trying to help the teacher improve. There are two potential dangers connected with this scenario. The principal may become so invested in being a partner in improvement that it will be almost impossible to make an objective summative evaluation. On the contrary, the principal may be so obsessed with making an accurate evaluation that it will be difficult to participate fully in trying to help the teacher improve. This dual role can be managed, but the principal needs to be aware of the pitfalls and also have access to other administrators who can help him or her navigate this difficult terrain. Whether assistance is provided by an individual principal or by a support team, the goal is always to meet the designated objectives for improvement as specified in the notice of deficiency within the allotted time.

We suggest that the intensive support team include an administrator (either the principal of another building or a central office administrator [if there are several of them]) and at least two other teachers (ideally, those with training as peer coaches if such a model exists in the district). The principal should assign one of the teachers to the team but allow the marginal teacher a choice in selecting the second teacher.

If possible, the administrator who serves on the assistance team should not also carry responsibility for summative evaluation of this teacher, for the reasons suggested above. The building principal who is responsible for summative evaluation confers with the members of the support team but is not a member of the team. This separation allows the principal to focus time and attention on the evaluation task. The support team undertakes a collaborative effort to conduct multiple observations in different teaching contexts, to provide concrete data for the teacher to analyze and reflect upon in collaboration with others, and to offer constructive feedback. The teachers can provide confidential peer support in a nonthreatening environment and offer modeling through the marginal teacher's observations in their classrooms.

***The Intensive Assistance Plan*** The intensive assistance plan includes clear goals, strategies for attaining those goals, some form of professional development intervention to help the marginal teacher acquire necessary knowledge and skills, and a time frame for these activities. At the follow-up meeting that occurs after the written notice of deficiency has been received or the superintendent has ruled on the teacher's appeal of the summative rating, the principal explains the process for formation of the intensive support team. The principal asks the teacher to choose a second teacher (in addition to the one chosen by the principal) to be placed on the support team. Once the support team members have been identified, the principal develops a draft of the intensive assistance plan and shares it with the support team members. After receiving feedback from the team members, the principal revises the plan and shares it with the marginal teacher.

In addition to classroom visitations for coaching purposes, there are a variety of professional development interventions that can be included in the plan to help the marginal teacher improve. The specific interventions that are tried should be connected to the data that are collected through the observations conducted by the intensive support team. Among the more common forms of intervention are the following: (1) opportunities to observe other teachers; (2) shadowing a successful teacher for a day; (3) provision of sample lesson plans from other teachers; (4) referrals to web sites and other resources for instructional ideas; (5) videotapes of effective teaching strategies; (6) written material on effective teaching from books or journal articles; and (7) workshops, either in-house or external to the school (Lawrence, 2005).

Although intensive assistance plans often provide the opportunity to observe teachers who are excellent models, this strategy is unlikely to be very effective unless other support is also provided. Bridges explains the problems encountered in asking marginal teachers to learn from observing others without support.

> *Marginal teachers are often unable to transfer learnings from one situation to another. When you use exceptional teachers as models to demonstrate teaching techniques, you must precede these visits by a conversation concerning what to look for and suggestions about why it is happening. You must also follow these classroom visits with a discussion that focuses on a particular objective. Weak teachers need several exposures to what exceptional performances might be, and these models should be with similar kinds of students at the same grade level or in the same content area. (Bridges, 1992, p. 59)*

The marginal teacher must also be afforded a reasonable amount of time to show improvement. The timeline will most likely be different in each situation, and perhaps for each identified goal. In setting timelines for improvement, one must balance the teacher's right to substantial time for remediation with the children's right to high-quality instruction. Typically, timelines for improvement require substantive improvement within a year for teachers who have received a rating of needs improvement and within one semester for teachers who have already received an unsatisfactory rating. If the desired results toward the stated improvement targets do not occur within this time frame, the administrator must take steps to remove the teacher from the classroom. Note that action leading to removal for incompetence can only occur as an outgrowth of an unsuccessful assistance plan.

The goal of intensive assistance is always successful remediation. The research literature does provide evidence that remediation can be successful. In one research study, principals reported that half of the teachers identified as marginal or incompetent improved after participating in a remedial process (Tucker, 2001). Although the principal and support team members work conscientiously to help the teacher improve, the teacher is likely not to recognize that the intent is to be helpful. More often than not, the emotional relationships are quite strained and difficult during the intensive assistance process. Bridges (1992) notes that attempts to "salvage" the marginal teacher are likely to be met with unmerited criticism, defensiveness, antagonism, and a refusal to accept responsibility for shortcomings. The teacher often places the blame for poor performance externally, that is, on teaching conditions, resources, or even the students. Bridges suggests that in responding to such behavior, administrators and support team members acknowledge the teachers' negative feelings but focus on the behaviors needed to bring about improved performance. Figure 11.4 gives an example of an intensive assistance plan a supervisory team might develop to work with Mr. Matthews.

**FIGURE 11.4** Sample Intensive Assistance Plan for the Marginal Teacher

**Purpose**  To provide assistance and support to Mr. Matthews, a 10th-grade social studies teacher with 15 years experience, so that he will attain a satisfactory summative rating.

**Team Members and Roles**  Building principal from building X, one teacher selected by Mr. Matthews, one teacher selected by the building principal. The administrator will conduct two formal observations each semester, preceded by a preobservation conference, and will provide feedback after each visit to help Mr. Matthews improve. In addition, he will conduct informal observations and may be requested by Mr. Matthews to conduct additional formal observations. The teachers will be available to conduct peer-coaching cycles with Mr. Matthews. Mr. Matthews and the coaches will arrange the number of observation cycles. Mr. Matthews may also observe the two teachers during his planning periods.

*Improvement Targets*

    A. To incorporate at least one but ideally two student-centered instructional strategies into each 50-min lesson.

    B. To use proximity to improve student engagement by circulating throughout the classroom to monitor student behavior and individual learning progress.

    C. To make maximum use of allocated learning time.

    D. To deal consistently with inappropriate student behavior (e.g., inattentiveness) through nonverbal and verbal interventions and logical consequences if needed.

*Timeline of Activities*

| | |
|---|---|
| A. Summer | Attend at least two workshops on differentiated instruction and classroom management, offered as part of the district's Summer Professional Development Institute. Identification of support team members and development of intensive assistance plan. |
| B. August | Intensive assistance planning meeting with Mr. Matthews. |
| C. September | Journal readings and recommended web sites on differentiated instruction provided to Mr. Matthews. He is asked to review his summer professional development notes and materials and combine them with this new information to craft lesson plans. |
| D. October | First semester support team observations by administrator and teachers begin. |
| E. December | Review of Mr. Matthew's artifacts collected to support growth toward the standards as well as all data related to the administrative classroom observations. Meeting with Mr. Matthews to review progress to date and to plan interventions for the second semester. A revised assistance plan timeline for the second semester will be developed at that time. Observations by administrators and teachers will continue throughout the second semester. |
| F. May | All observations will end by May 1. Mr. Matthews will provide portfolio with additional data sources to the building principal by that date. |
| G. June 1 | A summative evaluation conference will be held between Mr. Matthews and the building principal. If Mr. Matthews achieves a Level 1 rating on all standards, he will receive a satisfactory summative rating and return to the regular supervision and evaluation process. If Mr. Matthews does not receive a Level 1 rating in all areas, he will receive an unsatisfactory rating and may be dismissed. |

It is imperative that the assistance plan become part of the district's file documenting the teacher's performance and the district's attempts to help him or her. It is also imperative that the district document all activities intended to help the teacher improve that take place during the course of the year (e.g., observations, workshops, provision of materials). This documentation will be an important aspect of proving that the teacher was granted due process rights if it becomes necessary to dismiss him or her.

**EXERCISE 11.2    Assisting Mr. Matthews**

Form a group with three other people. Assume that each of you is a principal (not Mr. Matthews' building principal) who is responsible for working on the intensive support team with Mr. Matthews to achieve the goals listed in the assistance plan. Each member of the group should choose one assistance plan job target (A–D) and identify at least two types of *observational* data you could collect to document his teaching performance in that goal area. Also identify any resources that you are aware of that might help Mr. Matthews to improve his performance on that specific job target.

Given this understanding of the key components of the supervision process, we now turn back to the process for summatively evaluating the marginal teacher's performance.

# EVALUATION OF THE MARGINAL TEACHER

Evaluation of the marginal teacher, like supervision, differs in several respects from the process for veteran teachers who are performing well. Although standards for effective performance remain consistent and similar data sources are available for use in the process, the legal issues involved in the process as well as the teacher's demonstrated difficulty in making appropriate instructional decisions make it imperative that the administrators play a much greater role in directing the evaluation process. Data collection for evaluation purposes is directed entirely by the administrative team and focuses on the deficiencies that caused the teacher to be placed in the intensive assistance mode of the evaluation system. The outcome of the evaluation process is a return to satisfactory performance status or potential dismissal from teaching.

## Roles and Data Sources

Some systems of supervision and evaluation place the responsibility for summative evaluation of the marginal teacher solely on the shoulders of the building principal. We believe that is an unwise arrangement. In Chapter 10, we made the case that the decision to grant tenure to a novice teacher was so important that the responsibility for it should be shared by an administrative team, instead of belonging to the building principal alone. Clearly, the decision to rate a teacher as unsatisfactory and move for dismissal is just as important as the tenure decision. Using a team approach accomplishes multiple goals. First, it increases the confidence of the administrator when the time comes to make that critical decision. Second, it provides an opportunity to collect a great deal more observational data that can be used to help the teacher improve as well as to document the validity of a decision to rate the teacher as unsatisfactory. If dismissal is the ultimate course of action, the argument that the decision was based on the whims of a single individual cannot be made. Finally, it demonstrates that the district has taken the issue of consistency of evaluation ratings across administrators very seriously. We suggest that the administrative evaluation team consist of the building principal and a central office administrator, either the assistant superintendent or the superintendent. As noted earlier, it is best to avoid having administrators responsible for summative evaluation serve as the administrator on the intensive support team if at all possible.

The primary data source for making judgments about the teacher's performance is the observations made by the administrators, augmented by a portfolio of other data sources. The two evaluators focus their attention on gathering observation data primarily on the problem areas identified in the initial notice of deficiency. They may also collect data concerning any other aspect of classroom teaching performance related to the district's evaluation standards. In addition, they direct the teacher to collect other types of evaluation data that can be used to make a judgment about the teacher's level of improvement. These data may include video-taped lessons, teacher artifacts, student artifacts, and information on student learning.

The role of the marginal teacher in the summative evaluation process is reduced significantly. The teacher's primary role is to participate in the observation process. Although the teacher also assembles all nonobservation data into a portfolio that is given to the administrative team, it is the administrators, not the teacher, who decide what data should be collected for the portfolio. In addition to the data specified by the administrative team, the teacher may include in the portfolio other data that he or she feels will help to demonstrate improvement. Observational data collected by teachers on the intensive assistance support team do not become part of the evaluation material unless the teacher chooses to include them. Observations conducted by teacher colleagues are purely for assistance.

Students, parents, and other stakeholders do not play a role in the evaluation process unless the administrative team decides that collecting such data is necessary in making an accurate judgment about the teacher's performance. When a district has decided that a teacher's performance is marginal or unsatisfactory, it is no longer necessary to ask for input from other stakeholders. This is the point where the expertise of professionals must come to the forefront in helping the teacher to improve and in making decisions about whether improvement is sufficient in order to allow the teacher to continue teaching. Data from other stakeholders can be useful in pointing out the existence of problems in teacher performance, but they are typically not very helpful in remediating the problems or in making the summative evaluation decision.

## Evaluation Standards

Although the evaluation standards remain the same as those used with all other teachers, the criteria for attaining a satisfactory summative evaluation rating are different. In order to attain a satisfactory rating, the marginal teacher must receive a Level 1 rating ("Evidence is clear that the standard is met") on all standards. As discussed in Chapter 8, a veteran teacher whose performance is satisfactory or beyond may receive a Level 2 rating ("Evidence is not clear concerning whether the standard is met") in one standard and still receive a satisfactory summative rating. The deficiency notice that is provided to the marginal teacher when he or she is placed into the intensive assistance mode makes clear that only a Level 1 rating will lead to a satisfactory summative rating. A Level 2 or Level 3 rating on any standard leads to an unsatisfactory rating.

## Evaluation Procedures

The evaluation process actually begins with the meeting between the building principal and the marginal teacher that follows receipt of the notice of deficiency or the superintendent's ruling on the teacher's appeal. In this meeting, the principal explains the evaluation process that will be employed by the principal and the central office administrator. Prior to or during the first week of school, the principal and teacher meet again to discuss specific aspects of the evaluation process. The principal explains that the two administrators will each be observing once a month, focusing their data collection on the evaluation standards in which deficiencies were noted but also including any other pertinent observation data. The observations will be a combination of announced and unannounced visits in order to capture both optimal and typical teacher performance. In addition, the principal directs the teacher to begin collecting nonobservational data that will be included in the teacher's end-of-the-year evaluation portfolio. Exercise 11.3 provides practice in directing portfolio work.

**EXERCISE 11.3    Collecting Data on Mr. Matthews**

Return to the case of Mr. Matthews. Assume that he has been assigned to the intensive assistance mode of supervision and evaluation and that you are his building principal. Given the deficiencies noted in his performance and the four improvement targets, what *nonobservational* data would you direct him to collect for inclusion in his evaluation portfolio? Why? Meet with a partner to discuss and defend your choices. In your discussion, explain exactly what evidence you would need to see to be convinced that Mr. Matthews had really improved.

In contrast to observations conducted as part of the intensive assistance process, evaluative observations of the marginal teacher are not preceded by preobservation conferences. The goal of data collection is clear to both the teacher and the administrators, and the task of helping the teacher rehearse and think through lessons more appropriately is being carried out by the intensive support team.

Each evaluative observation is followed by a postobservation conference. The purpose of the postobservation conference is to provide the teacher with concrete feedback on his or her improvement or lack of improvement in the deficiency areas. The administrators take a directive role in the conference by explaining their interpretation of what they have observed as well as the subsequent actions that should be taken by the teacher. When improvements have been made, they provide positive reinforcement and suggest additional specific steps that will be needed to meet the improvement targets. When no improvement is evident, they redirect the teacher's attention to the improvement targets as well as the timeline that has been set.

Following the conference, the administrator completes a written summary of the observation that characterizes the improvement or lack of improvement, specifies steps to be taken, and summarizes the discussion during the postobservation conference. The teacher and both administrators receive a copy of the summary, and a copy is placed in the teacher's personnel folder.

At the end of the evaluation period (either a semester for a teacher previously rated as unsatisfactory or a year for a teacher previously rated as needing improvement), the administrators compile all the observation data and conference summaries as well as the portfolio produced by the teacher. These data become the foundation for the subsequent summative evaluation decision. We suggest that both administrators read through all of the data and rate the teacher's performance independently, and then meet to compare notes and complete the summative evaluation form together. Obviously, when the two administrators agree that improvement has occurred or has not occurred, the summative evaluation is easier to complete. A clear decision can be made whether to return the teacher to satisfactory status or to rate the teacher unsatisfactory and move for dismissal (if the teacher has received a previous unsatisfactory rating).

When the two cannot come to an agreement, the wisest course of action is probably to continue in the intensive assistance mode for the following year. We suggest that other administrators in the district review the decision reached by the two administrators on the evaluation team before the decision is announced to the teacher. This strategy not only makes it more likely that an accurate decision will be reached, but also gives the administrators an opportunity to "get on the same page" in terms of how they interpret evaluation data. It is particularly critical that the superintendent and the district solicitor be well informed and concur with any decision to seek dismissal of a teacher. If they are not clearly supportive of a dismissal decision, it is better to continue providing intensive assistance and perhaps to try to induce the teacher's exit through one of the mechanisms discussed below.

**FIGURE 11.5** Notice of Return to Satisfactory Status

---

Dear Mr. Matthews,

As discussed in our summative evaluation conference on May 28th, you have received Level 1 ratings in all eight district evaluation standards for this school year and have received a satisfactory summative evaluation. Congratulations! As a result of your improvement in performance, you will be allowed to return to the supervisory options of our supervision and evaluation system for the next school year. You will need to inform me in writing by the beginning of the next school year whether you will participate in classroom observation, peer coaching, self-directed development, action research, or a collegial development group. Your next formal evaluation will occur in 3 years, but as you know, it is appropriate to begin gathering data for your portfolio at any time. I look forward to working with you in the future and helping you to become an even more effective teacher.

---

**FIGURE 11.6** Notice of Unsatisfactory Rating

---

Dear Mr. Matthews,

As you are aware as a result of our summative evaluation conference held on May 28th, your teaching performance has resulted in an unsatisfactory summative rating for this school year. The unsatisfactory rating is based on your inability, despite substantial and ongoing attempts to help you improve your performance, to meet Standard 3 ("The teacher uses a wide variety of instructional strategies to engage students in learning and promote deep understanding of content") and Standard 5 ("The teacher creates a positive classroom climate that is well organized and conducive to student learning and manages student behavior effectively") of the district's evaluation policy.

(*For first unsatisfactory*) Issuance of this unsatisfactory rating means that you will continue in the district's intensive assistance mode of evaluation for the next school year. Failure to attain a satisfactory rating by the end of the first semester (January 27th) will result in issuance of a second unsatisfactory rating and a recommendation for your dismissal from this school district.

(*For second unsatisfactory*) As this marks your second consecutive unsatisfactory rating, I am recommending that you be dismissed from this school district.

As mandated in the collective bargaining agreement between the school district and the teacher's association, you have 7 days from receipt of this letter to appeal this rating to the Superintendent of Schools.

---

The summative evaluation rating is announced to the teacher in a conference with the building principal and also communicated in writing. If the evaluation is satisfactory, the teacher returns to the supervision options for the following year. If the decision is unsatisfactory, either the teacher continues in the intensive assistance mode or the district moves for dismissal. Examples of written notices of a satisfactory rating and an unsatisfactory rating are provided in Figures 11.5 and 11.6.

# WHEN REMEDIATION DOES NOT WORK: REMOVING THE MARGINAL TEACHER

If the intensive assistance process is successful and the teacher returns to satisfactory status, everyone can rejoice because the hard work paid off. If, on the contrary, the marginal teacher's performance does not improve despite significant attempts to provide assistance, the principal and other administrators are left with the gut-wrenching decision of what to do next.

## Responses to Continued Unsatisfactory Performance

When remediation is unsuccessful, Bridges (1992) identifies three alternative paths that school districts take in dealing with incompetent teachers: (1) tolerance and protection; (2) induced exit; or (3) dismissal. We believe strongly that removing the teacher from the classroom, that is, from teaching children, should be the district's primary goal. All too often, the option taken, in education and elsewhere, is that of tolerance and protection. "In a study of Fortune 500 companies, the flagships of American business and industry, 97 percent of responding administrators indicated that they were currently supervising an incompetent subordinate. Moreover, the most common response to this problem in all professions, organizations, and societies is to tolerate and protect the inept" (Bridges, 1992, p. 19). Administrators tolerate incompetence because they fear the costs of dismissing veteran teachers, because they are afraid that the evaluation criteria are not clear or strong enough to support dismissal, and because they have a natural desire to avoid conflict and hostility (Bridges, 1992).

Strategies for protecting incompetents include repeatedly moving the teacher from one grade level to another or from one building to another and assigning the teacher to those students whose parents seem least likely to complain about an ineffective teacher. Kaye labels this type of response as a compensatory response and includes the strategy of assigning the teacher to smaller classes and to classes with fewer students who have special needs (2004). Factors that lessen this tendency to protect incompetent teachers include small school size (there are not as many places to move the teacher), parental complaints, and a high value attached to teacher evaluation by the school board and superintendent (Bridges, 1992). Our position is that protection of incompetent teachers is immoral because it damages children. Though tolerating incompetence may be less stressful psychologically, accepting a position that includes evaluating teacher performance implies accepting the responsibility for removing incompetent teachers.

The second alternative, inducing the teacher's exit from the profession, can be carried out in various ways (Bridges, 1992). Administrators can apply indirect pressure by changing the teacher's working conditions to make work life less attractive for the teacher. Incompetent teachers may be assigned to the least desirable school buildings and to teach the least desirable subjects or students. The morality of this strategy can certainly be questioned as the students who need the most support may end up with the worst teachers. The incompetent teachers may also end up with the least desirable extra duties. They may find that their requests for supplies are frequently denied or that they end up with the least desirable teaching schedule in terms of when extra duties and planning periods occur. All of these factors may convince the teacher that it is time to go elsewhere.

Pressure to induce exit may also be much more direct. According to Bridges (1992), the usual progression in communication between the building principal and the incompetent teacher goes from gentle persuasion to improve, to increased negative feedback, to threats of an unsatisfactory evaluation, to an actual unsatisfactory rating, followed by counseling that it is time to get out of the profession before the administrator has no choice but to move for dismissal. Other forms of direct pressure include written reprimands that are placed in the teacher's personnel file and suspension of the teacher without pay (Owen, 1999). Often indirect and direct pressure are applied in tandem.

Some districts even enter into negotiations to induce the incompetent teacher to leave the district (Bridges, 1992). For example, the school district may offer the teacher a sabbatical leave with the understanding that the teacher will then leave the district without returning for the customary year required to pay back the sabbatical. The district may also agree to pay the teacher's fringe benefits (e.g., health care) or to allow the teacher to continue participating in the district's group fringe benefit plans for a specified period of time after the teacher has left the district. Some districts have even made one-time cash payments to encourage the incompetent teacher to leave. Although most people see teachers' unions as protecting incompetent teachers, Bridges asserts that the evidence relating to exit inducement indicates that the union is often a partner in applying subtle pressure to get the teacher to accept the recommendation to resign voluntarily (1992). The issue of teacher reaction to marginal and incompetent teaching is rather complex.

Kaye (2004) studied the perceptions of veteran teachers toward marginal teachers through surveys and interviews. The teachers in this Canadian sample identified three different types of marginal teachers. Kaye labeled the three types as flotsam, jetsam, and club med marginal teachers. Flotsam marginal teachers (a nautical term that refers to items lost by shipwreck and found floating at sea) were viewed as temporarily marginal because they were either new to the profession or teaching a new context. Teachers felt that this was a very hopeful situation in which intensive assistance would work. Jetsam marginal teachers (a nautical term that refers to items thrown overboard and abandoned at a time of danger) were viewed as teachers who become increasingly discouraged and unmotivated over time due to a constant stream of new innovation and demands. They have the skills to be competent but are tired and lacking motivation. Teachers tended to view this type of marginal teaching very sympathetically. Counseling was seen as the appropriate type of intervention. Club med marginal teachers were those who made a career of marginal teaching and who did not have the skills to be effective but were not even aware that they lacked the skills. They appeared to be in it just for the money or the security. Teachers advocated strong disciplinary reactions to this type of incompetence.

All of these attempts at inducement are intended to protect children from harm, to allow the teacher to save face, and to protect the district from involvement in a protracted court battle that could prove costly and whose outcome is not certain. Based on his extensive personal experience in working with teacher dismissal cases, Mr. Don Owen, a lawyer with the Pennsylvania School Boards Association, estimates that for every teacher dismissal that goes through the hearing process, there are approximately 10 resignations through induced exits (Owen, 1999).

The third option available to the school district is to seek the dismissal of the veteran teacher. Dismissing a veteran teacher is not a pleasant experience for anyone. It is emotionally and fiscally draining for all parties involved. Some administrators are reluctant to move for dismissal because they have heard horror stories of dismissal attempts that have been extremely costly and have been eventually overturned by the courts because of some minor procedural error. As a result, the evidence seems to indicate that dismissing the veteran teacher is the alternative least likely to be employed. "Despite conservative estimates that 5 percent of teachers are incompetent, the termination rate, which includes resignations, dismissals of tenured teachers and non-renewal of probationary teachers, is less than 1 percent" (Tucker, 2001, p. 52). Is this fear of dismissal warranted? Experts who have followed dismissal proceedings through the courts suggest that it is not.

> *The legal boundaries for performance evaluation of professional educators in the public schools, especially those drawn by the courts in the substantial spaces left open by state statutes and regulations, are much broader than are realized by the typical evaluator or evaluatee. Both often confuse the pertinent law with the professional lore. Rather than feeling fearful or hamstrung by the rulings of state and federal courts, school officials should focus on doing the right thing. (Zirkel, 1996, p. 18)*

Moreover, Strike and Bull (1981) note, "In our judgment, the legendary impossibility of dismissing a tenured teacher is much exaggerated. The causes of dismissal specified in most state statutes provide sufficient latitude for any plausible charge. The procedural requirements usually require care, patience, and perhaps courage. They are far, however, from unexecutable" (p. 323). If the district has a clear set of evaluation standards that are applied regularly, has sufficient (you can never have too much) documentation of the deficiencies noted in the teacher's performance, has provided the teacher with notice of the deficiencies as well as significant attempts at improvement, and has accorded the teacher the appropriate due process procedures, the chances of losing a dismissal case are quite slim. "Case law, in reference to all reasons for teacher dismissal, indicates that a school board's decision to terminate a professional employee is upheld the vast majority of the time by the state department of education and the appropriate courts" (Owen, 1999, p. 2). This evidence should provide any administrative team the courage it needs to protect children from incompetent teachers by moving for dismissal when attempts at remediation do not work.

## Crossing the Legal Ts and Dotting the Legal Is

As noted above, courts have typically allowed school districts great latitude in terms of professional judgment concerning the substantive reasons for dismissing a tenured teacher. As long as the district has reasonable standards for competent performance and clear documentation that the teacher has failed to meet the standards, the substantive aspects of dismissal should not be a problem.

The procedural aspects of dismissal are a different story. Courts generally keep a very close watch on the procedural aspects of due process. The school district must not only safeguard the teacher's rights to due process, but also document the fact that it has done so. Thus, documentation for dismissal takes two forms, documentation of deficiencies in performance and documentation of the procedural safeguarding of due process rights.

It is important to keep copies of the initial deficiency notice, of all subsequent correspondence with the teacher including summaries of all conferences and meetings, of the intensive assistance plan, of all summative evaluation ratings, and of all notifications of unsatisfactory ratings and the recommendation for dismissal. In most systems, the building principal is responsible for making sure that all of this documentation is available. Once the recommendation for dismissal has been made, materials are typically turned over to the superintendent and the school district solicitor, who oversee the dismissal proceedings. The principal then assumes the role of witness against the teacher in the actual dismissal hearing. Figure 11.7 gives a set of 10 questions adapted from Lawrence (2005) that the district must be able to answer in the affirmative in order to demonstrate that the teacher's due process rights have been protected by the evaluation process. An administrator who can answer all of these questions affirmatively should feel confident in moving for dismissal.

**FIGURE 11.7**   Due Process Rights Questions

1. Was the process for evaluation made clear to all teachers?
2. Was the process applied consistently to all teachers?
3. Was the teacher in question treated the same as other teachers and not singled out?
4. Did evaluation data include all aspects of the teacher's performance?
5. Is there a continuous and accurately dated record of all meetings and conferences with the teacher?
6. Did the teacher receive written notice of deficiency specifying exact concerns?
7. Did the teacher receive a list of specific suggestions for correcting deficiencies and ways to achieve a satisfactory rating?
8. Was an intensive assistance plan established and implemented using district resources?
9. Was the teacher given a reasonable time period to improve his or her teaching performance?
10. Was the teacher informed in writing that failure to achieve an acceptable level of performance would result in an unsatisfactory summative rating?

# CHAPTER SUMMARY

Working with a marginal teacher can be one of the most challenging responsibilities any administrator has to face. The ultimate goal of working with the marginal teacher is to bring about improvement in the teacher's performance. The administrator who works with a marginal teacher is in a paradoxical situation in that he or she must operate as if the deficiencies are amenable to remediation and will be corrected, but must simultaneously keep one eye on the legal requirements that will come into play if improvement does not occur and the teacher must be dismissed.

The initial step in working with the marginal teacher is notification of the specific deficiencies that led to the low summative evaluation and placement in the intensive assistance mode of supervision and evaluation. The principal must be clear, direct, and precise in setting benchmarks or goals for improvement within a prescribed time frame. Marginal teachers often benefit from a team approach to remediation and an intensive assistance plan that includes goals, strategies for attaining those goals, and some form of professional development to help the marginal teacher acquire necessary knowledge and skills. The intensive support team is directive in working with the teacher. Team members collect data, model data interpretation, identify changes required in the teacher's behavior, and follow up to ensure that the prescribed changes occur.

Administrators exercise more control over the evaluation of marginal teachers than that of other veteran teachers. The building principal and central office administrator work together to collect observation data concerning the teacher's performance. The teacher is directed by the administrators to collect other types of data for inclusion in a summative evaluation portfolio. Based on the observations and the portfolio, the administrative team decides whether sufficient improvement has occurred and the teacher has regained satisfactory evaluation status. If improvement is not observed, the teacher receives an unsatisfactory rating. Consecutive unsatisfactory ratings lead to dismissal of the teacher.

Though many school districts fear that teacher dismissal will be too costly and difficult to execute, the evidence indicates that the courts allow great leeway to school districts in terms of substantive aspects of teacher dismissal. Because the courts are very watchful in terms of the teacher's right to due process, following established due process procedures and documenting their existence is especially important. In addition to possessing skills for effective supervision and evaluation, administrators responsible for teacher evaluation must have a clear understanding of the legal ramifications of working with a marginal teacher.

# DISCUSSION QUESTIONS

**1.** Review the ideas that you and your partner generated concerning the initial case study of Mr. Matthews in Exercise 11.1. Then revisit the intensive assistance plan provided for him in Figure 11.4. Compare the plan you developed with the one suggested in Figure 11.4. How are the plans similar? How are they different? What accounts for the differences between the two? Do you think each plan would help Mr. Matthews improve? Why or why not?

**2.** Marginal teachers must be given a reasonable period of time to improve their performance. What factors would you take into consideration in deciding what a reasonable time period for improvement would be?

**3.** Assume that you have just accepted the assignment as the principal of a building in a new school district.

Will you read the summative evaluations of the teachers completed by the previous principal? Why or why not? If you do read them, in what ways, if at all, will they factor into how you assess teachers' performance during the coming year? Explain?

**4.** Are there any conditions or factors that would lead you to adopt the strategy of tolerating or protecting an incompetent teacher? If so, what are they and why do they justify your strategy? If not, why do you think so many other administrators in a variety of occupations choose to do so?

**5.** Many individuals argue that teacher tenure protects incompetent teachers. What are the advantages and disadvantages of teacher tenure? Do you support teacher tenure? Explain?

# THEORY-INTO-PRACTICE APPLICATIONS

**1.** Check your school district's teacher supervision and evaluation plan. Is there any mention of remediation for teachers who are assessed as marginal? If there is a remediation component, share this plan with the class and identify its strengths and weaknesses. Share your analysis with your district.

**2.** Identify a school principal or administrator who has worked with a marginal teacher to successfully remediate that teacher's performance. Without asking him or her to divulge confidential information, interview him or her about the process. In the interview investigate topics including the following: the factors that led to the marginal rating; the supervision and evaluation procedures used; the assistance provided to the teacher; the improvements that the teacher made; and the emotional aspects of the process.

**3.** If possible, identify a school administrator who has successfully dismissed a teacher on the basis of incompetent performance. Without asking him or her

to divulge confidential information, interview him or her about the process. In the interview include questions on the initial unsatisfactory rating, what was done to assist the teacher, what documentation was used to make the decision to dismiss the teacher, the actual dismissal hearing, and the emotional aspects of the entire process. Be sure to ask whether from the administrator's view the process was worth it or not.

**4.** With two or three colleagues conduct an Internet search using the term "teacher dismissal." How many of the references you found deal with dismissal for reasons of teaching incompetence versus dismissals for other reasons? What conclusions can you draw from this? How much of the focus in the resources is on legal aspects of dismissal as compared to ethical, personal, school culture, or other aspects of process? Why is this the case? What could be done, if anything, to change the tenor of the conversation so that legal issues do not occupy the most prominent role?

# REFERENCES

BRIDGES, E. (1992). *The incompetent teacher: Managerial responses.* Philadelphia, PA: The Falmer Press.

DANIELSON, C., & McGREAL, T. L. (2000). *Teacher evaluation to enhance professional practice.* Alexandria and Princeton: ASCD and ETS.

GOOD, T., & BROPHY, J. (2007). *Looking in classrooms (9th ed.)* New York: Addison, Wesley & Longman.

HAZI, H. M. (1998). Policy and legal considerations in supervision. In G. R. Firth & E. F. Pajak (Eds.), *Handbook of research on school supervision.* New York: Macmillan.

KAYE, E. B. (2004). Turning the tide on marginal teaching. *Journal of Curriculum and Supervision, 19*(3), 324–358.

LAWRENCE, C. E. (2005). *The marginal teacher: A step-by-step guide to fair procedures for identification and dismissal, (3rd ed.).* Thousand Oaks, CA: Corwin Press.

OWEN, D. (1999). *The four Ds: Documentation, discipline, demotion, and dismissal.* New Cumberland, PA: Pennsylvania School Boards Association [Workshop handout]

RATHS, J., & LYMAN, F. (2003). Summative evaluation of student teachers. *Journal of Teacher Education, 54*(3), 206–216.

STRIKE, K., & BULL, B. (1981). Fairness and the legal context of teacher evaluation. In J. Millman (Ed.), *Handbook of teacher evaluation.* Beverly Hills, CA: Sage Publications.

TUCKER, P. (2001). Helping struggling teachers. *Educational Leadership, 58*(5), 52–55.

ZIRKEL, P. (1996). *The law of teacher evaluation: A self-assessment handbook.* Bloomington, IN: Phi Delta Kappa.

# SUGGESTIONS FOR FURTHER READING AND RESEARCH

ANDERSON, L., & PELICAN, L. (2001) *Teacher peer assistance and review: A practical guide for teachers and administrators.* Thousand Oaks, CA: Corwin Press.

McGRATH, M. J. (2000). The human dynamics of personnel evaluation. *The School Administrator, 9*(57), 34–38.

PAINTER, S. R. (2000). Easing dismissals and non-renewals. *The School Administrator, 9*(57), 40–43.

TUCKER, P. D. (1997). Lake Wobegon: Where all teachers are competent. *Journal of Personnel Evaluation, 11*, 103–126.

# CHAPTER 12

# DEVELOPING YOUR OWN SYSTEM OF TEACHER SUPERVISION AND EVALUATION

**T**HE FINAL chapter of this book serves as a blueprint for combining and translating the conceptual knowledge base and skill development exercises, and applications presented in this book into a fully functioning system of teacher supervision and evaluation. This chapter examines four critical pieces to building the system:

- Collaboration fostered by forming a districtwide task force that represents multiple stakeholders
- A strategic planning process to design a system to match the district's particular needs
- Initial and ongoing professional development during implementation
- Periodic evaluation and revision for implementing and maintaining the system

This chapter offers concrete examples from systems that incorporate separate but complementary processes for teacher supervision and evaluation. Whether your role is that of a teacher or principal who serves as part of such a task force or as a central office administrator or consultant providing expertise to guide a task force in its work, our hope is that by understanding the step-by-step process for building a system, any school district's vision for a high-quality system of teacher supervision and evaluation can become a reality.

## GUIDING QUESTIONS FOR PREREADING AND JOURNALING

- Based on your reading and understanding of this text, describe what you might anticipate as your first steps in developing a high-quality system of supervision and evaluation.
- What are the resources (fiscal, personnel, commitment of time, etc.) that would you view as necessary to the process of creating and implementing a coherent supervision and evaluation system?
- Think about any questions that remain unanswered for you as you contemplate translating your conceptual understanding of supervision and evaluation into practice.

# INITIATING THE PROCESS: FORMING A TASK FORCE TO INVESTIGATE SUPERVISION AND EVALUATION

According to Standard 1.2 of the Educational Leadership Constituent Council (see Appendix B), administrators should possess knowledge and ability to develop, articulate, and communicate a shared vision through data-based research and strategic planning processes. In keeping with this standard, the first step toward creating a strategic plan for an effective supervision and evaluation system is to ensure that it is a cooperative effort blending together the voices of all stakeholders.

As a starting point, we recommend the formation of a supervision and evaluation task force comprised of participants from key constituencies. The stakeholder groups may vary depending upon the district's size and culture, but the task force should in any case include board members as representatives of the community, central office personnel, administrators, supervisors, union leaders, and teachers from a wide variety of buildings, grade levels, and subject or specialty areas.

In districts with strong unions, teacher representation is particularly crucial to the success of any change in evaluation procedures. In fact, without the support of union leadership, proposed revisions to supervision and evaluation systems are frequently stalled in the planning process. Several of the districts with which we worked actively involved the union from the onset by asking its president to select one teacher per building to serve on the task force and to personally participate as well. Additionally, the faculty in each school nominated and voted for a second teacher representative to voice building concerns to the task force.

Once membership is decided, the task force needs to select facilitators to direct the process and set a schedule of task force meetings. Again, in the spirit of collaboration, we advocate co-chairpersons representing administration and teachers. As the task force begins its work, it needs to consider some key questions such as those listed in Figure 12.1.

**FIGURE 12.1** General Questions for the Task Force to Consider

1. Why are we engaged in reviewing, researching, and revising our present supervision and evaluation system? Is it a top-down mandate, a grass roots effort, or a combination of both? What are the long-term vision and the goals of our work?

2. What role are task force members expected to play? How will we function as a group? How will we make decisions?

3. How effective is our current system of supervision and evaluation? How will we gather evidence concerning its strengths and weaknesses? What data will guide us in our decision making?

4. What is the present organizational climate in the district? Is it conducive to change in supervision and evaluation? Is there evidence of trust and collaboration among the school board, administration, and teachers, and among teachers themselves, or is a change in climate an end to which the revisions of the supervision and evaluation system could lead?

5. How much knowledge about best practice in teacher supervision and evaluation exists among our task force? How can we go about familiarizing ourselves with the most recent research? What kind of knowledge and skills exist in the district? Do we need the help of an outside consultant to get us started?

6. What additional resources are available to us in our work?

7. What other competing initiatives and change efforts are currently taking place in the district? How might they affect any changes in teacher supervision and evaluation?

8. In view of the organizational climate and competing initiatives, is the time right for us to devise and implement a revised supervision and evaluation system or should we temporarily delay the process?

We suggest that the task force begin with an overview of its goals and roles (questions 1 and 2). After laying the initial groundwork, the task force can then enter an awareness phase in which it searches for answers to questions 3, 4, 5, and 6.

The task force members begin by familiarizing themselves with the processes and procedures of the supervision and evaluation system currently in practice. This familiarization should include a document analysis of the written policy, with all the accompanying forms and requisite paperwork. Another aspect of awareness is to uncover the perceived strengths and weaknesses of the existing system, including climate. That task can be accomplished through designing and administering a needs assessment or self-study survey. Although the scope of the assessment can vary, we suggest dissemination of surveys to all administrators and faculty. Depending on the size of the district and the results of the data collected and analyzed from the initial survey, the leadership team might also conduct informal interviews or lead focus groups to elicit more specific feedback.

Data collected through the needs assessment drives the second phase of the process. In Figure 12.2, we offer questions a task force might use as they begin to construct a needs assessment instrument. Our questions can be revised and other questions can be added to tailor the survey to the specific needs and challenges of the individual district.

**FIGURE 12.2** Sample Items to Include in a Districtwide Needs Assessment Survey

---

**Directions** For each question, choose from these four responses:
(a) clearly evident, (b) somewhat evident, (c) not evident, and (d) uncertain.

*Category I*
District leadership, specifically the role and the commitment of central office personnel in communicating about and implementing the current supervision and evaluation system
1. Central office personnel clearly articulate the system's various goals, processes, and procedures in discussions with administrators and teachers.
2. Central office personnel allocate adequate resources for maintaining and assessing the system.
3. Central office personnel periodically collect data to provide feedback for evaluating the system.
4. The supervision and evaluation system is integrated with and supported by ongoing professional development efforts.

*Category II*
Operational and internal consistency, including the degree to which administrators consistently implement the written policy among teachers and across buildings
5. A written policy exists to describe the supervision and evaluation system, including underlying values, functions, roles, and processes.
6. The procedures and paperwork used for supervision and evaluation are consistent with the written policy.
7. The written policy is operationalized consistently among personnel and across buildings.

*Category III*
Organizational climate in the district
8. For the most part, the relationship between administrators and teachers is based on trust, mutual respect, and support.
9. The function of supervision encourages inquiry, reflection, risk taking, and continuous growth in a nonthreatening environment.
10. Opportunities exist for teachers and administrators to work in collaboration with one another.
11. Professional development opportunities provide teachers with the knowledge, skills, and choices to take an active role in a supervisory option that meets individualized needs.

12. The evaluation process makes expectations and criteria for satisfactory performance clear.

*Category IV*
Shared understanding by the multiple stakeholders as they reflect upon their philosophy and experiences

13. The various stakeholders have a voice and feel a sense of ownership in the teacher supervision and evaluation system.

14. Teachers and administrators alike can articulate the differences in processes used to supervise and processes used to evaluate.

15. Teachers and administrators alike can describe the procedures used for novice, experienced, and marginal teachers.

16. Teachers and administrators alike can explain the connections among the district's supervision and evaluation system, professional development efforts, teacher growth, and improved student learning.

Adapted from the work of the Supervision Committee of the Pennsylvania Association of Supervision and Curriculum Development, 1995.

Although needs assessment data are being collected and compiled, the team should simultaneously work on increasing its knowledge base. A better knowledge base ensures a shared understanding of current research and best practice. For a start, we recommend some type of formal presentation, attendance at an off-site workshop, or a mini retreat that provides an overview of the knowledge base. This learning process may be facilitated by an outside consultant; knowledgeable resource persons within the district; an educational association such as the Association for Supervision and Curriculum Development, which offers professional development opportunities; or by the task force members' own work reading and researching supervision and evaluation. Selected pedagogy from this textbook or any of the sources provided in each chapter's culminating reference section, "Suggestions for Further Reading and Research," can provide the knowledge and skills for thoughtful reflection and discussion.

Based on their data from the assessment of the current system and a newly updated understanding of the knowledge base, the task force is ready to tackle the final two guiding questions about the impact of competing initiatives and organizational climate. It is critical for the task force to pause at this point in their work and take stock of what they have learned through their initial investigation. Before moving forward, the task force must make an informed decision as to whether the time is right for change. The anticipated scope of the system revisions will play a major role in the decision whether to proceed. Exercise 12.1 suggests a method for examining whether the time is right for designing and implementing a new supervision and evaluation system.

Depending on the results of the data obtained, the task force may choose to confine its work to improving some specific aspect of an already good system of supervision or evaluation. For example, if the data indicate that the system is generally sound but that the organizational climate fails to sufficiently honor individual differences and preferences in teachers' learning styles, then the task force can focus on strengthening the supervision function by adding supervisory options for experienced teachers. Clearly, because this narrowed focus on one component of the system is much less complex and time consuming, the task force may not need to be overly concerned with competing initiatives.

If, however, the data awareness phase leads the task force to a decision to create a new system, climate and competing initiatives play a far more important role. For example, if the data collected during the awareness phase indicate that teachers are extremely frustrated by stalled contract negotiations, or if several competing initiatives are causing teachers and/or administrators to feel overextended, the task force may find it preferable to

**EXERCISE 12.1**  "Four Hats" Activity for a Supervision and Evaluation Task Force

**Directions**  This activity is especially helpful for a group considering any change effort. First, write the central question for consideration on a large sheet of poster paper for all to see and ponder. In this case the question is, "Is the time right for us to devise and implement a revised supervision and evaluation system?" Second, divide the task force members into four smaller subgroups. Assign each subgroup a hat color. Each subgroup selects a recorder to take notes and a reporter to share its findings with the committee as a whole. Regardless of the personal opinions of the subgroup members, each subgroup looks at the question and reflects on the implications of the change process through its assigned lens (hat color):

- White hat = *data*. Justify the need for the change in reference to needs assessment data and your understanding of the research.
- Yellow hat = *caution*. What are the possible downsides of this proposed change effort? What might present the biggest stumbling block in implementing the change?
- Green hat = *growth*. What are the positive aspects of this proposed change effort? Who might benefit as a result? How could it affect the growth for individuals as well as for the school district?
- Blue hat = *process*. What information will the teachers, administrators, school board, and community members need in order to understand this proposed change? How can we best introduce this idea to the various stakeholder groups?

After each group is given ample time to reflect upon the question through its particular perspective, the reporters will share their subgroups' findings with the whole group and a general discussion will ensue.

Adapted from York-Barr, Sommers, Ghere, & Montie, 2001.

---

temporarily delay their charge. Forging ahead when climate and/or context are not suitable may be counter-productive. The remaining sections of the chapter address this major task of developing and implementing a new system.

# FASHIONING A SYSTEM TO MEET THE DISTRICT'S NEEDS: THE STRATEGIC PLAN

If the leadership team makes an informed decision that the time is right to overhaul the current system, the next step is to collaboratively develop a strategic plan for doing so. A well-crafted strategic plan begins with a platform of clear beliefs as an underlying philosophical rationale that guides the efforts of the task force. This platform is a written statement. The statement clarifies the values on which the supervision and evaluation system will be built, much as our platform of beliefs, articulated in Chapter 2, guided our writing of this textbook. For example, one school district's platform gives the following rationale for including differentiated supervision as part of its system:

> *Differentiated supervision is a process designed to promote continuous improvement in the quality of instruction provided to our students. Since professional employees have varied learning styles, we must be cognizant of these differences if supervision is to be effective. Like educators who individualize programs for their students, a differentiated supervision program provides greater individualized supervision for professional employees by offering various options. Our program is based on the premises that outstanding educators constantly seek professional improvement and that meaningful change must come from within. Most educators, if given the choice, will involve themselves in growth producing experiences based upon their desire for their students to be successful. Differentiated supervision is also effective in*

*addressing the various growth needs of professional employees at different points in
their career. (Southern York County School District's Differentiated Supervision and
Evaluation Plan, 2001)*

Once the platform is in place, the task force must next determine whether to fashion
its own original system, to investigate models and adopt a system that has been tried and
proven elsewhere, or to adapt from several models, revising components to build an eclec-
tic system that takes into account the district's unique strengths, needs, resources, and climate. All three approaches have positive aspects.

Some would argue that creating a system when many models already exist is akin to
reinventing the wheel. They would point out that a tremendous amount of time and energy
is saved by adoption, that is, importing the tenets and procedures of a successfully implemented system that matches their platform of beliefs. Choosing to adopt has the distinct
advantage of learning from others' past mistakes access to all the necessary "trial-tested"
forms and other paperwork is another advantage.

On the contrary, task force members who are in favor of creating a system from the
ground up can counter with the fact that the investment of time and energy is worthwhile
because it fosters collaboration and builds a sense of ownership and shared understanding
among the participants. In their thinking, the *process* becomes as important as the resulting
*policy* because it contributes to professional dialog, community building, and a positive
climate for change.

Thus, perhaps the most beneficial course for districts to follow lies somewhere in
between. To adapt a system is to engage in the slow and deliberate process of designing a
supervision and evaluation plan that meets the needs of their specific context. By exploring, experimenting with, and modifying selected components from a variety of existing
models that share similar platforms, the task force gradually shapes a unique system.

In determining whether to create, adopt, or adapt, the task force might consider the
following questions:

1. In our work, how much of a factor is time? Do we have the time and the resources
   to engage in creating our own system by degrees? Or are our time and resources
   limited?

2. Based on our work uncovering perceptions about the existing climate, how critical to
   the successful implementation of the system is a process for building trust and developing a sense of ownership over time?

3. How and where can we find thriving systems of supervision and evaluation to study?
   Can we conduct site visits? Can we meet with representatives from the various
   stakeholder groups in other districts to learn firsthand about their experiences and to
   discuss the challenges they faced?

If the task force decides to create a new system or adapt a model from several existing
systems, dividing the task force into two separate working subcommittees on evaluation and
supervision would be prudent at this point. As discussed in Chapter 7, the evaluation subcommittee would begin with a review of various sets of performance-based standards or
basic criteria for competent teaching performance. In developing any list of standards, the
subcommittee must be sure that they conform to state guidelines and contractual obligations. After their work on standards, the subcommittee then explores how the procedures
for evaluating novice teachers, competent veteran teachers, and marginal teachers might be
differentiated. Next, the members must agree on some evidence-based system of data collection and compilation so that teachers can demonstrate achievement of those standards.
They also determine a process for summative evaluation. Finally, they consider the resources

needed to implement their evaluation plan. (see Chapter 7 for a specific step-by-step approach that can help guide the evaluation subcommittee).

Meanwhile, the supervision subcommittee can explore various supervisory options, including classroom supervision, peer coaching, self-directed growth, action research, and collegial development groups. In planning for each option, the group should consider the following:

- What are the potential benefits of incorporating this supervisory option into the system?
- What are the potential obstacles to incorporating this supervisory option into the system?
- What expertise and professional development do we need to implement this differentiated supervisory option?
- If we lack in-house the expertise, what resources can we draw on to develop this expertise?
- What roles and responsibilities are assumed by the teachers who choose this option?
- What roles and responsibilities are assumed by the administrators who collaborate with and support the teachers who choose this option?
- What resources will we need to implement the proposed supervisory plan? Are the costs within our budget?

The two subcommittees then report their findings and proposed drafts of the supervisory and evaluative functions. The task force as a whole reviews the reports and makes adjustments to ensure that the two functions fit logically together as one comprehensive system.

Following their work drafting the supervision and evaluation components, the task force completes a long-term strategic plan (Figure 12.3 offers a proposed outline of a strategic plan).

**FIGURE 12.3** Components of a Supervision and Evaluation Strategic Plan

---

1. Clearly written philosophy or platform of beliefs that underlies the system
2. Detailed description of the evidence-based evaluation system
   A. Mutually agreed upon core standards of professional practice
   B. Explanation of the varied tracks for the novice, veteran, and marginal teacher
   C. System for data collection and data compilation
   D. Explanation of the summative evaluation process
   E. Framework for professional development necessary for implementation
3. Detailed description of the available supervisory options
   A. Definitions of all supervisory options and related terms (e.g., self-directed teacher growth, job-embedded learning, individual action plan)
   B. Eligibility for choosing the option
   C. Responsibilities of the teachers and the administrators collaborating within this mode, including a timeline for completion of all tasks
   D. System for record keeping and accountability
   E. Framework for professional development necessary for implementation
4. Timeline for step-by-step implementation of the strategic plan
5. Statement of required resources
6. Plan for collecting data about the quality of the system and for periodic review
7. Appendix with all the forms that will be used

---

In addition to the already existing platform and the proposed drafts of the supervision and evaluation functions, the task force must now decide on an appropriate timeline. Do they implement the system all at once or incrementally? For example, one school district with which we worked revised a system that had previously depended solely on administrative observation (two classroom supervision cycles a year for each tenured faculty member) for both supervising and evaluating teachers. As a result of their needs analysis and research during the awareness phase, the goal of the task force was to separate processes for supervision from those for evaluation. The strategic plan provided the opportunity to promote continuous growth and established an evaluative focused assistance track for assisting new and marginal teachers. The timeline introduced the system incrementally.

During the first year of implementation, the district introduced a small-scale pilot program of peer coaching and self-directed professional growth. The departmental chairpersons (who served as part of the task force) volunteered to attend the necessary training during the summer and become the first group of peer coaches. During year 2 of the strategic plan, the peer-coaching program was carefully expanded. Teachers in the pilot group each shared their experiences with a trusted colleague and invited that colleague to engage in the requisite training to join them as a partner. By the end of second year, this step-by-step introduction to peer coaching had received favorable feedback from the teachers and the administration alike, including teacher union leadership and the district's professional development committee.

At the same time the department chairpersons were engaging in the peer-coaching pilot, the superintendent and two of the principals initiated a parallel pilot program by inviting a small contingent of outstanding teachers to write and implement self-directed professional growth plans. Acceptance in this program was based on a written individualized action plan that in some way linked personalized goal setting with district-identified professional development initiatives and that clearly outlined proposed impact upon student learning.

During the third year of implementation, peer coaching and self-directed teacher growth options were open to all qualified faculty. The focused assistance evaluative track for novice and marginal teachers was not implemented until the year 5, after most tenured faculty were engaged in various supervisory options. Freed from the responsibility of conducting two classroom observations per year with *every* teacher, the administrators and supervisors could take a more hands-on, sustained role in working with novice and marginal teachers who could most benefit from one-on-one support.

An important step in finalizing the strategic plan for supervision and evaluation is to consider the impact of the new system on the workload of teachers and especially administrators. If the preexisting system has included only observations by the principal (as in the preceding example), then creating a system with differentiated growth opportunities will definitely increase teacher workload. As these growth opportunities are more likely to meet teachers' needs and to result in enhanced performance, we believe that the workload increase is justified. Creating a new system is likely to shift administrator efforts from observing every teacher for evaluative purposes to observing some teachers for evaluation while conferring with others to facilitate their participation in the supervision options. Before a final plan is put into place, the task force should look across all of the supervisory and evaluative options within the system and determine exactly what each principal is responsible to do. If the workload seems too demanding for principals, the best approach is to cut back on the number of options and to implement more options gradually as the administrators gain confidence in their ability to meet the demands. The task force must also consider whether other professionals (e.g., department chairpersons or supervisors) could pick up some of the responsibilities that principals normally undertake. Such a move can give principals more time for the important task of facilitating teacher growth.

The last step in devising a comprehensive system is presenting the strategic plan to the board, administration, and faculty for approval. Approval will be far more likely if the task force members sustain open communication throughout the entire system-building process. To that end, the task force can use building level meetings and written communication to periodically update the subgroups that they represent. To lay a foundation for shared understanding, it is particularly important that they seek input and elicit feedback *before* implementation begins.

## SUPPORTING THE SYSTEM: IMPLEMENTING AND SUSTAINING THE SYSTEM THROUGH ONGOING PROFESSIONAL DEVELOPMENT

In Chapter 2 in our espoused platform, we described our fundamental belief that all educators, administrators, and teachers alike must possess a deep understanding of the teacher supervision and evaluation system as well as the skills necessary to carry out their roles successfully. The only way for this to happen is by ensuring readiness through initial training designed to impart the needed specialized knowledge and skills. With that training, educators will be able to engage in any of the processes described throughout the text.

We advocate a strong program of professional development as an integral component of system implementation. In each chapter of the book introducing various options for supervision and evaluation (Chapters 3–10), we provide specific step-by-step procedures and guidance for implementation. In Chapter 3, for example, Figure 3.2 provides a sample format for a 2-day peer-coaching workshop to prepare teachers to engage in productive classroom supervision of one another. Similarly, Figure 10.1 in Chapter 10 explains how to structure a 3-day workshop for mentors supervising novice teachers. Depending on the variety of supervisory options the system includes, we find it especially useful to design a professional development framework, including a timeline, that will equip administrators and teachers alike with the knowledge and skills to productively engage in supervision and evaluation.

Many supervision and evaluation plans fail because although the district conscientiously provided initial professional development, it made no provision for sustaining the efforts through ongoing training and support. For a system of supervision and evaluation to be successful, participants' specialized knowledge and skills must be updated as newly hired teachers and administrators join the district.

## MAINTAINING THE SYSTEM: LEARNING THROUGH PERIODIC EVALUATION

To ensure that the system continues to be implemented with consistency and integrity over time, the school district needs to make a long-term commitment to periodically monitor, assess, and reshape its efforts based on newly acquired data. Periodic data-driven evaluations refine the system as it is operationalized in practice. For example, the task force can reconvene annually to discuss how the system is functioning. Principals can closely monitor end-of-year reports from teachers engaged in various supervisory options. Central office administrators could review teacher evaluation portfolios and summarize the results for the task force.

Formal data gathering in the form of internal surveys and interviews or external audits should occur every 3–5 years. Figure 12.4 revisits the evaluation criteria introduced in Chapter 1 and provides specific, observable indicators for use in assessing the overall quality of a system. The district can conduct a self-assessment by collecting and analyzing data and comparing the results to the knowledge base in a process similar to the one described as part of the task force's charge earlier in the chapter.

**FIGURE 12.4** Evaluation Criteria to Assess the Teacher Supervision and Evaluation System

*Criterion 1* The processes for judging competence (evaluation) are clearly separated from processes for enhancing growth (supervision).

*Indicators*

1. People, time, and/or procedures are used to separate the two functions.
2. The procedures for judging competence focus on accountability, evidenced-based evaluation, and the overall quality of teacher performance.
3. The procedures for enhancing growth focus on continuous improvement beyond a teacher's current level of performance.

*Criterion 2* Supervision and evaluation are high district priorities.

*Indicators*

1. To promote shared ownership, the process involves a variety of stakeholders.
2. Ongoing review and assessment of the supervision and evaluation system take place.
3. Administrators have a reasonable supervision and evaluation load.
4. Fiscal and human resources are devoted to implementing, maintaining, and evaluating the system.
5. Clear connections are made between supervision and staff development.
6. Individual teacher goal setting is aligned with the district's vision, mission, and goals.

*Criterion 3* Opportunities for differentiated supervision are provided by the system.

*Indicators*

1. The processes for novice, experienced, and marginal teachers are clearly differentiated.
2. The system provides a variety of options for experienced teachers, including but not limited to classroom supervision, peer coaching, self-directed growth, action research, and collegial development groups.

*Criterion 4* The process for evaluation makes expectations and criteria for satisfactory performance clear.

*Indicators*

1. A clear and explicit set of criteria exists for describing quality teaching performance.
2. Consistency in understanding and using these performance indicators exists across administrators and schools.
3. Evaluators receive ongoing training so that a high degree of reliability in assessing teaching performance can be maintained.
4. A remediation and assistance component is available for marginal teachers.

*Criterion 5* The organizational climate is conducive to effective supervision and evaluation.

*Indicators*

1. The district concerns itself with the readiness phase before attempting to implement a supervision and evaluation system.
2. Supportive relationship building is evident; trust, collaboration, mutual respect, and a sense of community are nurtured.
3. A shared language and common understanding of supervision and evaluation exist across board, central office personnel, principals, other supervisors, and classroom teachers.

*(Continued)*

**FIGURE 12.4** (*Continued*)

4. Stakeholders value teacher risk taking, reflection, and inquiry as necessary to continuous professional growth.

*Criterion 6* The entire supervision and evaluation system is aimed at enhancing student learning.

*Indicators*

1. Supervisory options and growth goals are data driven and aimed at increased student performance.
2. A built in mechanism allows teachers to share with one another the results of successful supervisory options.
3. Districtwide documentation procedures are developed for recording and reporting evidence of impact upon student learning.

Another option is external review. In our state, the Supervision Committee of the Pennsylvania Association of Supervision and Curriculum Development, a team consisting of professors, assistant superintendents, and principals trained in supervision and evaluation, serves as an external review board. A district may submit its supervision and evaluation plan to our committee. After examining the written plan and other supporting documentation, we conduct a 3-day site visit to the district, interviewing teams of teachers representing each building, as well as principals and central office administrators, to uncover their perceptions and share their experiences. After the interviews, the team meets as a whole to compare the data. Finally, the audit team develops a composite profile for the district that identifies strengths and areas in need of improvement according to the evaluation criteria. In the next section, we feature one school district that availed itself of the external review process.

# CASE STUDY: ROSE TREE MEDIA SCHOOL DISTRICT

Rose Tree Media School District is a suburban school district that encompasses nearly 400 professional staff and over 4000 students. In 1995, at the request of the superintendent, the district set up a task force to create a differentiated supervision and evaluation model. The composition of the task force included wide representation from a variety of stakeholder groups: a school board representative, seven teachers from across the district, who represented various grade levels and subject areas, three building principals, parents, and a central office administrator who served as the facilitator. Their rationale for change was based on two underlying goals: (1) to emphasize, nurture, and support continuous growth and learning for every member of the professional staff; and (2) to strengthen the quality of instruction and services rendered to students.

The task force spent the year in an awareness phase, reviewing their current system of supervision and evaluation as well as many others. They developed a guiding philosophy or platform as a starting point for change. Their platform included the following tenets:

- Participatory planning by a group representative of all stakeholders
- Fostering a safe environment that promotes teacher collaboration, risk taking, and -self-direction;
- Administrative partnering in the professional learning of all staff

- Encouraging reflective practice
- Provision of a mechanism for continuous follow-up and assessment of the system (Rose Tree Media School District, 2001)

In the second year the task force developed a strategic plan consisting of three programs or tracks. Program I, the evaluative track, included all non-tenured teachers, all tenured teachers in their first year with the district, all teachers identified as marginal, and enough other tenured teachers to add up to approximately one third of the total number of faculty. Every experienced teacher cycles into Program I once every 3 years. In Program I, principals, supervisors, and/or central office administrators conduct an in-depth analysis of the professional's performance. The analysis involves a formal cycle of preobservation conference, classroom observation, and postobservation conference at least once per semester, plus frequent informal observations.

Programs II and III, representing years 2 and 3 of a 3-year cycle, are a time when experienced, tenured teachers commit themselves to an individualized professional growth plan chosen from an extensive number of supervision options. The system's 2-year growth programs foster maximum flexibility in meeting teachers' varied needs and levels of experience. The menu of differentiated choices includes peer coaching, reflective journaling, self-appraisal through videotape analyses, action research, collegial development groups, curriculum and instruction projects, relevant and applicable graduate coursework to enhance performance, a process portfolio that includes evidence demonstrating growth in planning, delivering, and assessing instruction, writing for publication, and a teacher internship with a business or community group to extend the concept of school-to-career.

During the 2 years in supervisory mode, teachers receive the support and encouragement of an administrator to explore, experiment, and attain the goals of their individualized plans without the fear that risk taking could lead to poor evaluations. While in the growth option, teachers continue to be issued an annual professional employee rating of satisfactory in accordance with the school code and the department of education regulations. However, unless the teacher specifically asks for a formal observation as part of the growth option, the supervisor works with the teacher in a consultative way. After 2 years in the supervisory mode, veteran teachers rotate back into Program I.

Rose Tree introduced the system on a pilot basis with a small cadre of teacher volunteers during the 1997–1998 school year. The system was implemented for everyone the following year. Figure 12.5 summarizes the system's three tracks for novice, veteran, and marginal teachers.

At the request of the central office team, our PASCD audit team conducted a site visit to evaluate Rose Tree Media School District's supervision and evaluation system in 2000, 5 years after the task force began its work. The strengths of the system were many; in fact, the district received commendations for exemplary achievement in five of the six evaluation criteria.

The PASCD team made two major recommendations under Criterion 4—"The process for evaluation makes expectations and criteria for satisfactory performance clear" First, although the district had a written instructional framework that delineated five criteria of outstanding teaching, the framework had been created and adopted by a team of central office administrators, principals, and supervisors. Few teachers were aware of the standards of excellence for teacher evaluation. Our team recommended that *all* stakeholder groups be represented and participate in developing a revised set of criteria and that the district communicate a shared understanding of what constitutes "good teaching." Second, no consistent, formalized mechanism for remediation of marginal teachers existed.

**FIGURE 12.5** Current Rose Tree Media Supervision and Evaluation Model

| Novice teachers | Veteran teachers | Marginal teachers |
|---|---|---|
| • Program I—a formal cycle of in-class observation at a minimum of once per semester; frequent informal observations<br>• Participation in an induction program/collaboration with a mentor<br>• A summative evaluation | • One third of the veteran faculty are evaluated annually, on a rotating basis (Program I)<br>• During the second and the third year following teacher evaluation (Programs II and III), faculty choose from among the following supervisory options:<br>• Peer coaching<br>• Reflective journaling<br>• Videotape analysis<br>• Action research project<br>• Collegial development group<br>• Curriculum and instruction project<br>• Graduate coursework<br>• Process portfolio<br>• Writing for publication<br>• Teacher internship | • Mandatory participation in Program I<br>• Assignment to a support team consisting of two teachers and two administrators<br>• A written plan of assistance that delineates area(s) of deficiency, strategies for improvement, and a timeline for upgrading performance<br>• A summative evaluation |

Although all marginal teachers received notification of their deficiencies and subsequent placement in Program I, the evaluative track, building principals handled the remediation process individually.

Since our audit, the task force has acted on both recommendations. One of the results is a revised Professional Option Action Planning Form for teachers in Programs II and III. The form now correlates the teacher's annual professional goal to one of five standards-based criteria of instructional excellence created collaboratively by the supervision and evaluation task force:

1. Promotes clear, high, and realistic expectations of what students know and should be able to do
2. Provides instruction that is varied and sensitive to the individual needs of students
3. Engages students as actively as possible in the learning process
4. Uses multiple assessments to focus on student learning
5. Uses data to provide students with consistent and quality feedback

As Figure 12.5 reflects, the district has also implemented a consistent intensive remediation plan. The plan identifies and communicates specific goals a marginal teacher needs to meet for improvement. Moreover, it establishes a support team composed of two administrators and two teachers, who in conjunction with the identified teacher develop a blueprint that includes strategies and a timeline for upgrading performance.

This example of a system in practice provides several important lessons about the development and implementation of a differentiated system of teacher supervision and evaluation. First, before implementing the new system, the district engaged in careful and deliberate planning by forming a task force representing multiple stakeholders. Second, the new system was built based on a platform that included the importance of differentiated growth opportunities and on the assumption that most teachers were eager to learn and grow. Third, the system offers a variety of opportunities for differentiated growth that ask teachers to connect their own growth to district goals and initiatives. Fourth, a clear set of criteria for quality teaching exists. Finally, this case provides an excellent example of a system that continually assesses its own effectiveness, is open to evidence concerning its quality, and uses feedback to make improvements.

# CHAPTER SUMMARY

This final chapter provides an action plan to guide school districts in developing, implementing, and maintaining a high-quality system of supervision and evaluation. The first step is the formation of a task force that represents and actively involves the various stakeholder groups in a collaborative process. The work begins with an assessment of the current system, including the perceptions of the various constituencies, a comprehensive needs assessment, and a compilation of data to drive informed decision making. Simultaneously, to ensure a shared understanding of current research and best practice, the task force familiarizes itself with the knowledge base on effective supervision and evaluation and compares that knowledge with the district's current practices. If the evidence indicates that the time is right to proceed, the next step for the task force is to compose a long-term strategic plan as a roadmap. The plan

begins with a platform of beliefs to serve as a foundation for all future work. Once the platform is in place, the next key determination for the task force is whether to create, adopt, or adapt a system. Regardless of which path it pursues, the task force needs to consider supervisory and evaluative functions separately. The task force then devises a timeline that not only provides for gradual implementation, but also suggests ways of maintaining the system through opportunities for professional development and periodic evaluation. The final step for the task force is to share the strategic plan with those it represents, to seek feedback, to make necessary modifications, and subsequently to take the final draft to the faculty, administration, and board for their support and approval. The chapter concludes with an example of a successful supervision and evaluation system in practice.

# DISCUSSION QUESTIONS

**1.** Return to the unanswered questions that you listed at the beginning of this chapter. Have they been addressed? If not, present them to the entire class for discussion.

**2.** The chapter discusses three strategies for developing a new system of teacher supervision and evaluation:

create, adopt, or adapt. Do you strongly favor one of these strategies over the other two? Why? If you do not favor one strongly, what factors would you use to decide which strategy you would use in a given school district?

# THEORY-INTO-PRACTICE APPLICATIONS

**1.** Review Figure 12.2 (items to include in a needs assessment survey), including the four categories and the specific items within each category. As members of the district's supervision and evaluation task force, what additional questions might you include to gather the data you need to inform your decision making?

**2.** Throughout the book, we have emphasized that developing a system of supervision and evaluation will

require a long-term commitment of resources. Divide into three groups. Have each group work separately as a task force to prepare a presentation for a different stakeholder group—the school board, the administrative leadership team, and teachers' union. Your job is to create and deliver a PowerPoint presentation to convince your audience that the time and resources needed to implement a revised system of supervision and evaluation would be well worth the investment.

# REFERENCES

Rose Tree Media School District (2001). *Differentiated supervision and evaluation plan.* Media, PA: Rose. Tree Media School District.

Southern York County School District (2001). *Differentiated supervision and evaluation plan.* Glen Rock, PA: Southern York County School District.

Supervision Committee of Pennsylvania Association of Supervision and Curriculum Development. (1995).

*Teacher supervision and evaluation: A process for school district self-assessment and improvement.* Lancaster, PA: Pennsylvania Association for Supervision and Curriculum Development.

York-Barr, J., Sommers, W., Ghere, G.S., & Montie, J. (2001). *Reflective practice to improve schools.* Thousand Oaks, CA: Corwin.

# SUGGESTIONS FOR FURTHER READING AND RESEARCH

Danielson, C., & McGreal, T. L. (2000). *Teacher evaluation to enhance professional practice.* Alexandria and Princeton: Association for Supervision and Curriculum Development and Educational Teaching Service.

Firth, G. R., & Pajak, E. F. (Eds.). (1998). *Handbook of research on school supervision.* New York: Simon and Schuster Macmillan.

Hall, G. E., & Hord, S. M. (2001). *Implementing change: Patterns, principles, and potholes.* Boston, MA: Allyn & Bacon.

# A WORD ON CLASSROOM WALK-THROUGHS

Peters and Waterman's leadership classic *In Search of Excellence* (1982) popularized the term "Management by Walking Around" (MBWA). Analyzing the characteristics of America's most flourishing companies, the authors focused on attributes that led to excellence. Among them was "organizational fluidity" brought about by open, frequent, and oftentimes, informal communication networks. Getting managers "out of the office" and into close contact with their employees appeared to be a simple, but important key to success.

Similarly, in the literature on effective educational leadership, administrators are encouraged to be highly visible on a routine basis in order to be true instructional leaders (Blasé & Blasé, 1998). Spending time in teachers' classroom gives principals a comprehensive "schoolwide picture made up of many small snapshots" (Richardson, 2001). Only by leaving the office and visiting classrooms can principals gain a true "feel" for the various types of teaching methods, instructional strategies, and assessment practices taking place throughout the building. They can also look for consistency of curriculum implementation and the use of district-identified effective teaching standards across classrooms (e.g., Danielson's (2007) domains). In a sense, time spent in classrooms is well worth it because principals can "keep a finger on the pulse of the school."

Unfortunately, the myriad pressures of management, including everything from bureaucratic demands to crisis management, do not always allow administrators to make spending systematic and frequent time in teachers' classrooms as much of a priority as they would like. Thus, the seeds were sown for the resurgence in popularity of "the classroom walk-through." A walk-through is described as a brief (from 2 to 10 min in length) classroom visit by the principal to gather information. Typically, feedback is provided to the teacher, in the form of a note, checklist, rubric, or question that is designed to encourage "reflection conversations" (Downey, Steffy, English, Frase, & Poston, 2004). Although we endorse the concept of walk-throughs as a means of visibility and informal monitoring for accountability, we offer a word of caution as school districts consider implementing walk-throughs with oral or written feedback to teachers as part of their supervision and evaluation plan.

In our espoused platform, we highlighted three central tenets that are crucial in the context of any discussion of walk-throughs: (1) the importance of an educational climate that fosters trust and mutual respect; (2) the complexity of the act of teaching; and (3) a shared understanding of the goals and processes of the supervision and evaluation system. The first of these principles of effective supervisory practice is a collaborative organizational climate. In Chapters 2 and 3, we discussed the fact that although teachers must open their doors literally to administrators, they do not necessarily have to "open themselves" metaphorically. In order for optimal two-way communication and a shared inquiry into practice to occur, principals must keep in mind the factors that facilitate adult learning. Among these factors are a teacher's sense of ownership and self-direction within the parameters of meeting building or district goals. From our viewpoint, feedback to teachers generated from walk-throughs should support a collegial rather than hierarchical approach. Thus, in any walk-through process *that involves observational data* (whether in the form of reflective questions about "teacher decision points," constructive criticism, or affirmation), teachers should be given a voice and a choice in the walk-through focus.

Why? The danger exists that walk-throughs that are poorly done can undermine the intent of a differentiated teacher supervision and evaluation system by confounding processes for judging compliance or competence (evaluation) from those designed to promote teacher reflection and growth (supervision). Walk-throughs that are top-down and principal directed put the administrator in control of what data to record. If decisions about what to look for and what to comment upon during a brief classroom visitation are top-down, teachers feel no sense of ownership. Although the intent of the administration may be nonthreatening, the perception of the teachers is what ultimately counts. Is the perception "us versus them" or a sense of "our being in this together?"

We are not condemning walk-throughs; in fact, we endorse the use of any technique that gives administrators more time in teachers' classrooms. However, we also feel strongly that they must be used judiciously as a communication tool. If the district currently employs a differentiated supervision and evaluation plan, walk-throughs with feedback to the teacher, whether formal or informal, make the most sense for competent, veteran teachers who are in the nonevaluative years or track of a differentiated supervision and evaluation cycle (typically, tenured teachers with satisfactory ratings are in the supervisory or professional growth tracks with no formal classroom observation 2 out of 3 years). With the principal's time and interest centered on an experienced teacher's chosen area of growth or individual action plan goal (e.g., the effective use of graphic organizers in reading comprehension), teachers would not feel as if they are working in isolation. Indeed, they could receive the follow-up to professional development that Joyce and Showers (2002) hail as a necessary part of successful transfer to classroom practice. Because of principals' frequent visits to these teachers' classrooms, they would remain well informed about the progress of the various peer-coaching efforts, self-directed growth and action research projects, and the work of collegial development groups taking place throughout the building. Classroom walk-throughs would provide more opportunity for offering tangible support ("How can I help you?", "What do you need to be successful?") and for mentoring faculty. Moreover, with proper preparation, pairs or teams of teachers conducting walk-throughs could easily be built into the system as a nonevaluative extension of peer coaching or the teacher induction program. Frequent teacher-to-teacher visitation has the potential to closely connect colleagues and stimulate substantive conversations about student learning. Teacher-led walk-throughs can serve as another avenue for building professional learning community (Blatt, Linsley, & Smith, 2005).

The second principle of effective supervision that applies here is recognizing teaching as contextual, recursive, multifaceted, and nonlinear. As we discussed in Chapter 7, historically the basis for making judgments about the quality of teaching has been the discrepancy model. In such a model, the district identifies a form of effective teaching, typically drawn from research, and uses that description as the criteria for best practice. Administrators then look for the amount of discrepancy between the model and observed teaching performance. Widespread use of discrepancy-based procedures simplifies the complexity of teaching into a neat little form. In the 1980s, Madeline Hunter found to great dismay that her model for seven essential elements of direct instruction was being reduced to a series of steps that teachers were expected to conform to in a lockstep approach, which was never her intention (Garman, Glickman, Hunter, & Haggerson, 1987). Any observation that attempts to relegate the complex act of meeting the needs of diverse groups of students into a list of generic teaching behaviors is a perversion of teacher supervision as we see it. Thus, it is important that administrators use the observations that are made during the short walk-through for engaging the teacher in subsequent, nonjudgmental conversation about what is occurring in the classroom and why it is occurring, rather than as evidence that can be used to judge the teacher's effectiveness. Although the majority of supervisors would agree to this in theory, a real danger exists for the data to be collected and used inappropriately.

Finally, our third caution pertains to the need for a shared understanding of and clear communication about the goals and processes of any form of teacher supervision and evaluation. If walk-throughs spring from universal understanding and a common commitment, chances of increasing their impact on teacher development and student learning are far more likely. Classroom walk-throughs should never be implemented without professional development for *both* the administrative team and the faculty. All stakeholders must understand the purpose for visiting classrooms on an ongoing basis and be part of the conversation about how and why walk-throughs fit in as an integral part of, *rather than an add-on to,* the district supervision and evaluation plan. Additionally, in order to feel nonthreatened, teachers must be familiar with the procedures used during and after each visit. Will data be collected? If so, what type of data? How will those data be used and shared? Could the data become part of a teacher's formal evaluation? The need for districtwide understanding, communication, and especially, operational consistency in practice is paramount.

In summary, classroom walk-throughs conducted in a collegial rather than hierarchical approach can be a positive, proactive means for principals to become a more integral part of the teaching/learning process. They can enhance the principal's role as an instructional leader by giving a clear sense of progress toward building goals and district initiatives that directly affect student learning. They can serve as a data-driven vehicle for identifying topics of discussion at grade level, team, or general faculty meetings and for assessing future professional development needs. As with any educational initiative, however, the potential of the tool lies with its implementation by the user . . . a point for reflection.

# REFERENCES

Blasé, J., & Blasé, J. (1998). *Handbook of instructional leadership: How really good principals promote teaching and learning.* Thousand Oaks, CA: Corwin Press.

Blatt, B., Linsley, B., & Smith, L. (2005). *Classroom walk-throughs their way.* Retrieved January 29, 2007, from http:// www.smp.gseis.ucla.edu/Resourcesforyou/ednews/ednews_2005_01.html.

Danielson, C. (2007). *Enhancing professional practice: A framework for teaching* (2nd ed.). Alexandria, VA: The Association for Supervision and Curriculum Development.

Downey, C. J., Steffy, B. E., English, F. W., Frase, L. E., & Poston, W. K. (2004). *The three-minute classroom walk-through: Changing school supervisory practice one teacher at a time.* Thousand Oaks, CA: Corwin Press.

Garman, N., Glickman, C., Hunter, M., & Haggerson, N. (1987). Conflicting conceptions of clinical supervision and the enhancement of professional growth and renewal: Point and counterpoint. *Journal of Curriculum and Supervision, 2*(2), 152–177.

Joyce, B., & Showers, B. (2002). *Student achievement through staff development* (3rd ed.). Alexandria, VA: Association for Supervision and Curriculum Development.

Peters, T. J., & Waterman, R. H. (1982). *In search of excellence: Lessons from America's best run companies.* New York: Warner Books.

Richardson, J. (2001). Seeing through new eyes: Walk throughs offer new ways to view schools. *Tools for Schools, 10*(1), 2–7.

# ELCC STANDARDS

**Standard 1.0** Candidates who complete the program are educational leaders who have the knowledge and ability to promote the success of all students by facilitating the development, articulation, implementation, and stewardship of a school or district vision of learning supported by the school community.

| Elements | Meets standards for school building leadership | Meets standards for school district leadership |
|---|---|---|
| 1.1 Develop a vision | a. Candidates develop a vision of learning for a school that promotes the success of all students.<br><br>b. Candidates base this vision on relevant knowledge and theories, including but not limited to an understanding of learning goals in a pluralistic society, the diversity of learners and learners' needs, schools as interactive social and cultural systems, and social and organizational change. | a. Candidates develop and demonstrate the skills needed to work with a board of education to facilitate the development of a vision of learning for a school district that promotes the success of all students.<br><br>b. Candidates base development of the vision on relevant knowledge and theories applicable to school-level leaders applied to a school district context.<br><br>c. Candidates use data-based research strategies to create a vision that takes into account the diversity of learners in a district.<br><br>d. Candidates demonstrate knowledge of ways to use a district's vision to mobilize additional resources to support the vision. |
| 1.2 Articulate a vision | a. Candidates demonstrate the ability to articulate the components of this vision for a school and the leadership processes necessary to implement and support the vision.<br><br>b. Candidates demonstrate the ability to use data-based research strategies and strategic planning processes that focus on student learning to inform the development of a vision, drawing on relevant information sources such as student assessment results, student and family demographic data, and an analysis of community needs.<br><br>c. Candidates demonstrate the ability to communicate the vision to staff, parents, students, and community members through the use of symbols, ceremonies, stories, and other activities. | a. Candidates demonstrate the ability to articulate the components of this vision for a district and the leadership processes necessary to implement and support the vision.<br><br>b. Candidates demonstrate the ability to use data-based research strategies and strategic planning processes that focus on student learning to develop a vision, drawing on relevant information sources such as student assessment results, student and family demographic data, and an analysis of community needs.<br><br>c. Candidates demonstrate the ability to communicate the vision to school boards, staff, parents, students, and community members through the use of symbols, ceremonies, stories, and other activities. |

| | | |
|---|---|---|
| 1.3 Implement a vision | a. Candidates can formulate the initiatives necessary to motivate staff, students, and families to achieve the school's vision.<br><br>b. Candidates develop plans and processes for implementing the vision (e.g., articulating the vision and related goals, encouraging challenging standards, facilitating collegiality and teamwork, structuring significant work, ensuring appropriate use of student assessments, providing autonomy, supporting innovation, delegating responsibility, developing leadership in others, and securing needed resources). | a. Candidates demonstrate the ability to plan programs to motivate staff, students, and families to achieve a school district's vision.<br><br>b. Candidates design research-based processes to effectively implement a district vision throughout an entire school district and community. |
| 1.4 Steward a vision | a. Candidates demonstrate an understanding of the role effective communication skills play in building a shared commitment to the vision.<br><br>b. Candidates design or adopt a system for using data-based research strategies to regularly monitor, evaluate, and revise the vision.<br><br>c. Candidates assume stewardship of the vision through various methods. | a. Candidates demonstrate the ability to align and, as necessary, redesign administrative policies and practices required for full implementation of a district vision.<br><br>b. Candidates understand the theory and research related to organizational and educational leadership and engage in the collection, organization, and analysis of a variety of information, including student performance data, required to assess progress toward a district's vision, mission, and goals. |
| 1.5 Promote community involvement in the vision | a. Candidates demonstrate the ability to involve community members in the realization of the vision and in related school improvement efforts.<br><br>b. Candidates acquire and demonstrate the skills needed to communicate effectively with all stakeholders about implementation of the vision. | a. Candidates demonstrate the ability to bring together and communicate effectively with stakeholders within the district and the larger community concerning implementation and realization of the vision. |

**Standard 2.0** Candidates who complete the program are educational leaders who have the knowledge and ability to promote the success of all students by promoting a positive school culture, providing an effective instructional program, applying best practice to student learning, and designing comprehensive professional growth plans for staff.

| Elements | Meets standards for school building leadership | Meets standards for school district leadership |
|---|---|---|
| 2.1 Promote positive school culture | a. Candidates assess school culture using multiple methods and implement context-appropriate strategies that capitalize on the diversity (e.g., population, language, disability, gender, race, socioeconomic) of the school community to improve school programs and culture. | a. Candidates develop a sustained approach to improve and maintain a positive district culture for learning that capitalizes on multiple aspects of diversity to meet the learning needs of all students. |

*(Continued)*

**Standard 2.0** (Continued)

| Elements | Meets standards for school building leadership | Meets standards for school district leadership |
|---|---|---|
| 2.2 Provide effective instructional program | a. Candidates demonstrate the ability to facilitate activities that apply principles of effective instruction to improve instructional practices and curricular materials.<br><br>b. Candidates demonstrate the ability to make recommendations regarding the design, implementation, and evaluation of a curriculum that fully accommodates learners' diverse needs.<br><br>c. Candidates demonstrate the ability to use and promote technology and information systems to enrich curriculum and instruction, to monitor instructional practices and provide staff the assistance needed for improvement. | a. Candidates demonstrate an understanding of a variety of instructional research methodologies and can analyze the comparable strengths and weaknesses of each method.<br><br>b. Candidates are able to use qualitative and quantitative data, appropriate research methods, technology, and information systems to develop a long-range plan for a district that assesses the district's improvement and accountability systems.<br><br>c. Candidates demonstrate the ability to use and promote technology and information systems to enrich district curriculum and instruction, monitor instructional practices, and provide assistance to administrators who have needs for improvement.<br><br>d. Candidates demonstrate the ability to allocate and justify resources to sustain the instructional program. |
| 2.3 Apply best practice to student learning | a. Candidates demonstrate the ability to assist school personnel in understanding and applying best practices for student learning.<br><br>b. Candidates apply human development theory, proven learning and motivational theories, and concern for diversity to the learning process.<br><br>c. Candidates demonstrate an understanding of how to use appropriate research strategies to promote an environment for improved student achievement. | a. Candidates demonstrate the ability to facilitate and engage in activities that use best practices and sound educational research to improve instructional programs.<br><br>b. Candidates demonstrate an ability to assist school and district personnel in understanding and applying best practices for student learning.<br><br>c. Candidates understand and can apply human development theory, proven learning, and motivational theories, and concern for diversity to the learning process.<br><br>d. Candidates understand how to use appropriate research strategies to profile student performance in a district and analyze differences among subgroups. |
| 2.4 Design comprehensive professional growth plans | a. Candidates design and demonstrate an ability to implement well-planned, context-appropriate professional development programs based on reflective practice and research on student learning consistent with the school vision and goals.<br><br>b. Candidates demonstrate the ability to use strategies such as observations, collaborative reflection, and adult learning strategies to form comprehensive professional growth plans with teachers and other school personnel. | a. Candidates demonstrate knowledge of adult learning strategies and the ability to apply technology and research to professional development design focusing on authentic problems and tasks, mentoring, coaching, conferencing, and other techniques that promote new knowledge and skills in the workplace.<br><br>b. Candidates demonstrate the ability to use strategies such as observations and collaborative reflection to help form comprehensive professional growth plans with district and school personnel. |

c. Candidates develop and implement personal professional growth plans that reflect a commitment to lifelong learning.

c. Candidates develop personal professional growth plans that reflect a commitment to lifelong learning and best practices.

**Standard 3.0** Candidates who complete the program are educational leaders who have the knowledge and ability to promote the success of all students by managing the organization, operations, and resources in a way that promotes a safe, efficient, and effective learning environment.

| Elements | Meets standards for school building leadership | Meets standards for school district leadership |
|---|---|---|
| 3.1 Manage the organization | a. Candidates demonstrate the ability to optimize the learning environment for all students by applying appropriate models and principles of organizational development and management, including research and data-driven decision making with attention to indicators of equity, effectiveness, and efficiency.<br><br>b. Candidates develop plans of action for focusing on effective organization and management of fiscal, human, and material resources, giving priority to student learning, safety, curriculum, and instruction.<br><br>c. Candidates demonstrate an ability to manage time effectively and deploy financial and human resources in ways that promote student achievement. | a. Candidates demonstrate the ability to use research-based knowledge of learning, teaching, student development, organizational development, and data management to optimize learning for all students.<br><br>b. Candidates demonstrate effective organization of fiscal, human, and material resources, giving priority to student learning and safety, and demonstrating an understanding of district budgeting processes and fiduciary responsibilities.<br><br>c. Candidates demonstrate an ability to manage time effectively and to deploy financial and human resources in way that promote student achievement.<br><br>d. Candidates demonstrate the ability to organize a district based on indicators of equity, effectiveness, and efficiency and can apply legal principles that promote educational equity.<br><br>e. Candidates demonstrate an understanding of how to apply legal principles to promote educational equity and provide safe, effective, and efficient facilities. |
| 3.2 Manage operations | a. Candidates demonstrate the ability to involve staff in conducting operations and setting priorities using appropriate and effective needs assessment, research-based data, and group process skills to build consensus, communicate, and resolve conflicts in order to align resources with the organizational vision.<br><br>b. Candidates develop communications plans for staff that includes opportunities for staff to develop their family and community collaboration skills.<br><br>c. Candidates demonstrate an understanding of how to apply legal principles to promote educational equity and provide safe, effective, and efficient facilities. | a. Candidates demonstrate the ability to involve stakeholders in aligning resources and priorities to maximize ownership and accountability.<br><br>b. Candidates can use appropriate and effective needs assessment, research-based data, and group process skills to build consensus, communicate, and resolve conflicts in order to align resources with the district vision.<br><br>c. Candidates develop staff communication plans for integrating districts, schools and divisions.<br><br>d. Candidates develop a plan to promote and support community collaboration among district personnel. |

*(Continued)*

**Standard 3.0** (Continued)

| Elements | Meets standards for school building leadership | Meets standards for school district leadership |
|---|---|---|
| 3.3 Manage resources | a. Candidates use problem-solving skills and knowledge of strategic, long-range, and operational planning (including applications of technology) in the effective, legal, and equitable use of fiscal, human, and material resource allocation and alignment that focuses on teaching and learning.<br><br>b. Candidates creatively seek new resources to facilitate learning.<br><br>c. Candidates apply and assess current technologies for school management, business procedures, and scheduling. | a. Candidates use problem-solving skills and knowledge of strategic, long-range, and operational planning (including applications of technology) in the effective, legal, and equitable use of fiscal, human, and material resource allocation that focuses on teaching and learning.<br><br>b. Candidates creatively seek new resources to facilitate learning.<br><br>c. Candidates apply an understanding of school district finance structures and models to ensure that adequate financial resources are allocated equitably for the district.<br><br>d. Candidates apply and assess current technologies for management, business procedures, and scheduling. |

**Standard 4.0** Candidates who complete the program are educational leaders who have the knowledge and ability to promote the success of all students by collaborating with families and other community members, responding to diverse community interests and needs, and mobilizing community resources.

| Elements | Meets standards for school building leadership | Meets standards for school district leadership |
|---|---|---|
| 4.1 Collaborate with families and other community members | a. Candidates demonstrate an ability to bring together the resources of family members and the community to positively affect student learning.<br><br>b. Candidates demonstrate an ability to involve families in the education of their children based on the belief that families have the best interests of their children in mind.<br><br>c. Candidates demonstrate the ability to use public information and research-based knowledge of issues and trends to collaborate with families and community members.<br><br>d. Candidates apply an understanding of community relations models, marketing strategies and processes, data-based decision making, and communications theory to create frameworks for school, family, business, community, government, and higher education partnerships.<br><br>e. Candidates develop various methods of outreach aimed at business, religious, political, and service organizations.<br><br>f. Candidates demonstrate the ability to involve families and other stakeholders in school decision-making | a. Candidates demonstrate the ability to facilitate the planning and implementation of programs and services that bring together the resources of families and the community to positively affect student learning.<br><br>b. Candidates demonstrate an ability to use public information and research-based knowledge of issues and trends to collaborate with community members and community organizations to have a positive affect on student learning.<br><br>c. Candidates apply an understanding of community relations models, marketing strategies and processes, data-driven decision making, and communication theory to craft frameworks for school, family, business, community, government, and higher education partnerships.<br><br>d. Candidates demonstrate an ability to develop and implement a plan for nurturing relationships with community leaders and reaching out to different business, religious, political, and service organizations to strengthen programs and support district goals.<br><br>e. Candidates demonstrate the ability to involve community members, groups, |

processes, reflecting an understanding that schools are an integral part of the larger community.

g.  Candidates demonstrate the ability to collaborate with community agencies to integrate health, social, and other services.

h.  Candidates develop a comprehensive program of community relations and demonstrate the ability to work with the media.

and other stakeholders in district decision making, reflecting an understanding of strategies to capitalize on the district's integral role in the larger community

f.  Candidates demonstrate the ability to collaborate with community agencies to integrate health, social, and other services in the schools to address student and family conditions that affect learning.

g.  Candidates demonstrate the ability to conduct community relations that reflects knowledge of effective media relations and that models effective media relations practices.

h.  Candidates develop and implement strategies that support the involvement of families in the education of their children that reinforces for district staff a belief that families have the best interests of their children in mind.

**4.2 Respond to community interests and needs**

a.  Candidates demonstrate active involvement within the community, including interactions with individuals and groups with conflicting perspectives.

b.  Candidates demonstrate the ability to use appropriate assessment strategies and research methods to understand and accommodate diverse school and community conditions and dynamics.

c.  Candidates provide leadership to programs serving students with special and exceptional needs.

d.  Candidates demonstrate the ability to capitalize on the diversity (cultural, ethnic, racial, economic, and special interest groups) of the school community to improve school programs and meet the diverse needs of all students.

a.  Candidates facilitate and engage in activities that reflect an ability to inform district decision making by collecting and organizing formal and informal information from multiple stakeholders.

b.  Candidates demonstrate the ability to promote maximum involvement with and visibility within the community.

c.  Candidates demonstrate the ability to interact effectively with individuals and groups that reflect conflicting perspectives.

d.  Candidates demonstrate the ability to effectively and appropriately assess, research, and plan for diverse district and community conditions and dynamics and capitalize on the diversity of the community to improve district performance and student achievement.

e.  Candidates demonstrate the ability to advocate for students with special and exceptional needs.

**4.3 Mobilize community resources**

a.  Candidates demonstrate an understanding of and ability to use community resources, including youth services, to support student achievement, solve school problems, and achieve school goals.

b.  Candidates demonstrate how to use school resources and social service agencies to serve the community.

c.  Candidates demonstrate an understanding of ways to use public resources and funds appropriately and effectively to encourage communities to provide new resources to address emerging student problems.

a.  Candidates demonstrate an understanding of and ability to use community resources, including youth services that enhance student achievement, to district problems, and accomplish district goals.

b.  Candidates demonstrate how to use district resources to the community to solve issues of joint concern.

c.  Candidates demonstrate an understanding of ways to use public resources and funds appropriately and effectively to encourage communities to provide new resources to address emerging student problems.

**Standard 5.0** Candidates who complete the program are educational leaders who have the knowledge and ability to promote the success of all students by acting with integrity, fairly, and in an ethical manner.

| Elements | Meets standards for school building leadership | Meets standards for school district leadership |
|---|---|---|
| 5.1 Acts with integrity | a. Candidates demonstrate a respect for the rights of others with regard to confidentiality and dignity and engage in honest interactions. | a. Candidates demonstrate a respect for the rights of others with regard to confidentiality and dignity and engage in honest interactions. |
| 5.2 Acts fairly | a. Candidates demonstrate the ability to combine impartiality, sensitivity to student diversity, and ethical considerations in their interactions with others. | a. Candidates demonstrate the ability to combine impartiality, sensitivity to student diversity, and ethical considerations in their interactions with others. |
| 5.3 Acts ethically | a. Candidates make and explain decisions based upon ethical and legal principles. | a. Candidates make and explain decisions based upon ethical and legal principles. |

**Standard 6.0** Candidates who complete the program are educational leaders who have the knowledge and ability to promote the success of all students by understanding, responding to, and influencing the larger political, social, economic, legal, and cultural context.

| Elements | Meets standards for school building leadership | Meets standards for school district leadership |
|---|---|---|
| 6.1 Understand the larger context | a. Candidates act as informed consumers of educational theory and concepts appropriate to school context and can demonstrate the ability to apply appropriate research methods to a school context.<br><br>b. Candidates demonstrate the ability to explain how the legal and political systems and institutional framework of schools have shaped a school and community, as well as the opportunities available to children and families in a particular school.<br><br>c. Candidates demonstrate the ability to analyze the complex causes of poverty and other disadvantages and their effects on families, communities, children, and learning.<br><br>d. Candidates demonstrate an understanding of the policies, laws, and regulations enacted by local, state, and federal authorities that affect schools, especially those that might improve educational and social opportunities.<br><br>e. Candidates demonstrate the ability to describe the economic factors shaping a local community and the effects economic factors have on local schools.<br><br>f. Candidates demonstrate the ability to analyze and describe the cultural diversity in a school community. | a. Candidates demonstrate the ability to use appropriate research methods, theories, and concepts to improve district operations.<br><br>b. Candidates demonstrate an understanding of the complex causes of poverty and other disadvantages and their effects on families, communities, children, and learning.<br><br>c. Candidates demonstrate an understanding of the policies, laws, and regulations enacted by local, state, and federal authorities affecting a specific district.<br><br>d. Candidates can explain the system for financing public schools and its effects on the equitable distribution of educational opportunities within a district.<br><br>e. Candidates demonstrate the ability to work with political leaders at the local, state, and national level.<br><br>f. Candidates can apply an understanding of how specific laws at the local, state, and federal level affect school districts and residents.<br><br>g. Candidates espouse positions in response to proposed policy changes that would benefit or harm districts and explain how proposed policies and laws might improve educational and social opportunities for specific communities. |

g. Candidates can describe community norms and values and how they relate to the role of the school in promoting social justice.

h. Candidates demonstrate the ability to explain various theories of change and conflict resolution and the appropriate application of those models of specific communities.

| | | |
|---|---|---|
| **6.2 Respond to the larger context** | a. Candidates demonstrate the ability to communicate with members of a school community concerning trends, issues, and potential changes in the environment in which the school operates, including maintenance of an ongoing dialogue with representatives of diverse community groups. | a. Candidates demonstrate the ability to engage students, parents, members of the school board, and other community members in advocating for adoption of improved policies and laws. |
| | | b. Candidates apply their understanding of the larger political, social, economic, legal, and cultural context to develop activities and policies that benefit their district and its students. |
| | | c. Candidates demonstrate the ability to communicate regularly with all segments of the district community concerning trends, issues, and policies affecting the district. |
| **6.3 Influence the larger context** | a. Candidates demonstrate the ability to engage students, parents, and other members of the community in advocating for adoption of improved policies and laws. | a. Candidates demonstrate an understanding of how to develop lines of communication with local, state, and federal authorities, and actively advocate for improved policies, laws, and regulations affecting a specific district, both directly and through organizations representing schools, educators, or others with similar interests. |
| | b. Candidates apply their understanding of the larger political, social, economic, legal, and cultural context to develop activities and policies that benefit students and their families. | |
| | c. Candidates advocate for policies and programs that promote equitable learning opportunities and success for all students, regardless of socioeconomic background, ethnicity, gender, disability, or other individual characteristics. | b. Candidates demonstrate the ability to advocate for policies and programs that promote equitable learning opportunities and success for all students, regardless of socioeconomic background, ethnicity, gender, disability, or other individual characteristics. |

**Standard 7.0** Internship. The internship provides significant opportunities for candidates to synthesize and apply the knowledge and practice and develop the skills identified in Standard 1–6 through substantial, sustained, standard-based work in real settings, planned and guided cooperatively by the institution and school district personnel for graduate credit.

| Elements | Meets standards for school building leadership | Meets standards for school district leadership |
|---|---|---|
| **7.1 Substantial** | a. Candidates demonstrate the ability to accept genuine responsibility for leading, facilitating, and making decisions typical of those made by educational leaders. The experiences(s) should provide interns with substantial responsibilities that increase over time in amount and complexity and | a. Candidates demonstrate the ability to accept genuine responsibility for leading, facilitating, and making decisions typical of those made by educational leaders. The experiences(s) should provide interns with substantial responsibilities that increase over time in amount and complexity and involve direct |

*(Continued)*

**Standard 7.0** (Continued)

| Elements | Meets standards for school building leadership | Meets standards for school district leadership |
|---|---|---|
| | involve direct interaction and involvement with staff, students, parents, and community leaders. | interaction and involvement with staff, school board members, students, parents, and school and community leaders. |
| | b. Each candidate should have a minimum of 6 months (or equivalent, see note below) of full-time internship experience. | b. Each candidate should have a minimum of 6 months (or equivalent, see note below) of full-time internship experience. |
| 7.2 Sustained | a. Candidates participate in planned intern activities during the entire course of the program, including an extended period of time near the conclusion of the program to allow for candidate application of knowledge and skills on a full-time basis. | a. Candidates participate in planned intern activities during the entire course of the program, including an extended period of time near the conclusion of the program to allow for candidate application of skills and knowledge on a full-time basis. |
| 7.3 Standards-based | a. Candidates apply skills and knowledge articulated in these standards as well as state and local standards for educational leaders. | a. Candidates apply skills and knowledge articulated in these standards as well as state and local standards for educational leaders. |
| | b. Experiences are designed to accommodate candidates' individual needs. | b. Experiences are designed to accommodate candidates' individual needs. |
| 7.4 Real settings | a. Candidates' experiences occur in multiple settings that allow for the demonstration of a wide range of relevant knowledge and skills. | a. Candidates' experiences occur in multiple district administrator settings and allow for the demonstration of relevant knowledge and skills. |
| | b. Candidates' experiences include work with appropriate community organizations such as social service groups and local businesses. | b. Candidates' experiences include work with appropriate community organizations, parent groups, and school boards. |
| 7.5 Planned and guided cooperatively | a. Candidates' experiences are planned cooperatively by the individual, the site supervisor, and institution personnel to provide inclusion of appropriate opportunities to apply skills, knowledge, and research contained in the standards. These three individuals work together to meet candidate and program needs. | a. Candidates' experiences are planned cooperatively by the individual, the site supervisor, and institution personnel to provide inclusion of appropriate opportunities to apply skills, knowledge, and research contained in the standards. The three individuals work together to meet candidate and program needs. |
| | b. Mentors are provided training to guide the candidate during the intern experience. | b. Mentors are provided training to guide the candidate during the intern experience. |
| 7.6 Credit | a. Candidates earn graduate credit for their intern experience. | a. Candidates earn graduate credit for their intern experience. |

*Note:* Length equivalency—The 6 month internship experience need not be consecutive and may include experiences of different lengths. However, all internships must include an extended, capstone experience to maximize the candidates' opportunities to practice and refine their skills and knowledge. This culminating experience may be two noncontiguous internships of 3 months each, a 4 month internship and two field practicums of 1 month each, or another equivalent combination. Full-time experience is defined as the number of hours per week required for attendance by a full-time student, receiving federal financial assistance (generally 9–12 h per week).

# INDEX

Breinigsville, PA USA
25 July 2010

242360BV00005B/11/P